Shakha to Nation

Shakha to Nation

The Greatest Speeches of the RSS

Edited by

Ram Madhav

with

Dnyanashri Kulkarni

JUGGERNAUT BOOKS
C-I-128, First Floor, Sangam Vihar, Near Holi Chowk,
New Delhi 110080, India

First published by Juggernaut Books 2025

10 9 8 7 6 5 4 3 2 1

P-ISBN: 9789353454937
E-ISBN: 9789353456153

Typeset in Adobe Caslon Pro by R. Ajith Kumar, Noida

Printed at Thomson Press India Ltd

Contents

Part 3: Sangh in Conversation

Preface

The year 2025–26 marks the centenary year of the Rashtriya Swayamsevak Sangh (RSS). Massive preparations are underway to take the organization's message to hitherto unreached sections of society as well as those who have less understood or misunderstood its mission and vision.

The RSS has thus far been understood largely from accounts of onlookers and observers, a majority of whom were neither sympathetic to it nor truthful about their reading of it. For its part, the organization itself has created vast amounts of literature to explain its raison d'etre and continues to do so. This collection of important speeches of RSS leaders over the last hundred years provides the reader with a distinctive and fresh opportunity to gain insight into their thinking and messaging. It helps in understanding the mission and vision of the organization from the proverbial 'horse's mouth', which has helped the organization grow in strength to reach where it is today.

We put together several speeches and a few interviews of the leading lights of the organization, starting from the founder Dr Keshav Baliram Hedgewar to the present-day leadership, to convey the flavours of the thought process that has guided this vast organization over the last century. By no means can we claim that it is an exhaustive list, nor can we conclude that these were the only great speeches. In the last hundred years, the organization has crossed many milestones and achieved many successes. Behind each such occasion lay the guidance and inspiration of its leadership. While there exists a vast amount of literature in the form of speeches in the private and public domain, this book offers just a few drops from that ocean.

Dnyanashri Kulkarni, a research fellow at the India Foundation, undertook the painstaking task of collecting a large number of important speeches delivered by the leadership over many decades. She accessed them from both published and archived sources. Most of that material was in Indian languages – mainly in Hindi and occasionally in Marathi. Kulkarni spent long hours to translating them in English and prepare the manuscript for publication. My job was to carefully scrutinize the text for inadvertent errors in translation, syntax and presentation. Since most of the speeches were delivered decades ago, there was some amount of editing involved to ensure that today's readers don't find the content amiss.

We are thankful to Juggernaut Books, publishers of this book, for their patience over delays in the preparation of the manuscript and for their professionalism in bringing out the publication in time for the centenary.

We hope that the compilation serves as a useful source of reference for those interested in understanding the world's largest voluntary organization – the RSS.

Introduction

The Journey of a Behemoth

The RSS, regarded by many as the world's largest voluntary organization, is celebrating its centenary in 2025–26. Founded in 1925 by Dr K.B. Hedgewar, a politically and socially motivated freedom fighter from Nagpur fondly known within the RSS as 'Doctorji', the organization holds the unique record of completing 100 years without ever experiencing any divisions. It has grown from strength to strength, turning every adversity into an opportunity and every opportunity into a mission. That is the reason why, at 100, the organization still looks remarkably youthful and strikingly agile. Millions of disciplined cadres, trained in tens of thousands of Shakhas across the country, run hordes of activities in every walk of national life with military-like precision and missionary-level dedication. And all this is done quietly, without any fuss and away from the glare of media and publicity.

To understand and appreciate the vastness of the RSS it is useful to look at the numbers and data. Shakha is the core activity of the RSS. It is the daily meetings of the Swayamsevaks held in open spaces across towns and villages of the country. This practice is unique to the RSS. No other voluntary organization in the world has daily meetings as its activity. As per the data released by the organization after its annual meeting in March 2025, the Shakhas are held in over 83,129 places across the country. In addition to these daily meetings, Swayamsevaks conducts weekly and monthly meetings at another 25,000–30,000 places, bringing the total number of regular meetings that the organization conducts to over a lakh.

Its ability for popular outreach was evident during the month-long country-wide fund raising drive it undertook in 2023 to support the construction of the Ram Janmabhumi Temple in Ayodhya. Around 5 million RSS cadre fanned out into more than half a million towns and villages and reached out to almost 200 million households – accounting for two-thirds of the total households in the country. On the day of the Ram Temple inauguration in January 2024, the RSS held devotional programmes in tens of thousands of temples and other public spaces across the country, drawing a record 280 million participants .

These numbers represent only a fraction of the reach of this vast organization. Initially focused on building a dedicated cadre for the organization through the Shakha, the RSS expanded, after independence, into various walks of national life. Thus began the story of the rise of its allied organizations, numbering more than 40 today, which are called the 'Sangh Parivar' organizations. Over decades of dedicated hard work, each of these organizations has emerged as a leader in its own field, earning massive public trust and support.

Despite its vast and commendable growth in the last century, the RSS remains an enigma to many. While millions have become Swayamsevaks and millions more are its admirers, there is a vast majority of the population that remains uninformed or misinformed about the mission of the organization. 'The RSS is difficult to understand and easy to misunderstand', observed Walter Andersen, an academic from the US who co-authored a book with Shridhar Damle on the history of the organization in 2019 by the name *RSS: The Brotherhood in Saffron*.

One unique aspect of the RSS is that it runs entirely on a voluntary basis, with no salaried employees and no public funding. The founder of the RSS, Hedgewar, was categorical from the beginning that 'Swayamsevak', the individual who is primarily responsible for building the organization, would be a unique type of activist, one who cannot even be called a volunteer, much less a member. For that matter, the RSS is an open organization without any formal membership, another unique characteristic that baffles many. Swayamsevaks are those citizens of the country, who come forward to dedicate their body, mind, and money – *Tan,*

Man, Dhan in RSS terminology – to the nation without expecting anything in return.

It is pertinent in this context, to quote Swami Vivekananda to explain the mindset of a Swayamsevak. 'Mark me, then and then alone you are a Hindu when the very name sends through you a galvanic shock of strength. Then and then alone you are a Hindu when every man who bears the name, from any country, speaking our language or any other language, becomes at once the nearest and the dearest to you. Then and then alone you are a Hindu when the distress of anyone bearing that name comes to your heart and makes you feel as if your own son were in distress. Then and then alone you are a Hindu when you will be ready to bear everything for them, like the great example I have quoted at the beginning of this lecture, of your great Guru Govind Singh. Driven out from this country, fighting against its oppressors, after having shed his own blood for the defence of the Hindu religion, after having seen his children killed on the battlefield – ay, this example of the great Guru, left even by those for whose sake he was shedding his blood and the blood of his own nearest and dearest – he, the wounded lion, retired from the field calmly to die in the South, but not a word of curse escaped his lips against those who had ungratefully forsaken him! Mark me, every one of you will have to be a Govind Singh, if you want to do good to your country', exhorted the saffron saint in one address. The Swayamsevaks, in this sense, are Hindus in Vivekananda's mould.

Incidentally, Swami Vivekananda's life and teachings have played an important role in the work and growth of the RSS. The concept of 'Hindu Rashtra' is largely drawn from his teachings on the civilisational and cultural identity and oneness of the ancient nation of Bharat, rather than from any religious or sectoral identity prism. The second Sarsanghachalak of the organization, Madhav Sadashiv Golwalkar, famously known as 'Guruji', was an ordained monk of the Ramakrishna Order started by Swami Vivekananda.

The founder of the RSS, Doctorji, was a political activist in the early 20th century. He initially dabbled in revolutionary politics against the British before joining the Congress movement in early 1900s, inspired by the Maharashtra stalwart Lokmanya Bal Gangadhar Tilak. The revolutionary streak in him did not endear him to Gandhi, the rising star of the Congress movement in the post-Tilak era of 1920s, with his politics of accommodation, compromise and emphasis on non-violence. However, as a committed leader of the independence movement, Hedgewar always followed Gandhi's leadership with due respect and continued to participate in various Congress Party activities. He played an important role as the local organiser when the All-India Congress Committee held its annual session in Nagpur in 1920, and he went to jail participating in the Forest Satyagraha in 1930, which was launched at Gandhi's call. Hedgewar encouraged all, including those joining his fledgling organization, to actively participate in the country's freedom movement.

But, his shrewd political instincts convinced him that the freedom achieved through compromises, without addressing the root cause of the nation's loss in the first place, would be weak and short-lived. He believed that the disunity within the national society, both political and social, was the main reason of slavery. While social divisions like caste, sect and religion led to weakening of the society against the advances of the proselytising Semitic religions, political disunity and quarrels among various rulers due to their corruption, greed and lack of character resulted in the surrender of country's sovereignty before the foreign invaders. Hedgewar's solution was to build a national society strong in personal character, imbued with a strong sense of national pride, providing an enduring basis for unity in an otherwise diverse society. It was with this mission that Hedgewar started the RSS in 1925 – essentially a socio – political movement, catering to the need of the hour, inspired largely by the works of reformers like Tilak, Aurobindo and Savarkar. In its early years, the Swayamsevaks were even asked to take a pledge that included 'securing independence for Bharat' as one of the objectives.

His successor, M S Golwalkar 'Guruji' added a new dimension to it after becoming the Sarsanghachalak in 1940. As the country moved closer to securing Independence, Golwalkar sought to reduce the political content and introduced a stronger religious and spiritual component into the organization's vision and mission. As mentioned earlier, Golwalkar was an ascetic trained in the Ramakrishna Order of Swami Vivekananda. He believed that while culture and religion are all-encompassing and uniting, politics in the Hindu scheme of things is only a minor part of the social life, often coming with the potential to divide. Thus, under his stewardship, the RSS evolved from a socio-political organization to a socio-cultural one.

This transition into non-political character was not easy. Vivekananda founded Ramakrishna Mission with a unique programme inspired by the one he witnessed in the Catholic ecclesiastical group of Jesuits. Jesuits were dedicated Catholic propagandists, who were not ordained priests, and thus were not confined to the churches and monasteries. They followed the path of teaching and service to spread the Christian message of love. Vivekananda appeares to have been influenced by their modus operandi, first during his interaction with Jesuit institutions in Goa, and later during his travels in America. He even delivered a couple of lectures praising their work in spreading love and universal religion, as opposed to the fundamentalist and sectarian interpretations of other Christian denominations.

Ramakrishna Mission, founded by Swami Vivekananda, followed a distinct approach. It did not create gurus who sat in temples and monasteries while the faithful are expected to come searching for religion. Instead, the monks of the Mission were tasked with carrying the universal Dharmic message of love and inclusion to every nook and corner of the country and teaching and serving the people. Golwalkar was a product of that order. One of the early dimensions he added to the RSS work was the 'Pracharak system', a band of dedicated activists, similar to the monks of his erstwhile order, who would offer themselves to the spreading of the socio-cultural work of the RSS. Described by Swami Chinmayananda, one of the great gurus of Sanatan Dharma in the last century, as 'White-clad Sanyasis', the Pracharaks became the sinews of the organization, building it brick by brick and shaping it into a vast socio-cultural force.

Hedgewar's active role in the freedom movement resulted in creating the perception that the RSS was a political organization with a political mission. That perception led the British administrators and their native officials to impose various types of restrictions on its activities during the 1930s. After the passing of the founder in 1940, Golwalkar consciously tried to give the RSS a non-political character, yet the challenge remained daunting in the decade of 1940s. Leadership of Independent India, led by stalwarts like Jawaharlal Nehru and Sardar Patel, too viewed the RSS from a political lens only. Nehru saw in it a challenge to his secular ideological politics and used the tragic assassination of Mahatma Gandhi in 1948 as an excuse to crush it. The RSS was banned by his government in 1948 linking it to the murder of the Mahatma. Patel, as the Home Minister, understood that the organization had nothing to do with the alleged crime. But, he too insisted that the organization must join the Congress Party, rather than maintaining an independent socio-cultural identity. However, Golwalkar stood his ground. His steadfast refusal to turn the organization into a political vehicle had resulted in temporary trouble for it in the form of continued ban and incarceration of a large number of its cadre.

Golwalkar did not detest politics. He, in fact, loaned important Sangh functionaries like Deen Dayal Upadhyay, Atal Behari Vajpayee and Lal Krishna Advani for political work to Shyama Prasad Mukherjee when the latter founded Bharatiya Jana Sangh in 1951. He constantly guided the rise of the new party, which pursued political goals that were in line with the socio-cultural mission of the RSS. However, he also assiduously maintained the nature and texture of the RSS as non-political. During that period, he and other RSS leaders were able to build cordial relations with leaders across the political spectrum.

Golwalkar's emphasis on socio-cultural over the socio-political earned the organization enormous goodwill. Despite initial ideological differences, Nehru invited then RSS to march shoulder-to-shoulder alongside the Indian Army in the Republic Day parade of 1963. Over 2,500 RSS volunteers participated in the marchpast upon the invitation of the government.[1] In 1965, prime minister Lal Bahadur Shastri sent a special plane to invite Golwalkar to Delhi for consultations during the India-Pakistan war.[2] In 1967, when prime minister Indira Gandhi set up a high-powered committee under retired Chief Justice A. K. Sarkar to examine the issue of a national ban on cow slaughter, that committee included Golwalkar too.[3] Golwalkar's demise in 1973 was condoled in Parliament, where Indira Gandhi paid her tribute, saying, 'Shri Golwalkar, an eminent personality who was not a member of the House, is no more. He held a respected position in national life by his force of personality and the intensity of his conviction, even though many of us could not agree with him.'

However, as the organization grew in strength, new challenges emerged. The political dilemma that haunted Golwalkar immediately after Independence returned to bother the organization in the post-Golwalkar era once again. For an organization whose *'pind'*, or the essential core, was socio-political, events such as the Emergency (1975-1977) and the Ram Janmabhumi movement of 1980s were powerful triggers to shed the socio-cultural *avatar* and return to Hedgewar's era of activism. When prime minister Indira Gandhi imposed of the Emergency in 1975, the democratic character of the country came under direct assault, Balasaheb Deoras, who succeeded Golwalkar as the Sarsanghachalak in 1973, had to mobilize tens of thousands of cadres of the organization in a prolonged fight against the draconian dictatorship. The RSS played a crucial role in the final defeat of Indira's dictatorship in 1977 and restoration of democracy.

However, the new leadership was quick enough to bring the organization back to its core socio-cultural work. Deoras encouraged cadres to focus more on questions like casteism, untouchability and social hierarchies aiming to rid Hindu society of those social evils. Deoras' famous speech at Pune in 1975, in which he gave a clarion call for eradication of untouchability 'lock, stock and barrel', became the new mantra for the organization. In the 1980s, nation-wide yatras were undertaken by the Sangh Parivar organizations to promote greater social equality and unity. The Ram Janmabhumi Movement, in which the RSS took a direct role, acquired massive national proportions and was also essentially used by the leadership to promote the cultural unity with the country that overcame all other social and political divisions.

Meanwhile, the Sangh Parivar organizations too grew in strength and popularity, particularly in the political field. It brought its own challenges to the leadership of the parent body. Unlike the Jan Sangh, the newly formed BJP started attracting many leaders with no RSS affiliation. At one stage, in mid-1980s, the new party officially adopted 'Gandhian Socialism' as its ideology, causing unease among the RSS cadres. Some irate leaders even openly proclaimed that the RSS was not 'permanently wedded to any political party'. The BJP's crushing defeat in the 1984 parliament elections, when even stalwarts like Vajpayee lost their seat, gave fodder to the rumour mills that the Sangh had abandoned the BJP for good. However, the BJP's decision under Vajpayee-Advani leadership in 1989 at Palanpur, Himachal Pradesh, to throw its weight behind the Ram Janmabhumi movement restored its standing with the Sangh.

As the BJP grew in strength and influence through the 1990s and the new century, such challenges continued to haunt the Sangh leadership. Should national interest be determined by a government of the day staffed with the Swayamsevaks, or should the organization itself step in to decide what constitutes national interest through its ideological lens? In all such difficult situations, the RSS leadership has demonstrated astuteness and ensured that its socio-cultural character remained intact, while the socio-political agendas were left to the Swayamsevaks in the BJP. The understanding was clear: neither was to step on other's toes. All the RSS chiefs after Golwalkar – from Balasaheb Deoras to Rajendra Singh to Sudarshan to Mohan Bhagwat – faced this dilemma. They all handled it with great skill and maintained the course set by Golwalkar.

There are two well-known ideological political models in the world. One is the Chinese Communist Party (CCP) model, in which, the Party is everything. It controls every sphere – students, peasants, workers, media and even culture. The Party stands above the government, decideds everything and the government's role is merely to implement it. Communist parties in different countries, and some others like the Janatha Vimukthi Peramuna (JVP) in Sri Lanka follow this model. The other model was practised in the United Kingdom by the British Labour Party. A party founded by the labour unions, it was under their total control until late 20th century. However, the labour unions' grip on the affairs of the British Labour Party is gradually diminishing. Currently, the unions elect only less than 50 per cent delegates to the party conference, and their voting power was reduced to one-third.

The RSS has presented a third model, wherein it relied on its Swayamsevaks to carry its vision and mantle forward in all walks of national life, including politics, without ever seeking to control them directly. Its faith in its own cadre, many of whom rose to occupy high positions of the social and political leadership in the country, has led it to grant sufficient freedom to them. Meanwhile, it continued to focus on its core mission of 'man making' as laid out by Hedgewar, building dedicated bands of Swayamsevaks ever ready to selflessly work for the good of the national society.

The secret of the great organization's success lies in its strict adherence to the core mission, never straying from it over the past century. Successive leaders have enriched its journey by adding various flavours to its core work while constantly striving to keep the organization up-to-date and relevant to the times.

It has been a fascinating journey of a century of an organization that came from the fringes to occupy the national centre-stage, which it does today. The path has been anything but smooth and an uneventful ride. On the contrary, especially after Independence, the RSS faced severe criticism and occasional onslaughts from its ideological and political adversaries. It endured acute and intensive scrutiny, not only from the governments led by adversaries and by political and public intellectual leadership, but also from the judiciary. Yet, in the end, it always emerged victorious. Many former adversaries, who once looked at it as a scourge, grudgingly admit today that it has emerged as the soul of this great ancient nation.

At its centenary, there could not be a more satisfying outcome for the RSS and its leadership.

Part 1

Sarsanghchalaks Speak

1

'Under This Sacred Saffron Flag, the Unification of All Hindus Is the Primary Goal of the RSS.'

K.B. HEDGEWAR, 'DOCTORJI'

The RSS – Rashtriya Swayamsevak Sangh – of Dr Keshav Baliram Hedgewar's time was an enigma, confining its activities only to the expansion of its mission all across the country without any publicity and fanfare. Doctorji was by nature self-effacing, and he sought to develop that culture of prasiddhi paranmukhta – disinterest in popularism – in the organization. His public appearances were rare, except those occasions when he participated in events related to the Independence movement of India. His travels and speeches were mostly confined to the RSS swayamsevaks.

The RSS was founded on the day of the Hindu festival Vijayadashami in 1925. Since then, that day has marked the foundation day of the RSS. Doctorji started the practice of organizing a public event of the RSS annually on that day, where an eminent social leader would be invited to grace the activities of the organization. As the sarsanghchalak, Doctorji used to deliver the main speech, highlighting RSS' vision and mission, a practice that continues to this day. As Hedgewar remained largely reticent about publicity, those speeches are the only major source available to understand his vision for the historic organization he had created for the Hindus and India.

Here is a summary of his vision and ideas as articulated by him during such annual Vijayadashami events.

It seems unnecessary to explain the principles or philosophy of the Sangh to the people of Nagpur or any Hindu in general. The Sangh is a Hindu organization. Among all the world's religions, Hinduism is unique in its emphasis on virtuous qualities and its teaching of the principle '*atmavat sarvabhuteshu*' (treat all beings as oneself), advocating love and compassion towards all living beings. Hinduism does not condone violence or injustice prevalent in the world today. Naturally, every Hindu wishes to put an end to such atrocities. However, mere preaching will not change the world's mindset.

When the Hindu society becomes visibly united and strong, the disrespect we face today will vanish, and the world will bow to us as we command. Hinduism has always upheld these ideals, and it is to protect this sacred religion and its culture that the Sangh was established. Presently, Hindu society is in a highly disorganized state. The aim of the Sangh is to unite this fragmented society, instil pride in being a Hindu in Hindustan and demonstrate to the world that the Hindu community is not a dying race.

The Sangh aims to cultivate a singular sense of identity – Hindutva. Although the Hindu community is divided into castes, the Sangh recognizes only one identity: Hindu. It does not see distinctions of Brahmin or non-Brahmin, touchable or untouchable, rich or poor, literate or illiterate. For the Sangh, nothing is as significant as Hindutva. The very creation of the Sangh is for the preservation of Hindutva. Under this sacred saffron flag, the unification of all Hindus is the primary goal of the Rashtriya Swayamsevak Sangh. I believe no other aim could be more noble, lofty or radiant than this. If anyone attempts to suppress Hindutva and build a new nationality, they are gravely mistaken. Such a thing can never happen. As long as the sun and moon exist, Hindustan will remain the land of the Hindus.

The Sangh aspires to spread the virtues of righteousness across the world. India's mission is to eradicate the demonic tendencies of mankind and teach humanity. The Sangh was not created to harbour hatred or to destroy anyone. Even those who oppose the Sangh cannot accuse it of such intentions, as is evident from the Sangh's history over the last several years. The Sangh has one sacred purpose: to make the Hindu nation united and powerful.

By 1933, the Sangh has been able to start 125 branches, with a membership exceeding 12,000. In Nagpur alone, there are 16 active branches. This work belongs to the entire Hindu society, and every individual must take responsibility for uniting Hindus. It is our collective duty to end the current pitiful state of Hindus and ensure that the world acknowledges their greatness. The Sangh works tirelessly towards the sacred goal of uplifting our Hindu society from its current plight and empowering it. We must all resolve to dedicate ourselves – with body, mind and wealth – to the revival of this ancient Hindu nation. This sacred duty of working for the Hindu Rashtra is the sincere mission of the Rashtriya Swayamsevak Sangh.

The Sangh's work transcends all political divisions. Any Hindu who upholds the goal of protecting the Hindu culture can contribute to the Sangh's mission with their body, mind and wealth. If every Hindu understands the Sangh's ideology and wholeheartedly believes that this organization is their own, then Hindustan's prosperity will flourish, and the golden day when the nation reaches the pinnacle of glory will not be far away.

It is the hallmark of humanity to live in this world with open eyes and to reflect on the direction in which the world is heading. From this perspective, it appears that we Hindus do not live with open eyes. If we did, we would have observed the world's progress and adjusted our actions accordingly. While we pride ourselves over our deep devotion to God, perhaps it is due to our religious rigidity that we have been unable to engage in activities like overseas travel or other means of understanding the world. However, through our organization, we can now study the practices and successes of the British, whom destiny brought to India.

This opportunity allows us to analyze the actions of those who have entered our homes and understand the key to their success. Anyone who observes with open eyes will realize that the British ability to subdue even powerful enemies like Germany, and their proud proclamation of the phrase 'The sun never sets on our empire', both stem from one essential factor: their exceptional organization.' Yes, their organization is exemplary, and their wealth and power are entirely dependent on it. At the very least, we must learn this simple lesson from them. Without organizing ourselves, Hindus cannot hope to survive in today's world. We have been emphasizing this for quite some time, and our efforts in this direction are visible to everyone.

Today, British rule in India is sustained by the strength of a well-organized police force. I often say that those working for the nation should always look up to the burning sense of national pride that the British possess. When the daughter of Emperor Shah Jahan fell ill, an English doctor cured her. The emperor, in gratitude, asked the doctor to name his reward. Had this opportunity been given to an ordinary Indian, they would have asked for personal gains. But the doctor requested that the British company be granted permission to trade in India. What does this signify? It reflects the British spirit of nationalism – a constant concern for national welfare, willingness to sacrifice everything for the nation and selflessness in service to their country. This is a truly admirable quality.

In a time when despair has engulfed the nation, and obstacles stand as mountains in the path of progress, the Rashtriya Swayamsevak Sangh continues to move forward undeterred. The experiences of the Sangh are so miraculous that it seems as if touching dust transforms it into gold. This reinforces our belief that the work of the Sangh is indeed divinely inspired.

The Rashtriya Swayamsevak Sangh aspires to perform only humble work. The Sangh has no desire to boast, no craving for publicity and no habit of making grandiose claims. It aims to do only what every individual is duty-bound to do – ensuring that our society, religion, culture and nation survive and thrive on this earth with dignity and pride. This natural desire and ambition align with the Sangh's vision.

Hindustan is the sole home of the Hindus. The Sangh works with the sincere intent that Hindus should live peacefully and securely in this homeland, free from the threat of any calamities. Its mission is to instil in every Hindu the pure spirit of nationalism – a sense that Hindustan is their rightful home and that its protection is their ultimate responsibility.

But the reality is that Hindus cannot live securely in their own home. Even though Hindustan is the home of Hindus, it does not feel like one. They lack security and are unable to live with self-respect. It's akin to the saying 'A golden name but holding a wooden broom!' Hindus are unable to ensure safety within their own house. What is the root cause of this? The primary reason is our weakness. When we observe other nations, we see that every society is strong, well-organized and lives with pride. In stark contrast, we find ourselves in a pitiable state, dependent on the charity of others due to our own frailty. This national crisis is entirely of our own making. If we wish to prevent others from plotting the destruction of the Hindu community, we must become strong and organize ourselves.

Making our society and nation capable of self-defence is not a sin. On the contrary, it is the most just and virtuous duty to protect our society and nation with unwavering effort and devotion. The Rashtriya Swayamsevak Sangh serves as a university for creating a strong Hindu organization in Hindustan.

The Sangh has been established solely for self-improvement. It has no other intention or purpose beyond this. Its only wish is to achieve its own upliftment. But before we can improve ourselves, we must consider how this improvement can be achieved. To uplift oneself, one must remain alive. A society that survives is the only one capable of improving itself and others. The foundation of the Sangh is rooted in this belief: the Hindu society must not only survive but must also be fit to survive, in accordance with the principle of 'survival of the fittest'.

The Sangh understands that the Hindu nation has been subjected to numerous invasions in the past, continues to face them in the present and may possibly face them in the future. The Sangh also knows that societies that invade others are often criticized by neutral observers, while sympathy is extended to those who are invaded. While this may be acceptable from an outsider's perspective, the society that is being attacked must not waste time blaming the aggressors. Instead, it must identify the reasons behind these invasions and eliminate them.

When we examine our Hindu society in this context, it becomes clear that the root causes of these invasions and atrocities are our weakness and ignorance. Today, Hindu society has become so ignorant that anyone can impose their will upon it and commit atrocities for their own whims. Despite this, we still show little concern or effort to address the disunity and lack of organization within our society. This negligence deeply disappoints the Sangh.

We are angered by the disgraceful mentality of Hindus – not the people themselves, for they are our own, and the very reason for our existence is their upliftment. However, the disgraceful mentality – the attitude of not protecting oneself – persists, which is why atrocities against Hindus continue to this day. Unless this mentality is eradicated completely, these invasions and attacks will not cease. The Sangh's mission is to eradicate this weakness, wash away this stain and instil a sense of strength and self-defence within the Hindu community.

Therefore, the Sangh seeks to spread a dense network of its branches across every corner of this vast Hindu nation, from the Himalayas to the southern seas, uniting the entire Hindu society into a powerful and self-reliant community. This is the sole desire of the Rashtriya Swayamsevak Sangh. The Sangh, with its unwavering commitment, is advancing rapidly to build the necessary strength for the rise of this sacred and beloved Hindu nation. With the blessings of our ancestors and the love and support of the people, we are confident that the Sangh will soon become a nationwide movement.

2

'Doctorji: A Steady Lamp in the Cause of the Motherland'

MADHAV SADASHIVRAO GOLWALKAR, 'GURUJI'

At 100, the Rashtriya Swayamsevak Sangh – RSS – is a well-known organization. Its ideology and activities are both admired and challenged. There is no field of social work that the RSS cadre have left untouched. Yet, the founder of this mighty and omnipresent organization, Dr Keshav Baliram Hedgewar, is quite an unfamiliar figure in the public discourse. A medical doctor from Nagpur in the Vidarbha region of Maharashtra, Dr Hedgewar, reverentially and affectionately called in the RSS circles as 'Doctorji', founded the organization in 1925 with a handful of young men. By the time he breathed his last, in 1940, which was 15 years later, at a relatively young age of 50, the organization had already acquired an all-India character, with 'shakhas'[1] spread across almost all the important states of British India.

Those who watch the RSS from outside are familiar with the name of M.S. Golwalkar, popularly known as 'Guruji', who is regarded as the ideological fountainhead of the organization. Admirers and critics alike turn to 'Guruji' for understanding and interpreting the vision and views of the organization.

The RSS is a top-down hierarchical organization, at the top of which remains the 'sarsanghachalak' – the supreme head of the organization. Sarsanghachalaks usually act as guides and philosophers, serving as father-figures for the organization, while the executive functioning of the organization is handled by the Akhil Bharatiya Karyakarini[2], led by the 'sarkaryavah'[3], an elected senior functionary equivalent to the executive head of the organization. Whereas the sarkaryavah is elected every three years by an electoral college comprising delegates from all over the country, the sarsanghachalak is nominated through consultations at the highest levels. The outgoing sarsanghachalak nominates their successor after consulting with a few senior colleagues.

Doctorji was the first sarsanghachalak of the RSS, who held that position until his demise in 1940. Before his passing, he nominated Guruji, a 35-year-old young ascetic at the time, to succeed him as head of the organization. Guruji remained sarsanghachalak for 33 years, until his death in 1973. Hugely respected not only for his scholarship and ideological perseverance but also for his asceticism, Guruji was instrumental in carrying forward the mantle of the organization handed over to him by the visionary founder himself.

While little was known about Dr Hedgewar 'Doctorji' – both to the swayamsevaks[4] of the RSS and to the outside world – it was Golwalkar, 'Guruji', who brought the founder's life to light, presenting it as an ideal for all patriots through numerous speeches.

Here is one such speech, in which Guruji aptly sums up the kind of organization that Doctorji intended to build through the example of his own life.

Dr Keshav Baliram Hedgewar, founder of the Rashtriya Swayamsevak Sangh, was born in 1889 in Nagpur. From early childhood until his final days, his life burnt like a steady lamp in service of the motherland. Even as a child of eight, he threw away in disgust the sweets distributed at his school on Queen Victoria's birthday, calling them a symbol of slavery. He would amaze his elders with strange questions such as, 'How is it that these Englishmen, coming from thousands of miles away, have become our rulers?' In high school, he was rusticated for igniting the flame of the Vande Mataram movement among the students. He had, as it were, imbibed the spirit of undiluted patriotism right from his mother's womb.

After matriculating from Poona (now Pune), he chose Calcutta (now Kolkata), then the home of revolutionaries, with the intention of observing the movement closely and participating in it. He soon became one with Bengali life and customs. He plunged into the vibrant political and social activities there and soon became a source of inspiration for a band of patriotic young men drawn from across the country.

When he returned to Nagpur as a young and brilliant doctor, many eyes were riveted on him with fond hopes for the 'bright career' that awaited him. Many matrimonial proposals were made to him. But his was not a life to be chained to the narrow confines of family. Seeking to put all such initiatives to rest, he wrote to his uncle Abaji Hedgewar, 'I have pledged my life to an ideal. I have staked my all at its altar. Where then shall I find time and energy to indulge in personal pleasures and family life?'

Let it be remembered that he was born in a family grovelling in stark poverty. We may come across persons born in affluence – free from worry for their bellies or for their kith and kin – who devote themselves to national service, though, of course, even such instances are rare. But Doctorji was the rarest among rare. Though extreme poverty and near-starvation was staring him in the face, he never thought of earning a single penny for himself or his family. He never practised medicine, though he was a medical doctor. Instead, he chose to become the 'doctor of the nation'.

Right up to his very end, dire poverty remained his faithful companion. For months on end, he carried on with hardly one full meal a day. Often, he would be in tattered clothes and lacked even the barest necessities of life.

One day, a gentleman called on Doctorji. As the conversation drew to a close, Doctorji requested him to stay for tea and sent word to his sister-in-law to prepare it. Minutes passed; no tea arrived. More time went by; still there was no tea. The gentleman was in a hurry to leave.

Doctorji went inside to find out what the matter was. And he found nothing except cold water and his sister-in-law quietly seated in a corner! There was no one else to go to the market and bring the necessary things. So, Doctorji himself went out, brought sugar and tea, and soon after, tea was served to the gentleman. That gentleman was perceptive enough to understand the situation. Till then, he had not the slightest idea of the monetary plight of Doctorji, though he had been acquainted with him for a long time.

In fact, looking at the ever-smiling face of Doctorji – his radiant enthusiasm, his infectious laughter and his captivating manners, spreading sweetness and joy all around – no one could imagine the extremities under which he was living. He was like a lamp that burns itself silently, yet sheds warmth and light in every direction.

Immediately after the incident, the gentleman sent word to me to inquire in detail about Doctorji's monetary condition. He was shocked to learn of the abject situation. He became restless and asked me angrily, 'Why have you not made arrangements to ease his financial worries?' I replied, 'How can Ekadashi[5] fill the belly of Shivaratri?[6]'

He grew somber for a while and told me, 'I simply cannot stand this. You must accept twenty-five rupees every month from me, at least to cover the expenses for Doctorji's guests. But take care, let this not reach his ears!' I suggested that he propose it to Doctorji himself. But knowing Doctorji's strong views on the matter, he too did not dare broach the subject with him, and the matter ended there.

In addition to his burning idealism, Doctorji was a glowing example of the rarest of virtues – the will to reform oneself in conformity with the chosen mission in life. He was born in a family known for its violent and fiery temper. Doctorji too inherited that ancestral 'heritage' in full. It is stated that inherited tendencies and habits die hard – *swabhavo duratikramah*. The saying, 'Man should be careful in the choice of his parents', expresses the same idea. But Doctorji proved all such self-defeating ideas false. From the day he resolved to build an organization, wherein people of varied natures and qualities were to be blended into an organized and harmonious whole, he decided to reform himself. Those who had seen him before were surprised to see a completely transformed man. After he founded the organization, it was rare to see him using a harsh word or getting upset in the face of even the gravest provocation. If anybody spoke to him harshly, he would just smile, and that smile would wear away the edge of opposition. Undoubtedly, his inner fire would erupt at times – but only when he witnessed insults and ignominy being heaped upon our nation, and its people mutely submitting to such indignity.

Steadily and through stupendous self-effort, Doctorji had transformed himself in every little detail of his behaviour, becoming a living example of a worker dedicated to the mission of national reorganization based on the highest values of our cultural heritage. He had realized from his experience that fiery public speeches, however thrilling in the moment, could never build an enduring organization of dedicated hearts that will burn like a steady flame amidst the tempests of temptations and adversities. On the contrary, such intemperate speeches would only harm the organization by inculcating, though unconsciously, a mentality of finding cheap satisfaction in criticizing and exposing one's opponents. Such a mentality could have no place in an organization like the Sangh, which sought self-reform in society, knowing as it did the one lesson of our history: that it is our own people, and not outsiders, who have been responsible for our degeneration and downfall.

Before the founding of the Sangh, Doctorji himself was a fiery speaker. In 1921, during the Non-Cooperation Movement, he was arrested for one such speech and produced before the court on a charge of sedition. After listening to his spirited defence, the magistrate remarked, 'His defence is more seditious than his speech!' But after the founding of the Sangh, he exercised full restraint in his expressions. Thereafter, his speeches, though charged with intense emotion capable of piercing through the hearts of the listeners, were never provocative or violent. Even in informal conversations, his words carried a wave of sweetness and heartfelt appeal. He had known by experience that sweetness of speech was a must for a national organizer.

There was nothing artificial or superficial about this transformation. It was so deep and enduring that it became the very texture of his nature, expressing itself spontaneously in thought, word and action. His was not the kind of 'long-distance popularity' that vanishes like a soap bubble on closer contact or scrutiny. There is a saying, 'No man is a hero to his valet.' But in his case, the opposite was true – the closer one came to him, the more would one love and adore him. His character was the same in private as in public – one sweet, harmonious whole. Such was his pure, noble, radiant and transparent character that even those who opposed him in the public sphere had not a word of reproach or abuse to direct at his person.

There was a famous barrister in Nagpur by the name Abhyankar, who was a leading political figure of that province. He had a voice of thunder and a knack for picking holes in his opponents' character, qualities he used in full measure during elections to expose and browbeat his opponents. Once, Dr Moonje[7] contested against him in elections. The barrister imagined that Doctorji and his Sangh were the main supporters of Dr Moonje and decided to attack them as well in his public speech. He launched a tirade against every supporter of Dr Moonje, but the moment he began referring to Doctorji, his tone softened at once. He openly confessed that he could not find a single word by way of abuse against Dr Hedgewar. Just imagine – a public confession of that kind amidst a virulent election campaign, and from such a person!

In fact, Doctorji's relations, even with his opponents, ran deeper than could be affected by any superficial differences. Right from his Calcutta days, he had cultivated an attitude of love, regard and co-operation towards all persons and organizations devoted to the cause of national emancipation, including those who did not see eye to eye with him. Political jealousies found no place in him. The flame of patriotism burning in his heart was too radiant to allow the shadows of parochial considerations to come anywhere near him.

Once a friend approached Doctorji to urgently secure a loan of 500 rupees. It was nearing midnight, and Doctorji was in a fix. He got up, went directly to Abhyankar and made a request. Without a word, Abhyankar brought the amount and handed it over to Doctorji. Doctorji asked him for paper and pen so that he could write a promissory note. Abhyankar replied, 'Doctor Saheb! Have I gone out of my senses that I should take a promissory note from Dr Hedgewar? All of Nagpur would laugh at me!'

Such was the absolute faith and confidence that his sterling character had inspired, even in the minds of his public adversaries. He was like Yudhishthira who would address even Duryodhana as Suyodhana. When the incredible news of Ashwathama's death spread in the battlefield, Drona decided to verify its truth from Yudhishthira, his chief adversary! Such was his rectitude, which made it easy for others, his friends and foes alike, to trust him.[8] Doctorji was, as it were, the modern reincarnation of Yudhishthira. He was verily a man with no foes and only friends – an Ajatashatru.[9]

Once, the government of the then Central Provinces and Berar became apprehensive that the growing strength of the Sangh might pose a threat to the 'communal peace' in the province. In 1932, it sent out a circular prohibiting its servants from taking part in the activities of the Sangh. Municipalities and district boards were also advised to take similar steps. There was an uproar in the province at the thoughtless and anti-national step of the government. It found its echo in the provincial assembly also, where a censure motion against the government was moved in the assembly. The motion was supported not only by the Hindu members but also by the Muslim, Christian, Parsi and all other members. It was preposterous, they all asserted in one voice, to imagine that an organization headed by Dr Hedgewar could be against any community. The ministry itself had to quit office shortly after that.

This feature of his character had endowed him with such a rare power of personality that even persons notorious for their arrogance and turbulence would behave in a decent and gentle manner in the presence of Doctorji. There was a person in Nagpur who used to call himself a 'general'. He had taken a vow not to allow any meeting that did not have him as the president to go undisturbed. The 'general' had an army of goons who would fall upon such an 'unauthorised' meeting, and within a few minutes, the meeting would end in confusion and chaos. During those days, a friend of Doctorji coming from outside was to address a meeting in Nagpur. But the promoters of the meeting had apprehensions that the 'general' would not allow the meeting to go on. Doctorji calmly assured them, which gave them the confidence to arrange the meeting. As the meeting commenced, the 'general' arrived with his 'army'. Seeing him coming, Doctorji rose and welcomed him with great warmth and made him sit by his side. The speaker too was in his full spirits and scathingly criticised the party to which the 'general' belonged. The 'general' was wild with rage, throwing his glances here and there; but seeing the calm, confident and majestic figure of Doctorji sitting just beside him, a cold shiver would pass through his body, and he would sit back helplessly in his chair. The meeting went on peacefully for over two hours. After the meeting was over, his followers pestered him, asking him why he had kept mum. He sheepishly replied, 'What could I do? That man was sitting beside me!'

What a mountain-load of anxieties and torments Doctorji must have been carrying in his bosom to be able to hold together countless number of men, mould each one of them after the image of an ideal national worker, and set up enduring conventions and inspiring examples as basis for the organized life of the whole nation. And all this under extremely hard conditions of personal existence! But the most amazing part was that no one could guess those deep undercurrents coursing through his being. Whoever came into contact with him would go back bathed in the fresh springs of joy and laughter gushing forth from him. Various and diverse were the types of persons who invariably surrounded him. His friends would jocularly say that Doctorji was maintaining a 'human zoo'! But no one in the 'zoo' felt out of tune in the company of Doctorji. The young and the aged, the orthodox and the modern, the educated and the uneducated, the rich and the poor would all find in him a note of common interest. Such was his ability to identify with others and the breadth of his skill in dealing with them. To him no man, however low and deficient in the eyes of others, was worthless.

At the root of that exceptional quality lay the spirit of complete humility, unsullied by even the slightest traces of ego. Infatuation for name or fame, position or power, never touched him. Right from the inception of the Sangh, he was constantly on the lookout for a suitable person who could be the head of the organization. He himself wished to remain only a humble follower, thus setting up a living example for all other swayamsevaks. In fact, he made repeated efforts to bring in a certain Hindu leader as its chief, but in vain. That eminent man, with all his virtues, could not grasp the potentialities of the Sangh or make up his mind for that historic role. Doctorji was sorely disappointed, but he continued his search. He remained, by the sheer merit of his qualities, the chief of the organization – like the lion, which is the natural king of the forest: *swayameva mrigendrata*. But he could not till the very end reconcile himself to that position.

Despite his towering personality, Doctorji never exhibited any airs. He would even discourage the natural and spontaneous expressions of adoration for him by his co-workers and swayamsevaks. He was severely uncompromising in that regard.

In 1940, he was returning to Nagpur after visiting the training camp at Poona. I had gone to the railway station to receive him. As the train arrived, we found him standing at the entrance of the compartment, his face beaming with a smile. Just as I advanced towards him to offer a garland, I met his stern forbidding glance. I stopped half-way with my hands half-stretched.

'I am coming to my own home. Where is the need for all this? In fact, we should welcome our honoured guest', he smilingly remarked and indicated towards the gentleman who was accompanying him.

I offered the gentleman that garland. I had no opportunity to honour Doctorji with a garland all through his life. I could only garland his body after he had left us.

He was equally averse to being photographed. It was only rarely and after a prolonged tussle with his co-workers that he would consent to his photograph being taken.

Though stern and unsparing to himself, what an ocean of love he was to each one of us! Words fail to describe the depth of that pure and selfless love. The boundless affection of the mother's heart, the sleepless care and diligence of the father and the inspiring guidance of the guru found their culmination in that single bosom. I, for one, feel it my proud privilege to worship him as my ideal. The worship of such a soul transcends the worship of an individual and becomes the worship of the ideal itself. He is verily my chosen deity.

Single-minded devotion, sterling character, matchless organizational skill, unflinching faith in the ultimate success of the cause he had taken up as his life-mission and limitless capacity for effort and exertion – that is how Doctorji can be summed up. His co-workers were torn with anxiety about his worsening health. Some warned that his body would not last long if he continued under such strain. But he would reply to all such concerns in a simple sentence, 'After all, my body is for the sake of work,' and would close the matter. He knew no rest or respite. His was the philosophy of action. He was for ceaseless and intense action, especially during one's youth. 'What is the use of resting during the days of youth, only to prolong one's life into old age when the body becomes useless for any active work?' he used to ask. Even if he agreed to rest at the insistence of his co-workers, he would not do so without starting a few shakhas in and around that place!

By 1939, his illness had become very acute. Doctors advised him complete rest. I was with him at the time. Treatment was going on, medicines were being regularly given, but to no result. The doctor who was treating him was perplexed. While checking the details of the treatment, he inquired at what time Doctorji usually went to sleep. I replied, 'As usual at 1 or 1.30 in the night.'

The doctor was shocked to hear that. He said, 'That is why he is not improving. Probably you are not allowing him to sleep early. He must go to bed by 10 o'clock.'

I confessed my inability to make him sleep so early. The doctor said, 'Well, if you cannot do it, I will myself come and do it.'

I welcomed his proposal. That day, the doctor came at 9 o'clock in the night. Doctorji had just taken his food and was alone in his room. As it wasn't advisable to sleep immediately after taking food, the doctor began chatting with Doctorji for a while. I was sitting outside the whole time. However, when the doctor began to feel drowsy and checked his watch, it was past 1 o'clock! He got up hurriedly, instructed Doctorji to sleep and stepped out. As he was leaving, I casually asked him the time. In an apologetic tone he said, 'I myself lost track of time,' and went away.

Doctorji stuck to that practice even during periods of serious illness. He would call the swayamsevaks at night and talk to them individually or in groups till late in the night. All our efforts to dissuade him proved futile before his grim resolve to expand the work at peak speed. Even the steel frame of his body could not cope for long with his intensely dynamic spirit. Within fifteen years of the starting of the organization, his body was completely consumed by the fire of idealism. It was not that he was unaware of the approaching end. In fact, he used to say, 'I know quite well the nature of my malady. I also know its remedy. But I have simply no time to spare for treatment. I do visualize its result. But I cannot help it. Let God's will be fulfilled.'

Just as a yogi finds fulfilment in offering himself as an oblation in the fire of yoga manifested in his body, so did Doctorji offer his body in the fire of suffering and sacrifice. That has been our glorious tradition. But today we often hear that we should not exert ourselves too much in our younger days, lest our lives be cut short. Doctorji ridiculed this advicc of wasting the precious moments of youth only to drag on in old age for some more years. One should in fact offer oneself at the altar of the motherland when the flower of youth is in full bloom, shedding fragrance and radiance all-round. It would be a sacrilege to offer a faded flower devoid of colour and fragrance in the worship of one's chosen deity. This was his concept of fruitfulness of human life; this was how he lived and this was how he died.

His was not an ordinary death. It was a steady and consuming fire that burnt through the entire period of his youth. There are some who sacrifice their lives in a flash of martyrdom. True, that too is glorious and inspiring. But to burn oneself every moment of one's life to light up countless other hearts is a *tapasya*[10] of the highest order. Like Shibi of the olden days, Doctorji cut his own flesh bit by bit in order to protect the 'dove', representing the society. Like Dadhichi who gave his bones to be forged into a deadly weapon to slay the demon Vritasura, Doctorji too smilingly transfused his lifeblood into society till the last drop.[11] That was how Shankaracharya died at the age of 32, Vivekananda at 39 and Shivaji at 50. Doctorji too died at 50. It is such men who live eternally!

Words get charged with irresistible power when uttered by such souls. Doctorji's words used to be very simple – as if he was speaking to a child. But what a force they carried! Once Dr Shyama Prasad Mukherjee[12] came to see Doctorji to discuss an important issue. Doctorji was too ill at that time – and that was to be his last illness – to engage himself in a long discussion. So, I requested Dr Mukherjee to have a preliminary talk over the subject with me and if anything remained, he could go to Doctorji for a final answer. He agreed. We had a prolonged discussion.

And although each one of his queries and doubts was answered, still he remained unsatisfied. So, we went to Doctorji and put the same question to him. Doctorji replied in a few words, conveying the same answer as I had given. But to my astonishment, I heard Dr Mukherjee say, 'Now I am completely satisfied.' That incident gave me the lesson of my life, that it was the character, the penance, the sacrifices of a person that impart power to their words. Arguments, discussions, flashes of intellect, all pale into dismal dimness before that supreme power.

Excelling though in all that goes to make an epoch-maker, he remained all through his life like a child – simple, unassuming, without any airs, speaking to one and all in a spirit of intimacy, laughing, joking and appreciating the smallest of virtues in others.

Once, in a weekly meeting of some advocates in the Sangh, several issues connected with the organization were being discussed in a free and informal manner – someone mooting a query regarding the future set-up of the Sangh, someone else suggesting the formation of a formal central committee and so on. Then abruptly, one of them posed a question, 'What, after all, is at the root of the Sangh?' 'Well, it is Doctor Saheb,' I simply said.

An old gentleman was present in the meeting who had known Doctorji from his boyhood. Doctorji would often go to him seeking his suggestions and guidance. Obviously, he was deeply moved to hear my words regarding Doctorji. He was surprised to find that all of a sudden, the 'Little Keshav' had grown to such heights. A flash of new realization, as it were, dawned upon him. After the meeting, he went to Doctorji and remarked affectionately, 'Doctor, how great you have become! All the while I was imagining you as the same old lad Keshav!'

The greatest of men who grace the world stage often cast that spell to make others unaware of their greatness, so that others may not shirk and shudder at their greatness, but come and freely mix with them in a spirit of comradeship. Sri Krishna, by his childish pranks, had cast a spell all over Gokula. No one, not even Yashoda, would remember that he was God Incarnate Himself.[13] Once, when he was reported to have eaten dust and Yashoda forced him to open his mouth, she saw illimitable universes dancing in that little cavity. She was shocked and dumbfounded. But that was only for the moment. The same old smiling, mischievous, teasing pranks of the child Krishna made her forget that fleeting realization.

Doctorji's disarming simplicity had cast a similar spell upon all those who came near him, even his nearest friends and co-workers. It was only rarely that they would remember, as if in a flash, that they were in the company of a great Indian of unsurpassable majesty, born but once in centuries for the redemption of the people. And they would be surprised and even shocked at the free and almost equal way in which they mixed with him, sometimes even taking liberties with him! But that was all for a moment. Again, the simple, smiling figure of Doctorji would cast its spell, and they would forget all about it.

Such was our Doctorji, the founder of the Sangh, the Hindu ideal of man in flesh and blood, the embodiment of the saying '*Kriyasiddhi sattve bhavati mahatam na upakarane*' (The great ones achieve great tasks not because of external aids but by their intrinsic merit), a guiding light for all generations to fashion their lives in its effulgence for a glorious and immortal national life.

3

'What We Lacked Was the Consciousness of Fundamental Hindu Unity'

MADHAV SADASHIVRAO GOLWALKAR, 'GURUJI'

This is the text of a talk given by M.S. Golwalkar, 'Guruji', in the Sangh Shiksha Varg[1] of RSS at Nagpur in May 1942. The talk was delivered when the country was still under British rule. In it, Guruji traces the reasons for the downfall and slavery of the country, seeking to attribute it to the disunity among the Hindus and emphasizing the need for the Sangh's mission of Hindu unity.

The very first thing that strikes us about ourselves is that we all belong to a great society called the Hindus, numbering 300 million, who dwell in this land of Bharatvarsha and on whose account the country is known as Hindustan. The Hindus were one of the most powerful and leading nations of the world in the past, adorned with glory and greatness. Until foreign powers came and polluted the soil of this land, we lived in peace and plenty. We had a galaxy of mighty empires, unparalleled religious philosophies and an enduring social fabric. Among us were great thinkers and statesmen, and also heroes and warriors, with powerful armies at their command. How is it that the same people today have lost all this power, glory and freedom? Many thinking people attribute different reasons to the downfall and decay of the great Hindu nation. Some say that the foreigners were too powerful to defeat and were well-equipped with manpower and material. They were armed with superior weapons and had more powerful, better trained and more disciplined armies than the Hindu forces. In short, they believe that our downfall was not due to our own inherent weakness and degradation but because of the superior force of the foreigners who descended upon this land to destroy our way of life.

But two significant chapters of our history lead us to an altogether different conclusion. The first was the large-scale and systematic invasion of Hindustan attempted by the so-called world conqueror, Alexander. The Greek emperor tried to invade Hindustan with his powerful army. He reached as far as the western bank of Sindhu River with the objective of plundering this land of gold. But Purushottama[2], a small Hindu king on the frontiers of Hindustan, resisted the march of the invader and successfully pushed back the hordes of invading Greeks. There is incontrovertible evidence to prove that Purushottama inflicted a major defeat upon Alexander. But this true history has been hidden from us by foreign writers and historians. They were not prepared to accept that Alexander's expedition was a failure. Instead, they came out with a version that the Greek forces defeated Purushottama and were about to cross the Sindhu. But that never happened.

After the first encounter with Purushottama, Alexander had to give up his grandiose invasion plan and retreat hastily towards Greece via Iran. Foreign authors came up with their own interpretations. According to them, Alexander was forced to return due to a sudden mutiny in his army, which wanted to return to Greece immediately. But that too never happened. Neither Alexander nor his army ever returned to Greece. Instead, they decided to settle in the green and beautiful meadows of Iran, while Alexander met his end on Iranian soil.

It is difficult to reconcile oneself to the distorted, fabricated version of the invasion as given by foreign writers. We are taught only that history in our school textbooks. But we must be able to check the facts and arrive at proper conclusions. Soon after the death of Alexander, another attempt was made by one of his lieutenants, Seleucus Nicator[3], to invade Hindustan, but he was so very badly mauled by Emperor Chandragupta[4] that, taking a lesson of his lifetime from his crushing defeat, he made peace with Chandragupta and offered his own daughter's hand in marriage.

Seleucus had to bow before the Hindu emperor because the invading forces found it impossible to withstand the might of his powerful Hindu army. But then, how is it that after some time, a new and dark chapter unfolded in the form of the Muslim invaders, who succeeded in defeating the same powerful Hindu armies and obtaining a firm foothold on our soil? Those Muslim invaders were, in fact, less powerful and ill-equipped in comparison to their predecessors, the Greeks. Why then did the might of the Hindus crumble before the Muslim onslaught, and why was their freedom lost? You will find the answer to the above question in another historical incident of equal significance – the dramatic episode from the life of King Prithviraj[5].

Prithviraj was the last Hindu emperor of Hindustan, who had a valiant army and a glorious empire. Muhammad Ghori[6] tried repeatedly, more than a dozen times, to invade Prithviraj's Hindu empire, and every time the Muslim invader was completely beaten back and put to flight. Ghori was captured by Prithviraj several times during those attacks. But he survived each time due to Prithviraj's generosity. What happened to Prithviraj's brilliant career in the end was a big lesson to Hindus. This powerful Hindu emperor fell victim to a petty family feud between himself and Jaichand Rathod, his father-in-law, who could not reconcile with the way in which Prithviraj had taken away his daughter, Samyukta, and married her. Individual or family feuds are, as a rule, a common feature of human society across time and place. But they were not allowed to assume a proportion that might prove detrimental to the interests of their country itself. When faced with external threats, people easily forget these feuds and unite as one to face the common enemy.

How is that we, Hindus, alone carry these feuds to such an extent that the result is utterly disastrous for our own national well-being? Why do our petty feuds lead to such a fatal fall? What is wrong with our body politic? Let alone a man on the street, even a responsible person of royal status like Jaichand had no national consciousness to place individual interests or personal honour in the background, and give priority to national interest and honour. He was prepared to go to unscrupulous lengths to avenge his daughter's marriage. Jaichand could not understand that by inviting a foreign power to help him against Prithviraj, he was not just harming Prithviraj, but the very Hindu nation itself. Whatever his differences with Prithviraj, Jaichand should not have stooped so low to invite the enemy of the Hindus merely to avenge the marriage of his daughter – a purely family affair. But he fell victim to the intense passions of hatred and vengeance and forged himself into a treacherous weapon in the hands of Ghori.

Thus, the invading Muslim rulers came to dominate this country not by dint of *their* strength, but with *our* help. We suffered from an acute lack of national feelings and hence were divided amongst ourselves. We could not present a united front to foreign aggression. It was this lack of Hindu national solidarity that had caused and hastened our downfall. A mere glance at our history of the last 1,000 years proves this contention right, again and again. If we have been under one foreign domination or other throughout this period, we have no one else to blame but ourselves. Whenever an effort was made to end this domination, it was our own Hindu brethren that forestalled that effort.

I would like to refer to other instances in our history in support of my contention. The East India Company[7] sent its agents to this golden land for the purpose of carrying out trade and commerce. Its directors in England had a keen and covetous eye upon the invaluable riches of the Hindus. It was an ordinary private trading company that had nothing to do with the government. It was not supposed to be its concern to maintain large armies and conquer countries. But as the company wanted more money it raised armies to loot people and exploit the financial resources of the country.

The company collected money from us and raised the armies, and then turned the same armies against us. How could it happen that an ordinary trading company could conquer this vast country and dominate over its great and ancient people? It happened because we were blind and indifferent to the national threat that was steadily eating our vitals. There were instances of many of our rich Hindus financing the nefarious activities of the company for their personal gains without the thought of the fatal effect that their actions might have upon the nation and its people. All these selfish factors ended in our own destruction. We not only allowed the foreigners on this soil but also helped them dominate us. We valued personal interest more than that of our country and people. Therein lies the root cause of our slavery and downfall during the last 1,000 years. We, in fact, never lacked in armies and weapons of war, which were always superior to those of our enemies. But our indifference was so great that we never cared who ruled us. We forgot to distinguish between a foreigner and a ruler of our own.

Many foreign travellers often observed that Hindus, though brave, were effeminate in character. They could not fight on their own initiative or for their own nation. One French traveller opined that a few thousand well-trained soldiers under an efficient commander could easily overrun the whole of this vast sub-continent. Hindus would fight bravely only when it was a fight amongst themselves. But they failed to present a united front to push back foreign invaders. The unbelievable historical story about Bhakhtiyar Khilji[8], who went from Delhi with just eighteen horsemen and conquered the whole of Bengal, speaks for itself.

And unfortunately, these conditions persist even to this day. We have never lacked in learning, wealth or bravery. But what we have lacked is the awareness of a fundamental Hindu unity – the sense of being one organic whole. We failed to make use of our great Hindu majority, which could otherwise have been our unique asset. Every Hindu thinks that they are alone, though the truth is the opposite. This feeling of isolation is responsible for the atmosphere of dread and cowardice prevalent in our midst. If we were to put a stop to our downfall, it should be our effort to fight these unworthy and perverted ideas, and develop a healthy and proper outlook.

4

'Cow Slaughter Is an Anti-India Act'

MADHAV SADASHIVRAO GOLWALKAR, 'GURUJI'

M.S. Golwalkar's tenure as sarsanghachalak saw many significant milestones, one of which was the campaign for a ban on cow slaughter. It was in a way the first major popular movement after Independence in which more than 27.5 million people of the country, from almost all walks of life, came forward to attest their signatures demanding complete ban on cow slaughter. The RSS cadre played a pivotal role in that campaign under the guidance of Golwalkar. During the course of that campaign, Golwalkar delivered several public speeches. The following is a summary of some of those speeches, capturing the essence and focus of the campaign.

Since ancient times, cows have been highly revered in India. The Vedas contain numerous references to the worship and protection of the cows. It is considered that cow protection is intrinsically linked to the overall well-being of humanity. Scholars are aware of these facts. Many such noble individuals have published concerned scriptures, verses and writings to impart accurate knowledge about this subject to the people of India.

Supporters of the ban on cow slaughter across the country, who are all of voting age, have provided their signatures demanding the same, the details of which are presented before you. A weeklong campaign has been undertaken to collect the signatures, and the RSS swayamsevaks have gathered these signatures in a transparent and authentic manner. Sometimes, such work is easily done by simply sitting at home. That was not the method adopted by the swayamsevaks.

Many saints and leaders have presented logical and forceful arguments regarding the cow slaughter ban. They have spoken with great intensity, like the flames of a fire. The greater the intensity of the feelings, the sharper the language naturally becomes. It is the circumstances that are the main reason for whatever strong views have been expressed here. Otherwise, none of them had any animosity towards anyone. Additionally, despite staying away from politics, it is natural for them to view issues like cow slaughter ban from a political prism. I have no objection to this. But personally, I do not see the cow slaughter ban movement from that prism.

Let me begin with the experiences we have had during this signature collection campaign. We took up this initiative during the auspicious period of Gopashtami.[1] Shortly after that, our prime minister accused that the cow slaughter ban movement was a political tactic. I never imagined that the cow slaughter ban movement would be branded as political. While working for this cause, I realized that strengthening Indian values and protecting Indian principles is extremely necessary. Without that, advancement of our nation is impossible. Cow is our mother and her slaughter is disgraceful for everyone. It must stop forthwith.

It is heartening that people of various religions, such as Muslims, Christians, Jews, supported this program. However, when Pandit Nehru[2] opposed it, some of their leaders began to feel that it was better to stay away from this campaign of the Hindus. The Muslim leaders, who were initially ready to support the campaign, also felt that staying away from Hindus would be beneficial to them. Some of them explicitly said so as well. Despite all this, millions of sensible Muslims still came forward to affix their signatures. They know that as citizens of India, they must align with the national mainstream here.

Their thinking is not only natural but also necessary. Take the example of America: if an Indian, living there as a naturalized citizen, were to say, 'The American Independence Day celebration is not mine; instead, Vijayadashami[3] is my national festival,' or 'I do not consider Washington as a national leader, I consider Rama[4] and Krishna as the true national leaders,' would the people there accept? Would such a person be able to live there as a citizen?

We did not take up this signature campaign thinking of any political strategies. We undertook this work driven by inner motivation. However, if the government ignores the significance of our sentiments and considers this work as a political strategy, how can we call this government our own? It is now clear that all the right-thinking people of our society support the demand for a complete ban on cow slaughter. Acharya Vinoba Bhave[5] said, 'The entire land belongs to the cowherds.' But I want to ask: Is this the land of the cowherds or the cow-slaughterers?

Our campaign is not new. Maharshi Dayananda[6] also took up this cause. Did he undertake it with a view to gain any political mileage? I am reminded of an incident from the life of Lokmanya Tilak.[7] He once visited Nagpur. Nagpur is the birthplace of an organization called the Cow Protection Society. When Tilak arrived, the organizers of the organization went to him and requested his support for the society. Lokmanya gave an interesting reply: 'Shivaji Maharaj did not establish any cow protection organization.' Not that he did not support the movement – he did that throughout his life – however, what he meant was that unless the rule of cow slaughterers is ended, how can the protection of cows be possible? Swarajya (self-rule) should mean cow protection – this has always been our conviction.

The Sangh has taken up this work with no self-interest. We seek no credit or benefit from it. Cow conservation is an important conviction for us and we want to imprint this conviction on everyone's mind. The Indian Constitution has promised a ban on cow slaughter. The relevant constitutional clause stated that all cattle, milch or dry, must be protected. The entire country was hopeful that their long-awaited wish would be fulfilled in the sessions of the Indian Parliament and state assemblies. However, nothing happened. The bill banning cow slaughter was not taken up. In fact, some states that wanted to pass it were dissuaded from doing so.

After Independence, it was expected that there would be a complete ban on the sale and slaughter of cows. However, due to the policy of appeasement, nothing was done in that direction. Therefore, to make the government aware of the feelings of the majority, we have undertaken this campaign. If the people want such a bill, we will ensure that it reaches the government through the signature campaign. For those who do not want it, we will explain the need for it. That will be our work. Rest is in the government's hands. If the government disregards the feelings of the majority to please a few voices, it will not be able to safeguard democracy. We are confident that such a bill will be presented in Parliament soon. This will be a test to see whether the government is truly democratic or not. This will be the moment of truth for the government.

We are adopting the most effective method to awaken the public. This is in line with our 27 years of work. We inspire the public with the feeling that this land, stretching from Kanyakumari to Kashmir, belongs to the Hindus. Hindus are the nationals of this country. We have repeatedly expressed this in various ways. There is nothing to hide in this, nor do we wish to make the topic difficult to understand. We say clearly that this is a Hindu nation. Some people do not agree with us, but they too understand this truth, though they do not have the courage to express it openly.

Democracy cannot be safeguarded by appeasing a few individuals and disrespecting the feelings of the majority. We are confident that such a bill will be presented in Parliament in the near future.

We are ordinary yet straightforward people, so we speak the truth frankly. Once, Shri Venkataram Shastri[8] called me 'blunt'. We speak in a blunt but clear manner. When we say that this is a Hindu nation, we also acknowledge that everybody has the right to live here, but they must adopt the appropriate conduct and way of life of this land. They should accept the valour of our ancestors, participate in the festivals and celebrations and maintain national harmony. They must truly become citizens of this land. They can worship their chosen deity. Hinduism grants every individual full freedom and recognition to develop according to their own way of worship, faith and belief. However, they should live in harmony with the national mainstream.

Hindus have always been liberal. Many centuries ago, due to the destruction caused by Western barbarism, the Parsi people came to live on the shores of Surat to protect their religion, sacred scriptures and the holy fire. At that time, the king of the region, Yadvaram, welcomed them with open arms. He consulted with the Shankaracharya of Dwarkapeeth[9] on how they should be accepted. They were accepted with the condition that they refrain from eating beef. And to this day, they continue to honour that condition while safeguarding their religion. On the other hand, some of our so-called progressive Hindus have become beef eaters. I do not consider them well-educated. Therefore, when people of other faiths wish to live with us, they must imbibe the values of this nation and integrate into the national mainstream. If we accept this truth, resolving all other issues will not be difficult.

During my travels for this cause, I once met a saint who told me that the government had adopted Emperor Ashoka's wheel as the national emblem, but he asked, during Ashoka's reign, was cow slaughter taking place? If not, then this government should also stop cow slaughter. Otherwise, the Ashoka Chakra should be removed from the national emblem.

Some people say that there is a large population of livestock here. But the reality is that India is a poor country with very little livestock. In this land of cowherds, the number of cows is very low. If I say that it is the lowest, no one should be surprised. Such a dire situation exists here. Therefore, we should think about how to stop cow slaughter. I have heard that before the Great War, the number of livestock here was much higher; but only 40 per cent remains now. We lost 60 per cent during the war. Nowadays, the craze for dollars has taken over everyone's minds, and some people are ready to do anything for it. Even pregnant cows are slaughtered. Some people claim that they do not slaughter milking cows. However, I believe that once a cow becomes pregnant, it does not remain a milking cow for some time, and they use this loophole in the law to justify slaughtering it.

Approximately one to one-and-a-half crore[10] cows are slaughtered every year. In the land of cowherds, no laws exist to ban it – how surprising? Therefore, considering all aspects – from economic to the more significant aspect of faith – cow slaughter should be banned. There should be strict punishment for those who slaughter cows. Great leaders in our country have said that cow slaughter is equal to human slaughter. Just as there are penalties for human slaughter, there should be similar penalties for cow slaughter too. Besides making such strict laws, the government must also develop a large-scale plan for cow rearing, cow conservation and cow protection across the country. That is necessary if we wish to prevent the slaughter of cows, bulls and other livestock in Gokul.[11]

The current provision merely states that state governments should take steps to ban cow slaughter – which is more of an instruction. However, how many states have actually followed it? Even those few rules that were made have been rendered ineffective. Therefore, it would be better if there is a nationwide, unrestricted law on this.

I believe that demeaning national life by encouraging the disgusting trade of cow meat out of greed for foreign currency is a great sin. I consider even touching those ill-gotten dollars as a grave offense. Such a heinous practice will ruin the entire national life. Wealth stolen and earned from sinful acts or external vices can never contribute to the prosperity of any family or nation. The slaughter of cows and the business derived from it will bury India so deep in the dirt that even if God himself comes to help, it will be a difficult task to uplift the nation. Therefore, we should leave behind the desire for riches from foreign currency.

People should not think that this work has been initiated by the RSS and hence the swayamsevaks will do everything. They are merely catalysts. The work belongs to the people, and the credit also will go to everyone.

We are aware that Mahatma Gandhi himself supported cow protection. He used to begin his prayers by reciting a verse for the protection of cows. That shows how seriously he regarded the issue of cow protection. The Congress, in its pursuit for freedom from the British rule, had decided to enter into a compromise with the India League, hoping that it would make things easier for attaining the goal of self-rule. When Shri Mahadev Desai[12] showed the agreement between the Congress and the India League to Gandhiji, he read it and returned it with his consent.

However, one of the conditions in that agreement was that after attaining self-rule, Muslims would have the right to continue cow slaughter. That caused great discomfort to Gandhiji. He could not sleep that night. In the middle of the night, he called for Shri Mahadev Desai and had him bring the agreement back. After reading it thoroughly once again, he said, 'I cannot accept the condition of cow slaughter. We are indebted to the cow, and therefore, protecting it is our supreme duty.' As a result, the agreement fell through at that time.

Some people argue that there is a command in the Quran regarding cow slaughter, but that is not true. If such a command existed, there would not have been a ban on cow slaughter during some periods of the Mughal rule in India. We know that Babur understood the sentiments of the local people and decided that it would not be appropriate to crush their feelings and hence imposed a ban on cow slaughter. If cow slaughter had been a religious sentiment for Muslims, Babur would have sincerely followed it.

The Muslims in our country were originally Hindus, and hence their behaviour should align with that of Hindus. Hindus regard the cow as their mother, and Muslims should also acknowledge it as a mother. In doing so, their Indian identity would be reaffirmed. Cow slaughter is an anti-India act.

Nowadays, people hesitate to refer to the cow as a mother. It has been a characteristic of our society to regard anything that nurtures us as a mother. That is why we have called this earth, which nourishes us with food and water, 'Mother'. We also regard the rivers of this land, which quench our thirst with their pure waters, as 'Mothers'. The term 'Ganga Maiya (Mother Ganga)' is very old. After a child stops taking mother's milk, it turns to cow's milk. It is only the cow's milk that we call as '*dudh*' (Hindi word for milk).

Some people provide references from the Vedas to support cow slaughter. They claim that the Vedas describe the *gomedh yajna*, where people used to slaughter cows and perform rituals with their meat. However, these references are based on misconceptions. Words must be understood in their true sense. If *gomedh* means slaughtering a cow and performing a ritual, then *pitrimedh yajna* could mean offering the parents as a sacrifice, and *grihmedh yajna* could imply setting the house on fire. But it's true meaning is something else. One should always take the true meaning. Supporting such a sinful act for personal gain is a greater sin.

Some argue that the increasing number of cows will reduce food for humans. This argument is irrational, because cows do not eat human food. After the harvest, they feed on the leftover husk and straw. In ancient times, people would leave a third of their land for pasture. This practice had a scientific basis. First, it allowed cows to graze, and second, it helped maintain soil fertility.

During the First World War, people of England thought of becoming self-reliant in terms of food grains. To achieve this, they brought the entire land under cultivation. Initially, the yields increased, but after some time, the fertility of the land started decreasing. Therefore, they had to leave some land for pasture again. Unfortunately, a similar practice is being implemented in India, and grazing lands are being eliminated. Animals are not allowed to graze in forests, and then the justification for continuing cow slaughter is made by citing shortage of fodder. This is completely unjustifiable.

In America, scientific studies on agricultural progress revealed that the excessive use of chemical fertilizers led to a decrease in soil fertility. Agricultural fields turned into deserts, where even a blade of grass could not grow. They also realized that cow dung increases crop yields and maintains soil fertility. Therefore, they started using more cow dung and reduced the use of artificial fertilizers. However, they are sending artificial fertilizers to our country.

By sending artificial fertilizers here, foreign countries achieve two objectives. First, by importing fertilizers, our foreign debt keeps increasing. Second, the fertility of our land is gradually decreasing due to the use of those fertilizers. Our people do not understand this. They think that foreign experts are helping us. What they do not realize is that these foreigners are not interested in our country's welfare, but only in their own.

They claimed that the milk of our cows is tuberculosis infected. If drinking milk from our cows can cause tuberculosis, what about eating the meat of those cows? The truth is that they want to destroy our livestock and make us dependent on them for milk powder. This is simply a policy to keep our country enslaved. Therefore, we must always keep our country's interests in mind and understand their motives. We should never accept any advice or subjugation from them. It is important to realize that when foreigners offer unsolicited advice, it is driven by their own interests. Thus, we must think independently. And that is true wisdom.

The butchers of our country consider slaughter as their ancestral tradition, and based on that conviction, they filed a case in the Supreme Court. The honourable judge ruled that young cows and bulls should not be slaughtered, and, at the same time, livelihood of the butchers too should not be taken away. On that basis, the judge stated that older cows can be slaughtered. Now, think about it: after the cows are slaughtered, how can one claim whether the meat is from an old or a young cow? It is difficult to determine. The second point is that when people in the state are corrupt, there is no need to be surprised if, for a little money, they certify a young cow as old. Therefore, our learned judges should not have made such a decision that leads to a result contrary to their own ruling. On one hand, they impose a ban on cow slaughter, and on the other, they leave a loophole. This is not correct. Hence, a complete ban on the slaughter of all cattle would be the just decision. Anything less than that will not be acceptable.

The union home minister had written a letter urging all states to enact laws banning cow slaughter. But Bengal and Maharashtra refused to do so. It is shocking that those who gain power by invoking the names of the descendants of Shivaji[13] today support cow slaughter in the very birthplace of Shivaji.

It is absolutely necessary for the central government to create a nationwide law for banning cow slaughter, even if it requires amending the Constitution. After all, the Constitution has already been amended 22 times. If the Constitution could be amended to grant the right to hand over the country's land to the enemy, why can't it be amended to ban cow slaughter? Recently, there has been some talk about amending the Constitution to make Sindhi a regional language, so it is not reasonable to say that an amendment cannot be made for the purpose of banning cow slaughter.

The Cow Protection Movement Committee has demanded that the government must amend the Constitution and create a law to ban cow slaughter. We should also resolve to ensure that this ban is implemented through legal means.

Those in power refer to our demand as a 'political stunt'. Respected people like Prabhudatt Brahmachari,[14] Shankaracharyas, Jain monks and others, who are leading this campaign, are saintly figures. What have they got to do with anything other than their prayers and worship? Jagadguru Shankaracharya even said in a gathering that if the government considers this a 'political stunt', then by immediately banning cow slaughter, it could gain the political support of the masses. Why doesn't the government take this simple step then? If Congress doesn't ban cow slaughter, it should not expect our help or votes. If the government thinks it must allow cow slaughter to win Muslim votes, we Hindus will not give them our votes. Let them win the elections with Muslim votes.

Some people think of me as a political leader. They believe that I am trying to become a minister. But I do not like politics. Fortunately, the field where I can serve my community is far more noble. I will dedicate my life to serving my community through that. I never even dream of entering politics. By the grace of God, my mind is clear, and a person who has drunk nectar would never long for buttermilk.

It was my wish that Prabhudatt Brahmachariji should not go on a hunger strike. Had I known before his declaration, I would have persuaded him against it. But now, since he has already announced it, he will surely stick to his decision. I know him well. He is very determined. Therefore, from the twentieth, he will definitely go on a hunger strike. It is not possible that while our saintly people fast we simply stand and watch. Hence, on the twentieth, let all of us also fast for a day. Let us all pray to God that this religious work is completed successfully. Let all of us raise a powerful voice together, demanding a law to stop cow slaughter.

As I travel across the country, I see that awareness regarding the issue of cow slaughter is growing among the people. However, my request to all of you is that this movement should not take an inflammatory form. Always remember the love and compassion of the cow, and without harbouring any anger, try to present our demand calmly. If the government's mind is clouded, it does not mean that we too should become like that. We must lead this movement with complete restraint. Threats to our national security from China and Pakistan are ever-present. In such a situation, we must be careful to ensure that this movement does not cause any catastrophic outburst. Let us awaken the entire society and raise awareness in such a way that the protection of the cow, which is the pride of our nation, becomes a reality.

There is no need to argue at length about the economic and social utility of the cow. We simply say that it is our pride, and it must be protected. If the cow is lost, then what will we do with our lives? Therefore, once again, I humbly request all of you to make it a firm resolution that we will stop it through law. This is the need of the hour.

5

'The Objective of the Sangh Is to Organize Hindu Society and Make It Powerful'

MADHUKAR DATTATRAYA DEORAS, 'BALASAHEB'

Madhukar Dattatraya, also known as 'Balasaheb' Deoras, was the third sarsanghachalak of the RSS, who succeeded Golwalkar, 'Guruji', in that position in 1973. He remained the chief of the organization for more than two decades until ill health led him to hand over the reins to his successor, Prof. Rajendra Singh, 'Rajju Bhaiyya'. Deoras' association with the RSS began when Dr Hedgewar, 'Doctorji', was alive, and thus he became one of the founder leaders of the organization. A forward-looking and reformist leader, Deoras introduced path-breaking initiatives in the organization, the most important of which was the push given to bring Hindu society out of caste-based divisions and animosity.

Like Golwalkar, 'Guruji', Balasaheb too contributed extensively to the dissemination of the Sangh ideology and vision through numerous public and organizational articulations. His views became the defining direction for the swayamsevaks not only during the years of his leadership but also far beyond that.

Herein are presented some of his thoughts on the idea and ideal of the RSS.

The work of Rashtriya Swayamsevak Sangh is a public endeavour. It is natural for its working methods to undergo slight changes according to circumstances. As situations change, the way the organization expresses its thoughts also adapts accordingly. Therefore, one should not be confused by certain modified approaches. Despite differences in examples before and after 1940, the fundamental ideology remains unchanged.

The objective of the Sangh is to organize Hindu society and make it powerful. Since this is an abstract thought, it may seem somewhat difficult to understand. In comparison, goals that can be achieved within a few years, such as ending British rule in India, are easier to comprehend. Because the Sangh's objective appears to be more complex, several questions often arise, such as: How long will the work of the Sangh continue? What is the nature of our strength? How much strength do we have? And so on.

To understand this, we must consider the ultimate objective of the Sangh. A natural order is necessary among individuals who act with a sense of collective identity because the true strength of society lies within that order. When such strength is awakened in society, it becomes naturally ready to solve its problems on its own at all times. The Sangh is working towards awakening this natural strength.

But the question 'how will this be achieved' arises. The example of England during the Second World War provides an answer and guidance in this regard. Several countries, such as France and Poland, collapsed within days under the impact of the War. England, too, withdrew its forces and fled from Dunkirk. It seemed as though England had been defeated. Many believed that it would soon make a treaty with Germany. In 1940, following the fall of France, Marshal Pétain[1] and Marshal Darlan[2] signed a treaty with Germany. However, by 1945, when England emerged victorious, these leaders were tried for treason.

What led to England's success? History testifies that the secret of its victory lay in its continuous and determined efforts. As the saying goes, 'God helps those who help themselves.' While several factors contributed to England's success, the most significant were its courage, determination and perseverance. Many attribute this victory to Churchill[3], but that is not entirely true. After the victory, a celebration was held in Churchill's honour by various institutions. During this event, a prominent leader, Clement Attlee[4], addressed Churchill, saying, 'You are the Lion of England.' Churchill, despite being a man of great ambition and ego, humbly responded, 'No, I am not the lion. You all are lions. I simply roared for you.'

The greatness of any nation does not depend on how great, wise or influential its leaders are. Rather, it depends on how strong, patient and capable its common people are. Their thoughts, values and behaviour determine the strength of the nation. A society where people are selfish and never consider the well-being of the entire nation cannot last long. This is why Hinduism teaches that one must forsake selfishness and work for the welfare of others: '*Ete satpurushah pararthaghatakah swarthan parityajya ye*.' Similarly, an ordinary person is one who engages in efforts for the benefit of others while ensuring that their personal interests remain unharmed.

In a society where the common people become selfless, a natural and inherent strength emerges. The history of the reconstruction of countries like England, Germany, Israel, Japan and India began after the Second World War. In these years, Germany achieved even greater economic progress than before. Japan and Israel also performed miracles. The Jews of Israel were historically regarded as people obsessed with money, greedy, cowardly and unfamiliar with the art of war. However, these very Jews fought in Palestine for 16 years. Half of Israel's population fought battles from their rooftops, while the other half operated factories from underground. They constantly lived under the fear of Arab attacks, yet today, they hold dominance over the Arabs.

In a short span, they strengthened their internal systems and also developed the capability to counter external aggression. How was this possible? There is only one reason – the natural strength within their society awakened in the behaviour of ordinary citizens.

In normal times, different societies may not appear significantly distinct from one another. However, when a critical moment arrives, their uniqueness is revealed. Times of crisis expose the distinction between strong and weak societies. The work of the Rashtriya Swayamsevak Sangh is directed towards awakening the natural strength within the common people of the society, who are the true source of power. The sooner this work is accomplished, the faster the mission of the Sangh will reach completion.

Across the world, societies that were more awakened, developed and naturally strong achieved progress with minimal effort and in a short span of time. However, the condition of Hindu society is different. Due to centuries of foreign rule, the natural state of our society has been completely eroded, leaving it in a fractured and weakened condition. India faces multiple challenges – regional differences, linguistic divisions, caste distinctions and more. When one issue is resolved, another new problem arises.

Today, Hindus are suffering not only in Pakistan and other countries, but even in Hindustan. If one were to focus only on despair, one might even think that being born into Hindu society is a matter of great misfortune. However, thinking in this way is not right. Until the society's natural, balanced state is restored, these painful circumstances c annot change.

During the time of Shivaji[5], a certain level of awareness had emerged. After the killing of Sambhaji[6], Rajaram[7] was taken to the fort of Jinji in the South for safety. When he was surrounded by Aurangzeb's[8] army, he managed to escape. Great commanders like Santaji Ghorpade[9] and Dhanaji Jadhav[10] continued guerrilla warfare. The entire society supported them. From the villages, they received young men to fight and food grains for sustenance. Information about the enemy's movements was regularly provided by the general public.

When Aurangzeb would learn that a particular village had supplied food, soldiers and weapons to the Marathas, supporting them, he would destroy that village. The residents were massacred, homes were burned down and crops were destroyed. Despite such oppression and cruelty, the society continued to actively support the struggle against the Mughals. However, such a state of society has only existed occasionally. The occasional flare-up of such sparks of public awakening is not enough. These sparks must be turned into a lasting flame.

During the thousands of years of foreign domination, our noble traditions were broken and our society declined. Ignoring this reality and only thinking about the future is not the right approach.

Various explanations are given regarding this decline. Some say that during the period of subjugation, long and exhausting struggles led to widespread despair among the common people. Others believe it happened due to the collapse of the varna system. Many such reasons can be proposed. But the truth is that these severe problems arose when our society's natural and inherent character was lost.

To resolve these issues, it is absolutely essential to rebuild the society's innate strength. The work of the Sangh will only be complete when the tradition of developing natural strength in society is firmly established.

In England, this strength has been passed down through generations as a tradition – almost like a value absorbed through one's mother's milk. There, through plays, cultural programs, cinema, education and all other mediums, everyone is shaped by the same set of values. In European countries, even though they experienced the Industrial Revolution, and countries like America underwent colonization, they always preserved their internal strength. In England, Clive[11] – who was once considered a thug and was sent off to India just to be gotten rid of – ended up becoming the 'founder of the British Empire' here. In those countries where values and character are instilled along with a mother's milk, even a thug like Clive becomes highly useful to the nation.

Another example is from Malaya. In a factory there, Chinese workers staged a violent uprising. Since their numbers were large, the British collector, out of fear, remained hidden for three days. He only came out after reinforcements had arrived. But by that time, a European manager from another factory – armed with just two pistols – had gone alone, fired some shots, and brought the riot under control. When news of this reached the higher authorities, the collector was dismissed and sent back to England. His wife even divorced him, saying, 'I cannot accept such a coward as my husband.'

Today in India, the approach is quite different. The average person here is not moulded in the same way. A strange notion about character has taken root – that it merely consists of what someone eats, how they dress or how they look at women. In truth, character is a much broader subject. A sense of responsibility towards society and the nation, and the readiness to sacrifice everything for its cause, are central aspects of character.

It is said about England's victory over Napoleon[12] at the Battle of Waterloo[13] that the Battle of Waterloo was won on the playgrounds of Eton. This means that the values instilled during childhood – through a mother's nurturing, a father's guidance, school playgrounds and classrooms – are what laid the foundation for that success. There must be a tradition of instiling such values from all corners of early life. Until such a society is built, India will continue to need the dedicated efforts of a unique organization like the Sangh.

No one else is currently working on rebuilding this natural, value-based structure of the society – in fact, most have ignored it. Creating natural strength within society is the foundation of our ultimate goal. Without understanding this clearly, many doubts and questions may arise. The daily functioning of a Sangh shakha is designed precisely to fulfil this goal.

Many of our traditions have been broken. Society has become disorganized. This is also why reform plans often do not succeed. The success of these plans depends not only on effort and hard work but also on the condition of the society. Today, the situation is not like it was during the time of Shankaracharya.[14] Public awakening and the task of spreading knowledge have become sluggish. For thousands of years, society has remained in this miserable state. No fixed time frame can be determined for a fragmented society to return to its natural state.

Our work is extremely essential, and therefore, it must be done. Two generations have already been dedicated to this work, and how many more will be needed is not our concern; we must continue our efforts relentlessly. Other plans are supplementary; our work is primary and foundational. The vision of the Sangh is to create a way of social life in which the collective consciousness of the people naturally turns towards society, effortlessly becoming capable of nurturing the society willingly and independently.

Given the current conditions of the country, it is also necessary to clearly understand the role of the Sangh. Along with building an invincible strength within Hindu society, the Sangh must also establish itself as a '*nityasiddha shakti*' – an eternally present and stable force. Our work is not like that of political organizations. Whatever immediate problems arise in the country, the Sangh does not attempt to solve all of them. Leaders with some degree of influence or strength may run around either genuinely or to show off, but the Sangh does not.

Why did Doctorji establish the Sangh? In 1927, when Hindus in Nagpur put up a strong resistance during a riot for the first time, everyone praised Doctorji. But just like the story of the blind men and the elephant – each one touching a different part and forming their own idea of what it was – people formed their own interpretations of the Sangh based on limited understanding. The same happened with many of Doctorji's associates who came close to him for various reasons. Some said that Doctorji was a revolutionary and had established the Sangh to uproot British rule. Others claimed that since Hindu–Muslim riots were common in those days, the Sangh was founded to help Hindus fight back.

Sometimes, when fights would break out in a neighbourhood, people would tell Doctorji to send all the swayamsevaks to fight and protect the residents. They believed that only by doing this would the deteriorating habits of society be corrected, and real change come about. Regarding the role of the Sangh, Doctorji would say, 'We will not do anything for you.' People were surprised that this soft-spoken man, who worked to unite Hindus, would say such a thing.

Doctorji would explain to them that society had gone astray. People neither wanted to take initiative nor understood their responsibilities. Whenever violence occurred, they expected Sangh swayamsevaks or the police to come, while they themselves stayed at home. If this mindset continued, society would become even more corrupt. The necessary transformation would not happen. If a neighbourhood was attacked, everyone should pick up a stick and defend it. Sangh swayamsevaks would come, but they would not be at the forefront. Doctorji used to say that even if everyone were to die, it was acceptable. The correct way to protect is to go ourselves and take everyone else along for defence. Only by doing this would the deteriorating habits of society be corrected and the right transformation take place. Doctorji had maintained this perspective on the Sangh's role from the very beginning.

The Sangh must remain continuously and tirelessly committed to the goal it has set before itself. When immediate issues arise, it is essential to carefully consider how much strength should be applied towards resolving them. It would be a mistake to think that all available strength should be thrown behind a single issue with the attitude of 'we'll deal with the rest later'. Viewing every minor problem as extremely critical is not the right approach.

In this context, the example of Napoleon is particularly relevant. He always kept a large reserve force with him. Sometimes this forcc was not used at all, or it would only be deployed at the very last moment of battle. Once during a battle, this reserve force was stationed on higher ground. Napoleon was there, calmly observing the entire battle. The soldiers in the reserve were getting restless watching the fight unfold. One of the officers became so impatient that he unintentionally shouted, 'Onward, onward!' Napoleon, standing nearby, struck the officer with the hilt of his sword and said, 'Who are you to give the order to advance while I am here? I've won many battles – I know when, where and how much force to use.'

Napoleon only used his reserve force when the time was absolutely right, even though the soldiers had been thinking since morning that they should have been sent into battle.

Those who engage in daily work, when faced with pressing problems, often feel that the Sangh's strength should be fully utilized to address those problems. Every time a crisis arises, such thoughts tend to emerge. When they see that Doctorji is not getting directly involved in resolving the immediate issue, various doubts arise in their minds. They begin to think that perhaps the organization is being preserved out of mere institutional attachment, that Sangh swayamsevaks are not concerned about the current problem, that only God knows when the Sangh's ultimate goal will be fulfilled, and that if the Hindu society itself collapses, then even the Sangh's goal will never be achieved – and so on.

In a healthy and ideal society, there are certain inherent qualities – qualities that, unfortunately, are still lacking in our own society. Furthermore, the Sangh's strength is not yet at the level that is truly required.

During the time of the Partition of India, there was widespread violence, conflict and horrific atrocities. Naturally, one might think that the Sangh should have prevented the creation of India. That thought is not incorrect. But despite everything, Partition did happen – it could not be stopped. The main reason was that the Sangh did not have the necessary strength at the national level to stop it.

In military operations, during a retreat, there is a role known as 'the guard action' – a unit assigned to ensure that all soldiers can return safely. Similarly, during Partition, the Sangh played a comparable role. With whatever limited strength it had, the Sangh defended people, resisted attacks and helped bring as many people as possible safely into India. In fact, in many places, the Sangh provided more effective protection than the government.

All of this was possible only because the Sangh maintained its existence with a distinct and determined strength.

It is not appropriate to hold the view that current or immediate problems have no significance for the Sangh. The correct approach towards them is to understand that the greater our strength within society, the more easily these problems can be resolved.

The Sangh has not taken any vow that it will *never* deploy its full strength in dealing with immediate challenges. However, the Sangh's ultimate goal is to transform this weakened society and help it attain a vibrant, natural form. Therefore, the Sangh must maintain its existence until this goal is fulfilled.

Once in a while, it might become necessary to deploy the Sangh's full strength to resolve an immediate issue. Even in such cases, the limits of our role must be considered. If a problem requires resolution at the government level, then efforts for its resolution should also be made at that level. The rest of the organizations, including the Sangh, can only extend support within a certain limit.

Immediate concerns continue to arise in society from time to time. It is not that the Sangh remains unaffected by them or feels no pain – certainly not. The Sangh does not close its eyes to these problems; it reflects upon them seriously. When people today feel troubled by such issues, the Sangh, which has been working for so many years, feels even greater pain. The very fact that such things continue to happen despite the Sangh's existence, despite the efforts made and despite the strength built over the years – and that this strength is not yet enough to prevent these problems altogether or resolve them immediately in the way we would wish – is indeed a cause of sorrow.

There is a significant role played by Dr Hedgewar behind the organization he created. Some people claim that Dr Hedgewar founded the Sangh to overthrow British rule. However, he always believed that by steadily increasing the Sangh's strength and moving towards the ultimate goal, such an outcome would naturally occur.

If needed, he would have even deployed the entire strength of the Sangh for that purpose. As a former revolutionary himself, he had come to realize that merely gathering a few people here and there, training them to use pistols and bombs and carrying out occasional acts would not bring about meaningful change.

Even the revolutionaries understood that the British Empire could not be overthrown merely by killing a few British officers in one or two places. Their vision was to establish centres across the country so that, at the right moment, coordinated action could be taken nationwide. However, when these young men got hold of pistols and bombs, they couldn't restrain themselves in the youthful fervour. If Lala Lajpat Rai was beaten, they were provoked by that; if some other incident occurred, they were agitated by that. As a result, premature explosions would occur here and there.

Having observed all of this, Dr Hedgewar decided to adopt a method of working that would allow the most open and visible activity possible, and that would involve as many young people as possible.

One objective behind this was also to drive the British out of the country. While working towards the societal transformation he envisioned, Dr Hedgewar certainly held the thought in his mind that if, during this process, an opportunity arose, the Sangh should be able to utilize its full strength to expel the British.

Various programs were planned by the people to drive the British out. Around that time, in 1939, a major world war broke out. Although Britain emerged victorious, the war had broken its back to such an extent that it was forced to decide to leave India. If a similar critical issue arises in the future, there would be no hesitation in deploying the full strength of the Sangh to address it.

The Sangh should achieve success through its own strength. However, the decision of where and how much strength to apply – and where not to – should be left to the leadership.

There are various perceptions about the Sangh in society. Those whose ideologies differ from that of the Sangh deliberately spread misconceptions about it. It is possible that some people may form misunderstandings after seeing the outer framework of the Sangh – such as the uniform, strict discipline and obedience. In one American book, the Sangh has been described as the 'Ku Klux Klan'[15]. Because of parading in uniform, some anti-Sangh individuals have even accused it of being Nazi-like. But the Sangh was founded in 1925, when the word Nazi hadn't even been heard of. We have never been bothered by the deliberate attempts to create confusion about the Sangh.

While articulating the vision of the Sangh, we speak of our ancient history, thousands of years of traditions, old systems and express pride in them. We are connected to the links of history. The perspective with which others look at their own history and traditions is different from that of the Sangh. Others tend to believe that all of this was useless – that there was no proper system in this country, no glorious history. They consider history to be one of defeat and downfall. They believe the traditions and systems were created without serious thought. For them, history begins only from the time Muslims arrived and established their rule. However, the Sangh does not agree with this viewpoint.

Our history is so ancient that even historians find it difficult to determine its exact age. It is only natural to feel pride in such a great history, in excellent systems and traditions that our country once had. That is why this sentiment naturally reflects in the language, speech and tone of the Sangh.

When the Sangh takes pride in this country's ancient culture, it sometimes creates a misunderstanding among certain sections of society that the people of the Sangh want to bring back exactly what existed a 1,000 or 2,000 years ago. Some think that the Sangh has no perspective regarding the new and emerging issues that arise in various fields across the country. In this twentieth century, they are seen as wanting to bring back ideas and practices from 2,000 or 4,000 years ago. Many perceive Sangh members as mere revivalists. This is the misconception people have about the Sangh and its work. Therefore, it is important to understand this matter clearly and properly.

For example, when some swayamsevaks of the Sangh entered the political arena, people formed an impression about them that they are very good individuals, full of character, highly nationalistic and that their thoughts are admirable, especially during times of crisis such as Chinese or other foreign invasions. However, when it comes to matters of national planning, social issues or economic policies, it is often said that 'this is not the domain of the Sangh members'.

This perception stems from a single reason: in the speeches given by Sangh members, one often finds the use of words like ancient tradition, culture, spirituality, religion, etc. There is nothing inherently wrong in this. Even today's highly modern people – whether they are communists, socialists or even members of the Congress – tend to use specific language and particular vocabulary in their speeches. Similarly, Sangh members also use their own distinctive language. But due to the conventional patterns associated with that language, misunderstandings arise among others.

We must now behave in a way that clears up these misconceptions. Others should feel that Sangh members, while taking pride in ancient traditions and observing their rightful dignity, are also well-informed about present-day realities – about the current era, prevailing circumstances, and social questions and challenges. A Sangh swayamsevak should not think only from the perspective that everything is already covered in the old Hindu traditions, and therefore, there is no need to think about materialism. If the swayamsevak, for any reason, holds such views, then the Sangh will not be able to exert the kind of influence over others that it intends to.

The Sangh is not a status quoist (conservative) organization that wishes to keep things as they are. It consists of Hindus who want a revolution in society so that the core values of Hinduism may be realized. There are many such people in the world who make lofty proclamations – 'What is there in this? What is there in that?' – and promote grand ideas like 'The world is one', or 'Brahma is the truth, the world is an illusion' with great force. But their actual understanding of spirituality and religion is extremely narrow and confined only to their kitchen and household rituals.

In today's world, a truthful and virtuous person is generally seen as someone who merely observes dietary rules and spends long hours worshiping in front of God. In reality, such thinking is very narrow.

During the period of slavery, our perspectives became very narrow, and as a result, the way of thinking in society also became restricted. Due to such narrow ideas – like 'Don't eat this', 'Don't marry into that' – a time of defeat and decline came upon our society. Taking pride in ancient traditions does not mean that we are also proud of the distorted lifestyle that emerged during this later period.

We hear that people from here went to Java, Bali and even reached as far as Mexico. If, from the beginning, this society had restrictions like the caste-based ones we see today – 'Don't go here,' 'Don't go there', 'If someone's shadow falls on you, you'll be defiled', 'Don't cross the ocean' – then such narrow-minded people could not have reached those places. Only those who were willing to undertake great experiments in society must have gone. It's not like they stood at the seashore, closed their eyes, chanted a mantra and opened their eyes to find themselves in Java or Sumatra. Even in those times, ships must have been built. They must have boarded those ships and shown great courage and patience. Due to changing wind directions, it might have taken them two to four months to reach their destination. They must have fought battles with the people there – or, if there was no war, they must have lovingly and warmly shared their culture with them. They must have taught them agriculture and how to build houses. People who only consider food and customs as religion, or those who give occasional spiritual discourses, certainly would not have been the ones to reach these distant lands.

The Hindu society has passed through many stages. There was a time when brave men from this very land, full of courage, patience and great aspirations, travelled abroad and influenced others through their noble way of life, guiding them along the right path. It is entirely natural to take pride in such a history. However, the distortions that emerged in the intervening period are not something the Sangh rigidly supports.

Take the caste system, for instance. Many people believe it was appropriate for its time. In those days, roads were scarce, and fast means of transportation such as we have today were absent. There was no question of an industrial revolution either. In that era, the caste system was perhaps the best and most necessary arrangement. To express a measured pride in it from that historical perspective is acceptable. But considering today's conditions and the forces of this era, the Sangh does not insist that everything should be restored exactly as it once was.

Our outlook must be such that it helps elevate the standard of human life. It is fine to recreate some of the older structures; but alongside that, there are new problems, the impacts of industrialization and many other issues that must be re-examined. If we display disregard for material progress and a higher standard of living, people will either call us outdated or say we are unaware of the changes happening in today's world.

Therefore, proper reflection on past systems and ideas is essential. Mere pride in the old ways is not enough. A true national figure is one who thinks about the times to come. For that reason, they do not simply allow the current state of affairs in their time to continue as it is.

Some time ago, two books by Savarkar[16] were published. In one of the chapters, it is written that when followers of Islam conquered large parts of India, destroyed many temples to build mosques and corrupted the people by forcing them to eat beef and convert to Islam, the Peshwas defeated them and advanced all the way to Kabul. Upon their return, they should have reconverted those Hindus who had been forcibly turned into Muslims by sprinkling them with Gomutra (cow urine), thus restoring them back into Hinduism. But they did not do this. Nor did they rebuild those temples that had been demolished and turned into mosques by the Muslims. In war, they were victorious, but the Hindus who had been converted to Islam remained Muslims.

The creation of India today is the result of this very mistake. In a way, the son had to pay the father's debt. The emergence of minority communities at both ends of the country was, to some extent, the consequence of a historical mistake made by our ancestors. The direct negative outcome of not bringing our converted brothers back into the Hindu fold is visible today.

In villages, it is said that, at night, some Christian missionaries would throw pieces of bread into a well, and the next morning, after people had drunk the water from that well, the Christians would claim that all those who drank the water had now become Christians because they had consumed 'bread' from the well. The Moplah community emerged from those who were forcibly converted to Islam. In India, a large number of Hindus were converted to Islam. When the king of Kashmir asked the Kashmiri Pandits to reconvert those who had converted and now wished to return to Hinduism, the Pandits refused, saying that the scriptures had no provisions for reconversion. These Brahmins went so far as to say that if the king declared these people Hindus again, they would all commit suicide, and *he* would bear the sin of *Brahmahatya* (Brahminicide). This was the mindset of that time.

However, RSS swayamsevaks do not follow such orthodox or outdated thinking. How absurd is the state of a society that once sent its people in small boats to Java and Sumatra, and proclaimed '*Krinvanto vishwam aryam*' – meaning, 'we shall make the whole world noble (Arya)' – yet later refused to accept their own people back into their fold?

When the Huns and Shakas (Scythians) invaded India, this society was able to assimilate them. At that time, society had the capacity to digest such influences. One other reason was that the Huns and Shakas merely aspired to become rulers through war. Unlike Muslims, they did not try to impose their religion and culture. Even after becoming rulers, they accepted the local religion and culture because it was superior. In those days, our society was powerful and thus assimilated them. Muslims, on the other hand, sought to forcibly convert others, while Hindu society held the belief that once someone became a Muslim, they were lost to the Hindu fold forever.

The current condition of our society has become so peculiar that the essential life-force seems almost entirely lost. The divisions instigated by Muslims and the British – such as untouchability and restrictions around food and contact – cannot be blamed solely on them. The Hindu society must also take responsibility. Whatever weaknesses existed in us were exploited by others. But in the current situation, we must contemplate these issues seriously and constructively.

It is no longer acceptable for generation after generation of a sweeper's family to continue carrying the society's waste. Nor should a sweeper think, 'Someone has to carry the waste, after all. My past ten generations have done this, so my future generations must continue as well.' In this rapidly changing world, it is extremely important to be aware of the forces of transformation and to remain alert to them.

While working in the field, when conversations and interactions occur with people outside the Sangh, a common thought expressed is that, among the forces being centralized in the country, the Rashtriya Swayamsevak Sangh (RSS) will undoubtedly become a significant centre of power. Many other forces currently dominate the centre of governance, but when these forces become fragmented, the Sangh will have to assume responsibility with considerable strength to ensure that anarchy does not arise in society and that society does not drift in a wrong direction.

Therefore, it is the duty of capable swayamsevaks to exert maximum effort now so that Sangh's work becomes even more powerful and effective before such a situation arises. Even today, the kind of and the extent of strength that the Sangh possesses is unmatched in society. However, there is a need to further increase this strength. If Sangh swayamsevaks maintain the necessary connections with various sections of society, then during the polarization of different powers, Sangh work will surely emerge as a major power centre, capable of keeping the entire society stable.

We must assess the current situation carefully and keep an eye on the emerging future conditions. The Congress party, for instance, has systematically attempted to label the Sangh as communal, and through deliberate propaganda, it has tried to implant false perceptions about the

Sangh in society. In addition to this, there is another ideological force that spreads even more misinformation against the Sangh – this ideology is Communism.

If one studies the conditions in our country and in other countries, it becomes evident that the ideology that spread under the name of Communism was driven by a momentary enthusiasm. Over time, that enthusiasm faded. Communism, which claimed to solve all the problems of society, has been proven a failure before the world. Its power is now in decline.

The wall that was built between East Berlin and West Berlin stands as evidence that Communism has failed. When Communism came into direct conflict with other ideologies, the Communists had to build a wall themselves in order to protect their ideology and their people. There may have been other reasons for building that wall, but it certainly signified the defeat of Communism. This new ideology had such an influence even on the educated class that they began to believe it could magically solve all the problems and questions of the world with a mere snap of the fingers. It was thought that all diseases, all sufferings, would be eradicated. The educated younger generation was particularly influenced, and Communism became a fashion, as they believed it was a new remedy, a new ideology. The educated youth who supported it were called 'progressive', but those thoughtful individuals who held different views were labelled as reactionary, communal and so on, creating misconceptions about them. Today, a significant turning point is rapidly approaching worldwide. People have come to realize that the claims made by this ideology – that everything could be solved through it – are false, deceptive and misleading. This realization is spreading across many nations, and it has reached our country as well.

In such a situation, we must present the ideology of our organization, our society's eternal life force, its ancient traditions and the changes we wish to bring about, in such a way that no one can call us outdated or old-fashioned. We must awaken the belief in society that the ideology of the RSS is the most appropriate and correct. It is on this foundation that society can become organized and powerful. And it is through this power that society will be able to solve all its challenges. To think in this way is neither communal nor regressive in any manner.

In the world, the older a country is, the older its history and traditions are. If we consider America, its history spans just two to two-and-a-half centuries. So, if any problem arises there, its background will not be older than 200 years. Russia, too, may have an old history, but the problems it faces today have relatively short historical backgrounds. Because of this short historical span, their problems are less complex and less intricate.

However, the situation in our country is entirely different from all others. Our history spans thousands of years. Even the smallest issues in our society have a background of 2,000–3,000 years. In such a context, neither a Russian model nor an American model can be effective. No foreign framework is going to work in our country. We have to find our own system through our own study and understanding. We must find solutions to our problems through our own intellect and creativity. This is the core idea of the Sangh.

In 1946–47, the events that took place in the country created a reaction across the entire Hindu society. The Sangh benefitted from this reaction in some form. During that time, hundreds of pracharaks[17] emerged, and within a year or two, numerous shakhas were established in various places.

However, the benefit of that reaction could not become permanent. If the assassination of Gandhi had not occurred on 30 January 1948, the Sangh would have had the time to absorb the large number of swayamsevaks who had joined due to the reaction. As a result, the strength of the organization would have greatly increased, and many social evils might have been eliminated.

This was directly experienced in Maharashtra at the time. When hundreds of swayamsevaks became pracharaks or vistaraks (expansion swayamsevaks) and went to different villages, a unique situation developed: well-educated youths from both Brahmin and non-Brahmin families started coming together to the Sangh gatherings. This alarmed those in society whose leadership was based solely on the Brahmin–non-Brahmin divide. They feared that if the Sangh succeeded in eliminating that divide, their power and leadership would collapse.

If the Sangh had gotten two or three more years, the swayamsevaks from both communities would have settled fully into the organization, and the division between Brahmin and non-Brahmin would have disappeared from all of Maharashtra. Even in other states, the Sangh had received so many new swayamsevaks that if they had been fully absorbed, the entire national landscape might have changed. However, perhaps destiny had something else in mind.

In the aftermath of the events of 1948, the unjust crackdown on the Sangh by the government – under the pretext of those events – meant that the large number of people who had joined the Sangh could not be fully assimilated.

Only the strength of the Sangh can maintain societal stability. Today in the country, whether it is those labelled as right-wing, left-wing or socialists, the Sangh interacts with all of them. In all other parties, there seems to be a kind of ideological untouchability, but the Sangh is the only organization in India that remains untouched by this mindset, and Sangh swayamsevaks make consistent efforts to connect with people from all walks of life.

During China's invasion, even military personnel used to ask, 'Can the Sangh's strength not be increased further?' They believed that the presence of such a force in people's minds is essential for the stability of society.

In this way, people have come to realize that the power of the Sangh will ultimately serve the nation and its society. The power to stabilize society at an all-India level lies only with the Sangh, but it does not yet exist in the quantity required. We must build such strength that, whenever an issue arises in any part of the country, we are able to resolve it by our own capacity. No other forces should be able to corrupt society or mislead it into a wrong direction.

Today, everyone's eyes are on the Sangh. The day is not far when all these people will rally around this Sangh power, and with their cooperation, we will certainly succeed in building a strong and resilient society.

6

'May All of Us Sincerely Feel That the Hindus Must Unite and the Basis for That Unity Can Only Be Social Equality'

MADHUKAR DATTATRAYA DEORAS, 'BALASAHEB'

In a path-breaking speech after taking over as the sarsanghachalak, Balasaheb Deoras articulated a powerful vision for the RSS on the questions of caste-based discrimination, social equality and social justice at the famous Vasant Vyakhyanmala (a lecture series) organized in Pune in May 1974. Through this address, Deoras sought to bring social harmony and social justice prominently on the RSS agenda. His categorical assertion that 'if untouchability is not a crime, nothing in the world is a crime' became the key motivation driving the cadres of the mighty organization to plunge into the work of ameliorating caste differences and the scourge of untouchability lock, stock and barrel from the face of the Hindu society. Reproduced here is the English rendering of his historic speech, originally delivered in Marathi.

The organizers of this program had suggested some topics for my speech. Out of them, I have chosen the topic 'Social Equality and Hindu Consolidation', as it has a vital bearing on the future of our nation. Hindu consolidation is a must for the welfare of the nation. Hence, all the aspects of it are important. Even among them, the aspect of social equality, being a delicate and currently relevant topic, appealed to me as one of great import.

While taking up this subject, the first question that naturally comes before us is: 'Who is a Hindu?' Many definitions have been given for the word 'Hindu', but none appears to be perfect. Each one of them, although carefully worded, suffers from the problem of being either 'too narrow' (*avyapti*) or 'too expansive' (*ativyapti*). That doesn't mean we can deny the very existence of the Hindu society just because it defies a definition. Although the word cannot be defined easily, we all know very well that the 'Hindu society' does exist. Also, all of us do have a definite and common understanding as to who constitutes that society. The government had formulated the Hindu Code Bill some years ago, which was approved by Parliament. Pandit Nehru and Dr Ambedkar[1] were the main architects of the bill. In order to make the bill applicable to the mainstream society of this country, they had to perforce name it as the 'Hindu Code Bill'. While defining its scope and applicability, they had to declare in the beginning itself that all citizens of the country, except Muslims, Christians, Parsis and Jews, will come under its purview and it was applicable to Sanatanis, Lingayats, Arya Samajists, Jains, Sikhs, Buddhists and all others who did not come under any of these categories. It was also made clear that anyone seeking exemption from it will have to bear the onus of justifying such an exemption. The only comprehensive term that could denote the people they had in mind was 'Hindu'.

We want to unite and organize all the Hindus. 'Organization' does not merely mean a crowd, a front or a meeting. It implies bringing people together and making them realize the purpose of their remaining together. This is not an easy task. We will have to furnish some basis for it. Some of those basic factors of unity will have to be necessarily emotional in content because the constitution of the human mind is such. Therefore, we start with our motherland: 'This is our motherland, we are its children, and we have been living here for the past thousands of years. During this long past, we have created in this land a glorious history, and also contributed to world thought, culture and civilization. We alone have been responsible both for its rise and its fall. Therefore, we, being the children of this soil, must come together and live together.' It is these realizations that should form the emotional basis for our unity. Even those who call themselves 'rational' would have to accept such an emotional basis.

There is nothing wrong in it. When Russia faced a terrible ordeal during the Second World War, even Stalin had to remind his compatriots that they all belonged to a single, great nation. He had to invoke the spirit of 'nationalism' and 'fatherland'. The necessity of such an emotional inspiration is beyond controversy. However, will that suffice? While actually working in the social field, we feel it necessary that there should also be a practical manifestation of this basis. It is, of course, essential that everyone must emotionally feel that we are all one and that we are all equal. But, at the same time, we should also always be able to naturally experience this oneness in our day-to-day life. So long as we do not have this living experience alongside the emotional appeal, the basis of our unity will neither be robust nor permanent.

Our history of the past hundreds of years tells us that just a handful of Muslim invaders and even fewer Englishmen could rule over us and could forcibly convert many of our brethren to their religions. They also created controversies like 'people of caste' (Savarna) and 'untouchables' (Asprishya). But we cannot just blame the foreigners for this and exonerate ourselves. What is the use of lamenting that it was because of the divisive machinations of the foreign invaders that our unity was shattered? It was inevitable that we would, sooner or later, come into contact with foreign societies and their cultures. There could not forever be a Berlin Wall between them and us. Only diffident people, afraid of the contacts and thoughts of others, seek to put up a wall around themselves. The greatness of any system is proved only when it can hold its head high even while in contact with outsiders. When a system encloses itself in an impenetrable shell, it is only declaring its own inferiority. Hence, instead of blaming others for our shortcomings, we should introspect within ourselves and try to know which of our failings enabled the foreigners to get the better of us.

In this regard, Dr Hedgewar, founder of the RSS, had a unique outlook. Whenever this topic arose, he used to say, 'We cannot escape our responsibility by simply blaming the Muslims and the Europeans for our downfall. We must seek out our own failings.' We have to admit that social inequality amongst us has been one of the major reasons for our downfall. Fissiparous tendencies like caste and subcaste rivalries and untouchability have all been the manifestation of this social inequality. For the activists of Hindu unity, this is a delicate and difficult issue since we are immensely proud of our dharma and our *sanskriti*, or culture. It is true that there are a lot of things that we can be justly proud of. The philosophy and values of life of this land have received the highest acclamation of thinkers across the world as an invaluable contribution to peace and progress of humanity itself. These values of life have stood the test of time. We naturally feel that these eternal life principles should be preserved. However, it is clear that even while cherishing this pride, it would not do to think that all that is old is gold.

Puraanamityev na saadhu sarvam (Not everything old is pristine). Just because something is old, it need not necessarily be good or eternal or the gospel truth. Neither should we think that since we have been living all these years on the basis of these old principles, we need not even think on new lines. *Taatasya koopoyamiti bruvaanaaha. Kshaaram jalam kaapurushaaha pibanti* (Only the cowards will drink salty waters of a well merely because their forefathers had dug it up). Such bigoted approach does no good to anybody. The saying speaks of such a person not as *satpurusha* (good person) but as *kaapurusha* (coward). Such a way of thinking is wrong.

The society is made up of various types of people. There will be some who will jump at any new thing as good and ideal; some others react to any new thing adversely and reject it outright as being useless and worthless. But those who have taken up the mission of eradicating social evils and reuniting the society should not take up either of these extreme attitudes. They have to adopt the attitude of '*Santaha pareekshya anyatarat bhajante*' (Wise men accept things after due diligence). They will have to distinguish, preserve and take up whatever is worthy and not feel sorry for those things that ought to die. The more our people adopt this rational way of looking at things, the sooner will the mission of Hindu consolidation be fulfilled.

For instance, according to a book I read recently, the Jews have reviewed their religious texts and practices after every century or two and re-evaluated them in the contemporary context. Of course, the wordings of the religious texts could not be changed, but fresh interpretations were provided to them in keeping with the times. They distinguished between what was eternal and what was changeable. I believe that in our country too, similar rethinking and re-evaluation of our religious texts must have been done in the olden times. Otherwise, there was no reason why so many different types of religious books – *smriti*s – should have come into existence.

We can see how many changes have taken place even in our gods and goddesses. Indra, Varuna, Agni and other gods have given place to Vishnu and Shiva. There was a time when the Shaivas (devotees of God Shiva) and Vaishnavas (devotees of God Vishnu) were at loggerheads, but Shri Shankaracharya established a harmony between the two and ushered in the puja of the Panchaayatan[2]. As a result, festivals like Shivaratri[3] and Prabodhini Ekadashis are being observed in almost every household today. That means, even in the past, efforts were made from time to time to establish harmony and bring in new interpretations, so that people would not insist upon sticking to every word and syllable of the old scriptures.

There are many stories narrated in the ancient texts and Puranas. But do we accept them all as literally true? For instance, it has been said in the Puranas that the lunar and solar eclipses are a result of 'Raahu[4] and Ketu[5] swallowing the Moon and the Sun'. But should we, in order to affirm our devotion to old religious texts, incorporate this story in the school textbooks to explain to children how the eclipses take place? We are bound to provide what is scientific and factual only in the textbooks.

It is not peculiar only to the Hindu society that religious texts are understood by the letter and believed in blind faith. In 1925, an interesting court case took place in America ('The Trial That Rocked the World', *Readers' Digest*, July 1962) – a country believed to be most scientific in outlook. A Christian citizen in one of the states filed a complaint against a teacher for teaching the theory of evolution, which was in contravention of the story of Genesis and Creation of Man as mentioned in the Bible. The teacher had taught the latest theory of evolution. But the court declared him guilty, and he was punished. However, today, no Christian gives credence to that story of evolution as narrated in the Bible; but still they have not given up their faith in that scripture. This may appear strange, but, has a great lesson for us.

Such problems are common to all countries. Solutions must be found for them. Whenever I speak like this, some people say that these are things created by God. Their intention is perhaps to impress upon us the idea that such things cannot be changed or amended because they are created by God. But how appropriate is this argument? God Himself declared, 'Whenever Dharma declines, I reincarnate myself.' However, the re-establishment of Dharma after its decline does not mean that the old order will be re-established without any change whatsoever. Unlike Prophet Muhammad, nobody in our country ever said, 'I am the last Prophet.' So, it is improper to think that since this is the 'Word of God' it is unchangeable. The re-establishment of Dharma can only mean that the same eternal life principles will be preserved, while its expressions and manifestations will change. We must be prepared to welcome these changes. We should also be able to think clearly and without bias about the genesis of the systems that came into vogue in the ancient past. There is no reason to think that our ancestors had no insight into things and created these systems arbitrarily or out of ignorance. We must keep in mind that the thinkers and leaders of society of those times had considered the needs of the society under those conditions and laid down suitable norms to ensure its solidarity and progress. If those systems are found unnecessary or unsuited for the present, we are free to reject them.

But it is also necessary to understand why a particular system was introduced in a particular period of time. Take, for instance, the '*varna vyavastha*' (the caste system). It is said no such institution existed in the olden times. But after some time, it was felt that some social arrangement was necessary to ensure proper and steady progress of the society. Leaders of those times thought that the society could progress only if four kinds of functions were properly and efficiently executed. Hence, the society was classified into four groups depending upon the specific qualities and aptitudes of individuals. Thus, the varna or caste system came into existence. It did not envisage any differences in the status of the people belonging to different groups. Classification is one thing and class-discrimination is another. According to some scholars, this classification was also not hereditary initially. But, as time went by, it must have become increasingly difficult to recognize and classify each individual based on his or her aptitudes in an extensive society, residing in such a vast stretch of land and having no means of quick transport or communication. Under such circumstanccs, birth in a particular family itself must have been taken as the indication of the aptitudes of the individual and a basis for classifying their varna. That is how the hereditary varna system must have come into place.

But, even at that time, there were no superiority or inferiority complexes attached to different varnas. On the other hand, the whole society was visualized as a single living entity, the very personification of the 'Virat Purusha' – Magnificent Being – with 'thousand heads, thousand eyes and thousand feet'. Such a glorious vision does not permit perverse and ridiculous notions like 'the thighs are superior to the feet, the hands are superior to the thighs, or the head is superior to the hands'. The idea was that all those limbs were equally essential for the proper functioning of the society. The sense of high and low that we witness today had no place in that concept of one integral and living social entity. To imagine otherwise would be to do grave injustice to our ancestors.

It was for this reason that the system was acceptable to one and all. Certain checks and balances evolved to carry it forward from generation to generation. For example, the group endowed with the intellectual power was asked to embrace poverty. The group with ruling power was denied wealth power. State power and wealth power were not allowed to combine in the same group. So long as these checks and balances were efficiently maintained, the system worked well. But defects crept in the system when these checks and balances were ignored in the course of time. Such defects are bound to creep into any system. It is well known that Communism is aimed at the removal of all types of inequalities, particularly the 'classes'. But Milovan Djilas (a top Communist leader of Yugoslavia), in his famous book *The New Class*, has written that a new class has come up in all Communist countries. This was the situation in less than 50 years of the inception of a system that avowedly worked towards doing away with all classes. Human nature is such. Vested interests develop in any system. The varna system too was no exception. The originators of the system should not be blamed for it.

Our ancient literature clearly shows that though our ancestors classified society on the basis of heredity, they were aware of the limitations of the inherited talent. It was said at one place, '*Shudropi sheelasampanno gunavaan braahmano bhavet; Braahmanopi kriyaaheenaha shudraat pratyavaro bhavet*' (By his noble conduct, a Shudra can become a Brahmin, and a Brahmin becomes a Shudra without that rectitude), or '*Jaatyaa braahrnana iti chet na*' (One cannot become a Brahmin because of birth alone). Great sages like Rishyashringa, Vishwamitra and Agastya[6] stand as illustrious examples of people who, though not born as Brahmins, became Brahmins by their penance, virtues and attainments. It is said in the Puranas that Mahidas, the author of Aittareya Brahmana[7], who became a Dwija[8], was the son of a Shudra woman. Jabala[9], who had no father to be named, was initiated into the Brahmin group by his guru through the Upanayana[10] ceremony. These things were possible only because our ancestors had recognized the limitations of inherited talents and hence had kept the system elastic and catholic in outlook. That was the reason why the system had lasted for centuries.

The situation has changed completely today. The changed situation demands changes in our way of thinking as well, in keeping with the times. Those were the days when every student had to learn his lessons at the residence of his teacher. The printing press had not been invented. The machine age had not set in. A blacksmith's son or a jeweller's son or a weaver's son used to learn their trades by observing their fathers at work. Home itself was their school. Hence, heredity and environment cooperated with each other in teaching the individual about their vocation. But today the printing press has arrived; and education is imparted in institutions, not at homes. The machine age has shifted vocations to factories where machines are used, rather than to homes where work was once done by hand. Science has progressed and new inventions have been made. The whole environment has changed. It is now recognized by one and all that, though heredity is important, environment also has an effective role in shaping human character.

Therefore, it is inconsistent with the demands of modern times to insist on the hereditary caste system.

Some people attach great importance to the differences arising out of natural and hereditary factors. To an extent, their contention is true. But to make these differences into a science is simply ridiculous. It is definitely not to the credit of man if he were to make efforts only to substantiate the hereditary disparities in individuals. His efforts should be to study nature's processes and devise ways and means for lessening these disparities and making them tolerable. Therein lies his greatness and his courage. Keeping in mind the limited importance of heredity, we should, by changing the environment and imparting education and training, and introducing suitable systems, try to remove any hereditary defects and handicaps in any section of the people. This is possible in the present times. The Japanese people were considered to be dwarfish in stature. But after the Second World War, they came into close contact with the Americans. Appreciable change took place in the eating and drinking habits of the Japanese people as also in their general style of living. As a result, their average height has now increased.

Before the First and Second World Wars, only certain groups of people in our country and also other countries were termed martial races. But during the two wars, massive mobilization and conscription of soldiers had to be resorted to in all the countries, and huge armies were raised. It was then observed that those people had fought better than even professional soldiers and standing armies. Nobody accepts the notion of 'martial' or 'fighting' races anymore. Hence, it is now futile to try to give heredity a philosophical basis. In fact, circumstances have changed so much that even the existence of that varna vyavastha, which served as a necessary basis for proper functioning of the society in the past, itself has become untenable. Castes, no doubt, exist, but they have nothing to do with the preservation of the social fabric. Caste is now confined only to marriage alliances. It exists only in form, while its spirit disappeared long ago. What exists now is not a vyavastha but only *avyavastha* – disorder! Time has come for all to put their heads together and think about how to guide this system – a system that has to die anyway and is in fact already on the path of its natural death – along the correct path to its termination.

'*Roti, beti, vyavahaar*' is a phrase that is in vogue in our country. In the olden days, even the *roti-vyavahaar*, that is, partaking of food, was restricted to within one's own caste only. That restriction has, however, broken down, and nowadays people of all castes have started partaking food together. The credit for such a change should go to English education, organizations such as the Jhunka-Bhaakar Sangh, community dinners, social workers taking up that task, etc. The RSS too deserves some credit for its camps and other congregational programmes that have subscribed greatly to the erasing of disparities among different castes. Inter-caste marriages have also started taking place. It can be said without hesitation that if the *beti-vyavahaar*, just like roti-vyavahaar, also takes place in greater measure, it will help hugely in wiping out caste-differences and bringing about integrity in the society.

However, beti-vyavahaar, or inter-caste marriages, are a more difficult proposition than inter-caste dining. Keeping this in mind, all should conduct themselves in a congenial manner without showing any unseemly haste. The reason is that in any marriage the question of a good match naturally crops up. Anyone cannot marry anyone else indiscriminately. It can be a good match if the bride and the groom can claim near-equality in educational, economic and social standards. This is possible when the residences of both are in close vicinity encouraging close contact with one another. Residential colonies like LIC colony, bank colony, railway colony and teachers' colony are coming up in good number nowadays; these help in building such an atmosphere. Along with this, when their economic status also rises and education becomes universal, such marriages too will become natural irrespective of caste differences.

Legislations, monetary temptations, propaganda tactics cannot bring about this change. This is a delicate matter that cannot have any instant solution. Everyone has to keep this in mind and contribute their might towards bringing about social transformation. This may take time, but it is bound to happen.

Untouchability is another saddening and unfortunate aspect of our social inequality. Some thinkers opine that it was non-existent in the olden times but gate-crashed into our social system with passage of time and took firm roots. Whatever be its origin, all of us consider that untouchability is a terrible folly and it must, of necessity, be thrown out lock, stock and barrel. There are no two opinions about it. Abraham Lincoln, who abolished slavery in America, said, 'If slavery is not wrong, then nothing is wrong.' Similarly, it is for all of us to declare that 'If untouchability is not wrong, then nothing in the world is wrong!' Every one of us must, therefore, aim at eradicating social inequality in each and every form. We must clearly explain to the people at large how our society became weak and disorganized on account of such social evils. We must also show them the way to get rid of them. It is necessary that every individual must make his or her contribution in this effort. That would remove a major obstacle in the way of Hindu unity.

In this task of bringing about social equality, we should be able to win over the support and cooperation of various types of people. We should, for that purpose, conduct ourselves with restraint and grace. Then only we will be successful. Our religious leaders, saints, sages and scholars hold a great sway over the popular mind. Their cooperation in this task is essential. Sometimes we feel that they are firmly attached to old customs and would not like to change. However, this should not make us mistake their good intentions. In other countries too, there are religious preachers pinning their faith on ancient systems. Nevertheless, people there do not ridicule them because of that.

We could approach our religious leaders in an appropriate manner and plead with them that they should, in their preachings and discourses, not only educate people about the facets of our Dharma that are of eternal value but also reflect on those facets that may require change. Such efforts from them would be more pervasive and impactful. We should also appeal to them that the responsibility of protecting the society is on them too and that they can discharge it only by coming out of their ashrams and unreservedly mixing with the society. Fortunately, there are already auspicious indications that our Dharma gurus have started working in this direction. Our late sarsanghchalak, *Param Poojaneeya* (most revered) Shri

Guruji[11] had brought all the religious leaders together on one common platform under the auspices of the Vishwa Hindu Parishad (VHP) and persuaded them to this viewpoint. As a result, many saints and religious leaders have started coming out and mingling with all sections of the society. They have given up their previous opposition to reconversion and come forward to take back the converted brethren of ours.

The enlightened section of our society has a great responsibility in this regard. They should also think and act in a manner that will help achieve equality and, at the same time, not give rise to bitterness in society. Those suggesting various revolutionary solutions to the problem of untouchability should also keep in mind the saying '*Upaayam chintayan praagnaha apaayamapi chintayet*,' meaning, they should think about the dangers that such solutions may lead us to. We want equality only for the purpose of an atmosphere of goodwill, harmony and mutual cooperation in the society. Those that speak, write or act without understanding this fundamental objective will only harm the cause they claim to be serving.

Many times, one particular section of the society is made the target of stinging attacks. It is highly improper to disgrace or demoralize any section of our society. Instead, examples of new and better social behaviour should be placed before them. Unfortunately, there are still some people in our society who believe in discrimination and are unable to understand the right attitude. But they are also a part and parcel of the Hindu society. It is not expected that we pounce upon such people or tackle them the hard way. There are certainly other ways of persuading and bringing them round. That was how revered Dr Hedgewar, the founder of the Sangh, used to work. I had the good fortune in my young age to work under his guidance.

During the initial year, we had many interesting experiences. I was present in the first Sangh camp. In that, there were quite a number of Mahaar[12] brethren. At lunch time, some participants of the camp began hesitating to sit along with them. They never sat for meals with the Mahaars before that. They shared their predicament with Doctorji. He did not react angrily enforcing discipline nor asked them to get out.

Instead, Doctorji simply told them: 'Our practice is to sit together. We shall sit accordingly.' All of us sat together for meals. Few of those that were hesitant sat in a separate line. But, when time for the next meal came, those very people came to Doctorji and apologized, and joined all others on their own accord. Had Doctorji taken some disciplinary action against them at the very outset and sent them out of the camp, they would never have transformed.

Another very instructive episode concerned my late friend, Shri Bachhraj Vyas.[13] He was a swayamsevak of the shakha for which I was the karyavaha.[14] He came from a highly orthodox family and would not come even to my house for meals. When he attended a Sangh camp, taking meals along with all others posed a problem for him. He could not partake the meals prepared and served for all. When I placed this problem before Doctorji, he did not quote any rule of the camp nor prevent Shri Bachhraj from attending the camp. He was certain that the desired reformation would definitely take place in him. He knew that Shri Bachhraj was a man of great calibre and utterly selfless at heart. Doctorji told me, 'Let him come to the camp. We shall give him the utensils and the ration; let him cook his own food.' That was how it went in the first year. But next year, Shri Bachhraj himself came and told Doctorji, 'I shall take meals with the rest!' Thereafter, as he involved himself more and more in Sangh work, his behaviour underwent a complete change in spite of his orthodox background. He became a trusted worker of the Sangh and served as the prant pracharak[15] of Rajasthan. Later, he rose to become the national president of the Bharatiya Jana Sangh.[16]

Many a time, at the root of the internecine quarrels and violent conflicts in the Hindu society lie political or personal rivalries. Election clashes and land and family disputes also take up that vicious form. Further, the politician or the interested person gives it the colour of a conflict between two castes just to save his skin and serve his political ends. On such occasions, unfortunately, many well-meaning people, including media persons, become pawns in this game out of innocence. In particular, journalists who are in search of a scoop, do not bother to obtain first-hand information about what happened and instead, weave out a story based on a single weak thread of information, giving it a sensational headline. When clashes take place between Hindus and Muslims, they are reported as a clash between two communities, whereas even petty quarrels among the Hindus are magnified and reported in an inciting manner. This is certainly not desirable. We should all exercise great care and restraint in all such situations if we wish to reduce social disparities.

It is a fact that the backward or untouchable brethren of ours have borne a great amount of misery, insults and injustice in all these centuries. That agony is there in their hearts. We have to find a way out of this. All of us feel that onslaughts on them are wrong and that they should stop forthwith. Our efforts, our talk and our behaviour should be conducive to the achievement of this goal. I appeal to the oppressed brethren also to exercise care and restraint. The faults and follies in our society must certainly be criticized. But there are different ways of criticism. When foreigners criticize us, it is with a sense of contempt. But when our own people criticize, it carries an element of pain born out of affectionate concern. Otherwise, if we begin to drag our past quarrels into the present, we end up placing our future in jeopardy. That will only hamper our progress towards equality and harmony.

They (the oppressed brethren) should feel that they are also a part and parcel of the same society and shall live as such with other members. If they stand up shoulder to shoulder with others who have similar ideas and feelings, then the combined efforts of both will make the task much easier and bring the goal much closer. In the past, some eminent leaders of the oppressed communities have severely criticized certain castes and certain religious texts. That was necessary at that time. In order to draw the attention of the people towards a specific point and rouse public opinion, an individual may employ strong language in the beginning. But it is not necessary that such tirades should continue forever. Times have changed, and transformation is evident today. In such a scenario, it is our responsibility to employ only such language that will help further the process of change.

I believe that the 'backward' brethren of ours do not ask for the mercy of anybody. They only desire an equal status with others and that too on their own merits. Since they have been backward all these days, they only want facilities and opportunities to be provided to them to advance. This desire of theirs is quite legitimate. And it is for them to decide how long these privileges should continue. In the long run, however, they will have to compete with others and earn an equal status only on the basis of merit alone. Perhaps, they also know this. It is for them to think and strive and chalk out a time-bound plan of raising themselves up. A day has to come when all of us will feel equal, both in our worth and capacities.

In spite of many drawbacks, the Hindus have their own specialties. They have certain concepts and attitudes with regard to life. Thinkers the world over concede that this society has established certain great and eternal values of life. If the Hindu society, believing in such eternal values of life and following them in practice, can stand up united, imbued with the spirit of social equality, then alone will those specialities live on forever and prove beneficial to the world at large as well. But unfortunately today, the Hindu society is weak and disorganized. Dr Ambedkar felt very much pained that, in this society – a society that considers all human beings as children of God, nay, as part and parcel of that Divinity Itself – there should be found a sense of high and low. He also said that there could be no better basis for equality than the basic faith in the existence of a common spark of divinity in all human beings.

Our society has a long history. Through all these centuries, there was absolute freedom of thought and action. As a result, a large number of things were written in our texts, some of which could even be misinterpreted. If '*Na stree swaatantryamarhati*' – woman is unworthy of freedom – is quoted to make it appear that the woman was despised in this society, then the saying '*Yatra naaryastu poojyante, ramante tatra devataaha*' – where women are revered, there the gods rejoice – is also available to show that women were held in the highest esteem. If one wants to establish unity and harmony in society, one has to think about what principles should be picked up from our religious texts and from our history, which would be conducive to the removal of disparities and the consolidation of Hindu society. May all of us sincerely feel that the

Hindus must unite, and the basis for that unity can only be social equality! With this conviction, may all of us come forward to make our society united and strong! This is my fervent appeal to one and all.

7

'We Aspire to Build an India That Is Self-Respecting, Self-Reliant and a Beacon of Wisdom for the World'

RAJENDRA SINGH, RAJJU BHAIYYA

In 1994, Balasaheb Deoras, the then chief of the RSS, decided to hand over the reins of the organization to his successor owing to his ill-health. Tradition of sarsanghachalaks picking up successors during their lifetime started with that decision of Deoras. Prof. Rajendra Singh, a renowned nuclear physicist from Prayagraj, who was until then serving as the sarkaryavah of the organization, was named as the fourth sarsanghachalak.

Rajendra Singh was an expert in nuclear physics and was offered a fellowship for advanced research by the legendary Sir C.V. Raman. However, Singh decided to give up his academic career and dedicate himself to the work of the RSS. He grew up in the ranks of the organization to rise to the highest position, which he held for six years, before handing it over to his successor in 2000.

His speeches were delivered in simple language, yet were filled with logical and scientific arguments. He provided a contemporary outlook to the organization during his stewardship. A summarized version of a couple of his important speeches during the annual Vijayadashami events at Nagpur is presented here.

Today is the sacred day of Vijayadashami. Thousands of years ago, on this very day, Lord Shri Ram defeated Ravana, the king of demons. This victory of truth over falsehood, of righteousness over unrighteousness, is still celebrated in every home and in every corner of the country. In hundreds of places, (effigies of) Ravana are burned today, reminding the entire society that in this land of Bharat, Dharma and justice are never defeated, even if they possess fewer resources. Ravana came fully equipped with a grand chariot to fight, whereas Ram fought him on foot. Tulsidasji[1] described this in a short couplet, '*Ravan rathi, virath Raghuvira / Dekh Bibhishan bhayo adheera*' (Ravana rode a grand chariot, while Raghunath [Lord Ram] stood without one / Seeing this, Vibhishan grew anxious).

Yet, despite the lack of resources, victory belonged to Ram. Similarly, in the Mahabharata, despite having a smaller army, the Pandavas emerged victorious. Today's day reassures those who work for righteousness that the final victory will be theirs.

It was for this reason that Dr Hedgewar, the founder of the Rashtriya Swayamsevak Sangh, chose this very day to establish the Sangh. His resolve was to awaken a spirit of victory throughout society and to engage people in the sacred duty of nation-building through the Sangh.

At that time, the atmosphere, from the perspective of the Hindu society, was filled with despair. Due to the cunning strategies of the British, a belief took root among the country's leaders that India could not attain Independence without the support of Muslims. As a result, efforts were made to appease them – the national anthem was altered, the design of the national flag was changed, and even the country's language was modified. However, these concessions only fuelled further demands, ultimately leading the nation to witness the tragic event of Partition.

Through his deep study of the rise and fall of our nation, Dr Hedgewar reached the firm conclusion that only through a united Hindu society could the country's bright future be secured. Hindu society's self-forgetfulness led to its downfall over the past thousand years. Therefore, by awakening a sense of national duty towards the country and drawing inspiration from our traditional culture, he resolved to once again elevate our nation to the pinnacle of glory. As a means to achieve this, he laid the foundation of the Rashtriya Swayamsevak Sangh.

In 1947, the country attained Independence. However, (the India–Pakistan) Partition led to a horrific massacre, forcing millions to flee, lose everything and become refugees in their own land.

It has now been 47 years since India became independent. Today, we can all see where we stand. The golden dreams we once had for an independent India now seem shattered, like broken fragments of a vision.

Let us take a broad look at the current state of our nation.

The foremost priority of any country is its security. What is the state of security for ordinary citizens in India today? Thousands of people have been provided with gunmen for protection, yet key national figures, especially Opposition leaders, continue to be assassinated. Over the past two years, hundreds of bomb blasts have rocked different parts of the country, claiming many lives. In Mumbai alone, multiple explosions in a single day killed hundreds of people and caused damage worth thousands of crores. The explosive used, RDX, is not an ordinary substance – it is manufactured in highly advanced government factories. The RDX used in these attacks was smuggled into the country by enemies of the nation and is still hidden at various locations.

Today, in places like Mumbai, Delhi, Kolkata or Chennai, these elements can trigger explosions whenever they wish. It is well known that the Pakistani intelligence agency, ISI, is involved in these activities; but simply stating this holds little significance. The real concern is that hundreds of people within India are aiding these foreign intelligence operatives. Among those caught are prominent smugglers with deep connections to political leaders. Yet, no legal proceedings have even begun against them. Some of the country's top lawyers are working to defend them. The TADA law under which they were arrested is now being challenged by the very leaders who betray the nation. Unfortunately, the Indian government is hesitating to take strict action against these traitors.

In our own country, 3 lakh Hindu brothers from the Kashmir Valley have been forced to flee their homes and properties, living as refugees to save their lives and dignity. The audacity of Islamic terrorists in India has reached to such an extent that they have even threatened to stop the Amarnath pilgrimage. Today, neither individuals nor communities are safe anywhere. The continuous massacres in Poorvanchal and the thousands of murders in Bihar paint a grim picture of the challenges that lie ahead.

Due to the government's short-sightedness, when the disputed structure in Ayodhya was demolished, hundreds of temples across the country were destroyed in retaliation. Riots broke out in various places, highlighting the growing strength and influence of anti-national forces. There is a well-known saying: 'Constant vigilance is the price of freedom.' As patriotic citizens, it is our duty to remain alert to all divisive and violent elements and to make every effort to thwart their activities in every possible way.

The economic condition of a country is the second criterion for assessing its capability and strength. Even after 47 years of Independence, India remains one of the poorest countries in the world in terms of per capita income – both India and Sri Lanka have a higher per capita income than India. At the time of Independence, India had no foreign debt. Instead, it had a foreign exchange reserve of 17 crore rupees. However, today, India has a foreign debt of 2.5 lakh crore rupees, meaning each citizen bears a debt burden of approximately 2,500 rupees – equivalent to their annual income.

To repay this debt, India has to pay an annual interest of 35,000 crore rupees, for which more foreign loans are taken. Nehru's socialist economic policies invested around 1.25 lakh crore rupees in government-owned factories, which could barely provide jobs to 20–25 lakh people, and today, most of these government enterprises are running in losses. Meanwhile, around 1.5 lakh crore rupees were invested in the private sector, generating employment for about 75 lakh people, and most of these private enterprises turned profitable. However, even with this approach, only about 1 crore people in India could secure jobs, while millions remain unemployed or underemployed throughout the year.

The failure of state-owned enterprises has become evident worldwide. Even socialist countries are abandoning socialist economic systems. In Western nations, the market-driven economy seems to be the only viable economic model. India's government policies are also moving in this direction. The removal of barriers such as quotas, permits, licenses and the 'inspector raj', which hinder domestic industries, is a welcome step. However, bringing in the entire Western economic model under the guise of globalization is not appropriate.

The United States (US), home to just 4 per cent of the world's population, consumes 40 per cent of the world's resources. Such an economic system is not globally sustainable. Despite this high level of consumption, the US faces significant unemployment, rising crime among youth and widespread drug abuse, which are major concerns for its government. This limitless race for consumption will rapidly deplete the world's resources and still fail to bring true satisfaction to humanity. The economic model based on excessive consumption is simply not feasible for Third-World countries.

Economically powerful nations continue to exploit other countries by exerting financial pressure. India's signing of the GATT (General Agreement on Tariffs and Trade) agreement stands as a testament to such coercion. Currently, India holds only 0.5 per cent of global trade, yet the government has signed this treaty under the illusion of increasing its share. As a result, India will have to reduce tariffs for multinational corporations. Soon, factories producing for products for fast-food chains, foreign soft drinks and imported electronic devices will flood the country. This will not only lead to the misuse of middle-class income but also force many indigenous industries to shut down.

Small-scale industries have the real potential to generate employment, but they will struggle to survive against the aggressive marketing and financial dominance of multinational corporations. Foreign trade could have been expanded through bilateral agreements, allowing both parties to safeguard their economic interests. However, the GATT agreement will primarily benefit economically powerful nations, bringing numerous crises upon India. The impact will be severe on agriculture, pharmaceuticals and the chemical industry, pushing the country towards economic subjugation.

Therefore, it is crucial to revive the spirit of Swadeshi and resist multinational corporations. To awaken and alert society on this issue, the Sangh has pledged full support to the Swadeshi Jagran Manch, a movement aimed at reaching millions of people across 1.5 lakh villages. We urge every citizen to recognize the looming economic crisis and counter this economic invasion with their patriotic spirit.

A person has no control over the caste in which they are born. However, developing one's qualities, enhancing one's skills and abilities, is certainly within one's control. But when caste-based considerations dominate, other virtues become invisible.

The true state of a nation can be assessed through its social structure. A progressive country aspires to have a hardworking, enthusiastic and harmonious society. However, in India today, the 85 per cent Hindu society that forms the backbone of the nation, appears to be entangled in internal conflicts rather than embracing these values.

When the country's great leaders framed the Constitution, they thoughtfully provided 22.5 per cent reservation for Scheduled Castes and Scheduled Tribes (SC/ST), who had long suffered from extreme social and economic backwardness. The expectation was that, as their educational and economic status improved and social harmony through awareness and regulations increased, the reservation percentage would gradually decrease. The idea was to remove those individuals who had already benefited from it or had reached parity with others in terms of education and economic standing, thereby allowing the remaining underprivileged members of these communities to avail the benefits more effectively.

However, instead of reducing it, the percentage of reservations has only increased. An additional 27 per cent reservation has been introduced in the name of educational and economic backwardness. Many individuals, even from so-called upper castes, also suffer from economic hardships, which in turn lead to educational disadvantages. Economic deprivation should be considered the most significant form of backwardness. Instead of job reservations, special educational arrangements should be made to address the educational gap.

If reservations in employment are necessary, society must be sensitized to prevent bitterness. A sense of unity and familial spirit should be cultivated so that privileged individuals willingly forgo certain benefits for their underprivileged brethren. However, today, the reservation system has expanded beyond the Supreme Court's 50 per cent limit, reaching 67 per cent in some states and even 80 per cent in others. This has led to violent conflicts and social unrest.

When the Supreme Court ruled that while granting reservations to educationally backward people, the creamy layer should be excluded from these benefits, the Kerala Legislative Assembly passed a resolution stating that no person in the Other Backward Classes (OBC) category in the state falls under the creamy layer. An IAS (Indian Administrative Service) officer, a doctor, a lawyer, an industrialist or an income taxpayer cannot be deprived of education due to financial constraints. Therefore, unless we exclude the creamy layer from reservation benefits on an economic basis, these benefits will never reach the truly deprived sections.

We acknowledge that Indian society has caste-based backwardness. Reservations are useful for uplifting the backward sections of society and for strengthening social harmony. However, it must be ensured that caste-based reservations do not lead to vested interests. Politicians primarily focus on electoral gains and hence ignore policies that would truly benefit the genuinely backward sections. This is all done to gain the electoral support of influential people included in the creamy layer.

Qualified individuals should be encouraged, and merit should hold a prominent place in the administration of the country. Therefore, it is absolutely essential that, as per the Supreme Court's decision, reservation should never exceed 50 per cent under any circumstances, and qualities such as character, competence and virtues should be given the highest priority.

Political leaders, driven by selfish motives, are further inciting young generations with provocative statements, aggravating the divide. It is crucial that responsible social leaders curb this political opportunism and work towards solutions based on mutual love and harmony. Economically well-off individuals should not receive reservation benefits, as they already possess the means for education and progress.

Today, the privileged sections of society must come forward to support the deprived communities by ensuring access to education, healthcare, employment and self-reliance. Through various service-oriented initiatives, social harmony can be fostered, strengthening the bond of unity and mutual respect. True progress will emerge from such service and compassion.

The Rashtriya Swayamsevak Sangh, through its swayamsevaks and supporters, is already running thousands of service projects in underprivileged areas. However, there is a need to expand these initiatives to tens of thousands. We aim to ensure both the upliftment of society and the cultivation of a service-oriented mindset among privileged individuals. Only in such a compassionate and inclusive environment can we neutralize the growing social discord. Until society is infused with complete harmony, the goal of social justice will remain incomplete and ineffective.

Since Independence, the political landscape of the country has been consistently marred by corruption. For many years, elected leaders would switch parties, primarily joining Congress, and no law was enacted to prevent such defections. It was only during Rajiv Gandhi's tenure that an anti-defection law was introduced – ironically, when Congress realized that their own members might start defecting.

In contrast, the United Kingdom (UK), despite not having an anti-defection law, has not witnessed a single instance of party-switching by a member of Parliament (MP) in the last 50 years. Meanwhile, in India, loopholes in this law have been exploited to bring the current government into a majority, despite it originally being a minority government. When lawmakers can be bought, there remains a dangerous possibility that foreign entities could also manipulate them.

Today, nearly every prominent leader in power faces allegations of corruption. States like Bihar, Karnataka, Andhra Pradesh and Maharashtra have all outdone each other in this regard. The extent of corruption has reached such levels that when an impeachment motion was brought against Supreme Court judge V. Ramaswami in the Lok Sabha, his lawyer defended him by arguing that misuse of government cars, telephones and resources were minor infractions – mere 'financial irregularities' rather than corruption. He downplayed the issue by stating that it involved only a few lakhs of rupees.

To make matters worse, the then law minister from Congress stood up and admitted that such 'irregularities' were common among all ministers, effectively branding the entire cabinet as corrupt. When the Lok Sabha convened as a judicial body to deliberate on Ramaswami's case, Congress MPs (members of Parliament) deliberately walked out, refusing to vote on his corruption charges.

If lawmakers and ministers themselves refuse to act against corruption, what precedent does it set for the judiciary? Can judges also adopt a similar approach when delivering justice? The state of politics in the country has reached a critical juncture, demanding urgent reforms to restore accountability and ethical governance.

The open use of money and muscle power in elections has become a widespread issue, with criminal elements increasingly aligning themselves with political leaders. This reality has been exposed by statements from government officials and social activists in Maharashtra, who have provided substantial evidence of this troubling trend. When a legislator is elected by spending excessive amounts of money and lacks a clean image, how can we expect them to uphold honesty and integrity in governance? Leaders who enter politics through such means are more likely to focus on recovering their investment rather than serving the public interest.

Additionally, funds allocated for public welfare and development often get siphoned off at various levels. The issue was starkly highlighted by former Prime Minister Rajiv Gandhi, who admitted that out of every 100 rupees sent from Delhi for development projects, only 15 actually reaches the intended beneficiaries, while the rest is lost to corruption among politicians and government officials. In such a scenario, no matter how many billions or trillions are allocated for social welfare, the common people will see little to no benefit. This rampant misappropriation of funds raises serious concerns about the country's development and calls for urgent measures to curb corruption, ensure accountability and promote clean governance.

Nowadays, the most concerning issue in the world is terrorism. Before the Atlanta Olympics, 250 innocent passengers travelling on America's TWA (Trans World Airlines) flight were killed in an explosion. Despite taking extreme precautions, a bomb blast in an Atlanta park injured hundreds of people. Since terrorists have begun targeting even programs meant for joy and entertainment, the shadow of fear looms even over moments of leisure and enjoyment in life. Therefore, the president of the United States, Mr Bill Clinton, expressed deep concern over this issue in his statement. Nowadays, such incidents are occurring in every corner of the world, from Japan to America. India, too, has been facing this menace for the past eight to ten years. Nearly 300,000 Hindus from the Kashmir Valley have become refugees in their own country due to this very reason. In the Northeast as well – particularly in Nagaland, Manipur and Assam – this cycle of senseless killings has been ongoing for many years.

A deep study on why terrorism arises and effective measures to stop it are unfortunately not being undertaken. According to the prevailing approach, the response to terrorism is also superficial, following what is commonly referred to as the 'the band-aid' method. Merely statements from rulers are issued, declaring that those responsible for such terrorist activities will not be spared at any cost.

One of the fundamental principles of democracy is the freedom to hold differing opinions. That is why Voltaire famously said, 'I do not agree with what you say, but I shall defend with all my might your right to say it.' In India, freedom of thought has existed since ancient times. There is not just one school of philosophy but at least six, and even atheists have held significant positions in philosophical discourse. True democracy lies in firmly holding one's beliefs while respecting the viewpoints of others.

However, unfortunately, certain ideologies have emerged in the world that claim that those who do not follow their path are destined for hell. They fail to grasp the simple question – before the arrival of their prophet, were all people condemned to hell? Both Islam and Christianity have developed this exclusivist outlook. Their systems are built around a specific mode of worship, a single scripture for guidance and absolute submission to a prophet. Because of their rigid adherence to a singular path, they begin to view all other paths with contempt. Their intolerance reaches such extremes that they see the destruction of others as a means of fulfilling their divine purpose.

History bears witness to the horrific massacres committed in the name of propagating Islam and Christianity. While passages promoting brotherhood and tolerance can be found in their scriptures, their followers have largely ignored them and acted in contradiction to these teachings.

Human nature varies from person to person. Therefore, how can all people, living in different corners of the world, follow a single path? This is why various sects have also emerged within Islam and Christianity. The hostility and conflicts between these sects can still be observed today. The persecution of Ahmadis and Shias in India, as well as the ongoing conflict between Catholics and Protestants in Ireland – despite the West being considered civilized – are recent examples of this phenomenon.

When it is not possible to eliminate an opponent through direct warfare, the next step manifests as terrorism. If terrorism is to be eradicated, we must address its root causes. The world must move beyond rigid, exclusive ideologies and embrace the Indian philosophical perspective of '*ekam sat, vipra bahudha vadanti*' (truth is one, but the wise express it in different ways) and '*sarve bhavantu sukhinah*' (may all be happy).

India has witnessed the rise of numerous sects and the birth of many great saints who have guided humanity on the path of righteousness. Yet, history shows that such sects have never led to bloodshed or violent conflict. It is precisely this unique characteristic of the Hindu society that has allowed democracy to flourish in India; whereas in its fragmented regions where Islam dominates, democracy has struggled to sustain itself. This inclusive Indian worldview and way of life are what define Hindutva. How unfortunate it is that instead of taking pride in our own heritage, we ourselves engage in criticizing it.

Nowadays, 'secularism' has become one of the most debated and significant topics in our country. In English, a state governed by a particular religious doctrine is called a theocratic state. Its opposite is a secular state, meaning that since the state is responsible for ensuring security, economic stability and justice, it should not consider a person's religion or sect when fulfilling its duties. This is a reasonable and just expectation from any government.

India has upheld this principle for thousands of years. Hardly any region in this country has ever been governed as a theocratic state. Given this history, accusing those who draw their worldview from Indian culture of being anti-secular is perhaps the biggest falsehood of this century. The Hindu society has inherently learned to respect all forms of worship. That is why, while both Bangladesh and Pakistan have declared themselves Islamic states, India can take pride in being a secular state.

Unfortunately, after Independence, many of India's top leaders were unfamiliar with Hindi and Sanskrit. As a result, they mistakenly translated the English word 'religion' – which refers to *mazhab* (sect) or *panth* (way of worship) – as 'dharma'. Consequently, they began calling a secular state as *dharmanirapeksha* (religion-neutral) governance. However, there is no exact equivalent of 'Dharma' in foreign languages, which is why many English texts refer to it as Dharma itself. In the Bhagavada Gita, Lord Krishna stated that the purpose of his incarnation was to establish dharma, yet today's rulers tirelessly advocate for a 'secular' state.

Perhaps these leaders have developed an aversion to Dharma, which is why corruption has taken deep root in the country. As faith in Dharma has declined since Independence, selfishness and moral degradation have risen, leading to an endless series of corruption scandals. Today, it is difficult to find an Indian politician who can speak with honesty and integrity. Even Mahatma Gandhi – whom most of today's leaders claim as their role model – said that politics without Dharma is nothing but garbage. Dharma is the collection of virtues and the foundation of moral values that empower individuals and society. How can we expect to build a strong and righteous nation by rejecting it? Politicians have even removed references to Dharma from education, fearing any mention of it. They have ensured that this ideological disorder continues to infect future generations as well.

The administrators of today have interpreted secularism as appeasement of Muslims while accusing Hindu society of social narrow-mindedness. They have no objection to paying salaries to imams or granting subsidies to Haj pilgrims. The formation of a minority commission and allocating a separate fund for its financial assistance does not hinder their secular sentiment.

During the struggle for Independence, the Congress adopted the path of Muslim appeasement to keep the country united, which ultimately failed completely with the Partition of India. That same misfortune still haunts them today. Just as an addict clings to intoxicating pills to indulge in unrealistic dreams – destroying their own health in the process – today's politicians are consuming the toxic drug of appeasement in their greed for power, hollowing out the nation.

One cannot attain political power solely on the basis of minority votes. Therefore, a conspiracy is also being hatched to divide Hindu society. Those who claim that casteism is the biggest enemy of this country and has caused immeasurable damage to society are, in reality, promoting casteism in a different manner. Whether it is college admissions, jobs or political elections – caste has been made the most important issue today.

Until the voters of our country rise above caste and cast their votes based on truth, integrity and moral values, we will continue to have corrupt administrators like today. For the nation's upliftment, I strongly advocate giving the highest importance to character in every field. I consider efforts towards character-building to be far more significant than the progress of industry, education and agriculture.

Examining all these issues, it becomes evident that the biggest problem in our country is the lack of good people. Employees in sectors like administration, education and healthcare do not seem committed to fulfilling their duties.

I recall that our very own countrymen used to perform their duties with far greater integrity during British rule. In the Vidarbha region, this year's matriculation examination results showed that 64 government schools had a pass percentage of zero. Can anyone imagine a school where those responsible for education and management have become so negligent in their duties that not a single student passed?

Therefore, the grand announcements of central and state governments hold no significance unless they are implemented by dedicated and morally upright employees. The creation of such individuals is possible only when there is a commitment to ideals on one hand and visible examples of integrity on the other. The lives of politicians have become devoid of inspiration due to their lack of moral values. They are seen chasing wealth so obsessively that expecting anything from them is utterly futile.

If we can ignite the spirit of cultural nationalism in politicians, it would be a remarkable achievement. India has been an ancient and great nation, recognized for thousands of years as an epitome of knowledge, prosperity and morality. There is a dire need to revive this memory and instil a sense of pride in our heritage.

In the midst of prevailing darkness, how can a nation progress? The Rashtriya Swayamsevak Sangh does not believe in mere criticism of others; rather, it follows the principle that darkness cannot be dispelled by cursing it but by lighting a lamp. As the Akhil Bharatiya Vidyarthi Parishad (ABVP) song says: '*Chalein jalayen deep wahan, jahan abhi bhi andhera hai*' (Let us go and light a lamp where darkness still exists).

The RSS instils self-confidence, patriotism, discipline and a spirit of hard work among its swayamsevaks. The belief that 'This is our ancient land, a Hindu Rashtra for centuries, which has witnessed many ups and downs, and we shall make it great again' is deeply embedded in their minds. It is through the awakening of such sentiments that real transformation occurs.

Anyone who loves this land, reveres its culture and respects its great personalities is a true Hindu and a national figure. On the contrary, those who lack faith in the nation and its heritage – regardless of their devotion to other causes – are akin to adversaries. Only through unwavering national devotion and a collective social consciousness can we eradicate corruption and awaken a spirit of action.

Through the experiences of swayamsevaks working in different fields, we see firsthand that the people of our country are second to none in terms of talent. What is lacking is a commitment to the nation, an emotional bond with it and that is precisely what the RSS seeks to cultivate.

Social harmony can only be achieved through this sense of belonging. When the entire Hindu society rises above personal gains and losses and begins to prioritize the interests of the nation, real change will take place. The purpose of the RSS is to awaken and mobilize the virtuous forces of society.

Among the ancient civilizations of Egypt, Iran and India, only the Indian civilization has survived. The other two perished as soon as they encountered Islam. The essence of India's ancient greatness and uniqueness is known as Hindutva – a tradition of thought and a way of life. Even the Supreme Court has acknowledged this. The Rashtriya Swayamsevak Sangh understood this and developed a method to instil nationalism, discipline and character among the citizens of the country. Today, its shakhas are spread across every corner of the nation. We firmly believe that the shakha system has played a crucial role in cultivating these virtues in many individuals.

Simple programs, when carried out with dedication and faith, yield astonishing results. History tells us that Ajamila,[2] simply by naming his son Narayan,[3] became accustomed to chanting the name and attained spiritual elevation, while Sage Valmiki,[4] by uttering *mara-mara*, ultimately became the author of the Ramayana. When swayamsevaks pray under the sacred saffron flag, which symbolizes India's entire historical essence, and keep the image of Bharat Mata in their hearts, it leaves a profound impact on them.

We have heard stories of swayamsevaks from Punjab and Kashmir who have risked their lives to protect their brethren. Patriotism and the spirit of sacrifice cannot be cultivated through selfish interests or material benefits. Leaders tirelessly proclaim that India is an integral part of India while simultaneously offering economic packages worth thousands of crores to instil patriotism. If, after spending 90,000 crores rupees and losing 90,000 soldiers and civilians, India's integration is still incomplete, then these new efforts following the same approach will likely meet the same fate.

A person's devotion to the nation can only be awakened by reminding them of the millennia-old bond between this land and its people, like that of a mother and her child. This is the only way to safeguard the unity and integrity of the country. Those who hesitate even to sing 'Vande Mataram', can they ever make sacrifices for the unity of the nation?

These days, there is much discussion about the Comprehensive Nuclear-Test-Ban Treaty (CTBT). Nuclear-armed nations seek to prevent other countries from advancing in this domain. Indeed, nuclear weapons are devastating instruments of destruction, possessing the potential to annihilate the entire world. However, instead of setting a concrete timeline for their own nuclear disarmament, these nations focus solely on preventing India from developing nuclear weapons.

Given that two of India's neighbouring countries possess nuclear weapons, it is entirely justifiable for India to prepare itself in this regard. If any one nation in the world deserves the right to possess nuclear arms, it is India – a country that firmly believes in non-violence and is equally concerned about the well-being of all. India harbours neither opposition nor hatred towards other religions or nations, and thus, it would never use nuclear weapons for destructive purposes.

India, with its philosophy of *Vasudhaiva Kutumbakam* (the world is one family) and its commitment to global welfare, must not remain weak or powerless. If India becomes feeble, the noble ideals it upholds will also vanish from the world.

Great principles also require the support of strength. That is why our tradition states '*Agratash chaturo Vedah, prishthash sasharam dhunuh*' (In the front, the four Vedas; at the back, the bow with arrows).

We aspire to build an India that is self-respecting, self-reliant and a beacon of wisdom for the world. However, we must never forget that this vision depends on our integrity, patriotism and organizational strength.

8

'We Have Forgotten Ourselves, and Those Who Forget Themselves Are Vulnerable to Any Attack'

K.S. SUDARSHAN

Kuppahalli Sitaramayya Sudarshan, the fifth sarsanghachalak of the RSS, addressed the audience at the release of a book *Hindus Under Seige*, authored by Dr Subramanian Swamy, an eminent politician, writer and economist on 18 September 2006. Revered Swami Jayendra Saraswati, chief pontiff of the Kanchi Kamakoti Mutt, was also present on the occasion. Following is the text of his address.

Just now, Subramanian Swamy spoke about the book and explained how Hindu society is currently facing numerous challenges from all directions. In reality, we had continuously faced such crises for over 800 years and successfully overcome them. It is true that due to our own weaknesses, we remained under foreign rule – nearly 500 years under the Muslim sultans and approximately 175 years under the British rule. However, the Islamic dominance over this land did not happen effortlessly. We are often told that they arrived, and the people here were defeated without resistance. But that is entirely false.

The first invasion of India occurred in 636 AD during the time of Caliph Umar[1], but it was repelled. After that, several invasions took place, and each one was successfully countered. Later, in 712 AD, Muhammad bin Qasim[2] attacked, capturing the Sindh province and surrounding regions. However, he too could rule only for three years before being defeated and driven out. It was almost a century after Qasim that Mahmud of Ghazni came, followed by Muhammad Ghori another 100 years later. In every instance, the people of this land resisted, fought bravely and sacrificed their lives to prevent foreign invaders from establishing their rule. However, in 1206 AD, following the defeat of Prithviraj Chauhan, Islamic rule was finally established in India.

Thus, although the first attack had occurred in 636 AD, there was 570 years of resistance before the invaders could establish their rule in 1206 AD. In contrast, in other countries, the invaders could gain complete control over the people quickly. In India, even after ruling for 500 years, they could not convert the entire population to Islam. Before their arrival in India, wherever the Islamic invaders went, they completely uprooted native cultures. Within 100 years of the advent of Islam, they brought regions expanding from Gibraltar to the Sindhu region under their control. This included all of Southern Europe, North Africa and Central Asia, which were fully absorbed into their empire.

They believed that the victory they had achieved was by the grace of Allah, and since Allah had declared their religion to be the final and supreme faith, it was destined to prevail. Their belief was that Allah had sent various prophets to different communities throughout history, but the last and ultimate prophet was Prophet Muhammad. Since he was the final prophet and no other would come after him, the religion he preached was also the final one. They believed that their religion had nullified all previous faiths, and it was their duty to establish the green flag over the entire world. With this conviction, they surged forward. However, later in Europe, Christianity also gained strength and stood firm in its faith. The Christians retaliated, leading to the Crusades[3], which resulted in their reclamation of significant parts of Europe from Islamic rule.

In India; although the invaders succeeded in establishing their rule, they could not completely erase the culture of the land. This raises an important question. How is it that in other countries, the invaders could successfully uproot entire cultures and convert the people to Islam, but in India, despite 570 years of continuous invasions and 500 years of rule, only about 12–13 per cent of the population got converted to Islam? Moreover, those converted to Islam were not the common or poor people. Dr K.S. Lal[4], in his book *Indian Muslims: Who Are They?* concluded that most of the converts belonged to the so-called higher castes – Brahmins, Kshatriyas and Kayasthas. Those from the so-called lower castes were, in reality, not the ones who converted to Islam. Dr Lal's research and statistics show how limited the conversions actually were, despite significant efforts by the rulers.

One of the main reasons for this limited conversion was the resilience of the social structure. Even though political power was lost, Indian society had another strong unifying force – what we call as the caste system. The caste system was a social and economic structure that assigned specific professions to different groups. Each caste was given a designated occupation, ensuring that no other group could take over their livelihood. Because everyone had a defined role, there was no fear of losing employment or resources. Unlike modern times, where entire industries can be taken over or companies acquired overnight, such corporate-style takeovers were impossible in that era. People were confident that their livelihoods were secure within their caste-based profession, and this interdependence created an intrinsically connected social fabric.

Moreover, the system dictated that those considered the most intellectual would have the least material consumption, whereas those engaged in physical labour would have no restrictions on consumption. This unique social arrangement contributed to the resilience of the Indian society, preventing widespread conversions even under centuries of foreign rule.

There are people who not only possess empathy but also go to great lengths to alleviate the suffering of others. They endure hardships, run around, put in effort and when the time comes, they are even willing to sacrifice themselves. Whether it is during a tsunami, a famine or a flood, we find many such people stepping forward to help. This attitude is not commonly found in the West. People in the West have become so individualistic that they only care about themselves and do not feel the need to be concerned about others. A recent example was the heavy rainfall in New Orleans, which led to massive flooding. People were stranded on the higher floors of their houses, suffering without food for five days, yet no one cared. Everyone in America lives only for himself.

In contrast, in our country, people take it upon themselves to help. Even before the government arrives, ordinary people reach out to assist. Such person is a *narottama* – the best among humans. And these narottamas advance further, expanding their consciousness so much that they embrace the entire humanity as their own, they become truly great. A prime example is Swami Vivekananda[5]. When he addressed the Parliament of Religions in Chicago in 1893, he began by saying, 'Sisters and brothers of America.' That one greeting had electrified the entire audience, who erupted in applause and gave him a standing ovation for five minutes. Why did this simple phrase create such a powerful reaction? Because, while in India, it is common to address each other as brothers and sisters, in the West, people typically say 'ladies and gentlemen'. When Swami Vivekananda addressed them as sisters and brothers, it deeply touched them. The next day's newspapers even said, 'Why do we send missionaries to India? In reality, people from India should be coming here to teach us.'

Swami Vivekananda embodied the Indian philosophy of *Vasudhaiva Kutumbakam* – the whole world is one family. He saw everyone as his own. Saints like Ramakrishna Paramahamsa[6] and Sant Dnyaneshwar[7] achieved such deep spiritual realization that they identified not only with living beings but also with inanimate objects. They felt the pain of everything in existence, transcending the human experience and embodying a divine state. Ultimately, such individuals attain the form of Narayana – the Divine – themselves. The essence of Indian culture is this transformation: from *nara* (human) to Narayana (Divine Being).

It was a constant endeavour in our country to cultivate such elevated souls in the society. Such values and virtues cannot be instilled merely through formal education in schools and universities. Hence, our tradition has relied on the wisdom imparted by revered figures like Adi Shankaracharya, saints, monks and other wandering ascetics. These sages travelled across the land, spreading knowledge through discourses and storytelling, teaching people about the ultimate truth and the duty of serving others. Because of this deep-rooted cultural education, even an uneducated villager in India, who may not be articulate or fluent or has a polished language, often demonstrates outstanding moral character through their behavior.

I will share one example. In the Saurashtra region of Gujarat, there was a severe famine for two consecutive years. Due to this, people took their cattle and migrated to other states. Only the elderly, the poor and women were left behind. It came to the knowledge of the swayamsevaks that these people were struggling to find food. The swayamsevaks in Gujarat decided to immediately send *sukhdi* for them. Sukhdi is a nutritious sweetmeat made by mixing wheat flour, ghee and jaggery. An appeal was made to the public that everyone should prepare sukhdi and bring it to designated collection centres in every city and town, from where it would be transported and distributed to the famine-affected people in Saurashtra. Soon, heaps of sukhdi started accumulating at these centres.

At one such collection centre in a small town, people were bringing sukhdi from their homes. Among them was an elderly woman, dressed in tattered clothes. Thinking that she was a beggar, and had come to seek sukhdi, someone told her, 'Mother, this sukhdi is not for distribution here. It is meant for the people of Saurashtra, where people are dying of hunger. If we eat it here, what will they get?' With great hesitation, she humbly said, 'I have not come to ask for sukhdi, but to offer it. Please ensure that my sukhdi also reaches those in need.'

How did this woman, a beggar, learn about this noble act? Perhaps she had heard a sermon somewhere. She had understood that feeding the hungry brings great merit. And so, despite herself living in penury, she too wanted to earn some virtue by contributing whatever little she had. This is the mindset of ordinary people in our country, a uniqueness that defines India.

This land embodies incredible diversity. Nowhere else in the world can one find such a vast range of geographical and cultural variety. We have the Himalayas, covered in snow throughout the year, and we have Kerala, where there is hardly any winter. We have Cherrapunji, which receives the highest rainfall, and Barmer and Jaisalmer, which receive almost none. We have fertile lands, deserts, coastlines and high plateaus – every possible geographical feature found elsewhere on earth exists here. Similarly, we have all kinds of people – tall, medium and short individuals; dark, fair and wheatish-skinned people; flat-nosed and long-nosed people; so many castes and tribes, each with unique traditions; a wide variety of cuisines and rituals of worship.

Our ancestors recognized this diversity and formulated the principle of 'unity in diversity'. They understood that God created diversity in the world. If He had wished, He could have made everyone the same, but He didn't. This is the divine beauty of creation.

Today, some people say they want to convert the whole world to Islam or Christianity. But why? God has created each one of us differently. Had He wished, He could have made everyone the same, but He didn't. God is the Lord of all, not just of Muslims or Christians alone. He did not create only one community; He created all. If everything was His creation, then trying to destroy others is an attempt to disrupt God's own creation.

Diversity exists in nature. Because the world was created from the three fundamental qualities – *sattva* (purity), *rajas* (activity) and *tamas* (inertia). When these qualities were in perfect balance, there was no world. The moment an imbalance occurred, creation took place. How did this imbalance arise? It came from a thought in God's mind: '*Ekoham bahushyam*' (I am one; let me become many). This thought led to movement, which resulted in the creation of the entire universe. And one day, everything will return to its original state of balance.

Since diversity is a reality, to ensure that it does not become a source of suffering, our tradition teaches us to treat everyone as our own. It teaches us to take only what is necessary for ourselves and to share the rest with others. There is no virtue in eating to our fill when others are starving. Instead, we should say, 'Let us share this bread – half for me, half for you.'

This way of thinking, shaped over thousands of years, is what we call as the Hindu consciousness. We also call it 'dharma', though the English language lacks an exact equivalent for dharma. The British mistakenly translated Dharma as religion because they saw religious rituals such as prayers, fasting and pilgrimages in Hinduism and assumed it was just another religion, like Islam or Christianity.

However, Dharma is not a religion. The Supreme Court of India has ruled in three different cases that Hinduism is not a religion but a way of life, an ideal of living, a process of experiencing life. Thus, Hindu Dharma encompasses everything – individual, society, nature and the divine. It establishes harmony among them, and the system that maintains this harmony is called dharma.

A person's relationship with society begins with the family, then extends to the community, the nation and beyond. Similarly, we also have a relationship with nature. Everything we need comes from nature, so we must maintain balance with it and take only what is essential. Nature has enough to meet our needs, but not our greed. Yet, in an attempt to satisfy our greed, we are destroying nature completely.

Today, because of economic reasons, slogans like 'save the environment' are being raised everywhere. In 2003, an Earth Summit was held in New York, attended by representatives from 106 countries. The summit lasted for four days. For the first three days, discussions took place and in the end, 40 points were identified as crucial for environmental protection. On the fourth day, the representatives were supposed to sign an agreement on these 40 points. The Indian delegation, led by Dr Karan Singh[8], distributed the English translation of the 'Prithvi Sukta'[9] from the Atharvaveda[10] to all the delegates. When they read it, they were amazed and asked why it had not been shared on the first day itself. The 'Prithvi Sukta' not only contained those 40 points but also 22 additional ones, including the principles of *Vasudhaiva Kutumbakam* (the world is one family) and *sarve bhavantu sukhinah* (may all be happy). Ultimately, the delegates acknowledged and praised the wisdom in that scripture.

Thus, our philosophy considers everything – individual duty, social duty, environmental duty and spiritual liberation – as the interconnected aspects of dharma. But the concept of the English word 'religion' captures only a small fraction of this vast idea. Due to our English-based education, we have been led to misunderstanding our own heritage. We have forgotten who we are; we have lost our identity.

This situation arose because of the education system imposed upon us. The British understood well that they were only a handful in number and could not rule over India unless they corrupted the minds of its people. There is a Sanskrit verse that states: *Shastrahata na hi hata ripavo bhavanti, prajnahatastu ripavah suhata bhavanti. Shastram nihanti purushasya shariram ekam, prajna kulam cha vibhavam cha yashash cha hanti.* (One does not truly die if killed by weapons, but if one's wisdom is destroyed, one is as good as dead.)' The British aimed to destroy our wisdom.

In April 1866, a meeting of the Royal Asiatic Society was held in London, chaired by Reverend W. Strong. The records of the meeting mention a discussion led by Mr. Edward Thomas, 'who spoke about successive waves of Aryan immigration from the Oxus region into the provinces of Ariana, across the Hindu Kush, and into Punjab. He described the pastoral races that entered India, suggesting that their crude chanting became the Vedic hymns and that the Brahmanical institutions later took shape along the banks of the Saraswati River.'

Such narratives were deliberately constructed to create self-doubt among Indians, making them believe that their own scriptures were merely songs sung by wandering cattle herders. This attempt to delegitimize Indian heritage was a systematic effort to make people feel alienated from their own culture. Even today, terms like 'Adivasi' (indigenous people) are used, as if some people belong to India while all others are outsiders. But in reality, are not all of us Adivasis – the original inhabitants of this land? No one came from outside. This has now been conclusively established that there was no separate race called the Aryans, nor did they invade India from outside. Even the BBC has acknowledged in its broadcasts that the theory of Aryan migration was false.

Despite this, confusion was deliberately instilled in our minds, making us question our origins and our own history. The glorious episodes of our history were never taught to us. Instead, only the instances where we were defeated or subjugated were extensively narrated. Our achievements and valour were never highlighted.

Rabindranath Tagore once said that an English child is well aware of the victories and conquests of his ancestors, their expansion of empires and their achievements in trade and commerce. This knowledge instils in him a sense of pride and a desire to emulate their courage in warfare, wealth and commerce. However, what is taught to our children? They are told that they are fools, that their ancestors were fools and that they never established any empire or achieved anything remarkable. But what they actually did is never revealed. As a result, a child born in our country remains only an imitator of the West and does not think independently.

Today, as the world stands on the brink of another great struggle, it becomes our duty to understand our heritage and history accurately. We are unaware of the treasures we possess. Just as a farmer's child, upon finding a gemstone, plays with it in the mud without knowing its worth, we too remain oblivious to the invaluable legacy we hold. When a king comes and offers a high price for it, only then does the farmer realize its true value. Similarly, we must recognize the importance of our heritage and educate our new generation about it.

We have forgotten ourselves, and those who forget themselves are vulnerable to any attack. A person in a coma does not feel pain, no matter what happens to him. Therefore, the first step is to awaken him. India, over the past several centuries, has entered a state of unconsciousness, a coma-like condition. Consequently, we no longer know who we are, what our purpose is, or why God has sent us into this world. Our role is to unify the entire world, but today, destructive forces are attempting to weaken and destroy us. We must defeat these forces, as this is our ultimate purpose.

In his book, Swamyji, an eminent intellectual, has detailed the various kinds of invasions we face – attacks that are not overt but hidden, making it difficult to detect them. These attacks are eating away at our nation from within, much like termites that hollow out a pillar, making it appear strong on the outside while weakening its core. No one knows when such a weakened structure will collapse. Therefore, we must remain vigilant. His book contains many facts about these invasions – how they are happening and, more importantly, how to resist them.

The Rashtriya Swayamsevak Sangh was founded precisely with this goal of awakening the Hindu society. This nation is a Hindu nation, and it has a purpose to fulfill; but we have forgotten ourselves. That is why we need to be reawakened. Since its inception, the RSS has grown into a vast organization, working in multiple areas as envisioned by its founders. At present, different wings of the organization are actively working across the country. Every challenge mentioned in the book is being addressed through these organizations.

If we fail to act now, we risk sharing the fate of civilizations that have disappeared – the Babylonian, Egyptian and Roman civilizations. If we do not take action, we too may become a mere footnote in history.

However, that is not going to happen. We are witnessing a transformation today. A new order is being born. With birth come labour pains. The world is going through such a phase of painful transformation. Sociologists have observed that before a major societal change, its symptoms begin to appear 15 to 20 years in advance. Some of these signs include:

1. Alienation: People feeling disconnected from their identity and roots
2. Increase in violent crimes: A rise in lawlessness and unrest
3. Mental disorders: Growing anxiety and psychological instability
4. Social disintegration: Efforts to divide society into factions
5. Increase in religious faith: A significant rise in religiocity and devotion

All these signs are visible today. There is violence, unrest and division, but at the same time, faith in religion is also increasing. When all hope fades, people turn to the divine. This surge in religious sentiment is a sign that a great transformation is near.

For example, in Kerala, earlier, only 15,000 people used to participate in the Sabarimala[11] pilgrimage. But last year, the number rose to one million. Similarly, in Pandharpur[12], the number of devotees has increased exponentially. During the month of Shravan[13], millions of Kanwariyas[14] undertake pilgrimages across North India. The Amarnath Yatra[15] continues despite terrorist threats. Similarly, despite a bomb blast, the Vaishno Devi[16] pilgrimage continues.

Whenever a major change is about to occur, these indicators intensify. Once the transformation point is crossed, everything stabilizes. And that moment is fast approaching.

Swami Vivekananda, around 1894–95, wrote to his disciples that a new golden age had begun with the birth of Swami Ramakrishna Paramhansa in 1836. Sri Aurobindo stated that the transitional period between two ages lasts 175 years. Just as dusk falls between day and night, a period of transition marks the end of one era and the beginning of another. Adding 175 years to 1836 brings us to 2011 – the year when India's fortune will begin to shine again on the world stage.

It is inevitable. However, at the same time, the forces seeking to weaken us will intensify their attacks. Every conscious individual in society has the duty to awaken his brethren, instil in them the pride of their heritage and organize collective resistance. People must be inspired to take charge of their own future, discard laziness and ignorance, and rise once again. India is destined to reclaim its place as a great civilization. It is our duty to kindle this spirit in every individual.

9

'We Must Perceive, Understand and Manifest [Mahatma Gandhi's] Idealism in Our Lives'

MOHAN BHAGWAT

Dr Mohan Bhagwat, the present sarsanghachalak of the RSS, is a visionary leader who has taken the message of the organization to previously unreached sections of the society through his targeted outreach programmes. He has sought to present the thought process of the RSS in a contemporary light and has demonstrated openness to engage with ideas and opinions from across the ideological spectrum. Addressing an event on 2 October 2019, commemorating the birth anniversary of Mahatma Gandhi, Bhagwat spoke about the need to understand Gandhi's vision and strive to emulate it.

The revered Mahatma Gandhi is prominent among luminaries whose names were etched in a glorious chapter in the history of the eternal and epochal journey of modern and rising independent Bharat. Bharat is the land of spirituality, and its progress rests on the same. Mahatma Gandhi sought to lay the foundation and build a polity for Bharat based on that spirituality.

Gandhiji's efforts were not limited to power politics. His focus was more on creating righteous behaviour (*satvik acharan*) in society and its leadership. He outrightly rejected the egoistic and corrupt global and domestic politics driven by selfish pursuits. It was his dream for the country and humanity that public life should be based on truth, non-violence, self-reliance and real freedom. Gandhiji lived by that vision throughout his life.

As a part of the nationwide protests against the arrest of Gandhiji, Congress had organized a rally in Nagpur in 1922. Addressing the rally, Dr Hedgewar, founder of the RSS, said that there was no disparity between his words and deeds, terming him as a sacred soul (*punya purush*) and added that Gandhiji was a man who was always ready to sacrifice everything for his principles and ideals. Hedgewar said that mere glorification through words would not advance Gandhiji's mission. He asserted that emulating Gandhian values in our lives is the only way forward to further the vision of the Mahatma.

Gandhiji was well aware of the detrimental impact of the slavish mentality that had developed among the countrymen during the course of the British rule. In his book, *Hind Swaraj*, he envisioned a Bharat free from this slave mentality and prepared to achieve progress and prosperity based on a purely *swadeshi* vision. At that time, Western imperialists had dominated the entire world with their dazzling materialism, promoting their systems and lifestyle by way of distorting the education system and making everyone financially dependent on their political power. In such a situation, Gandhiji endeavoured to give a new thought to all spheres of national life based on our own identity. However, those people immersed in a slavish mindset couldn't appreciate Gandhiji's efforts, they continued to accept Western values as a credible model and denounced our ancestors, history and culture as inferior and disgraceful. Massive influence of the West is visible in the country's direction and condition even today.

Many contemporary world leaders had drawn ideas and inspiration from Gandhiji's thoughts and contributed to their own nations' progress. On Gandhiji's demise, Albert Einstein[1] had said: 'Generations to come, it may well be, will scarce believe that such a man as this one ever in flesh and blood walked upon this Earth.' Gandhiji had placed his life as an example before us through his pure thought and action.

Gandhiji had visited a Sangh camp held near Wardha in Vidarbha region of Maharashtra in 1936. Dr Hedgewar visited him at his Wardha Ashram the following day. The contents of the long question-and-answer session and discussion that took place between them are now in the public domain. Gandhiji had also visited a shakha near his place of residence in Delhi during the tragic days of Partition. He spoke to the swayamsevaks in the shakha. A report of that visit was published in the *Harijan*, dated 27 September 1947. Gandhiji expressed his joy over the discipline of the Sangh Swayamsevaks and complete absence of any divisive feelings of caste and creed among them.

Gandhiji, who believed in the *swa*-based reconstruction of Bharat, firmly stood for social equality and harmony and translated his vision into action by setting a personal example through his life. Even those who might have had minor differences of opinion with him viewed him with reverence. We must perceive, understand and manifest that idealism in our lives.

Right from the beginning, the RSS has had a tradition of remembering the great personalities of our national life through the recitation of a *stotra* every morning. In 1963, this stotra was revised by adding several new names including that of revered Gandhiji. Nowadays, it is known as the Ekatmata Stotra. The swayamsevaks recite it every morning and recall Gandhiji's life of above-mentioned values.

While remembering the Mahatma on his 150th birth anniversary, we shall take a pledge that we will emulate his sacred, dedicated and transparent life example, and his Swa-centric life vision, and through that we shall imbibe the qualities of dedication and renunciation in our lives with a mission to make Bharat the *vishwaguru*.

10

Vijayadashami Speeches, a Decade Apart

MOHAN BHAGWAT

It has been a tradition in the RSS that the sarsanghachalak delivers an important address annually on Vijayadashami, the foundation day of the organization. This long-standing practice, followed for decades, helps not only the swayamsevaks, but also the wider public understand the views and policies of the organization with respect to contemporary issues and challenges that the nation and the world are facing. Continuing this tradition, Dr Mohan Bhagwat, the present sarsanghachalak, delivers the annual Vijayadashami address at Nagpur presenting the organization's perspective on contemporary national and global issues.

Presented below are two of his important speeches delivered 12 years apart, the first one in 2010–11 and the second in 2023.

Vijayadashmi 2010–2011

The festival of Vijayadashami is celebrated in our country with great gaiety and enthusiasm from time immemorial as a day of victory of Dharma, that is, virtue, service and righteousness. This year the festival comes at a time when the entire nation is heartened by the court verdict on the Ram Janmabhoomi issue, delivered on 30 September 2010. This verdict of the Lucknow bench of the Allahabad High Court will ultimately facilitate the construction of a magnificent temple at the Ram Janmabhoomi.

Maryada Purushottama Ram is the manifest divine for Hindus all over the world. At the same time, he is also the manifestation of our national culture and honour that is at the core of our country's identity, ethos, integrity, urge for freedom and vigour. That is why in the first copy of our Constitution, among the pictures attested as description for the events that reflect our ideals, aspirations and traditions, the first individual picture that finds place – after the pictures of Mohenjo-Daro and life in a hermitage – is that of Sri Ram. History of the Sikh Panth clearly records Sri Guru Nanak Devji's visit to Sri Ram Janmabhoomi at Ayodhya in 1526 AD. It is now acknowledged – on the basis of historical, archaeological and physical evidence – that there existed a sacred Hindu monument at the site of Sri Ram Janmabhoomi prior to 1528 AD.

The legal battle over Sri Ram Janmabhoomi dragged on for 60 years, causing serious disharmony, severe conflict and pain in the entire society. However, setting aside the past, we all have to come together as one people to build a grand temple at Ayodhya for Maryada Purushottama Sri Ram. That should also put an end to all the pain and uncalled for acrimony.

The Sangh views the verdict as an opportunity granted by destiny to every section of our society, including Muslims, to make a fresh start in the spirit of affectionate coexistence. Let us rise above our petty divisiveness and the obstinacy born of prejudices and suspicion. Let us embrace our unique, all-inclusive and tolerant culture – one that inspires in us an unwavering and intense sense of patriotism and respect for our ancestors, and preserves, promotes and validates all our diversities – and come together to build the temple at the birthplace of Sri Ram who, in the words of Sri Lohia, is the catalyst for the integration of the north and the south of Bharat. This is the desire of the entire society, which has manifested amply in the unity and restraint displayed by it after the verdict.

But we also witness efforts being launched from day one, to distort this opportunity for national integration into an instrument for achieving political self-interest through appeasement. Some people, who have mastered the art of creating conflicts by exploiting our diversity – be it religion, region or language – for the sake of securing votes, are again resorting to petty conspiracies that threaten social harmony, all under the guise of lofty yet misleading rhetoric and clamour in the name of secularism.

They always create impediments in any efforts and initiatives for harmony. There are also a few people among our intelligentsia and media, who, overcome by their egoistic feeling towards their own illusive thinking and their prejudices against the Hindu thought and activism in support of Hindus, have shamefully abandoned all concern and fear for truth. The sole guiding factor for them is their self-interest or business interest. One can easily identify them by studying the difference in their language and behaviour until 4 p.m. on 30 September and after the verdict was announced. Their attempts to create fear and mistrust among various sections and organizations of our society always take place under the garb of weird arguments in the name of humanity and secularism. We must always be wary of these forces. In fact, these are the very people who are responsible for not allowing hoary ideals, such as universal brotherhood, harmony and freedom from exploitation to blossom, by resorting to the use of those very ideals for achieving their own self-interests and evil objectives.

It is now evident that due to these tendencies a dangerous conspiracy is afoot to bring into vogue phrases like 'Hindu terror' and 'saffron terror' under the pretext that some Hindu individuals were allegedly involved in incidents of terror here and there. There are attempts to drag the Sangh also into it. This is a sinister conspiracy to mislead Hindus through a campaign of lies and to defame Hindu saints, noble citizens, temples and organizations. We have not bothered to find out who is behind all this and who is going to be the beneficiary of this vilification campaign. But what is certain is that, instead of benefitting anybody, this campaign would certainly bring disrepute to our nation and pose a serious danger to it.

This sinister campaign to defame the saffron colour – which adorns our constitutionally-ordained national flag and represents sacrifice, hard work and wisdom – targets not only the Hindu society and its saints, who always stay away from such militant activities and fight the forces of terror our country Bharat; and the swayamsevaks and Sangh-inspired organizations that stand at the forefront both during natural calamities as well as man-made disasters like terror attacks and wars, often risking their lives to support the administration. These organizations also run 1.57 lakh service projects for the deprived, without any self-interest or discrimination. This campaign is bound to fail. Before the judicial trial had even commenced, the media trial was unleashed against the Sangh by spreading canards. Those indulging in this malicious campaign should first look into their own defaced self. This is not the time to push the country into depraved electoral conspiracies.

The powerful countries of the world make every effort to exploit international circumstances to establish their hegemony. This explains the current unhealthy rivalry between the US and China as they compete for global supremacy. In the name of war on terror, America's active intervention has now extended into Pakistan, right into our neighbourhood.

Corruption and misrule of the ruling class, that has caused a wave of mass anger and brought in regime change in some countries in the Middle East, is also seen in some corners as an effort to promote the interests of America and other Western countries. Communist China, our northern neighbour, is also enhancing its strength to establish dominance over the world. Naturally, we cannot remain untouched by the turmoil created by this power game. We have always regarded the entire world as one family and sought genuine friendship with all, rather than dominance. Countries around the world acknowledge this through their experience of the exemplary conduct of Indians living abroad. That is why they trust and welcome us wholeheartedly. While not compromising on our sovereignty, dignity and security, we should take the initiative to transform the current volatile global situation into one of mutual trust and co-operation, in keeping with our traditional world view.

We have a deep cultural relationship with our neighbouring countries particularly in Southeast Asia. Even today this relationship is remembered with gratitude, joy and happiness. We are bound by common economic interests. There is a general consensus in these countries that Bharat should lead them and stand by them through thick and thin. We should strengthen our economic, diplomatic and cultural ties with all these countries. We will have to be more focused in our efforts to help stabilize neighbouring Nepal and foster a relationship that is more favourable to us. We should also initiate efforts to alleviate the suffering of Sri Lankan Tamils and create conditions that enable them to contribute to Sri Lankan society and national life on equal footing, with their civil rights protected and their status intact.

We must tighten our security along the Bangladesh border, prevent it from remaining porous, and stop infiltration and illegal trafficking of arms, cattle, fake currency and drugs, while also ensuring that the atmosphere in Bangladesh becomes more favourable to us.

Tibet continues to remain under illegal occupation of China. We must help the Tibetans living there, as well as in Bharat and other parts of the world, by helping to give voice to their sentiments and by protecting their human rights, faith and traditions, both in their homeland as well as in the world.

The crisis in Kashmir has become very serious and complicated. Due to our negligence, Baltistan and Gilgit have become part of Pakistan, and now China is trying to complete the encirclement of Bharat by positioning its army in those regions. Meanwhile, the United States is working towards a safe and honorable exit from Afghanistan, while seeking to secure a foothold in Kashmir with the help of Pakistan.

We should move fast before this shadow of sinister international politics overtakes the Valley. We have to create an atmosphere in Afghanistan that aligns with our interests, and strive to turn the situation in the Valley towards greater integration with the rest of Bharat. This is the mandated duty of any national government towards its integral territories.

The sovereign state power of Bharat should not be seen as buckling under the designs of separatist-sponsored stone pelters. Removing Army bunkers or curtailing the powers of our forces is not going to help in protecting the integrity and security of our country. The direction of our policies should be guided by the unanimous resolution passed by our Parliament in 1994. We must not forget that the accession of Kashmir to Bharat, through the Instrument of Accession signed by Maharaja Hari Singh, is final and non-negotiable.

The Kashmir Valley is not the whole and sole of Jammu and Kashmir state. Even in the Valley, it is only a tiny minority that is clamouring for autonomy and dreaming of *azadi* by promoting secessionism. Engaging and patronizing only these secessionist groups and their leaders in various dialogues is not going to help in resolving the crisis. In fact, it will only aggravate the problem. Besides the Valley, we have to think seriously about the problems being faced by Jammu and Ladakh for decades and the discrimination that they are being subjected to. We have to undoubtedly talk to the youngsters and people of the Valley who have come under the secessionist sway. But at the same it is imperative on our part to appreciate the feelings, needs and aspirations of various other sections of the state, like the nationalist-minded Muslims, Gujjars and Bakarwals, Shias, Sikhs, Hindus including Kashmiri Pandits and Buddhists.

There is an urgent need to pay attention to the long-standing demands of the refugees from the Pakistan-occupied Kashmir (PoK). Kashmiri Pandits must be enabled to return to their homes and hearths with honour and safety and assured livelihood. All these sections want complete integration of the state with rest of Bharat. That is why when we think of Jammu and Kashmir, we must take into account security, development and aspirations of all these sections. Dialogues taking place in the context of Jammu and Kashmir will be representative and fruitful only when these sections are also included and listened to.

Since Independence, people of Jammu and Kashmir have been craving for peace and a good government that doesn't discriminate. It is necessary to ensure that they soon get such a government and administration which is free from corruption and discrimination.

Hand in hand with Pakistan – whose military establishment has an avowed enmity with us – China has entered into Gilgit–Baltistan region in the northern areas of Jammu and Kashmir. We have failed to grasp the geopolitical importance of this northern part of Bharat, wherein meet the boundaries of six nations, and have allowed them to be exploited by the aggressors.

Terrorists are being instigated to infiltrate and disturb peace in Jammu and Kashmir at the behest of Pakistan. Truth is that even the constitution of Pakistan and the highest court of PoK do not recognize Jammu and Kashmir as a part of Pakistan. Yet, Pakistan is engaged in creating trouble in Jammu and Kashmir. Why despite all this, our central government and the interlocutors appointed by them insist time and again that Kashmir is a political problem?

Kashmir is not merely an internal political problem. It is a problem created by aggression and terrorism instigated from across the border and fanatic fundamentalism, as also by our weak-kneed and indecisive policy. The Centre and the state governments should pursue a policy of strengthening the voice of patriotic elements as opposed to this aggression. The Hindu refugees of 1947–48 should be speedily resettled with full citizenship rights, and the displaced Kashmiri Hindus should be able to go back to the land of their ancestors with full preparedness and with impeccable guarantee of their safety so that they can live there as Hindus and Indians. There should be a sensitive and transparent administration in the state of Jammu and Kashmir, which should end discrimination against various castes and classes in the population as well as against regions of Jammu and Ladakh. Article 370 that hinders integration of Jammu and Kashmir with rest of Bharat must be abolished. The mentality that harps on the pre-1953 status and seeks separation of Kashmir from Bharat must be crushed. The central government and its interlocutors should change their mindset. The pre-1953 situation cannot be the basis of the solution to the Kashmir problem. The unanimous resolution passed by Parliament in 1994, that PoK be restored to Bharat, should alone be the basis of the tone of discourse on the Kashmir problem.

China, which used to equate its forced occupation of Tibet with the Kashmir problem to justify its illegitimate action, has now registered its presence in Gilgit and Baltistan. It attempted to meddle in our internal affairs by declaring that citizens of Jammu and Kashmir and Arunachal Pradesh need not ask for visas to enter China. At least now there shouldn't be any confusion or illusion in the minds of any about the real intentions of China. Its military, political and economic designs to encircle, pressurize and weaken Bharat are too glaring to be missed. In contrast, we need to do a lot more in our military, political and economic strategy, the alertness of our leadership and the preparation of public opinion. Any further delay in these matters would be tantamount to inviting grave threats to the nation in the near future.

Occasionally, guided by its own interest, China seems to be taking some initiative to strengthen its economic, diplomatic and cultural ties with Bharat. However, recent events reveal its real intention to expand its influence – not only in the Asian continent but also in Bharat – even through the use of military power.

The incursion by Chinese troops in Leh and Ladakh, the demolition of our bunkers, threats to our ships in the South China Sea in blatant violation of the principle of international law, and efforts to prevent Bharat from oil exploration are some of the recent examples of the same. China objects when we improve our relations with countries like Vietnam. It is published in media that as per our intelligence sources China has forged links with terrorists in the Northeast of Bharat.

It is true that we want neither enmity nor war with anyone. But we must not forget that our own naivety and innocence once made us the victims of shrewd and crafty war tactics of China in 1962. Hence, while maintaining cultural ties that we have been enjoying with China since the time of Bhagwan Buddha and also our current economic relations, we must remain vigilant, build necessary infrastructure along the border and not allow any slackness in our military preparedness. Also important is to influence international diplomatic dialogues more effectively in order to garner global support for us in any possible eventuality.

China has sponsored and promoted Maoist insurgency in Nepal. Maoists of our country have close links with the Maoists of Nepal. The government is stuck in internal squabbles over the question of firmly dealing with the Maoists. We have yet to see credible efforts being initiated to make the administration transparent and accountable and to accelerate development activity in the Maoist-infested areas. At times, even this grave issue seems to exploited for ulterior political benefits, such an approach will prove costly for our national security and democracy.

It is imperative now for our political class to understand the pain and sufferings of the people of our Northeast. They should deepen their understanding and knowledge, and develop a more thorough and informed approach as to how to solve the problems of those people. Terror groups that completely lack any mass base and are practically defunct are being given a fresh lease of life by the Centre and the state governments by initiating dialogues with them.

Even a 60-day blockade of Manipur some years ago did not show any impact on the government, nor is there any visible willingness to take action against the raging terrorism there. The Riyang tribe, displaced from Mizoram to Tripura, is facing total extinction; but the administration is not even remotely aware of it. Without trying to understand or even listen to the problems of the people in the region and despite the problems arising out of the large-scale infiltration, the government of Bharat seems over-eager to cede its territory in its talks with Bangladesh. Our incomplete and superficial understanding and awareness about the challenges of the region and our indifference to the difficulties of the people, our lack of a clear-cut national perspective and our mentality to exploit anything and everything for political gains have compounded the problems of the Northeast, just like in Jammu and Kashmir.

In the Northeast too, separatist forces get all the attention and those loyal to our country are grossly ignored. This policy has provided a golden opportunity to the separatist terrorist outfits like the National Socialist Council of Nagaland (NSCN), who had lost all public support and were almost defunct, to once again raise their ugly heads. Arunachal Pradesh, which has long withstood Chinese machinations and is standing like a protective wall on our border, is today a victim of gross neglect.

Patriotic people of Manipur suffered immensely from the shortage of essential commodities when blockades were imposed for long durations by the separatist forces, leading to them feeling tired of appealing for help and finally becoming dejected and anguished. Do our leaders not realize the cost of pampering separatist forces while neglecting our own people, especially along sensitive borders that are in the shadow of the expansionist designs of China? Continued negligence towards the machinations of foreign missionaries in the region has further complicated the situation.

On one hand, there is this vacillation and lack of willpower displayed by our ruling establishment; and on the other is the unmitigated influx of the Bangladeshi infiltrators from across the borders that have been left porous even after 60 years of Independence. The courts as well as the intelligence agencies have repeatedly asked for detection, deletion and deportation of these infiltrators. However, the experience everywhere is that our leaders at both the state and central levels, who can stoop to any low for the sake of votes, lack basic willpower and courage to initiate even the first step of detecting. This infiltration is completely changing the demographic profile of the Northeast and of the border districts of Bengal and Bihar. This has led to a rise in fundamentalism. Violent and anti-social elements have been emboldened by this attitude, and the local tribes and Hindus have become victims of the high-handedness and atrocities of these elements. Latest example of the plight of the patriotic Hindus in this region is the murderous attack on them at Deganga in West Bengal. Neither the state government nor the central government is bothered about the suffering of the Hindus. All that they are bothered about is their votes. The government and the policy makers have realized from several experiences that deterioration in the internal law and order situation and security of Hindus in the border districts is fraught with serious implications for our border security. Yet there is no change in the attitude.

One wonders if the government is really bothered about this issue at all. The way provisions have been made in the census data collection this time for people to claim nationality without providing any proof, any illegal migrant could claim nationality easily. All the citizens are going to get a Unique Identity Number soon. But where is the arrangement to verify whether those securing it are truly the citizens of our country or not? We shouldn't allow such mistakes or casual approach in these serious policy matters.

We make tall claims about creating a society free from caste by birth identity. Then why are we introducing policies that include the collection of caste data during the census – a process meant for one nation, one people – thereby reinforcing caste consciousness once again? Prominent scholars and social activists have appealed to the countrymen that in order to create a united and coherent national society, they must declare their caste as Hindu, Hindustani or Bharatiya. Why should the government, which is duty-bound to bring in emotional integration, act to the contrary and ask each citizen about caste? If necessary, the government may find another independent, temporary and limited plan to collect necessary caste data for the sake of its schemes.

What do we proclaim about the future of this nation and where are we actually leading it? The common man of this country, whose economic well-being we all talk about, is a simple farmer, a small-time shop owner, a push-cart vegetable vendor or a footpath trader. He is an unorganized worker in a town or a village, an artisan or a tribal. But the Western economic model that we follow is big business-centric, village-uprooting, employment-displacing, environment-destroying, high energy-consuming and expensive. It is not centred around the common man. Nor is it environment, energy and investment saving, or employment generating.

On one hand we talk about education to all. But on the other hand, we have turned education into a business, making it unaffordable for the poor. We want our education system to impart values like humanity, social responsibility, duty-consciousness and patriotism effectively in our society. But at the same time, we have discarded all that once nurtured these values, and instead promote books and syllabi that fuel a race for more money, selfishness, materialism and insensitivity.

At the root of this gap between our words and deeds is the gross ignorance of and complete disrespect for the real identity of our nationhood, unity and global mission, further aggravated by our selfishness and disharmony. Only an alert and awakened society, committed to shaping the mindset in the leaders of the nation and guarding against ideological distortions, can rescue the nation from this crisis.

The RSS has been engaged in creating individuals capable of building such a society for the last 85 years. It is now universally accepted and becoming increasingly clear that Hindutva is the core identity of this ancient nation, and an imperative basis for its integrity and security, basis of the unity of the society and its vigour, and the catalyst for lasting peace in the world.

Twenty-five years ago, on the same occasion of Vijayadashami, and from the same platform, the then sarsanghachalak, Sri Balasaheb Deoras, had said that secularism, socialism and democracy are still alive in our country only because this is Hindu Rashtra. Today eminent thinkers like M.J. Akbar and Rashid Alvi are also saying the same thing.

Hindutva alone can awaken us to the underlying oneness in the manifest diversity around us, enabling us to protect and respect it, and organize all that diversity in one unified thread. Let the Hindu society, which is the progeny of this land, internalize this comprehensive, universal welfare-oriented, non-reactionary idea of Hindutva in thought, word and deed. Let us unite and fearlessly proclaim loud and clear the honour of our sacred motherland Bharat, its glorious history and traditions and the eternal Hindu culture. The necessity of time makes it imperative that all of us unite. Let us get rid of selfishness and disharmony and make all our efforts for building an eminently glorious and victorious Bharat. Let us free the whole world from its problems and lead it on the path of peace.

The objective of Sangh's work is to impart Hindu values and pride in every individual through daily shakhas; inspire and equip the person to have a clean and selfless heart and offer their entire life for the country, Dharma and culture; and build a strong and united society. Sangh has no other objective or ambition except to fulfil this mission.

Vijayadashami 2023

We celebrate Vijayadashami Utsav every year as the festival of strength (*shakti parv*) and a celebration of complete triumph of humanity over demonism. This year has witnessed several events that have been encouraging to all of us, making this year's celebration one of greater pride and joy.

This year, Bharat, as president, played host to the annual summit of the G-20 group of major countries. Throughout the year, several programs involving heads of states, ministers, officials and intellectuals of the member countries were organized at various places across Bharat. Naturally, the warm hospitality of the people, the glimpse into Bharat's glorious past and the exciting developmental march that is underway in the country left a deep impression on all the participants from across the world.

Everyone witnessed Bharat's genuine goodwill and diplomatic heft in securing membership for the African Union in the coveted G-20 and also in getting the G-20 Declaration passed unanimously on the very first day itself at the Summit held in New Delhi in September this year. '*Vasudhaiva Kutumbakam*', the guiding principle of Bharat's distinct thought and vision, has now been incorporated into the philosophy of the entire world. Thanks to Bharat's efforts, the economy-centric forum of G-20 has now been transformed into a human-centric forum. By successfully holding the G-20 Summit, our leadership has done a commendable job of firmly establishing Bharat as a major nation at the global stage.

Recently, our country's sportspersons also brought us great pride and joy by winning 107 medals (28 gold, 38 silver and 41 bronze), leaping past the 100-mark for the first time in the Asian Games. We extend our hearty congratulations to them. Successful launch of Mission Chandrayaan has also gloriously showcased resurgent Bharat's strength, intelligence and capability. The determination of the nation's leadership has seamlessly combined with the scientific knowledge and technological prowess of our scientists. Bharat's Vikram lander touched down at the Moon's South Pole – a first in the history of the Space Age. The scientists who accomplished this historic feat, boosting the nation's pride and confidence and the leadership that supported them, are being applauded and congratulated across the country.

All endeavours of a nation are driven by the national ideals that serve the overall purpose of that nation. That's why a temple for Sri Ramlala, whose picture is depicted on a page of the original copy of our Constitution, is being built at Ayodhya. It has been announced that Sri Ramlala will be consecrated in the sanctum sanctorum of the temple on 22 January 2024. Due to practical difficulties and security reasons, only a limited number of people would be able to be present in Ayodhya on that auspicious occasion. Bhagwan Sri Ram is the epitome of dutifulness and Dharma, and symbolizes love and compassion. Same type of environment should be created at our respective places on this occasion. We should celebrate the consecration ceremony at a small scale in various places across the country. This will awaken the spirit of Ram in every heart, and embellish the Ayodhya of the mind, creating an atmosphere of love, responsibility and goodwill in the society.

Bharat has emerged stronger after battling centuries of challenges, and our nation is now certainly moving forward on the path of material and spiritual progress. We are all extremely fortunate to witness the unfolding of events and incidents that mark Bharat's unstoppable rise.

We are commemorating the 2,550th year of the *nirvaan* of Sri Mahavir Swami, who showed the path of non-violence, kindness and morality to the entire world through his exemplary life. This is also the 350th year of coronation of Chattrapati Sri Shivaji Maharaj, who showed us the path of liberation from 350 years of foreign subjugation, by establishing the Hindavi Swaraj based on justice and public welfare. This year also happens to be the 200th birth anniversary of Maharshi Dayanand Saraswati, who gave a clear and true vision of our *swa*, or self, to the people of the country through *Satyarth Prakash*. The coming year is also the year of remembrance of two great personalities who remain a source of eternal inspiration for our national efforts and endeavours. This year would be the 500th birth anniversary of the indomitable Rani Durgavati, who made supreme sacrifices for protecting the identity and Independence of our country. She is an icon, remarkable for her enterprise, courage, patience, intelligence, strength and bravery as well as for her administrative skills and care for the welfare of her subjects. She was a shining example of efficiency, leadership, unimpeachable character and burning patriotism for the women of Bharat. This year also marks the 150th birth anniversary of Chhatrapati Shahuji Maharaj, the ruler of Kolhapur (Maharashtra), who, with his welfarist vision and administrative acumen, dedicated his life to rooting out social inequality.

Further, we have just completed the bicentenary celebrations of the Tamil Saint Srimad Ramalinga Vallalar, who began to awaken people to the cause of the country's Independence right from his youth. The stove he lit to feed the poor through *annadan* still burns in Tamil Nadu. Besides his struggle for the country's Independence, he persevered for Bharat's spiritual and cultural awakening as well as for a complete eradication of social inequality.

As we complete the Amrit Mahotsav of Bharat's Independence from British colonial rule, remembrance of the remarkable lives of these inspirational personalities gives us the message of social equality, and unity and integrity and defending the 'swa' or 'selfhood'.

It is a natural desire for human beings to make every effort to safeguard their 'swa' – the core identity. As the world is shrinking, nations are increasingly becoming worried about challenges to their identities, their 'swa'. Attempts to homogenize the entire world or to create uniformity haven't succeeded so far, nor will they succeed in the future.

Thus, the desire to preserve the identity of Bharat and the identity of Hindu society is only natural. It is no surprise, then, that a crises-ridden world expects Bharat to emerge with a new vision that is conducive to the changing times and is based on its own value systems, so that it can meet the contemporary needs and challenges of mankind. World is facing the scourge of fanaticism, arrogance and hysteria stemming from religious sectarianism. Solution to conflicts like the war in Ukraine or the Gaza Strip, which arise due to a clash of interests and extremism, remains elusive.

A lifestyle of unabashed consumerism, out of sync with nature, is leading to a string of new physical and mental health issues. Individual vices, social evils and incidents of crime are on the rise. Families are breaking apart, as the sense of individualism is deepening in the society. Pollution, global warming, imbalance in seasonal cycles and the resultant natural disasters are increasing every year as a result of unrestrained exploitation of natural resources. Terrorism, exploitation and totalitarianism are having a free run wreaking havoc. It has become abundantly clear that the world cannot counter these problems with its inadequate vision. Therefore, it is looking towards Bharat expectantly to lead by example and show a new path for peace and prosperity based on its own *sanatan* (eternal) values.

A smaller version of above-mentioned events can be witnessed in Bharat as well. For instance, we recently witnessed a series of devastating natural disasters in the Himalayan region, from Himachal Pradesh to

Uttarakhand to Sikkim. It is already being feared that these events could be a prelude to some serious and massive ecological crisis brewing in the future. This area, which is on our northern border, is critical to country's border security, water security and environmental health, and must be protected at all costs. We need to consider the entire Himalayan region as a single unit from the standpoints of security, environment, demography and development. This naturally picturesque area is geologically new, still forming and hence unstable. Arbitrary development plans were implemented without fully understanding the nature and characteristics of its topography, geology, biodiversity and water resources. As a result of this messy planning, this region and also the entire country is standing on the brink of a crisis. We all know that this is the region that serves as the source of water to all the countries of East and Southeast Asia, including Bharat. We are also long aware of China's presence on our northern border. Therefore, this area has special geological, geo-strategic and geo-political significance. Keeping that in mind, this area needs to be tackled from a different perspective.

Although these incidents of natural disasters are occurring more in the Himalayan region, they hold a clear message for the entire country. Due to the development trajectories based on inadequate, excessively materialistic and consumerist approach, humanity and nature are slowly but surely moving towards destruction. There is a growing concern about this all over the world. Bharat will have to abandon those unsuccessful paths or gradually turn back, designing its own distinct development path, in tune with the current times but also based on Bharatiya values and the overall unified and integral vision. Such a model of development would be eminently suitable not just for Bharat, but for the entire world. We must shun the tendency of dogmatically imitating old and unsuccessful paths.

We ought to rid ourselves of the colonial mindset and embrace only that which suits our country. Need of the hour is to adopt our own *swadeshi* (indigenous) path of development based on 'swa', by making what is already available in our country appropriate and relevant to the times. It is observed that some policy changes have recently been enacted that align with this distinct vision of development.

In the broader society too, an increasing number of new and successful experiments and innovations are taking place in areas like agriculture, industry and trade-related services, co-operatives and self-employment. However, in the field of administration, there is a greater need for a similar awakening among the policymakers who shape the direction and vision of various fields of human activity. It must be remembered that only 'swa-based', time-tested government policies, the prompt, consistent and people-oriented functioning of the administration and the co-operation and support of the larger society – in thoughts, words and actions – can bring about a meaningful transformation in Bharat.

However, efforts are being made to derail this transformation, to rupture social cohesion and unity, and increase conflicts. Due to our ignorance, imprudence, mutual distrust or carelessness, such undesirable disturbances and divisions are being increasingly witnessed in the society. The mission of Bharat's rise has always been the welfare of the entire world. As a natural consequence of this rise, the selfish, destructive and deceitful forces seeking to fulfil their sectarian interests are facing severe curbs and restrictions. Hence, there is continuous opposition from them. Although these forces wear the mask of some ideology or the other, and claim to be working for some lofty goals, their real objectives are something else. People of credibility who genuinely, work selflessly, irrespective of their ideology and the kind of work they do, always prove to be a hindrance for such deceitful and destructive forces.

These destructive, all-devouring forces call themselves as cultural Marxists or 'woke', the awakened ones. But they have forgotten Marx as early as in 1920s itself. They are opposed to all orderliness and morality, beneficence, culture, dignity and restraint in the world. In order for a handful of people to have complete control over the entire human race, they reward, promote and spread anarchy and indiscretion. Their modus operandi involves taking control of the media and academia, and plunging education, culture, politics and social environment into confusion, chaos and corruption. Such an environment enables the creation of a vicious cycle of fear, confusion and hatred. A society that is divided and entangled in mutual conflicts and confusion becomes weak, and easily and unknowingly falls prey to these destructive forces that are seeking their own dominance everywhere. In Bharatiya tradition, this style of functioning that creates disbelief, confusion and mutual hatred among the people of any particular nation is called *mantra viplav*.

To achieve narrow political gains, attempts are being made to forge alliances with these undesirable forces in the country to defeat political rivals. This is unwise and harmful for the country. The society has already become amnesiac, ravaged by all sorts of divisions, and is caught up in the deadly pursuit of selfish interests seeped in jealousy and hatred. That is why these demonic powers are able to get the support of internal or external forces who want to break the society and the nation.

If we look at the current situation in Manipur, this fact becomes obvious. How did this mutual discord and hatred suddenly erupt in Manipur, which had been peaceful for almost a decade? Were there extremists from across the border also among those who committed violence? Why, and by whom, was an attempt made to give a communal tinge to this conflict between the Meitei and Kuki communities in the state? Who was apprehensive about the future of their existence? Who has a vested interest in trying to drag and besmirch an organization like the Rashtriya Swayamsevak Sangh, which has been engaged in serving everyone without any bias for many years, into this unfortunate incident without any reason?

Which foreign powers may be interested in taking advantage of such an unrest and instability in Manipur – a state that shares borders with Nagaland and Mizoram in this sensitive Northeastern border region? Did the geopolitics of South Asia also play a role in these events? Despite there being a strong government in the country, on whose strength and instigation has this violence continued unabated for so many days? Why did this violence erupt and continue even though there was a state government that wanted to maintain peace, which had been prevailing for the last nine years?

Now, when people on both sides of the conflict are seeking peace, which are the forces that continue to trigger hatred and violence by causing some violent incident somewhere in the state as soon as any positive step is seen as being taken in that direction? Multipronged efforts will be required to solve this grave conflict.

To resolve this vexed problem, we need strong political will, concurrent actions and efficiency. At the same time, enlightened leadership of the society will also have to play a special role in bridging the gap of mutual distrust that has arisen due to the unfortunate situation between the two communities. The swayamsevaks are continuously and dedicatedly serving everyone and organizing relief work, while appealing to the positive and influential people of the society for helping restore peace. It has been the endeavour of the Sangh to keep everyone safe, united, harmonious and peaceful by treating everyone as its own, even if it entails great sacrifices. We are proud of our swayamsevaks and other activists, who have made tremendous efforts in a calm and composed manner to help and take care of everyone in this terrible and disturbing situation in Manipur.

Appropriate response to this mantra viplav has to be only through the unity of the society. This permanent and unfailing sense of unity is the key to keeping the conscience of the society awake. The Directive Principle of our Constitution also exhorts us to achieve this emotional unity. In every country, the milieu and ground conditions that create this feeling of unity are unique. It could be the language of that country, the common worship or belief system of the residents of that country, common business interests or a strong bond of central power that binds the people of the country together. However, we must not forget that unity built on man-made artificial structures or on the basis of common self-interest is not durable or sustainable. Our country's diversity boggles the mind, so much so that it takes time for people to understand the existence of this country as one nation. But this country of ours, as a nation and as a society, is still surviving, thriving and prospering, even after undergoing several ups and downs in history, maintaining an unbroken link with the threads of its glorious past.

We are fortunate to have inherited a tradition of unity that not only surprises the minds of the outsiders but also attracts them. What is the secret behind such unity? Needless to say, it is our all-inclusive culture. It is our conduct and way of life that transcends the differences between worship, tradition, language, region, caste, etc., and extends the circle of our affinity from that of our own family to the entire global family.

Our forefathers realized the truth of the unity of existence. Thus, they became aware of the principle of Dharma, which fuels the progress of the body, mind and intellect, and which leads to *Moksha* by balancing both *Artha* (Means) and *Kama* (Ends). Based on that realization, we evolved a culture that implemented the four eternal values of *Dharmatattva* – truth, compassion, purity and penance. This became possible because our motherland was prosperous, bountiful and secure from all sides. That is why we devoutly worship our motherland Bharat, considering her as the presiding deity of our values and traditions.

Recently, we respectfully remembered great personalities of the freedom struggle on the occasion of the 75th anniversary of our Independence. Those great people who protected our religion, culture, society and country; made necessary improvements in them from time to time; and enhanced the glory of our nation, were our perseverant ancestors who remain an abiding source of pride for all of us. These three elements – devotion to the motherland, pride in our forefathers and a common culture – make us stand out proudly as one nation by tying together all the diversities of language, region, sect, caste, sub-caste, etc.

The permanent unity of society stems not from any selfish pursuits but from a sense of belongingness.

Ours is a very large society, with a remarkable breadth of diversity. Over time, some aggressive and violent traditions from foreign countries infiltrated into our country, yet our society remained one based on these three elements. Therefore, when we talk about unity, we must bear in mind that this unity will not be achieved through any transactions or deals. If this unity is be attained by force, it will get ruptured again and again.

In today's environment, many people are naturally worried after seeing the efforts being made to spread discord in our society. We come across people who identify themselves as Hindus, and also those who are called Muslims and Christians because of their way of worship. They believe that, setting aside *fitna, fasad* and *kitan* (discord, strife and violence), it is best to pursue *sulah, salamati* and *aman* (reconciliation, security and peace).

An important thing to keep in mind in these discussions is that they are not about different communities coming together in one land by chance and seeking to become one. We are the descendants of common ancestors, children of one motherland and inheritors of one culture, but have forgotten our mutual and inherent unity. We have to understand our inherent unity and get connected again on that basis.

Do we not have problems with each other? Don't we have needs and expectations for our own development? Don't we compete among ourselves to achieve development? Do all of us behave by following these principles of unity in thoughts, words and actions? We all know that this is not the case for everyone. But those who wish for this unity to take hold cannot insist that all problems should first end, all questions be resolved, before we can think about unity.

It is easy to understand that if we change our behaviour by embracing the vision of belongingness, then solutions to problems will automatically emerge. We will have to work peacefully and with restraint, without getting distracted by the sporadic events happening here and there. Sure, the problems are real, but they are not limited to one caste or class alone.

Along with the efforts to solve those problems, an enthusiastic and committed mindset of affinity and unity will also have to be nurtured. To forge such a lasting unity in society, we will have to shed the sense of victimhood, stop looking at each other with suspicion and avoid manoeuvres aimed at political dominance. Sadly, politics becomes a hindrance only in such noble initiatives. But when we call upon the people to shed their sense of victimhood, or ask them to shun mutual distrust, this is not a form of surrender or compulsion. This is not a call for ceasefire between two warring parties. Rather, this is an exhortation to all to recognize the thread of cultural continuity and unity that runs through our country's vast diversities.

This is the 75th year of the Constitution of our independent Bharat. This Constitution also points in the same direction. If we pay enough attention to the two speeches given by Dr Babasaheb Ambedkar in the Constituent Assembly at the time of delivering the Constitution, we will arrive at the same essence of cultural continuity and unity. This is not a task attainable overnight. Bitter memories of old conflicts continue to fester in the collective psyche. The wounds of the dreadful horror of

Bharat's Partition run very deep. The resentment caused in the minds due to the 'action and reaction' cycle over the horrific Partition often manifests in our utterances and actions. There exist bitter experiences, ranging from not being able to get a house in each other's localities to being treated with mutual contempt. A blame-game ensues over every incident of violence, riots, harassment. Misdeeds of an individual are extrapolated to blame the entire community. A war of words follows, leading to provocations and incitements for retribution against each other. Forces that want to break the country by making us quarrel also take full advantage of this situation. We often see that a small incident gets exaggerated and publicized in a dramatic manner. Statements expressing concern and warning emanate from within the country and abroad. 'Tool kits' that incite violence are activated and mutual suspicion and hatred are further intensified.

All those who are committed to harmony in the society need to be wary of these nefarious games. Solutions to all these problems will only emerge gradually. But for that to happen, a climate of trust and harmony is a prerequisite. It is important that we increase dialogue and understanding between communities with a calm and stable mind, and develop respect for each other's beliefs. We must strive for harmony among all, and our minds, words and deeds must be in complete alignment with that larger objective of attaining deeper social cohesion and unity in the country.

We will have to work hard in this direction, looking at the ground reality and not be misled by propaganda or guided by assumptions. We must persevere in our efforts for a long time – with patience, restraint and tolerance, resolutely shunning extremism, anger and fear in our words and actions.

Regardless of the provocations, it is important and mandatory to follow the rule of law and abide by the Constitution. In an independent country, such behaviour is considered an expression of true patriotism. It is not advisable to get caught up in or swayed by inflammatory propaganda carried out through the media, and the volley of allegations and counter-allegations that follow. Media should be used to propagate truth and promote harmony in the society. The correct solution to violence and hooliganism is for society to become an organized force, take the initiative to uphold law and order and extend appropriate support to the government and administration.

The country is going to hold Lok Sabha elections in the early months of 2024. Attempts to harvest votes by inflaming emotions are not desirable, yet they keep happening. Let us avoid these things, as they hurt the unity of the society. Casting the vote is the duty of every citizen, and we must fulfil that duty. Cast your vote keeping in mind the vital issues of unity, integrity, identity and development of the country.

The year 2025–26 marks the centenary year of the Rashtriya Swayamsevak Sangh. Preparations are underway for the swayamsevaks to endeavour to fulfill these goals. Let the words and deeds of the society strengthen the love for the country and forge a deeper social cohesion and belongingness. Any discrimination that might still exist with regard to access to temples, water or crematorium must end.

We should deepen our relationship with nature by saving water, discarding the usage of plastics and increasing greenery in and around our homes. Let us strengthen our reliance on 'swa', or selfhood, through swadeshi. Wasteful expenditure ought to stop too. Employment opportunities in the country should increase, and the country's capital should be used within for the welfare of our own people. Practice of swadeshi should start from home.

Respect for the rule of law and other responsibilities as a citizen should be observed by all. A climate of harmony and co-operation should prevail in the society. It is imperative to make a sustained effort to make this behaviour a part of our basic nature by starting with small things and practising them regularly and conscientiously. Besides serving the needy members of the society themselves, the swayamsevaks will, in coming days, strive to make the entire society a participant in these endeavours. As always, the swayamsevaks will continue to co-operate with and contribute to whatever the government, administration and the public-spirited members of the society are doing, or would like to do, in the interest of the society.

A nation prospers only when the society remains united and vigilant, and makes selfless efforts in all domains of human enterprise. A nation attains glory and radiance when the governance is welfare-oriented and the administration is people-centric, driven by sustained co-operation based on the ideals of 'swa'. When a nation, full of vigour and glory, has a culture like Bharat's sanatan culture – which embraces everyone as its family, which guides us from darkness to light, from untruth to truth and which leads us from mortality to the immortal life of meaningfulness – then that nation restores the balance of the world and brings to the world the blessings of a happy and peaceful new life. This is the real purpose of the revival of our immortal nation of Bharat in the present times.

11

'The Thought of the Sangh Is Synonymous with Hindutva Thought'

MOHAN BHAGWAT

The Delhi unit of the RSS had organized a three-day lecture series at Vigyan Bhavan, New Delhi, in September 2018. The series was addressed by Sarsanghachalak Mohan Bhagwat. Speaking to an audience of over a thousand – including many of Delhi's prominent figures – Bhagwat delineated the views of the organization on various important and contemporary issues. He also responded to numerous questions from the distinguished gathering in the most candid manner.

Here is the text of his speech from the second day, which deals with many important issues of contemporary relevance.

Our work is fundamentally man-making. Swayamsevaks have entered and started working in almost all walks of our social life. They have also built various organizations and institutions. All these organizations and institutions are independent, autonomous and self-reliant. None of these organizations or institutions is run according to the decisions taken at the meetings of the Sangh. These have been started by our swayamsevaks on their own accord, and they also run them without depending on others. They keep in touch with the Sangh and also get suggestions and co-operation. The swayamsevaks also develop the sense to extend co-operation to whoever is doing some good work with honesty for the sake of society, irrespective of whether they are our supporters or opponents.

Questions concerning the relationship between the Sangh and politics are being raised time and again. Is the Sangh nurturing any political ambition? The common trend nowadays is that when a person acquires capabilities and creates their own identity in the field that helped them achieve their capabilities, they will be keen on joining politics. However, the work of the Sangh is to organize the entire society. Politics, political parties and the work of organizing the society can go together only to a limited extent. Hence, the Sangh has, from the very beginning, made a strong resolve to keep itself away from politics. The Sangh will never involve itself in competitive politics, will never fight elections and the office-bearer of the Sangh will never take up any official responsibilities or positions in any political party. The Sangh will always keep itself aloof from politics.

Dr Hedgewar himself was an accomplished political worker. As a student in Kolkata, once, he had even thwarted a plan of the British government, conducting an agitation using the newspapers. The British government had planned to bring in legislation to declare invalid the degrees conferred on students of the National Colleges who had played some role in the freedom movement or agitations. It was not easy to organize an agitation against the British on this issue. Dr Hedgewar visited every nook and cranny of Kolkata, talked to prominent people, took them into confidence and convinced them to say yes, if some government officials came and enquired if any meeting was held at that place against the proposed legislation. They were also requested to respond in the affirmative, if they were asked whether they had taken part in the meeting. He also gave them the names of different people to invoke, in case they were asked to give the names of the people who had addressed the meeting. They were also supposed to inform the officials that the meeting was attended by a large number of people, and a resolution was passed unanimously, calling for the restitution of the degrees. He then got news reports about these so-called 'meetings' published in newspapers saying that they were held at so-and-so places and were attended by so many people and that resolutions were passed against the government.

When the reports of the meetings started appearing in newspapers day after day, the British government panicked and sent its own people to verify the veracity of the reports. And those people, who got enough proof of the meetings having taken place and also that there was large scale resentment against the government on the issue, reported back that any attempt to go ahead with the proposed legislation would be tantamount to inviting the wrath of a bull. As a result, the government withdrew the proposal.

Dr Hedgewar was an adroit political leader and was highly popular among the youths in Vidarbha. But, as the mission of the Sangh is to organize the entire society, from its very inception, he made a strong resolve not to indulge in day-to-day politics. It is for the people to decide who should rule them. When we talk about abstaining from politics, that does not mean that we will remain silent on questions like infiltration or other national issues. Politics has to play its own prominent role in the matter. But the consequences of tackling or not tackling such national issues properly will be felt by the entire nation. Hence, the Sangh keeps making its stance clear about national challenges from time to time.

Why then is it that there are so many swayamsevaks in a particular political party? Also, that political party has so many swayamsevaks as its office-bearers. The incumbent prime minister and the national president of that party are also swayamsevaks. So, many people start speculating that everything is decided from Nagpur. This is a totally wrong perception. Let us not forget that the swayamsevaks who are active in the political arena are very senior karyakartas, workers. Their political experience too is far expansive. They don't need somebody's advice to manage their political affairs. Also, we are not too well-versed about politics and hence incapable of giving any advice. However, being known to each other, we occasionally enquire about mutual well-being. If at all they are in need of any guidance, they can ask us and, if possible, we will give it. However, it cannot be construed as our exerting influence over their politics or policies. As swayamsevaks they share our vision and are quite capable of giving practical shape to this vision in their own respective fields. And they are doing this in an independent, autonomous and self-reliant manner. It is also our desire that they should work in their own way. We never want to act as an outside power-centre.

So, what is the relationship of the Sangh with politics? Why are there so many swayamsevaks in a particular political party? This is not at all our problem. Why swayamsevaks are not inclined to join other political parties, it is for them to think. We never ask our swayamsevaks to work for any particular political party. We only tell them to stand with those who keep the nation and the national interests foremost in their minds and adopt policies accordingly. Any political party can do so, and that is happening also. Our swayamsevaks, on their part, as citizens, are doing whatever is possible in the national interest. Those who hold responsible positions in the Sangh are not expected to indulge in politics. However, other swayamsevaks have the freedom to join or not join politics. Swayamsevaks lead their day-to-day life with utmost discretion. As the work of the RSS progresses, its influence gets reflected in every field – including politics. We never intend to create this influence, but it happens on its own. What can we do?

We voice our views on national policies and also use our strength to get the good policies implemented. Swayamsevaks, being the responsible citizens of this nation, are expected to be active in all fields of national life. They have no vested interest either in any political philosophy or in any political party. Their only concern is national interest. They will not have ill-will for anyone nor will they be over-friendly with anyone. This is the nature of the Sangh.

From ancient times, our nation has bestowed highest honour on women. From a purely philosophical point of view also we always viewed women as the personification of strength (*Shakti swarupa*) and the Universal Mother (*Jagadamba*). However, in practice it is not so. Also today, there is no need or expectation to install them in temples in the form of a goddess and offering worship to them; nor is it necessary to keep them tied to the chains of household slavery. Being a part of the society, they are equal partners in all social activities and also share equal responsibilities. Hence, they must be treated as equals. But it should not be with the attitude that 'we are here to ensure your deliverance or salvation'. It is our common experience that in certain matters women are more competent than men and they can do certain jobs more efficiently than men. So, the need of the hour is to provide them more strength, giving them more freedom and opportunity, and help them to be enlightened.

It is the desire of the Sangh that, right from our homes to every walk of our social life, the work of awakening the collective strength of women (*matrushakti*) should be carried out. Man and woman are complimentary to each other, and for life to be meaningful both have to work together as equal partners. Right from decision-making to sharing responsibilities, they should be equal partners. Also, they have to play their own role in the national reconstruction. This is the considered opinion of the Sangh about women.

The thought of the Sangh is synonymous with the Hindutva thought. That does not mean that Hindutva is the find of the Sangh. It has been the traditional thought of our nation for ages. However, so many delusions have been created about it.

The biggest role in creating this delusion about Hindutva was played by the Hindu society itself. Hindutva is the name of the value system consisting of values like unity in diversity, harmony, sacrifice, temperance and gratefulness. Truth is its foundation. When the entire world was searching for happiness in the outside world, our ancestors had turned their attention inwards. In the Bharatiya system, besides conducting scientific experiments to explore the transient material world, we have also undertaken studies into the eternal spiritual world. Rooted in both logical exploration and practical experience, our ancestors realized the one Truth that permeated all existence. The tradition of great realized souls has continued unbroken from our venerable past to this day.

We are never satisfied by holding discussions on logic and philosophy merely at the intellectual level. That's why Swami Vivekananda had asked his guru Sri Ramakrishna Paramahamsa as to whether he had seen God! Although Vivekananda asked the same question to many others, no one was able to give him a satisfactory reply. Of course, with the help of logic, so many people can explain it. However, such explanations are of no use. Vivekananda had asked the same question to Rabindranath Tagore's father, Debendranath Tagore, but could not get a convincing reply. 'You have the eyes of a yogi,' Debendranath said. 'No sir, I want a straight answer to the question whether you have seen God?' Vivekananda persisted. But he could not get a correct answer.

Once, Vivekananda's professor was explaining the meaning of the word 'trance' in philosophy class. 'If you want to know the real meaning of the world, then go to Dakshineswar,' the professor said. Vivekananda visited Sri Ramakrishna at Dakshineswar. After one or two visits, he put the same question to him: 'Sir, have you seen God?'

To this, Sri Ramakrishna, who had not even passed the fourth standard, replied: 'Yes, I have seen God, more intensely so, than I see you. I have talked to God, more intensely than I am talking to you. If you follow the path I show you, you can also do it.'

Truth can be explained in different ways, and, at times, the description can even be contradictory. But Truth is one, and that is the Truth of the unity of existence. Accept the diversity in the world based on that Truth, have respect for it and celebrate it. Be dedicated to your own diversity, have respect for the diversity of all and live together. It is Hindu, or say Hindutva, that is giving the message of this value-system.

The word Hindu cannot be found in any of our ancient scriptures. It is a fact that we got the name from outside. There are many scholars and saints even today who do not use the word 'Hindu' and, instead, use the word 'Sanatani'. Even for Dharma, they say Sanatana Dharma. Religions like Buddhism use the word Dhamma. It was due to some unique circumstances that we came to be known as Hindus later on.

In his article written in 1929, Mahavir Prasad Dwivedi had written that when Zoroaster reached Persia (present-day Iran), people made him their Guru and requested for his introduction. 'We are a people who believe in human unity and so how can I give you my introduction? However, if you want to know the land from where I am coming, I must tell you that my ancestors had come from the banks on the other side of the River Sindhu.' In the Persian language, the letter 's' is pronounced as 'h', and for this reason, they made their guru, Hindu Guru.

During those days Iran had bilateral trade with Israel, and through the traders this name came to Israel. Our traders, who were doing maritime trade, came to know about it, and gradually the name reached our intellectual sphere as well. We find mention of the word in our scriptures of the ninth century AD or so. However, this word was still not available in our dialects. When invaders started attacking our traditions and norms one after the other to establish the dominance of their way of life, that set our people thinking: 'How is this happening? In spite of our belief in impersonal and formless God, as they also do, why are they attacking us?' They got the answer: 'You are all Hindus, and we are out to convert you to our faith.' It was from that time onwards that the word Hindu became a part of our dialects also.

As, by tradition, saints and great men are the first to use the words in our dialects, and this word Hindu first appeared in their sayings. Guru Nanak Dev ji said : '*Khurasan khasamaan kiya, Hindustan daraya, kaya kapad tuk tuk hosi, Hindustan samalsi bola*' (Lord, Thou takest Khurasan under Thy wings, but yielded Hindustan to the wrath of invaders. The clothes will be torn apart into shreds, and then Hindustan will remember these words.). This word gained popularity among our people and now it clings on to us. Although we have not been given our respective names with our permission, our names stick with us. If we are called by some other names, we won't even respond.

I have, although not from any direct source, heard that Muslims from Bharat going for Haj pilgrimage are being registered there as Hindvi Muslims. Also, in the discussions held in the intellectual circles such thoughts are termed 'Indic thoughts'. The word Indic also means the same.

When we say Bharatiya, it is not merely a geographical expression. Because the geographical boundaries of Bharat may change when it either expands or contracts. The word Bharat represents a nature. In short, all these words are synonymous. Hindu is the word that clearly reflects the sum and substance of all these words.

Hence, the Sangh is very particular about the word Hindu. However, that does not mean we have any quarrel or enmity with those who use the word Bharat, India or Arya. We know they prefer to use those names. For us, the word Hindu is very dear. But if others prefer some other name that is also fine, and there need not be any quarrel about it, because what is most essential is to accept the principle of unity in diversity.

As the word Dharma is available only in Bharatiya languages, there is so much of confusion about it. Dharma and Dhamma are the gifts of Bharat. You cannot find these words anywhere in the world. As the word 'Dharma' has connection also with rituals, it is close to the word 'religion', which is concerned with certain types of rites, modes of worship, certain types of scriptures and prophets. So, while talking in a foreign language, we use the word religion. And when we translate the word religion into our language, we use the word Dharma to denote the word religion, and hence the confusion. Dharma is not the legacy of any particular country or society. Dharma is universal, belonging to the entire humanity. What is presently known as Hindu Dharma is not the Dharma of Hindus only. Hindu religious scriptures are not known as 'Hindu' scriptures, but as Human Code of Social Conduct (Manava Dharma Sashtra). Those were written even before the word 'Hindu' was coined. They are not intended for any particular section of people, but for the entire humanity.

Religious sects and spiritual orders born in Bharat, like the Sanatani, *Bauddh*, Jain, Sikh and Arya Samaj, speak about universal welfare, because we have never treated ourselves as different from the rest of mankind. '*Mata cha Parvati Devi, Pita Devo Maheshwarah/Bandhavah Shivabhaktash cha, Swadesho Bhuvanatrayam*' (Goddess Parvati is our mother; Lord Maheswara is our father. The devotees of Shiva are our relatives; for us, all the three worlds are our homeland).

The whole world is our family. *Vasudhaiva kutumbakam.* This is our nature, because Bharat is born with the mission of realizing the unity of existence. Bharat exists to proclaim the message of this unity to the whole world. We remain as a single social unit, as a *rashtra* (nation), carrying along all forms of diversity.

Our Rashtra is very ancient. If we try to define 'Rashtra' using Western concepts, it can exist only where there is State. In the absence of State, Rashtra also will cease to exist. But we never accepted this concept. In our concept, State may change from time to time, but Rashtra will be a permanent cultural entity.

As far as the concept of Dharma is concerned, that part which deals with eternal values constitutes the eternal Dharma (s*hashwat* Dharma). The part related to conduct and customs (*aachara* Dharma) is an ever changing one, because aachara Dharma depends upon place, time, circumstance and the person practising it. During the debate on the Hindu Code Bill in the Parliament, Dr Ambedkar asked those who were opposing the Bill: 'What do you mean by Dharma? Values or code? You are taking code for Dharma. Code changes, and it should change. And I am changing it. Values remain the same.'

In our Hindu tradition, we changed our gods and goddesses. The gods of Vedic age are not worshipped anymore. Form of gods underwent changes during the middle ages. New sects have now come up.

The concept of Hindutva never binds one to any particular food habit, nor does it support any specific mode of worship. It is not limited to any particular language, province or region. The concept of Hindutva combines social and individual happiness with that of the entire creation. It recognizes the importance of monetary and material desires (*Artha* and *Kama*). Everyone has desires, which, if fulfilled, lead to happiness. Economic resources are necessary to fulfil those desires. Thus, economics also became a part of our fourfold goals of life (*purushartha*). However, both Artha and Kama must go hand in hand. Also, one should not merely aim for one's own progress. Along with one's own development, one should think about the development of others. To have this feeling in mind is what is called discipline. That discipline is Dharma.

To lead a life of discipline and achieve harmony is Hindutva. However, being very ancient, there are so many creeds amongst us – each claiming, 'This is our Dharma.' We accept all such claims. We accept all forms of diversity, and that has become Bharat's identity. Ours is a universal Dharma, which is not confined only to Bharat. Bharat has realized it through penance and a deep exploration, and is engaged in imparting the knowledge of it to the entire world, merely as a trustee.

During the time of the Vedic Rishis, the message of spirituality was carried all over the world. In the era of Tathagata Buddha, inspired by his example, the same Dhamma was propagated all over the world. Even today, we find our saints and sages continuing the same tradition. But they have never sought to convert people. When Paul Brunton approached

Sri Ramana Maharshi with the request to convert him into a Hindu, Sri Ramana said: 'You are a good Christian and should remain a Christian. That will make your life meaningful. There is no need for you to become a Hindu, as we treat all diversity, divine knowledge and philosophies as true.' Realized souls like Sri Ramakrishna Paramahamsa used to say: 'As many faiths, so many paths.' He practised every religion and, after achieving the ultimate experience, proclaimed that all that was nothing but Hindutva.

All diversity will remain; differences too will remain; they will all be welcomed and honoured. Being the progeny of Bharat, who has taught us to rise above discord, these differences will never create dissonance or fissiparous tendencies among us.

Patriotism is another feature of that value system which we call Hindutva. We consider it as the identity of Bharat. The very existence of Bharat is for it, and that is why we have been upholding it under every circumstance. Even while foreign invaders trampled upon our freedom, we had taken care to uphold it to the extent possible. When some of our own people, out of their selfishness, corrupted it by acting against the values, there arose a host of saints and sages, who took up the task of restoring that value system.

In the process, many creeds emerged, each interpreting the philosophy, method and aachara Dharma differently in accordance with their place, time and circumstance. Over millennia, by living in harmony and recognizing underlying unity – what is called Hindutva – this way of being became a habit. Nobody is insignificant, and the interest of all should be taken care of. Going beyond the Western motto of 'maximum good of the maximum people', our ancestors said: '*sarwepi sukhinah santu*', which means 'the well-being of all'. When you take Bharatiya religions and sects, you will only see the thought 'of all'.

The world is now badly in need of this thought. We have to build a society that puts this all-encompassing thought into practice. Wherever we have gone in the world, we have neither quarrelled with anybody nor conquered anyone nor usurped the wealth of anyone. Wherever we went, we only shared our knowledge and civility with them. Generally, in the world, when people of some country go to another country, establish dominance and return after some time, they leave behind memories that are unpleasant. People will never speak well of them or remember them fondly. Only exception to this rule is Bharat. Wherever we have gone, the people there remember us with joy and gratitude. Even now vestiges of that bygone era are available at some places in the form of idols or relics, and also in the form of stories from the Ramayana and the Mahabharata, and as the Ramlila. Modes of worship have changed in many of those countries. They are no longer Shaivites nor even Buddhists. Many of them are Muslims now. Yet they say, 'We have not changed our ancestors!'

Why are such sweet and wondrous memories recalled about Bharat only? It is because Bharat has carried its sense of equity, discipline, sense of oneness with all others and the desire for universal well-being everywhere. We have to rekindle that spirit here once again. Our motherland, bestowed with plenty of water, abundance of agricultural crops and the cool and soothing breeze of the Malaya Mountains, has, from the ancient times, never ever entertained the thought of invading others. We were protected on all sides. In the distant past, unlike now, modes of conveyance were extremely sparse. So, we were safe and prosperous. We also welcomed all those who came from outside without any hesitation. As we were already having so many languages, goddesses and gods, we never sensed any danger from newcomers. We expected all to live according to the tenets of the Manava Dharma.

'I have not borrowed the ideal of liberty, equality and fraternity from the French Revolution. I have taken it from the teachings of Tathagata Buddha, rooted in this very soil,' said Dr Ambedkar in the Constituent Assembly. When freedom comes, equality is at stake and if you try to bring equality, freedom has to be compromised. To carry both equality and freedom together, fraternity is necessary. And that fraternity is what is called Hindutva. What is the basis of this fraternity? The feeling that our ancestors are the same, our cultural heritage is common, and our motherland is one.

When I sincerely express my feeling that we treat all who are in Bharatvarsha as Hindus, at times, some people object to it. Everyone has the freedom to identify as Hindu or not. And even if someone wants to be known by some other name, not only do we respect that choice, but it does nothing to affect our affinity towards them. Our shared identity remains the same. From the point of view of our Rashtra, we call this identity as Hindu.

Some people feel proud of calling themselves Hindu. But there are others who may not be so enthusiastic about that. There are some others, who, out of some material considerations or 'political correctness', are unwilling to openly say that they are Hindus, but would be ready to acknowledge it in private. There are yet others who have forgotten all about it. But they all are our own people and belong to Bharat. In our point of view, organizing Hindus is synonymous with organizing the entire society.

While appearing for an examination, we tend to answer easy questions first and then deal with the tougher ones. Likewise, we are uniting those who consider themselves as Hindus first. We are uniting them not against anybody else, but for their own sake. We do not have enemies anywhere in the world or in our own nation. There may be people who have enmity towards us. Except for protecting ourselves from them, we can never even think of harming them. In fact, we seek to walk alongside them, and in time, bring them too into our circle of kinship. That is Hindutva in action.

Not everything that has come to be associated with Hindu customs and traditions necessarily reflects Dharma. Because the gradual decline of the real concept of Dharma began from the period of the Mahabharata itself. That is why I said that the main role in constricting it is played by the Hindu society itself, because we began to confuse values with rituals. As a result, several sins like profanity, wicked practices and untouchability entered the social fabric of Hindus. It is our desire to rectify those defects. We are for resurrection of the Eternal Human Dharma in a new form, suited for the place, time and circumstances of the present day.

We can't even think of wishing bad for anyone. Hindutva is founded on three bedrocks: patriotism, respect for ancestors and culture. There should be no reason for any controversy over these. Knowingly or unknowingly we all practise them.

The Sangh thinking is based on this very Hindutva. There is no need for us to think about anything new.

We adopted a Constitution when we opted for a democratic polity for our nation. This Constitution, created by our own people, reflects our national consensus. Hence, it is incumbent on everyone to maintain the spirit of the Constitution. From the very beginning, the Sangh has wholeheartedly accepted it. I never said anything against the Constitution but only tried to communicate in my own words whatever is there in it. We have always honoured the spirit behind all symbols and the Constitution of independent Bharat. Our Constitution is also one such symbol. It was after so many centuries that we got an opportunity to adopt our own system, and the leading thinkers of our nation sat together and created this Constitution. It didn't come out of any thin air. Those leaders who were instrumental in making it had discussed each and every word of it threadbare and spared no stone unturned to achieve unanimity of opinion. Only then was it adopted.

Our Constitution contains the Preamble, the Fundamental Rights of Citizens, the Directive Principles of State Policy and the Fundamental Duties of Citizens. The Constitution has provisions to amend laws enacted under it. The forum for that is the Parliament. The laws are interpreted by the court. The Constitution has several other provisions as well.

Now let me refer to the Preamble:

> WE THE PEOPLE OF INDIA, having solemnly resolved to constitute India into a SOVEREIGN, SOCIALIST, SECULAR, DEMOCRATIC REPUBLIC (*We all know, the words Socialist and Secular have been inserted later on. Since they continue to remain a part of it, I have read those words also*) and to secure to all its citizens:
>
> JUSTICE, social, economic, political;
>
> LIBERTY of thought, expression, belief, faith and worship;
>
> EQUALITY of status and of opportunity; (*Hereafter, there is an important matter told by Dr Ambedkar Sahab in his address at the Constituent Assembly*)

and to promote among them all

FRATERNITY assuring the dignity of the individual and the unity and integrity of the Nation;

Dr Ambedkar had said in the Constituent Assembly that it was because of our internecine quarrels that the foreigners had conquered and made us slaves. He said: 'We are sitting in warring camps as mutual enemies. Limitation of our system should be blamed for it. If we fail to create such a fraternal feeling, I can't say, what sort of fate awaits us.'

Sangh is engaged in creating that sense of fraternity. Unity in diversity can only be the basis of that fraternity. This thought process that has come down to us by tradition is called Hindutva. Hence, we say that ours is a Hindu Rashtra. This does not mean that there should be no Muslims here. The day we say Muslims are not required here, Hindutva will be lost. Hindutva speaks about viewing the entire world as a family. So, the moment we say only the Vedas are acceptable and the Buddhists, who do not recognize the Vedas, are not acceptable, Hindutva will be lost. Because, in our nation, we have incessantly been in the pursuit of Truth, and all the different spiritual systems have arisen out of that process. All those diverse systems deserve respect. This is our conviction, and it should be so. As Hindutva is the only source that provides the feeling of fraternity with an ideological foundation, we have been following it.

When Sir Syed Ahmad Khan returned to Lahore after becoming a barrister, the Arya Pratinidhi Sabha of Lahore accorded him a reception. When introducing him, the introducer said: 'Among Hindus, there are plenty of barristers, but he is the first Muslim to become a barrister. Hence, we are felicitating him.' In his speech, responding to the manner in which he was introduced, Sir Syed Ahmad Khan said: 'I am very much pained that you have not counted us among you. Are we not the sons of Bharat Mata? Although our mode of worship has changed due to historical reasons, what else has changed?'

We were aware of this sentiment until the 1880s but gradually erased it from our minds. It is necessary to revive this feeling once again. If you don't want to call him a Hindu, don't call him so – there is no problem;

but call him a Bharatiya. We feel that Hindu is the only word useful in creating such a culture, and hence, we are sticking to that word. Even if it proves a losing proposition, we are ready to bear it. Because we believe that, as long as this word exists, this nature of Bharat will also not become moribund. People of Bharat will move forward taking everybody along.

Question of respecting or disrespecting the Constitution should not arise at all. We are all bound by thc discipline of the Constitution. Let me say that our universal Dharma, Bharat's Dharma and the present-day customary Dharma, all have been incorporated in our Constitution, and we are all bound by it. The Constitution is so liberal that it provides for discussion on its contents. Such discussions keep taking place as well. The Sangh has the highest regard for the Constitution and law. There is not even one instance to show that the Sangh has acted against them.

We are not egotistical to claim that the Sangh will single-handedly achieve the redemption of Bharat! And no one should entertain such sort of egotism, because, no individual, no institution, no organization and no government can take the nation forward all alone. The destiny of the nation changes only when the whole society becomes meritorious and organized, and, forgetting differences and selfishness, becomes ready to live and die for the nation. History tells us that all those nations that have risen from the abyss to attain greatness in modern times have done so only because of a minimum of hundred years of relentless efforts in that direction. I have read the history of countries like England, America, France, Cuba, Japan and China, and whatever I am telling you is based on the conclusions I have drawn after reading that history.

I will give one example. *The Incredible Japan* is a book written on Japan. When the book was written, Japan was a leader in world trade. The book was written by two sociologists and two economists after studying Japanese markets. The book is worth reading. In the last page of the book, they have drawn nine conclusions, of which the first five are not at all concerned with economics. They write: First, the Japanese people are disciplined and, hence, could progress. Second, when the Japanese think of welfare, rather than thinking only about their individual welfare, they think about the welfare of their entire village and plan accordingly. Third, the Japanese are ever ready to display dauntless courage for the sake of their nation. Fourth, the Japanese are prepared to undergo any sort of sacrifice for the sake of their country. And fifth, they take special care to perform every work in an excellent way.

We also have to infuse such a culture in our society. Only when the whole society gets imbued with this spirit, the fortune of the nation will change. Otherwise, for a few days everything will be hunky dory and then the decline will start again. The Sangh is working with this goal in mind.

Recently, I had been to Chicago for the World Hindu Congress. I also had the opportunity of addressing the people there. When Swami Vivekananda started his address with the words, 'Sisters and brothers of America', the whole place reverberated with the applause of the audience for full three minutes! But if I say the same words today, nobody will clap. Why? Because, it is necessary to have the backing of the effort (*tapasya*) behind those words. To achieve welfare of the world, it is necessary for Bharat to acquire competence economically, morally and socially. Stringing the flowers of diversity into a beautiful garland, we have to bedeck the nation with it. The factor that will be uniting us all is what is called Hindutva.

In Rabindranath Tagore's celebrated collection of poems, *Gitanjali*, there is a portion titled 'Naivedya'. At the end of one of those poems, Tagore addresses the Supreme Father and asks for Him to deliver a blow on our nation with His harsh hand and wake it up to this very world!

The English translation of the poem is thus:

Where the mind is without fear and the head is held high; Where knowledge is free;
Where the world has not been broken up into fragments by narrow domestic walls;
Where words come out from the depth of truth;
Where tireless striving stretches its arms towards perfection;
Where the clear stream of reason has not lost its way into the dreary desert sand of dead habit;
Where the mind is led forward by thee into ever-widening thought and action –
Into that heaven of freedom, my Father, let my country awake.

Tagore was from Bengal. But in Maharashtra, Swatantrya Veer Savarkar had said the same thing in his poem 'Swatantrata Bhagavati' (Goddess of Freedom), 'Whatever is best, sublime, great and powerful, let they all incarnate with you, in this very country, Bharat.' The picture of independent Bharat in the minds of our freedom fighters was the same.

Even when I speak on the type of society that is required for building up such a Bharat, I don't want to express any ideas of my own. Speaking on dealing with the defects in our society, Mahatma Gandhiji has mentioned about the seven sins we have to eradicate earnestly, for which reformation is necessary. What we call as man-making is the same. Here are the seven sins mentioned by Gandhiji:

1. Wealth without work
2. Pleasure without conscience
3. Knowledge without character
4. Commerce without morality
5. Science without humanity
6. Religion without sacrifice
7. Politics without principles

If we take a look at our social life today, we will see that many good things have happened since Independence. However, unless and until we are able to eradicate the sins mentioned by Gandhiji, it will be difficult for us to derive the full benefits of this Independence. The entire society must make concerted efforts towards this. These sins do not exist outside us; they reside in our minds. We have to make efforts for eradicating them, and that itself is the Sangh's message.

To rewrite the history of our sacred motherland, we will have to earn the requisite merit and help others become meritorious as well. And then, we all have to collectively decide what needs to be done and act accordingly. The result will be proportionate to our strength.

That is the vision of the RSS.

Part 2

Thinkers Speak

12

'True Swarajya Is Emotional and Spirited'

UMAKANT KESHAV APTE, BABASAHEB

Umakant Keshav Apte, fondly called in the RSS circles as Babasaheb Apte, was a veteran leader of the organization. He began his journey in the organization during the time of the founder Dr Hedgewar, 'Doctorji', and continued to serve in various important capacities under the guidance of Golwalkar, 'Guruji', also. He too was one of the thought leaders of the movement in the initial tumultuous decades, providing foundational ideas to the swayamsevaks across the country.

What is '*swarajya*'? The literature produced over the last 70 years does not provide correct guidance on this matter. The literature created during the renaissance of 1905 presents an excellent discussion of it. However, that literature seems to have faded from view today.

An ordinary person might say that a government of one's own people is swarajya. But does this definition truly capture the essence of swarajya? Suppose someone asks, 'How does an electric bulb light up?' and the answer is, 'Just press the switch and the light will turn on.' Is that answer sufficient? If the bulb is faulty, pressing the switch will not make the light turn on. Even if the bulb is fine, but the wiring connected to the switch is defective, or there is some short circuit, the light still won't turn on when the switch is pressed. If there is some issue at the powerhouse itself, the same result follows. For an electric bulb to light up, the bulb, the wiring system and the powerhouse all need to be in proper condition – otherwise, there will be no light. In the same way, merely saying that swarajya is 'a government of one's own people' does not convey the complete meaning.

The words 'swarajya' and '*pararajya*' both contain the word '*rajya*' (rule or state). If we set aside rajya, the focus in 'swarajya' is clearly on '*swa*'. Swa means one's own. The word swarajya carries within it a deep pride in one's own identity, a profound love for it and a commitment to live an entire life inspired by it. It suggests that every drop of one's blood is proud of that 'swa (selfhood)', that life without its protection is insignificant. Such an intense conviction forms the basis of the idea of 'self-respect'.

Where there is no such self-respect, no reverence for one's own identity, no ideal in life for its development, no heartfelt emotion connected to it – such a situation may be termed rajya, but it cannot be called swarajya.

So, was pararajya (foreign rule) bad simply because fair-skinned people ruled us? That was indeed a common belief earlier. But why is foreign rule truly bad? Because it involved exploition and looting. In the period after 1920, even respected scholars began to argue that the demand for swarajya was to end exploitation by the British. Their grievance was that we got fewer pieces of bread. They defined swarajya as 'freedom from deprivation' – that we should have enough to eat and drink, and adequate clothing to cover our bodies. In other words, they equated swarajya with prosperity. In this sense, they sought economic swarajya.

But before 1905, the understanding of swarajya was different. At that time, it was said that no revolution is possible without swarajya. Foreign rule was seen as an obstacle to our development. What we wished to do could not be done. In such a condition, we were unable to express our inner convictions, nor could we accept or reject anything purely out of our own will, whether good or bad. Pararajya was a hindrance to the development of our potential. Therefore, swarajya was seen as essential.

There is a beautiful example related to this. I once visited Dalmiya Nagar. There are large factories there, and residential quarters have been built for the workers. Around 5,000 people live there. The company has installed loudspeakers along the roads at its own expense. These loudspeakers continuously blare for fixed hours during the day (perhaps 10–12 hours). Whether you wish to hear it or not, whether you're sitting inside your house doing whatever you like, they keep blaring. I asked the residents there, 'Does this bring you any joy?' Everyone answered, 'No, it causes great discomfort.' Normally, who would say that a loudspeaker is a cause of discomfort? People enthusiastically install them at home. They listen to songs, speeches, dramas, even the running commentary of a match or event on the radio for hours. Who would call such a loudspeaker unpleasant?

But what I saw there convinced me that even a loudspeaker can be a source of pain. Why? Because at home, you turn your loudspeaker on or off at will. You can tune it to Delhi or Calcutta (now Kolkata) as per your choice. That gives happiness. But in Dalmiya Nagar, there's no such joy in listening to it, because it doesn't operate according to your will. You have no right to tune it to the Delhi station, nor to switch it off. It keeps running. No matter how you try to block your ears, you'll hear it. It's a continuous nuisance. Can this be called freedom?

In swarajya, one acts according to one's own will. That will is naturally inclined towards the development of good qualities within oneself. This leads to joy, and the feeling awakens that one's life should have a meaning. At the root of all these things lies self-respect – a sense of pride in one's identity.

Swatva (selfhood) refers to one's country, one's people and the ancient history that connects the two – history shaped by our great ancestors, their sacrifices, valour and achievements. All these together form *sanskriti* (culture). Culture includes art, skill, literature, social customs – everything. Pride in our own culture is the foundation of the nation.

If people feel pride in this culture, and let it inspire their actions, then the tendencies we see today – of avoiding responsibility, of wanting to reap without sowing – will disappear from our nation.

After the country attained Independence, for some time a certain attitude began to emerge – 'Now what is left to do? We've got swarajya.'

Once, I was travelling by train from Jhansi to Kanpur. A discussion was going on in the compartment. Someone said, 'Now no one questions us anymore. The train is ours now. Why even bother buying a ticket?' I intervened and said, 'Let's say the train is ours – but just as you can't harvest a crop without sowing seeds, how can the train run without purchasing a ticket? Merely calling it our own won't make the engine run. If you don't put coal in the engine or provide it with water, will it move? Then there's the entire railway system – there are employees who need salaries. Looking at all this, one must buy a ticket.' Hearing this, those discussing the issue fell silent.

People have misunderstood swarajya to mean that they no longer need to work. That just like rain falls from the sky without effort, all pleasures and comforts will now fall into their laps. People said that swarajya meant freedom from scarcity, but what they actually meant was freedom from effort.

Nothing can be gained without hard work – this is true for both material and spiritual happiness. When the sources that inspire hard work are completely ignored, and a person is told, like a two-legged beast, 'Do the work!', then they work merely for bread. But a person doesn't always work just for bread. They are driven by a higher purpose. They try to improve their life and follow the path of their innate nature. Sometimes, whether or not they get food is not even their primary concern.

When the cultural purpose of human life is completely ignored and people are simply told to work, they lose the motivation to do so. Not only that, even those who are already working begin to do less. A mindset of doing less work and wanting greater enjoyment forms. As a result, conflict and competition arise. It is precisely due to such tendencies that some people believe, 'Now that we've got swarajya, we're free from work.' They don't care what happens in society. Whether there is social degradation, disease, poverty – they don't bother. They don't think about what people around the world must be saying upon hearing such news.

Earlier, under British rule, whatever problems arose, the blame was put on the British. But now, if the world asks, 'The British have left. Why is there still famine?', what answer will we give?

It is natural to ask – do people no longer have the tendency to work? Are they inherently lazy by nature? In truth, people's nature is not lazy. Fifty years ago, the life of an average person was full of hard work and diligence. The real issue today is the absence of *swabhimaan*, or self-respect. Where there is no self-respect, there is no industriousness. And where there is no industriousness, there can be no self-reliance.

Swabhimaan is a feeling of the heart; *swavalamban* (self-reliance) is the result that arises from hard work.

Earlier, leaders would say, 'This product is foreign – don't use it. Produce it in our own country.' But now that insistence is gone. They no longer see any reason to differentiate between foreign and indigenous goods. Today, we say, 'We'll eat only if food comes from abroad.' At the very least, earlier we had grains grown on Indian soil – nectar-like food born of Bharatbhumi.[1] But now, our food comes from Australia, Brazil, Canada and who knows where else. Whether this food is meant for humans or for horses, we no longer even care. This nutrition-less grain, which we receive in the form of rations, is what fills our stomachs today.

We are dependent on others even for food and drink. We are also dependent for knowledge, for inspiration and motivation and certainly for ideas and thoughts.

In the past, efforts were made to make us self-reliant. In 1905, a four-point formula for self-reliance was proposed: national education, *swadeshi* (use of indigenous goods), boycott of foreign goods, and swarajya (self-rule). This national education was inspired by swabhimaan. National schools were established in various places. But today's education system doesn't even mention the glory of India.

One of my friends once shared that many professors in our universities do not even know who Mirabai[2] is – the same Mirabai whose devotional songs are sung by little children. This is a result of the absence of national education.

Let's say some foreign country decides not to send us a certain product anymore – after all, you cannot force them to do so. The choice is either to produce that product in our own country, or to have the pride to say that we will manage without it. But even that kind of resolve is no longer visible among us.

People often interpret swarajya (self-rule) and *swatantrata* (freedom) as the same thing. But what does swatantrata truly mean? Every nation has its own unique way of life, its own distinct worldview and its particular ideology. A societal structure based on that ideology – that is swatantrata. Whether in the spiritual, political, artistic or scientific realm, the consistent application of one's own system across all spheres is what constitutes swatantrata.

When swatantrata expresses itself in the political realm, it is called swarajya. Swarajya is merely one part of swatantrata. True swatantrata is when it is manifested in every aspect of life – and naturally, it will then reflect in governance as well. Swarajya does not merely mean having someone of our own in power. A person is not 'our own' just because they have a native name, were born here, have dark skin or consume the food and water of this land. Truly, one who holds pride in the nation in their heart – that person alone is truly our own.

We have attained swatantrata in our country. But is this truly swatantrata? Have we made any real progress over the past years? In fact, the situation has worsened compared to before. This decline did not happen suddenly – it has deep underlying causes. The very foundation of our swarajya was flawed. It was not based on swatva, or a sense of selfhood. Where the development and protection of swatva takes place, where there is readiness to sacrifice everything for its sake and where one finds life's true meaning in living and dying for it, only there can swarajya be firmly rooted. That, unfortunately, is not the case in our nation.

What kind of swarajya is this? It's like a hunter who either accidentally or deliberately left the door of a cage open. But is a cage made only of iron bars? No – the real cage resides in the bird's own mind. As long as that cage remains, it doesn't matter whether the bird is held behind iron bars or is seemingly free. If its heart is enslaved, if it has no desire to experience the bliss of soaring in the sky, then it will fear stepping out of the cage. It will think, 'The cage was better. Food and water came on time. There was no fear of cats or dogs.'

In its mind, the cage was not a symbol of slavery – it was a protector. And when that protector vanishes, sometimes it feels sorrow. That's the condition of our current swarajya. Can this truly be called swarajya? When the bird steps out of the cage, it thinks, 'Now that I'm out, what do I do? A cat might come and eat me.' But the real question is – what *should* you do? *Fly!* But the bird doesn't even know that it has the power to fly, that its wings have strength and that it belongs to the skies. It doesn't have that self-confidence. That is exactly the state we are in.

India's ancient glory still endures – but even after attaining swarajya, we have not enhanced that glory. We do not do what ought to be done. We have so many resources, such a large population and so many intelligent people. Yet there is no real effort to engage the good people in meaningful work or to eliminate those who harm society. The reason is that we lack a solid foundation and mutual affection. The absence of a foundational ethos is a serious matter. We must awaken the dormant sense of pride in being born in *Bharatvarsha* (India), fan that fire into a blazing force, and channel it into effort, courage and a sense of duty. Only then can the nation become *swavalambi* (self-reliant) and *swayamshasit* (self-governed), both internally and externally.

It is incorrect to claim that our country never had a swayamshasit or self-sufficient way of life. Not only the nation but its very villages were swayamshasit and *atmarnirbhar* (self-dependent). Even under external rule, our villages preserved their swatva, their autonomous way of life. Before the arrival of the British, the level of education in our country was higher than that of any European nation. We had wisdom, industry and effort, because the foundation of swabhimaan (self-respect) was intact. Until we rebuild this foundation of swabhimaan, and erect upon it firm and load-bearing stones, the temple of the nation cannot be built. And this swarajya of Bharat will remain only a name without substance.

To say that swarajya arrived just because the British left is to understand it in a negative sense and not as something affirmative or deeply felt. True swarajya is emotional and spirited, where people are eager to contribute, not disinterested in work or caught in petty conflicts. Our neighbouring countries do not suffer from this malaise. They work with the feeling and determination that their nation must never be lowered in the eyes of the world. Their governance aligns with their swatva. In our case, people's desires go in one direction, while the rulers' imaginations head elsewhere. Laws and schemes are devised without people's support. It has been India's tradition that the power to make laws does not lie with the rulers. The king's duty is simply to ensure that the people follow the law and to punish those who do not. But today, the situation is the reverse. Wrongdoers enjoy every kind of protection and support, while good people are left without help.

Swarajya is not merely necessary because progress does not happen under foreign rule. The value of swarajya lies in the freedom to grow and evolve. It means having the right to work harder and the freedom to act in harmony with the nature (*swaprakriti*) of one's own nation. But today, we look to others at every step. Every decision we make depends on someone else's cues. Is this what we call swarajya?

The external obstacle of foreign rule has now been removed from the path of our nation – but does that mean we have reached our goal? A person who truly wishes to walk will surge forward once the obstacle is gone. The removal of a stone from the path should inspire greater movement. Our task now is not to determine the path – it has already been clearly laid down by our ancestors – our task is to walk it.

People ask, 'If the path has been set by our ancestors, why aren't we walking it?' But how can we? Food nourishes life, and life gives rise to *purushartha*[3]. Where is that food? Even basic sustenance is hard to find. More than even nourishment, what is urgently needed today is to present the radiant image of our ancient heritage before society and awaken its swabhimaan.

When everyone joins hands to work, then food, clothing and all other essential goods will be produced. We will generate four times what we actually need. The country will become entirely *swavalambi*. There is no other land in the world as inherently self-sufficient as our own. We have every type of climate and intelligent people. This land is superior even to heaven – but if people do not work, then even heaven will turn into hell due to their inertia.

When the form of society becomes sound and whole, it flourishes in every direction. Swavalamban arises in every sphere of national life. The light of the sun of swatantrata begins to shine across every area of life. Without this, Bharat cannot ascend to the peak of prosperity and greatness. If we strive for this, we will witness the presence of *Bhartiyata* (Indianness) in every aspect. Without it, swarajya has no real meaning.

13

'While Organizing Hindus Is a Noble Task, Who Will Solve the Terrifying Problem of Poverty?'

UMAKANT KESHAV APTE, BABASAHEB

In this next thought-provoking essay, *Umakant Keshav Apte, fondly called as Babasaheb Apte* delves deeper into the economic thought of ancient India and how it distinguishes itself from the Western economic models in terms of achieving holistic development of man.

Life has many aspects, such as politics, economic policy, education, knowledge, art, scriptures, customs, food, attire and more. The society that moves forward by weaving all these aspects into a cohesive whole truly deserves to be called a nation. From this perspective, when we declare that Bharat is a Hindu nation, we mean that the foundational principles of our national life were discovered in ancient times through all these facets, and efforts should be made to ensure that they continue to guide us in the future as well.

It is not appropriate for us to completely entangle ourselves in just one contemporary issue. For example, why should we give the highest importance to politics? Whether we place politics second or consider it to be the guiding force behind economic life, or the Bharat's poverty problem, we must also reflect seriously on these matters. This is a question that people often ask. People often ask: while organizing Hindus to counter the attacks on Hindu society and religion is a noble task, who will solve the terrifying problem of poverty that looms over us?

Some people even go as far as to say that the only problem we face now is poverty. During British rule, solving the problem of poverty in India was difficult. Now that political domination has ended, everything else will be fine. This kind of thought is gaining considerable strength in the country, and naturally, people are raising questions about this.

It is an accepted fact that poverty exists. Everyone experiences the suffering caused by poverty. It must be eradicated, and there can be no doubt about that. Now, the argument often goes that if we must eliminate poverty, why not emulate the progressive nations of Europe and America, which have completely eradicated poverty and where poverty is no longer an issue?

While the political control of Western countries was not a good thing, they have built a unique social structure and an economic framework, which has resulted in a society where no one goes hungry or lacks clothing. In a population of 20,000–25,000 people, you won't find even one who doesn't have enough food to eat or clothing to wear. So, why not imitate their economic structure? In truth, this question requires deep and serious contemplation.

There are two aspects to consider in this direction. The first question is, has India always experienced poverty from the beginning? The second question is, did this poverty arise due to our cultural value or was poverty ever given a prominent place in our philosophy? When we study history to find answers to these questions, we discover that both of these assumptions are entirely false. Our philosophy never gave any respect to poverty. Whether one is poor or wealthy was considered of little importance. However, poverty was considered highly undesirable, and being wealthy was not regarded as a bad thing. The idea that our country and society should remain poor simply did not exist here.

If proof is needed, history itself testifies that 200 or so years ago, such a state of poverty never existed in our country, no one who wanted food would go hungry and no one who desired clothes would remain unclothed. The land was filled with prosperity and happiness. Evidence of this can be found in the accounts of foreign travellers who came to India at various times in ancient history. During that period, there were no restrictions – as in Russia and other countries – on what could or could not be seen. The doors of cities, villages and forests were open to all. These travellers visited all places, and whatever they experienced, they recorded in their memoirs. In their travel accounts, there is no mention of poverty in India. On the contrary, they describe a prosperous and happy India. India had two names: one was *Dharmabhumi* (the land of righteousness), and the other was *Swarnabhumi* (the land of gold). Where there is Swarnabhumi, why would there be poverty?

A third piece of evidence is that in ancient times, all the invasions of India were primarily motivated by the desire to loot the vast wealth of this land. The wish to destroy the culture came to their minds only later. This is a historically proven fact that cannot be denied. Now the question arises: How can the philosophy and social structure, under which India was wealthy and prosperous, and where poverty had no place, be blamed for the current state of poverty in India? On the contrary, if we turn to that same philosophy, why should we not be able to create the same prosperity as in ancient times?

In the present context, there is a need to once again reconnect with the foundational principles of our ancient social structure. That foundation is this: the land of Bharat is our motherland, and the society that regards it as such is the Hindu society. What is needed is the building of a united, nationwide, organized and strong society – one that rises above caste, creed, province and sect; one that fosters a sense of brotherhood towards every individual; one that shares in one another's joys and sorrows.

If such a society is established, then through the collective effort of its members, it can surely recreate a life that is once again rich, golden, prosperous, peaceful, progressive and respected – just like in the past. There is no room for doubt in this. This is the right path. That is, in the haste to eliminate poverty, it is not wise to uproot the very foundation of our national life. Our old foundation is strong. If we hold on to it, then even if not in 5 years, certainly in 25 or 50 years, we can rebuild our nation to be as strong and prosperous as before.

We have a vast society – intelligent and hardworking. Our land is fertile. We have skill and craftsmanship. Everything is favourable. Then why should a prosperous life not be possible? It certainly will be. People ask, 'It's been so many years since we gained *swarajya*, yet poverty has not gone away.' This cannot be blamed on the Indian social structure or its philosophy. When no one has even attempted to rebuild society based on that philosophy, how can prosperity be expected to follow?

If we build our society on Western foundations, the prosperity we achieve will not align with the true aim of our life. The goal of our life is the realization of God through the full development of our humanity. Prosperity is only a means to that end, not the end itself. When there is prosperity, the body becomes capable of performing devotion, worship and spiritual practice to attain God. It is through the body that we can worship the Divine. Our philosophy encourages us to strive only for as much prosperity as is required to keep the body capable and healthy – for adequate food, rest and the essentials of life – not for indulgence or excess.

In our tradition, four major *purusharthas* (goals of human life) are identified: Dharma, *Artha*, *Kama* and *Moksha*. In that, *Artha* – material wealth – holds only a partial place, metaphorically like 25 paise in a rupee. Even that comes after Dharma. Dharma is our foremost duty, and it takes many forms.

For example, elders in the family often serve young children with great care and effort. In return, it becomes the moral duty of the grown children to serve their aging parents. This is a debt (*rin*) we owe them, and we must strive to repay it. If, due to their passing, that repayment isn't completed during their lifetime, then honouring their legacy by continuing their values, passing on noble values to the next generation and teaching them to walk in the footsteps of their forebears becomes our way of discharging that debt.

Raising our children with good values, making them capable of serving others and setting an example through our own lives – even amidst adversity – so that we never abandon our source or purpose: all this is part of the effort to become free of the debt that we owe to our ancestors (*pitr-rin*). This falls under *Dharma purushartha*, the pursuit of righteous duty.

Dharma does not merely mean attaining God or salvation after death. It also includes *abhyudaya* (well-being) in this life. But even that worldly well-being is only the first step of Dharma. Our aspiration is to rise even beyond that.

The next purushartha is Artha – but for what purpose? The ultimate aim of human life is the realization of God. However, this is not an easy task. Though a human is not an animal, onc is still born with many animalistic tendencies – lust, anger, greed, attachment, pride and jealousy. Rising above these, one must attain true humanity, and from there ascend towards divinity.

To reach that divine state, one must cultivate divine qualities: generosity, compassion, tolerance, selflessness, fearlessness, a sense of duty, discipline, purity and renunciation. Developing these virtues requires great effort and discipline. The body must be maintained as a fit instrument for this intense *sadhana* (spiritual practice). And if that means arranging for food, clothing and shelter to keep the body healthy and steady, so be it. But even in fulfilling these basic needs, one should not end up spending 12–14 hours a day merely working for material gain.

Hence, our social structure was designed in such a way that one could work for just a few hours, earn enough to meet the body's essential needs, and then devote the remaining time to the cultivation of *sattvic* (pure) qualities and spiritual growth.

A person should build a family not for indulgence, but as the first step on the path of duty. That is, the individual should sacrifice personal comforts for the welfare of the family – be ready to embrace sorrow with a smile for the greater good. Family life is the first stage of spiritual broad-mindedness. If the flow of family life is disrupted, then the continuity of the nation and culture also breaks. Without this, a person reduces themself to a two-legged animal. To prevent such a decline, our tradition envisioned the *grihastha ashrama* (householder stage).

In this ashrama, the wealth earned should be enjoyed – but only to the extent that it aids one in progressing on the path of Dharma and spiritual realization.

It is not necessary that all the countless people in society must sit cross-legged, holding their noses, engaged in meditation and other spiritual practices in order to progress towards spirituality. People are diverse. Some may find concentration and inner focus through art, others may attain the experience of *Sat–Chit–Ananda* (truth–consciousness–bliss) through deep study and learning. For some, the path to God may lie in embracing all of humanity as their own; for others, it may come through developing a sense of kinship with even non-human creation.

In this way – whether through scripture, art, knowledge or service to mankind – all these paths require peace in the country. There must not be chaos or disorder. Only then can a person enjoy the wealth they have earned and build conditions to grow further.

This next purushartha is called Kama. But the inclination for sensory enjoyment (*bhoga-vritti*) is not considered the ultimate in our tradition. It is merely a necessary step on the path of progress. Therefore, Lord Krishna himself says in the Bhagavad Gita: '*Balam balavatam caham kamaraga vivarjitam/Dharmaviruddho bhuteshu kamo'smi Bharatarshabha*' (I am the strength of the strong, free from desire and attachment. I am the desire (kama) that is not opposed to dharma, O best of the Bharatas). (Gita 7.11).

Even after achieving the first three *purusharthas* – Dharma, Artha and Kama – it may still feel like one's hunger has not been fully satisfied. The body's needs may be met, but the mind still lacks peace. The intellect remains unsettled. The soul has not yet found tranquility.

At this point, a person turns towards the path of *nishreyasa* – the ultimate good – for the peace of the soul. This final destination is called Moksha – liberation. It is the fourth and final purushartha.

Thus, the structure of life as envisioned in our tradition is deeply balanced. No one goal is considered higher or lower than the others. Talking about moksha at the very beginning while neglecting one's duties is not appreciated in our tradition. Similarly, completely rejecting the idea of moksha and becoming totally absorbed in the material world has also never been encouraged. Such is the thoughtful, layered and purposeful design of our way of life.

In the West, the approach is quite the opposite. There, the idea of Dharma as a duty-bound moral principle is practically absent. Families are disintegrating. What might have existed 200 years ago is uncertain, but today the situation is such that when parents grow old, their children feel no sense of gratitude towards them. Their behaviour resembles that of animals and birds – once grown, the offsprings forget their parents.

Just as we in India have shelters (Pinjrapol, Gosamrakshan Sanstha) to care for lame, crippled or elderly cows, so too in the West they have institutions like 'Old Men's Homes' and 'Old Women's Homes' for the elderly. These are run with government aid or donations from the wealthy. In such places, old people must spend the remainder of their lives at the mercy of paid staff. One can easily imagine how much love and attention they might actually receive in such conditions.

Just as animals have no concept of 'mine' or 'yours' when it comes to food, a similar mindset prevails in Western life. Their focus remains solely on the production and consumption of material pleasures. But just like fire never gets extinguished no matter how much ghee is offered into it, similarly, even if life comes to an end while indulging in pleasures, the desire for enjoyment remains unfulfilled.

They have conquered the external world and created an enormous system just to consume pleasures – and in doing so, they end up spending their entire lives in this pursuit. For them, only two purusharthas exist: Artha (wealth) and Kama (desire/pleasure). If someone feels that family becomes a hindrance in this pursuit, they do not hesitate to abandon it.

Why this difference in conduct between East and West? Because in our tradition, enjoyment is not the ultimate goal of life, whereas in the West, it is. That is why there is a vast difference between the social organization in their culture and ours.

The purpose of social organization in our tradition is to create conditions favourable for every individual to progress towards the ultimate goal of human life – self-realization and liberation. In contrast, their social organization exists primarily so that when many people come together and collaborate, they can produce a much greater quantity of material pleasures.

The second purpose of their organization is that the power generated by society or the nation should be used to establish dominance over other countries. By doing so, they can seize the wealth and material resources of others and bring them back for their own enjoyment. They have no hesitation in exploiting others – draining their blood – to fulfil their own desires. This has been the consistent behaviour of almost all Western nations: attacking others, enslaving them, exploiting them, seizing their resources and enjoying the luxuries of life without effort. Their entire history is filled with such accounts.

The so-called 'advanced' Western nations have all gained their wealth and prosperity through such acts of plunder – by draining others of their resources and strength. There is no historical evidence to suggest that they achieved this affluence purely through honest effort and sincere labour.

Another point is: even if they desire enjoyment, do they ever consider its long-term consequences? Not at all. Why is there a mad rush among them to rapidly exhaust the wealth that nature has accumulated over millions and millions of years? Coal is being steadily depleted. Petrol is running out. Now they have turned to atomic energy. But the minerals needed to generate that power, like thorium, also exist in limited quantities. A time will come when living the way they do today will become impossible. Without coal, trains won't run; without petrol, vehicles won't move. Even the means to harness atomic energy will eventually be exhausted. In other words, they lack a long-term vision.

That's not the case in our tradition. We make limited use of limited natural resources – like metals, gold, silver, brass and minerals. But we extensively utilize resources that regenerate continuously – such as wood from trees, cow dung and similar materials. Hence, a balance is maintained between taking from and giving back to nature. This cycle of mutual exchange ensures lasting happiness. Their Western vision, however, is not farsighted. They do not aspire for sustained, enduring joy. The pleasure of eating and indulging the senses is fleeting. A person only finds joy in food when hungry. If one keeps eating after the stomach is full, then even the food that gave pleasure just 10 minutes ago becomes a source of discomfort. Therefore, food should be a means, not an end. It is meant to strengthen the body, not to become the purpose of life. Working like a machine all day just for the body and indulging like an animal is not right. Such a life does not bring true fulfilment.

If there is no concern for parents and family, then who will care about the rest of the world? On one hand, millions of people in Asia and Africa are dying of hunger, and on the other hand, in America, wheat is burned to prevent prices from falling. If all the butter reaches the market, prices will drop – so they dump mountains of butter into the sea. They use science to grow more crops from the land – but to what end? Despite hoarding and consuming material goods, they are not satisfied.

A human being has more than just a body – they also have emotions. There is hunger of the body, mind, intellect and soul. When a sense of humanity occasionally awakens within them, it brings a surge of anguish. They commit suicide. And even more than those who die by suicide, many go insane. In that population, 10 per cent of people are becoming mentally ill. The rest are plagued by the problem of leisure. It takes them just two or three hours of work to earn money – then what is the problem? It's the problem of free time that stands before them, wide open. They read books, watch television and radio, but still, they can't sleep. Sleeping pills are taken. Isn't all this a sign of illness? Is this what a healthy society looks like? Whether they go to the Moon or to Mars, one thing is clear: they have not been able to tame the beast within the human heart.

In contrast, our efforts have been directed towards the development of *manushyatva* (true humanity), and even beyond that, towards the cultivation of *daivatva* (divinity). It is said: *Atmanam rathinam viddhi shariram rathameva tu/Buddhim tu sarathim viddhi mana pragrahameva cha* (Kathopanishad). In other words, know the soul to be the passenger in the chariot of the body. The intellect is the charioteer, the mind is the rein and the senses are the horses. One should, in the light of the intellect, control the senses through the reins of the mind.

But in the West, no one listens to the intellect, which is the charioteer. The horses (senses) run wild in every direction. They hurt themselves and break their limbs. What then would be the condition of the chariot-rider? What will become of his life? It's not hard to imagine.

Why did we fall into decline? We became engrossed in nurturing the family. We forgot our debt to society. The obligation towards family took precedence, and the peace and welfare of society faded away. Our *rin*, or debt, tradition ended at the family level. The spirit of living as an integral part of society diminished. Hence, we must not be hasty. Do we wish to live like the West, merely to escape poverty? No, we do not. Then, rushing will not solve the issue.

For a 1,000 years, we were under foreign rule. Foreigners and those of alien faiths enslaved and looted us, leaving behind extreme poverty. But to destroy this poverty, adopting their societal structures, ideals, systems and mindset would be self-destructive. We must resolve these problems from the very root, based on this understanding.

Before building a house, one must lay a strong foundation. That foundation is our Dharma, our culture and our traditions. Even if people do not fully understand them today, we must not discard them. There should never be a feeling of shame or contempt about our past. The thought that being born in India is a misfortune must be dispelled. We must reawaken the conviction that taking birth in India is a great blessing.

We must reach out to every child of Bharat and help them understand that, driven by fervent devotion to the motherland, people of every caste, sect and belief system should, with one voice, chant '*Bharat Mata ki jai* (Hail Mother India)'. We must stand shoulder to shoulder, walk together and cooperate in our endeavours. When this unified, organized strength is built, the current disbelief, chaos and intellectual anarchy will vanish, giving way to a harmonious and prosperous social order.

Only then can each individual progress meaningfully in life, in alignment with their inclinations and capabilities. There are many people in society who find fulfilment in agriculture, cow protection, trade and other industries. Some are manual labourers, others work solely with their intellect. But the idea is that together, they form a single national organism.

Just as the human body is made up of various parts, the nation too is formed of such integral parts. If someone says, 'The hands do the labour, like a worker, and the stomach is like a capitalist,' how would that make sense? It's true that the hands do the work, and the food goes into the mouth, and then to the stomach. But the blood produced from that digestion is equally distributed to the hands and legs, is it not? According to a Greek story, if the hands, legs and other body parts boycott the stomach, the stomach will die – but so will they, shrivelling and becoming lifeless. Hence, such a divisive ideology is completely misguided.

In our tradition, we did not think in terms of isolated parts, but always holistically. Each individual was given the opportunity to work according to their nature, qualities, preferences and abilities. No one was seen as a rival; everyone was seen as complementary to one another. That was the structure of our society in the past. Today, it lies in ruin. Only the remnants remain, and those too, in a completely distorted form.

The cause of our decline was not the original social structure, but our slavery. However, ignoring this truth, people are criticizing the past and blindly imitating foreign ideologies, spreading concepts of class struggle and owner–worker conflicts in the country. Our nation's enemies are also involved in this propaganda. We must be cautious of them and strive to ensure that we do not forget our own *svadharma* (self-dharma), social structure and traditional ideals. The feeling of joy and pride should arise in our hearts for being born as sons and daughters of this land.

It was due to the outstanding structures of ancient times that we were able to withstand numerous invasions and survive until today. This sense of gratitude should be awakened. Based on this pride and reverence, we must resolve to change the present situation and take responsibility for rebuilding that ancient, excellent structure. We must make an effort to awaken the sense of responsibility in every heart, for constructing a society that is unified, filled with self-respect and reverence for the past.

If we succeed in building such a society – one filled with self-pride and respect for the past – a divine life will emerge on Indian soil. The entire world will be astonished by this, and the very problems that have driven the West to despair, to the point where they are contemplating suicide, will be solved. America and Russia have developed nuclear, and hydrogen bombs capable of destroying the world. Isn't this the path to self-destruction? There, the individual may be suicidal, but the entire society is headed towards self-annihilation.

We will only be able to demonstrate the ability to solve these problems when, based on the foundation of our culture, we reach a balanced state in our society and create a life that is prosperous, peaceful and progressive, right here in our own country. Destroying poverty will then be a minor achievement. Just like when a person buys a ticket from Delhi to Madras (now Chennai) and boards the train to Madras, they will inevitably pass through Jhansi without needing another ticket or changing trains.

Thus, our efforts should be to create a national life in which there is no animosity, no sense of injustice or exploitation and no ill will towards others. We will strive for our own development and that of others, creating a society based on a broad-minded perspective. This will also give us the strength to guide others. If others refuse to follow the right path due to obstinacy, our nation will not be harmed. If they dare to attack us, we will have the power to defend ourselves effectively.

We must understand this comprehensive outlook well and create our individual lives based on this perspective. In our tradition, the entire life of an individual has been planned with the welfare of society in mind. The stages of life – *brahmacharya* (celibacy), *grihastha* (householder), *vanaprastha* (retirement) and s*anyasa* (renunciation) – all contribute to the permanent happiness of the individual, as well as the peace and prosperity of society.

If an individual works for eight hours for the family, they should also work for at least eight hours for society. When an individual's life is planned from the perspective of social welfare, prosperity comes naturally, poverty is eradicated and peace is established.

14

'The Programme of Our Sangh Is to Revive the Healthy Flow of National Life'

EKNATH RANADE

Eknath Ranade was a senior RSS pracharak who served as the sarkaryavah of the organization before being entrusted with the gigantic task of raising a befitting memorial for Swami Vivekananda at Kanyakumari in Tamil Nadu. His years of dedicated efforts resulted in mobilizing support for the project cutting across political and religious lines, and a grand national memorial was constructed on the rock where Swami Vivekananda had undertaken a three-day penance before setting off on his historic journey to Chicago in 1892–93.

Ranade established Vivekananda Kendra with Kanyakumari as the headquarters, which mobilized a large number of dedicated workers to promote Swamiji's thoughts across humanity through educational and social service projects. Ranade was also a profound thinker and authored several thoughtful works.

In this compilation of his addresses, Ranade talks about the mission of the RSS and the role of swayamsevaks in achieving it.

The work of the Sangh is to build capable karyakartas or workers who can re-establish a well-organized Hindu society and an invincible Hindu nation with dignity in the world. This is the task of national reconstruction – to rekindle the ideals of Hindu life-values and Hindu worldview in the life of this nation once again.

When we say 'reconstruction', it implies that at some point in the past there existed a proper structure, which, over time, developed flaws and errors, and therefore requires reconstruction now. On the other hand, if we say 'new nation-building', it conveys the meaning that there was never a national life in India to begin with, and now, a completely new nation needs to be created on the strength of several new ideologies born in recent times.

In recent years, many such 'new nations' have emerged, but with regard to the national life of our country, we cannot say the same. A civilized and cultured national life has existed in India for thousands of years – this fact is as clear as day through the testimony of history. What is true for an individual is equally true for a nation. If a person lives life without any purposeful achievement, even if they live for many years, it will be said about them: 'They were born human, but wasted their life in vain.'

Living for the attainment of a noble ideal brings to life the true spirit of humanity in a person's life. Otherwise, it is a life of a rock or a stone, and not that of a human. A life spent chasing after the fulfilment of one petty desire leads to ten more desires, and in trying to fulfil those, one runs like a mirage-chaser, lost in delusion. Their life ends merely in the pursuit of personal gratification. A person who sets a clear purpose for life and lives thoughtfully in pursuit of that accepted goal spends every moment of their life for it. A purposeless person wanders here and there all life long. Like a wanderer making aimless journeys, boarding one train after another upon being dropped at a station, with no clear destination – such is their drifting life.

They see, hear, eat, drink and even sleep anywhere – they perform all physical activities of a human being, but they have not truly lived as a human. A child's life too is like this before understanding dawns on them. But the moment they realize the purpose of their human life, in that very moment, they are reborn as a human and the formation of their personality begins. Their speech and conduct become regulated. They begin to live the life of a human being with purpose.

What is true for an individual is equally true for a society as a whole. For social life to be real, there must be a collective ideal, a clear direction and a goal to be attained. Otherwise, it is merely a herd of beings who happen to be called humans. Such a herd lives a nomadic life. If all people do not stand united with a firm resolve to achieve a specific goal, then it cannot be called a nation. Only when all components of society share a collective experience, when a group consciousness exists among all, and when they stand together like limbs of a single body – unified in mind and fully channelled in their strength towards achieving a common goal – only then can that society be called a nation. Through shared aspirations, it becomes not just a community but emerges as a nation.

The unified collective life of all segments of society, their common sense of friend and foe, their natural tendency to come together to resolve issues faced by the society and their shared aspiration to live with the single ideal of national upliftment – these are qualities that naturally manifest in a true national life. In other words, merely the desire to stay together in the hustle of life is not enough to live as a nation. Even animals live in herds, but they do not possess a sense of group consciousness. When a grave danger arises, animal herds scatter and each animal flees in its own direction. Animals lack the awareness needed for confronting challenges together while staying united.

A society that is referred to as a nation possesses, within its collective consciousness, the ability to understand and articulate – in appropriate terms – its own national life and how it relates to other societies and nations around it. On the basis of this group consciousness, the society develops its own philosophy of life and undertakes the search for eternal truths. It sets its own independent principles and rules of conduct. It presents an ideal of *Maryada Purushottama* – the Supreme Being of righteousness – that can be accepted by all. It strives to cultivate shared aspirations among all components of the society.

Questions like when the world came into existence, who created it and why, are reflected upon by the wise and knowledgeable individuals within that society. They decide what truly constitutes the welfare of society. To achieve the goals of its national life, all members of the society move forward along a predetermined path and direction.

From this perspective, Swami Vivekananda's profound words are especially meaningful: 'Every nation has a destiny to build, it has a message to deliver and a mission to accomplish.' If we reflect from this point of view, we understand that just as an individual has a distinct identity, so too does a nation. With this identity come unique aspirations, beliefs and objects of reverence; distinct ways of thinking; and a particular sense of what is right and wrong.

The goal of collective life is not decided by any one person. It evolves, generation after generation, within the life of the nation itself. It is transmitted from one generation to the next. Our ancient saints and sages sacrificed their personal lives and placed this great nation before us. For swayamsevaks like us, who step out in service of society, it is essential to deeply imprint within our minds these fundamental thoughts – the purpose of the nation, its goal and the message it seeks to offer to the world. Only then will we clearly understand the true nature of our Sangh work.

Earlier, I had mentioned a few types of service work; among them, this is the highest form of service. Organizing the entire society in such a way that every component of it can attain both worldly prosperity (*abhyudaya*) and ultimate well-being (*nishreyasa*) – and developing such a social structure and system – is the noblest form of social service. It is said, '*Yato'bhyudayanishreyasasiddhih sa dharmah*' (That which ensures both worldly prosperity and ultimate liberation is Dharma). (Gautama Dharmasutra)

And as Shankaracharya says in his commentary on the Brahmasutra, '*Praninamabhyudayanishreyasahetuh sa dharmah*' (That which leads to the material well-being [abhyudaya] and ultimate liberation [nishreyasa] of living beings is Dharma). (Brahmasutra Bhashya)

Such service is eternal. A society where no individual faces any obstacle in attaining the highest goal of both material and spiritual life is the ideal social system. Because in such an organized society, flaws like competition, envy and exploitation – which hollow out the social fabric – can never arise. Just as different limbs of a body, through mutual cooperation, contribute to the pleasant functioning of the entire body, in the same way, an organized society thrives and constantly progresses through mutual cooperation. The idea of class struggle cannot even arise there.

Our noble ancestors built and sustained such a conflict-free, robust social life in India for a long time. With the loss of consciousness

The site of the first shakha, Mohite Wada, Nagpur

Dr Hedgewar (third from right), M.S. Golwalkar (second from right) and V.D. Savarkar (extreme right) with others

A young Dr Hedgewar

(L to R seated) Appaji Joshi, Dr Hedgewar, M.S. Golwalkar and others

Dr Hedgewar addressing a gathering

M.S. Golwalkar

Dr Hedgewar (extreme left)

M.S. Golwalkar (right) with Swami Amritanand

M.S. Golwalkar at the Mathura Gohatya Virodh Rally

Pracharaks of RSS deputed to Jan Sangh

Vajpayee with Deendayal Upadhyaya

A young Atal Bihari Vajpayee

Deendayal Upadhyaya

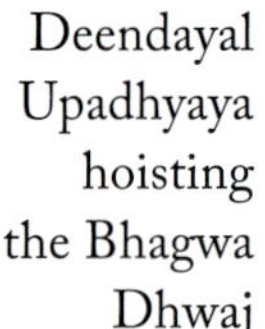

Deendayal Upadhyaya hoisting the Bhagwa Dhwaj

Atal Bihari Vajpayee during a convention of Janta Party workers to form a new party, the Bharatiya Janata Party, at Firoz Shah Kotla Road, New Delhi, 5 April 1980

Balasaheb Deoras (speaking), Atal Bihari Vajpayee, Vijaya Raje Scindia and others at the foundation laying ceremony of houses for Deendayal Dham service projects of Nagla Chandrahan, 13 July 1982

Balasaheb Deoras addressing swayamsevaks

Balasaheb Deoras

Rajendra Singh in 1978

Dattopant Thengdi addressing a gathering at India Gate

In 1985, Dattopant Thengdi led a Bharatiya Mazdoor Sangh delegation to China on the invitation of the All-China Federation of Trade Unions

Dattopant Thengdi (centre) at a meeting of the Swadeshi Jagran Manch

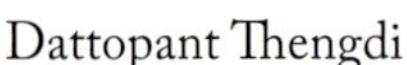

Dattopant Thengdi

Eknath Ranade

Ranga Hari

K.S. Sudarshan

Dattatreya Hosabale

K.S. Sudarashan and Mohan Bhagwat

Mohan Bhagwat

PM Narendra Modi, Mohan Bhagwant, UP CM Yogi Adityanath (extreme right) with others at the Ram Mandir Pran Pratishtha in Ayodhya 2025

Suresh Soni

regarding this distinctive form of Hindu social life, humanity became disoriented. To re-organize that again is the task of our Sangh.

Across the world today, many thinkers are striving earnestly to construct a society free from competition and envy, where interpersonal relationships are harmonious and balanced, where life is content and free from exploitation. Such efforts aim to develop a social structure where not only are the basic needs of a person fulfilled, but their inner quest for satisfaction is also addressed.

Our ancient sages had already built such a social structure long ago, and it functioned effectively in India for centuries. During that time, India's scholars, with great self-confidence, called out to the entire world. In the words of Maharshi Manu[1]: '*Etaddeshaprasutasya sakashadagrajanmanah / Svam svam charitram shiksheran prithivyam sarvamanavah*' (Let all human beings on earth learn the ideals of character from the eldest and noblest born in this land). (Manusmriti 2.20)

This statement of Maharshi Manu reflects the self-confidence of our visionary and reflective ancestors. Without rejecting any specific national identity, they successfully created a well-structured society – regardless of worship practices or life philosophies – that uplifted individuals and established a society free from exploitation and conflict. All necessary principles and codes for such a society were once effectively implemented by our great ancestors in India. This is history.

China, Russia and America are each attempting to build an ideal social system based on their own ideological foundations. These efforts are still in the experimental phase, as is evident from reports in newspapers and the accounts of people who have visited those countries. However, the ancient sociologists of India indeed constructed such an ideal system in this country that could be suitable for any country or society.

Along with ensuring food, clothing, shelter and life-essential education for every individual, our scriptural scholars recognized and respected the unique identity that exists at a higher level beyond just body, mind and intellect. They discovered a process to regulate all three and cultivate the experience of consciousness that dwells in the innermost being of man. A social order was developed here in India that fostered the complete growth of a person, including the body, mind, intellect and soul.

Our visionary thinkers declared with confidence that if these societal principles were accepted by any community across the world, they would undoubtedly progress in every respect. Western scholars are only now beginning to understand this; that is why Einstein[2] confidently stated, 'India will guide us.'

It is our inherited responsibility to give direction to the world, and we must accept this role. There are certainly many obstacles today – some beyond our control – but we must stand firm with patience and overcome every challenge to fulfil this duty. At one time, we successfully created such a social structure and showed that it was suitable for the entire world; it is necessary today to reiterate that same confidence. We have already demonstrated such an organized social system through the model of the Sangh. It is our duty now to organize the entire society on the same ideological foundation. The program of our Sangh is to revive the healthy flow of national life. Today, it is our task to eliminate the forgetfulness of this duty that has occurred in our society.

All nations of the world, big and small, are longing for a peaceful life. History tells us that such a life existed in India since ancient times. Foreigners tried to destroy this national life through invasions. They forcibly eradicated the faith of our society, trampled upon the land and dismantled our cultural symbols. But India never launched such barbaric attacks on anyone. The noble people of India went out into the world as messengers of peace. These sages travelled across the globe to teach the knowledge of a life filled with inner contentment and eternal joy.

Even today, it is our responsibility to give this message and this mantra of peace to the world. The reawakening of an ideal social order is the greatest gift India can offer to humanity. We must work with this conviction.

To reorganize the fragmented life of our Hindu nation and to create capable swayamsevaks for it is the task of our Sangh. When many people reside together in a particular area, it does not automatically make them a nation. They may establish a government system, but that is not enough. It is only when people, living with a shared heart, come together to live as one that they form a 'nation'. A society motivated by the desire to achieve a higher purpose in life, aiming to deliver its distinctive vision to the world, becomes a 'nation'. This is the idea we present. We have previously discussed how all the components of such a nationalist society, men and women alike, work together with a single-minded effort to achieve their high goal.

When many people live together in a particular area, their primary concerns are their basic needs and outward life – food, clothing and other necessities. Once these needs are met, the thinkers of society engage in deep contemplation about one's worldview and the ideal way to achieve it in practical life. They study and reflect on what the collective goal of society should be and present it to the society as a grand and divine objective. Their efforts are directed towards making all aspirations align with this goal. In this regard, the vision of our ancient sages, who reached great heights in their wisdom, is remarkable. Even today, scholars around the world are astonished by their guidance of eternal truths. By leading a pure, sattvic life and through rigorous penance, they documented their experiences for the welfare of society. These are not mere intellectual or imaginative exercises based on study of scriptures, they are the nectar of societal welfare revealed through impartial contemplation. The essence of their thoughts is encapsulated in the four *purushartha*s, the four goals of human life. Based on this, they presented the framework for human life in the form of the '*purushartha chaturthaya*', the fourfold purpose of life, to their society.

These four purusharthas, when achieved in life, guide the style of thought and contemplation of each individual. However, everyone agrees that these four purusharthas are the sole aim of life. Similarly, when striving to achieve them, the ultimate goal of life – *Mukti*, or liberation – is the ultimate aim, as experienced in the lives of great Rishis, or sages, through their penance and purity. To be freed from the endless cycle of birth and death, to be liberated from the cycle of joy and sorrow, is what they called *jivanmukti*. Achieving that state is the final goal of every human life, and living within the framework of the four purusharthas is considered essential for it.

Swami Vivekananda's definition of Mukti is distinctive. He says, 'Every soul is potentially divine. The goal is to manifest this divinity within, by controlling nature, external and internal. Do this by work and worship, psyche control or philosophy – by one, or more, or all of these – and be free.' The true nature of the human mind is described as a 'bundle of desires and cravings'. In order to satisfy these desires, humans have the creativity and external resources available. These desires are referred to as *Kaam* in our tradition. The means to control and fulfil these desires while adhering to moral conduct is called *Artha*. The entire functioning of the world depends on both Kaam and Artha. It is impossible for a human to satisfy all desires. How can limited resources fulfil unlimited desires? If one attempts to do so, confusion and disorder are inevitable. Attempting to satisfy desires only increases them. Hence, control over desires through Dharma is necessary. By regulating the fulfilment of desires within the boundaries of Dharma, the ultimate goal of Mukti can be attained. This is the life-system established by the rishis of India. The life journey of man, from birth to death, flows within the boundaries of the two shores of Dharma and *Moksha*. Every individual has experienced many births before, and after death, many more births will follow. Freedom from this cycle of '*punarapi jananam, punarapi maranam*' (cycle of births and deaths) is Moksha.

This liberation is the goal of every human life, as taught by our great sociologists, and has been translated into direct practice in Bharat.

When we accept that there are many paths to attain Moksha, the main consideration that arises is that we must determine our own path. The journey of life in this world is something we must complete ourselves. When thinking of following any path for Moksha, the practical entanglement of illusions (*Maya*) and attachments is of no use. The accumulation of wealth is of no utility in this regard. There is a verse from the Brihadaranyaka Upanishad where Yajnavalkya tells Maitreyi, '*Amritatvasy tu na asha vittena*' (4.2), meaning that the hope of attaining immortality through wealth is futile. The course of a person's future life entirely depends on their own actions. The love and affection of relatives and friends is of limited use.

The ascension of the Pandavas[3] to heaven illustrates this well. Only Dharmaputra Yudhishthira was able to take his dog with him, while the other Pandavas gradually fell away on the journey. The task of every social reformer and thinker is to develop a social system that allows each individual to follow the path of liberation freely and without hindrance. I must live and die alone. No matter how many desires I may have, I cannot live another's life or accept another's death. The life journey will only be successful when the social environment is conducive to it.

It is not only spiritual thinkers who have presented this idea. Our scientists, relating to worldly life, have also accepted the same goal. Thinkers from various physical fields such as economics, political science, fine arts, Ayurveda and others have also proposed that the ultimate goal of life is Moksha. This unity of thought among the philosophers from all fields is found only in India and nowhere else. As per Ayurveda, '*Jivem sharadah shatam, modam sharadah shatam, nandam sharadah shatam.*' In other words, may we live for a 100 years, may our body remain strong and healthy and may we pass this 100-year-long life with happiness, contentment and joy.

In each textbook of fine arts or any other science and knowledge branches, the subject of '*Anubandha Chatushtaya*' (The fourfold connection) is discussed at the beginning, emphasizing the eligibility of the reader, the purpose and the interconnection of all these elements. Every author of these scriptures has written that the purpose of studying is 'that knowledge which leads to Moksha.' Books that discuss subjects like military science, political science, security science, astrology, dance, music, grammar and others begin with the author's presentation of Moksha as the primary goal of study. To achieve Moksha, it is instructed that, having lived a long life of a 100 years, one should lead a life that is prosperous, healthy and content, enjoying all aspects of life in moderation and with joy. This is the ultimate directive presented in all these scriptures.

It is universally accepted in India that the welfare objective of social institutions and organizations is to assist each individual in achieving the goal of Moksha according to their capacity. However, whether indirectly or directly, every branch of knowledge and every scripture emphasizes the importance of making each individual capable and competent for this purpose. If every individual in society becomes so, the entire society will also become capable and competent. If attention is paid to every penny, the rupees will accumulate. (An English proverb that conveys this meaning is: 'Take care of the pence, and the pounds will take care of themselves.') This same principle applies when rebuilding the entire nation. If efforts are made to align the thoughts and actions of every individual to be beneficial for the life of the nation, the entire nation will undoubtedly become powerful and prosperous. The goal of the Sangh is to make our nation strong. Our effort to inspire each individual with values is precisely for this reason. Other societal works follow after this standard.

Service performed with a selfless attitude and a proper perspective on life is what truly deserves to be called service in its truest form. Therefore, it is the responsibility of every volunteer organization to provide each individual with sufficient opportunities to engage in various forms of social service. Due to the practice instilled by the most revered Doctorji in our collective work, thousands of swayamsevaks have made their personal lives secondary and have become pracharaks. We continue to witness them working year after year. Our duty is to ensure the overall progress of our nation. Therefore, the primary need is to create swayamsevaks who can organize and systematize social life. Our effort is to realize our dream of organizing the entire social life. Our task is to build a new, appropriate social order based on the finest principles that enhance both social and individual lives, in line with the current circumstances.

What is important to remember is that we are mere instruments in the hands of the Almighty God, and this pure sense is what drives us to carry out our work. Our organization is a voluntary one. Assisting people suffering from natural calamities like famine, flood and cyclones is indeed service, but if we begin to regard only this as true service, we would have to pray to God to create such natural disasters in order to have the opportunity to serve. In truth, the creation of well-educated and well-cultured individuals is the real and best form of service in accordance with the ideals of Indian life. This is the essence of the thought process that underpins the work of the organization.

15

'Akhand Bharat . . . Is the Foundation of Our Entire Philosophy'

DEENDAYAL UPADHYAYA

Deendayal Upadhyaya was one of the senior RSS leaders of the last century who provided a strong ideological foundation for the organization through his speeches and writings during the 1950s and 1960s. He was among the early leaders delegated to work in the Bharatiya Jana Sangh (BJS) by Golwalkar, 'Guruji', in 1950. He became the organizing secretary of the newly formed party under the leadership of Dr Shyama Prasad Mukherjee and continued in that position for a decade and a half before being elevated to its president in 1968. Under Deendayal's leadership, the BJS emerged as the principal opposition party in the country to the then dominant Congress Party not only politically but also ideologically. Deendayal presented a new and alternate ideological vision in the form of 'Integral Humanism' in 1964–65 that emerged as the main challenger to the prevailing Nehruvian worldview. The promising career of this idealist and intellectual leader came to an abrupt end in early 1968 when he was found dead under mysterious circumstances by the side of the railway tracks near Mughalsarai station in Uttar Pradesh.

Akhand Bharat – Undivided India – remained one of the important cornerstones of the RSS ideology. In this lecture, Deendayal explains the phrase and its meaning.

The Bharatiya Jan Sangh has set the goal of Akhand Bharat before it. Akhand Bharat is not just a representation of the geographical unity of the nation, but also a symbol of the Indian worldview that sees unity in diversity. Therefore, for us, Akhand Bharat is not a political slogan that we adopted because it was popular in a particular context; rather, it is the foundation of our entire philosophy. It is a fact that when India was divided on 15 August 1947, and its unity shattered, people had to endure dire consequences of this fragmentation. That led to an intense hunger for reunification of India. However, if we carefully study the inner flow of the age-old life-stream of this nation, we realize that our national consciousness has always strived for unity, and in that endeavour, we achieved considerable success too.

'Uttaram yat samudrasya himadreschaiva dakshine / Varsham tad bharatam nama bharati yasya santatih' (The land that is situated to the north of the Indian Ocean and south of the Himalayas is called Bharat and its children are called Bharatiya.) That was how our ancient sages described the land of Bharat. It was not merely about the land but also about people and their culture. We never saw land, people and culture as separate. Instead, through their unity, we realized the nation.

The fundamental beliefs about national and cultural unity of India held by the Jan Sangh are all encapsulated in the term 'Akhand Bharat'. The feeling of considering every particle of the land, from Attock[1] to Cuttack[2]; Kutch[3] to Kamrup[4]; and from Kashmir[5] to Kanyakumari[6], as sacred, pure and dear is implicit in Akhand Bharat. The people who have emerged from this sacred land since time immemorial, and those who are here today, have always experienced a fundamental unity in their entire lives. In spite of their superficial differences, this unity is something every devotee of Akhand Bharat continues to uphold even today. They share each other's joys and sorrows. The sons of Akhand Bharat, born from its womb, have, through their contributions in various fields, maintained the thread of unity. Our religious policy, economic policy, politics, literature, art, philosophy, history, Puranas, Upanishads[7], our memories and scriptures – all, despite outward differences in forms of worship, have consistently upheld the unity of the devotee's spirit. The realization of this cultural unity is essential for the worshipper of Akhand Bharat.

Our history is all about this experience of the unity of life and the creative efforts to remove any obstacles in its path. Slavery was the biggest obstacle to our sense of unity. Consequently, we fought against it. The attainment of *Swaraj* (self-rule) should have strengthened this sense of unity. Unfortunately, it did not. Today, there is a struggle of opposing emotions within our lives. 'Akhand Bharat' is the true nature of our nation. A fragmented India is a distortion. Even if we seek to experience the illusion of joy in this distortion, the true joy will never come. Once we accept this reality, our internal conflict will immediately end, and our efforts will acquire more strength.

Many people have doubts about whether Akhand Bharat will ever be realized. Their doubts are the result of a defeatist mindset. They witnessed the defeat of their attempts at maintaining unity in 1947. Victory of the separatist policy has broken their spirit, and now they want to make their defeat permanent, which is not possible. No one can go against the basic nature of the nation. Doing that will result in self-destruction. The defeat of 1947 was not the defeat of the Indian spirit of unity per se, but only the defeat of the efforts that were made in the name of national unity. We did not fail because our goal was wrong; we failed because we chose the wrong path. When the goal is not achieved due to defective means, the goal itself cannot be discarded as unworthy or impractical. Those who are questioning the practicality of the idea of Akhand Bharat are the very same people who adopted those faulty means and still do not want to abandon them.

The greatest obstacle in the path of Akhand Bharat has been the separatist and anti-national mentality of sections of the Muslim community. The Partition of India and creation of Pakistan was a victory for that mentality. Those who are sceptical about Akhand Bharat assume that Muslims will not change their policy. If their assumption is true, will the 60 million Muslims that are living in India also pose a great challenge to the nation's interest? Would the Congress leaders say that Muslims should be expelled from India? No. Instead, they must be assimilated into Indian national life. If this unity can be achieved in partitioned India, it will not take long for the rest of the territory to reunite. If the country was divided due to the lack of a sense of emotional unity, it can be united on the basis of the same sentiment. We should strive for that. To make every Muslim feel like an Indian, we will have to change our policy of the past half-century. The Congress had attempted Hindu–Muslim unity on an incorrect basis. Instead of emphasizing on the innate eternal sense of cultural unity and making everyone experience it, it accepted that we are all different and attempted to build unity on the basis of political bargaining. Such efforts could not succeed because a synthesis of nationalism and anti-nationalism is not possible.

16

'In Our Tradition, the Nature of the State Has Always Been Envisioned as a Dharma Rajya – A Righteous State'

DEENDAYAL UPADHYAYA

In this address, Deendayal Upadhyaya attempts to explain the concept of Dharma Rajya and the need for re-establishing it in India.[1]

A nation is formed by the confluence of land, people and culture. It is the people and culture that transform inert land into a living, conscious entity. Through land and culture, mortal people attain a sense of immortality. The direction and definition of their lives, along with the norms and rules of conduct, are established on this basis. Culture is, in essence, the result of the interplay and interactions between people and land over millennia.

According to some scholars, people are born with certain distinctive qualities as a non-random creation of the Divine, and the evolved expression of that original element is what constitutes culture. Others believe that when the interactions between individuals take a certain ideal-oriented direction, the impressions they leave on the mind – which in turn guide future behaviour – become known as culture. Thus, culture is both the cause and consequence of a person's duties.

The bond that people develop with the land – of belonging, of mutual purpose, of nurturer and nurtured, protector and protected, milker and milked – is what adorns and enriches culture. The essential point is that land, people and culture are interdependent. While scholars may prioritize one or more of these aspects, just as body, soul and life are all integrated and inseparable, we cannot consider any of the three – land, people or culture – to be less important than the others. A nation cannot exist without all of them.

The foundation that protects, enhances and prospers the nation born of the union of these three elements is Dharma. Dharma is what sustains. Through it, both *abhyudaya* (worldly prosperity) and *nishreyasa* (ultimate liberation) are achieved. It is through Dharma that the interests of the individual and the collective are harmonized. Just as a person who follows Dharma strengthens the body while realizing the soul, thereby attaining both material and spiritual bliss, a nation that adheres to Dharma brings welfare to land, people and culture alike.

Because of this conception, rituals like *bhumi-pujan* (worship of the land), pilgrimages, mother-worship, societal systems and Vedic sacrifices are all included in our Dharma. This Dharma governs the relationships between the individuals, between individual and society, between one society and another and even between the animate and the inanimate, making these relationships mutually harmonious. Dharma permeates our entire life.

Given the supreme place of Dharma, all our institutions have traditionally been established upon its foundation. The state, which originally arose for the protection of the nation, cannot function by disregarding Dharma. Just as a cook appointed to prepare food cannot fulfil his duty by ignoring fuel and its heat, similarly, a state that becomes indifferent to the sustaining force of Dharma will fail to protect the nation. Therefore, in our tradition, the nature of the state has always been envisioned as a *Dharma rajya* – a righteous state. All other classifications of governance are secondary. As long as a state is founded upon Dharma, irrespective of whether it is a democracy or a monarchy, it will ultimately be benevolent and welfare oriented. On the contrary, history offers numerous examples of how both democratic and autocratic systems were used to oppress the people.

In a Dharma rajya, unity and integrity of the land, along with deep reverence towards it, are always imminent. A Dharma rajya can never be narrow-minded or sectarian. Dharma has the quality of sanctifying even the smallest and humblest of beings. This very quality gives rise to deep reverence and devotion towards the land. Selfless patriotism cannot exist outside the framework of Dharma. *Lokaradhana* – service to the people – remains the sole objective of a Dharma rajya.

A ruler who follows Dharma has no right to his meal as long as even a single citizen remains hungry. The very term 'raja' (king) was conferred upon the rulers because of their duty of *lokaranjana* – bringing joy to the people. The ethics of Dharma are essentially social ethics. Dharma does not divide people, rather it considers them as a unified whole. Just as the body and its limbs are inseparably related, so too are the people and their institutions. Neither can any limb be neglected, nor the body. A flower exists because of its petals, and the petals attain their beauty and purpose by being part of the flower. There is no room for separatism here. From a cultural point of view too, Dharma is integrating and unifying. The experience of oneness in life is the unique feature of Indian culture, and the code of conduct imbued with this spirit of oneness is what we call as Dharma.

Undoubtedly, the mission of this code of conduct is both the protection of the collective and the development of the individual. To focus exclusively on either the individual or the society is a partial approach. Indian culture simultaneously and equally promotes the well-being of both. Systems like democracy and socialism have failed to reconcile this dual goal. Dharma, however, makes this balance naturally possible.

The nature of a Dharma rajya is fundamentally different from that of a *panth rajya* – theocratic state. Dharma and panth (religion) are not the same. Confusion arises because the word 'Dharma' has often been incorrectly translated into English as 'religion'. But Dharma is much broader. Religion and sects concern only one aspect of life – way of worship. A panth typically deals with only one of the four *purusharthas*[2] from an individual standpoint. Dharma, while being one of the four purusharthas, is also the foundation of all four. Hence, a Dharma rajya is not a theocratic state. Theocracy arises when the king himself becomes the religious head. India never allowed that position to the kings. In fact, when all powers are concentrated in the state, theocracy is the result. If the ruler holds a theistic belief or is associated with a specific sect and uses that as the basis to govern all aspects of social life, then the state becomes a panth rajya.

In Europe, both non-Christians and Christians who spoke against Biblical doctrine faced persecution by the state. Galileo[3] was imprisoned for this very reason. The Caliphate[4] and Papacy[5] are the outcomes of this approach. Even today, what is happening in Russia and China is not much different from a theocracy. Though Communists are not theists, their system exhibits all the characteristics of a dogmatic belief. Those who strive for socialism as an end goal, if successful, will also establish a similar sectarian state in which socialism becomes their sect.

By contrast, a Dharma Rajya believes in decentralization or systematic distribution of powers. The principle of 'whatever the king does is justice' does not apply here. Instead, the king is expected to act justly, while what is justice will be determined not by him, but by Dharma. In modern terms, one may equate this to a constitutional government, but with a crucial distinction – today's constitutions are created by ordinary humans and have become mere playthings in their hands. They are altered arbitrarily. As a result, instead of governance being guided by the constitution, the constitution itself is tailored to suit the government. In contrast, Dharma's principles are not man-made, but rather insights realized by enlightened sages through their inner experience of the profound mysteries of the universe. In such a system, unwritten laws are more authoritative than written ones. Society expresses its soul through conduct, and the rules or *smriti*s should be reflections of this inner rhythm. Because society naturally follows a Dharma-aligned, ethically endorsed conduct, anarchy or arbitrariness does not arise. Thus, a Dharma Rajya avoids the extremes of mobocracy – rule by the chaos of masses; and autocracy – rule by one dictator.

The Dharma Rajya is not based on any one book. It is not static but dynamic – yet its dynamism is not to be mistaken for instability or lack of direction. It evolves with time and place but remains unchanging in matters of fundamental principles of life. In this system, the legislative power of society does not lie with the king, but with Dharma. Dharma rajya is generally equated with the 'Rule of Law', but if the authority to make laws lies solely with the ruler, then it essentially becomes 'rule of law to be framed by the ruler'. Such authority is not granted under a Dharma rajya.

Dharma rajya is different from today's democracy. Though the king is responsible for public welfare, he too is governed by Dharma. People are also subject to Dharma. Just as a king has no right to punish or remove a righteous subject, the people do not have the right to remove a Dharma-abiding king. Democracy, based on the assumption of constant conflict between the interests of the ruler and the ruled, keeps a sword of perpetual rebellion hanging over the ruler's head in the form of the political opposition. Such a model of democracy, which probably stemmed from the dualistic Christian worldview of God and Satan, is not suitable for human development.

People can remove the king only if he acts against Dharma. Removing the king is not the people's duty; their duty is to follow Dharma. When the king comes in the way of that, removing him becomes Dharma. Many accept the importance of Dharma, yet do not see the need to proclaim a Dharma rajya. If they were to introspect, they would see that such hesitation stems from confused notions about Dharma and the politics of the past half-century. If we wish to change this course, we must clearly declare the character of our state. Many slogans have been raised – secular state, welfare state, socialist state – but those being inherently contradictory to the Indian tradition and ethos, they failed to create anything meaningful. There is no consensus today on what Dharma rajya should look like. Even though Dharma is the eternal truth, its manifestations have always been subject to differing opinions. The same can be expected for Dharma rajya.

But this is also true for socialism and other ideologies – there are as many forms of socialism as there are socialists. However, all these ideologies are fundamentally foreign, and accepting them turns our gaze outward. In contrast, Dharma rajya is an essentially Indian conception, and even if there is disagreement, we are encouraged to look within.

17

'The Answer to World's Problems Is Not Socialism, but Hindutva'

DEENDAYAL UPADHYAYA

In this address, Deendayal Upadhyaya examines Western political concepts such as socialism and democracy from the perspective of Hindutva.[1]

Although socialist thought and socialist parties have existed in India since the time European ideas began influencing the educated class, socialism, as a theory, never succeeded in securing a significant place in the political or social life of our country. However, after the Avadi[2] session of the Indian National Congress – where it officially declared the formation of a socialist society in India as the ultimate goal – there is a change in the situation. As far as the general public is concerned, socialism remains an enigma. The Congress' resolution failed to enthuse the masses about socialism. But the policies of the government began to gradually tilt towards socialism causing anxiety to those involved in politics and policy making.

Today, socialism is enjoying disproportionately high importance than the actual number of people who believe in it. Moreover, prime minister's popularity and stature led to a feeling as though socialism had become the nation's favourite way of life. Calling oneself a socialist has become fashionable these days. Fair weather political parties are competing with each other to prove their socialist credentials. Even the Hindu Mahasabha[3] has started talking about 'Hindu socialism'. Some Vedic thinkers started digging into the ancient texts to discover something that they can claim as Vedic socialism.

In India, the Congress was not the first party to raise the slogan of socialism. Even before the Congress adopted Avadi resolution on socialism, there were socialist parties active here – and they still exist today. Dissatisfied individuals from those parties have formed various factions, each one of which would claim to be the true and authentic socialists. This situation is leading to further confusion about socialism.

In Europe, different forms of socialism have always existed. Roosevelt, Hitler, Mussolini and Stalin – all called themselves socialists. There are also many, who, though not involved directly in politics, formulated their own theories of socialism. We can find followers of all these various types of socialist ideologies in our country. Efforts were also made by some of them to create an Indian version of this European concept that fits our social and cultural life.

Jayaprakash Narayan[4] still considers himself a socialist. Although M.N. Roy,[5] in the final phase of his life, completely renounced socialism, he was still known as a radical socialist until his demise. Along the way, ideologues and politicians have created such diverse interpretations of socialism that people are left confused, unable to understand where they themselves stand.

Once, it was sarcastically remarked that socialism is not a philosophy of life but merely an awkward habit. If we analyze the thoughts of socialists, this statement might appear quite accurate. Universal desire of all socialists is to raise the standard of living of the common man. They stand in opposition to those whom they consider lazy or those, in their view, who obstruct the rightful earnings of hardworking labourers.

We might be surprised to learn that Swami Vivekananda had also called himself a socialist, and to support his belief, he offered arguments quite similar to those of modern socialists. In one of his speeches, he said, 'I too am a socialist. Not because socialism is a complete philosophy, but because I believe that even a single morsel is better than starving. Redistributing happiness and sorrow is indeed better than a state where only a select few experience all the joy or all the suffering. In this painful world, everyone should have a chance to see better days.'

This deep sympathy for the hungry, and the desire to give them a place of dignity and equality in society, continues to inspire every true socialist even today.

Karl Marx's[6] good intentions are commendable. In this world filled with pain, suffering, inequality, injustice, sorrow, torment, oppression, slavery, exploitation, hunger and deprivation, anyone who has a humane conscience cannot help but adopt a socialist attitude. However, socialism is not limited to just that. It is true that one wants to end this painful situation. This person has analyzed the situation, diagnosed the problem and devised a remedy for it. Here comes the discipleship of Marx.

Marx developed contemporary socialist ideas and presented a broad ideological framework that had the potential to attract future generations. Even socialists who disagreed with Marx could not reject his irrefutable arguments. He proposed a practical plan, using which the Bolsheviks had successfully seized power in Russia to make that dream a reality. However, from the Bolshevik Revolution to the present, the history of Russia, despite some successes here and there, has been a testament to the limitations of this method.

The first attack of socialism was on democracy. With the exception of those who lived behind iron curtains, socialist thinkers around the world were alarmed by this. They had faith in democracy. In fact, it was because of democratic ideals that they had developed sympathy for the common people and talked about ensuring equality for them. Democracy had granted political equality to all. However, scientific discoveries and mechanized production methods had resulted in huge economic disparities. In that new political environment, equality lost its significance. Marx raised the slogan of a classless society. For the interim period, he spoke of the dictatorship of proletariat. There was plenty of room for suspicion in this. People were asked to give up what they had already achieved (political equality) for the sake of something uncertain. They had no idea that socialism would take away even what they had. They were already destitute. Socialism should have given them something, not taken away what little they had. But before giving anything, socialism took away their personal freedom and political equality.

On 28 April 1919, Prince Kropotkin[7] wrote a letter to the workers of Western Europe,

> I owe it to you to say frankly that according to my view, this effort to build a Communist Republic on the basis of a strongly centralized state, Communism under the iron law of party dictatorship, is bound to end in a failure. We are learning to know from the Russian experiment how not to introduce Communism . . . As long as the country is governed by a party dictatorship, the workers and peasants' councils evidently lose their entire significance . . . It (USSR) develops a bureaucracy so formidable that French bureaucracy, which requires the help of forty officials to sell a tree, broken down by a storm on the national highway, is a mere bagatelle in comparison.

Efforts of the European socialists gave rise to a new philosophy now called democratic socialism. They opposed the communists and asserted that socialism should emerge in a democratic manner. They wanted to worship both socialism and democracy together. But the fundamental question is whether socialism and democracy can coexist. Idealists are hopeful about it while the progressives are not. Socialism asserts that all sources of production should be under the control of the state. Since socialists believe that the political, intellectual and social life of a society is shaped by its sources of production, it is essential for the socialist system that the state has complete dominance in economic, political and other spheres. This creates a situation where it will not be possible to effectively exercise democratic rights against those in power. The first victim of the socialist bullet will undoubtedly be a democrat. Socialism and democracy cannot coexist. It is impossible for the lion and the goat to drink water from the same pond.

The confused state prevailing in the socialist camp today is largely due to this new philosophy. No thinker has yet succeeded in presenting a flawless and comprehensive picture where the coexistence of these two elements would be possible. Moreover, when we consider various forms and limitations of democracy, alongside the different social and cultural structures of different countries and varying levels of economic development, this confusion compounds. Due to this complex entanglement, it is near impossible to resolve the confusion.

Non-socialist countries have also contributed to increasing this confusion among the socialists. In recent years, their liberal policies and new economic thinking have left the socialists in a state of bewilderment. Today, an average farmer and worker in America or England, who, according to the communist definition, would be called the proletariat, are not in the oppressed state that existed a century ago. Welfare state ideas are being accepted in the capitalist systems also. Marx's predictions about both capitalist and socialist countries have proven false. The capitalist nations have developed their systems well, while the socialist countries remain stuck at the very point where they began their journey. Even if they took a few steps forward, it was not in the right direction. Capitalist countries, due to their democratic systems, have the flexibility to correct their mistakes and accept new ideas, whereas the socialists lack this kind of flexibility in their approach to problems. Their ideology does not inspire new thinking. Like followers of a religion based on messianism and immutable superstitions, rigid socialists prefer to stay away from new ideas. That is why, in the communist world, such liberal thinkers are often met with insults. Thoughtful humans cannot remain thoughtless. If there is no system to guide their thinking in a proper direction, the inevitable result will be confusion in all directions.

The debate on socialism that has arisen in India today is mainly focused on the merits or futility of expanding state-run industries. Advocates of private industry and socialist thinkers stand opposed to each other. However, an interesting fact is that both are eager to leave adequate and fair space for each other. In an underdeveloped economy, the government must take control of certain industries that might have been left to private entrepreneurs in ordinary circumstances. But, in a planned economy, private industrialists cannot be given the same level of freedom that their counterparts in the West have been enjoying for centuries. In fact, if this competition is kept under control, it can help in establishing proper balance between the two.

The main issue is not whether we accept socialism or the principles of free industry. Socialism and democracy cannot be compared, but they are not our only options either. They are merely means, not ends. So, what is the end? We must first define the destination and then determine the path. All thoughtful humans have considered human welfare as the end goal. In the attempt to make humans happy and prosperous, both socialism and democracy acquired a grotesque form. They stripped away all the unique qualities of humanity. René Fülöp-Miller[8] discusses this in his pamphlet *Dehumanization in Modern Society*. He writes, 'Democracy, although it gave us the right to vote, trial by jury, a free press, religious freedom, the freedom to choose their jobs and the freedom to speak their mind, (it) also gave us the "economic man".'

This concept gave birth to capitalism, where the emphasis was placed on increasing production capacity. But the ability to lead a purposeful life was completely neglected. On the other hand, socialism and communism raised the slogan of collective security and protection of the working-class interests, but in doing so, they also gave birth to the 'war-hungry man'. This war-loving man is a product of the socialist state, and he has neither the freedom to think nor the freedom to make decisions for himself. Under this system, the value of human life is considered no more than that of a helpless animal.

Both socialism and democracy have focused only on the physical aspect of human beings and their needs, and both have a great reverence for modern science and technological advancement. Both fall prey to modern inventions. The result is that the determination of means of production is no longer based on human welfare and needs, but rather on machines. In a centralized system of production, whether it is controlled by individuals or the state, the free personality of the human being disappears. He is reduced to nothing more than a part of a machine. If we were to protect humanity, we must free the individuals from the slavery of machines. Today, the individual does not rule over the machine, the machine rules over the individual.

Reason behind this love for machines is the desire to fulfil the ever-increasing material needs of humans. But we must not forget that material prosperity alone cannot make humans happy. The problems faced by materially prosperous nations are also before us today. We must consider all aspects of human life and treat production, distribution and consumption as one unified entity. We must create a system where, while engaging in production and consumption, a person also leads a meaningful life. A person is not just a sum of physical needs; he has spiritual needs as well. Any way of life that neglects this spiritual aspect of human life can never be complete. We must remember that the idea of progress in both material and spiritual terms is not a mere fantasy; it is a responsibility to fulfil the needs of society while preserving human dignity. Both socialism and democracy have accepted one-sided paths, and instead of developing the personality of man by harmonizing these two different tendencies, they have created a confusing situation and prepared a battlefield for different powers.

The Hindu way of life, based on the four pursuits of Dharma, Artha, Kama and Moksha, is the only way to free us from this crisis. The answer to world's problems is not socialism, but Hindutva. This is the only philosophy that does not divide life into fragments but considers it as a whole. While reflecting on the Hindu ideals of life, we must not associate them with lifeless rituals prevalent in Hindu society. It would also be a grave mistake to think that Hindutva is opposed to scientific progress. Science and machines should be used in a manner that aligns with our social and cultural life principles.

Following the ideas of Mahatma Gandhi, thinkers like Vinoba, Jayaprakash Narayan and Rajagopalachari presented the concept of trusteeship. This is in line with the Hindu way of life. It is an idea that can be equally useful for both socialist and non-socialist societies. If we blindly follow the Western mechanistic system, neither the idea of *sarvodaya* (welfare of all) nor socialism will be able to preserve our culture or solve the problems before us. We will have to face this mechanization on all fronts – political, economic, social and ideological. Our goal should be to establish a dharmic state with democracy, social equality and economic decentralization. The combined result of these principles will provide us with a philosophy of life that will offer security amidst today's turmoil. You may call this by any name – Hindutva, humanism or any new ideology – but this will be the only path that is in harmony with the soul of India and can inspire new enthusiasm among the people. Other paths and ideologies do not align with the progressive nature of this country's life; they will lead us towards distortion and destruction rather than development. It is possible that this path can also serve as a guiding light for the entire world that is at a crossroads today.

18

'Some People Claim That a Hindu Nation Is Being Established Today, but We Say That There Is No Need to Establish What Already Exists'

DATTOPANT THENGDI

Dattopant Thengdi was a senior pracharak[1] of the RSS who served in various capacities in the organization since 1940s until his demise in 2004. He was a senior leader of the organization and the founder and motivator behind the formation of three important organizations of the RSS family – Bharatiya Mazdoor Sangh (BMS), Bharatiya Kisan Sangh (BKS) and the Swadeshi Jagaran Manch (SJM). He was also an author and a prominent thought leader, contributing many important original ideas for various labour and the farmers' movements he spearheaded. He wrote and spoke extensively and helped spread the RSS school of thought far and wide.

In this address sometime in 1990s, Thengdi examines the concept of secularism and its applicability in the Bharatiya context.

I am a Hindu. Reading newspapers and listening to the speeches of our political leaders, one comes to the conclusion these days that perhaps if there is anyone in this world who is most communal, it is the Hindu. Hindus are considered extremely narrow-minded and conservative. Some politicians have become so progressive that they say, 'Call me a donkey if you wish, but do not call me a Hindu.' Being a Hindu myself, I consider it quite unfortunate.

I visited Karnataka some time ago where I met a social worker named Lakshmi Narayan Alva. He had dedicated himself to uplifting the Bunt community, a small and underprivileged group. Since this community was largely uneducated and backward, he had worked tirelessly to improve their condition. During that time, newspapers and politicians widely praised him for his efforts in uplifting a marginalized community. He was even invited to an international conference, where he was honoured and referred to as an 'internationally renowned social worker'.

Until then, he was working for the upliftment of the Bunt community only. However, later he realized that while helping one community is commendable, the broader Hindu society also needed support. With that motivation, he joined the Vishwa Hindu Parishad (VHP)[2] and accepted an official position within the organization. But the moment he became a VHP office-bearer, politicians began labelling him as narrow-minded and communal. The same man who was celebrated as an international humanitarian leader until then for working towards the upliftment of one small community was suddenly branded as narrow-minded when he chose to work for the upliftment of the larger Hindu society. That is the tragic situation that the Hindu community faces.

These days, terms like anti-communalism and secularism are being widely used. Even in the labour sector, when the Ram Janmabhoomi[3] movement started gaining momentum, leaders like E.M.S. Namboodiripad[4] called upon the communist trade unions to organize anti-communalism rallies. The Samyukta Morcha[5] includes communists, socialists and others. They informed us about their plan to hold an anti-communalism conference. We responded through a letter, appreciating their initiative and stating that since eliminating communalism is the need of the hour for the entire nation, we would fully support the conference. However, we made one request: 'Please provide us with your definition of communalism.' We thought that it would be helpful to understand what exactly they meant by it. Instead of providing a definition, they sent us a pamphlet – full of hyperbole, but nowhere any definition. We wrote to them again, pointing out that while their pamphlet was elaborate, it failed to provide the definition that we had sought. If they provided a definition, it would help us assess whether the organizations they branded as communalist – such as the RSS, VHP and BJP (Bharatiya Janata Party) – were indeed communal, and if so, how do they fare in comparison to organizations like the Communist Party of India (CPI) and Communist Party of India (Marxist) (CPI-M). But they refused to respond in writing, arguing that they would only answer verbally, but do not wish to commit anything in writing. Eventually, due to a firm stand taken by us, their entire effort failed to gain traction in the labour sector. Their grand plan of mobilizing an anti-communalist wave across the country through the labour sector ultimately led to nothing.

Nowadays, this topic is on many people's minds because of the frequent occurrence of communal riots in various parts of the country. There were riots in Ahmedabad, Hyderabad and in several places across Uttar Pradesh and Bihar. Every ordinary Hindu thinks that riots are not good. The very nature of a Hindu is that they abhor violence. A Hindu never acts when it comes to violence; they only react.

There is widespread discussion over terms like anti-communalism and secularism, especially in our media. However, the problem is that those who discuss these issues do not go to the root of the problem. There is a saying that correct diagnosis is half the cure. If a disease is diagnosed correctly, half the battle is won because once the diagnosis is clear, planning the treatment becomes easy. But if the disease is in one place and you are treating something else – if someone has typhoid but you are giving him medicine for influenza or malaria – he will not get cured.

It is not that our political leaders lack intelligence and are therefore unable to diagnose the issue. The problem is that they do not want to diagnose the real issue. A true diagnosis of this problem would go against their vested interests. That is why they avoid it. The politicians are extraordinary people. If they are not diagnosing the disease and it is spreading, then we, as ordinary, ignorant and uneducated people, should at least try to understand what the real problem is. We are not more intelligent than politicians. But our qualification is that we genuinely want to know what the real problem is.

If we look at it simply, during riots, the emotions of both Hindus and Muslims are inflamed. People attack each other, murders happen, and some are killed in police action too. Those who incite violence sit comfortably in their air-conditioned rooms, while ordinary people take to the streets and get killed. Outwardly, it is the common people who are indulging in riots. But if we examine carefully, we realize that ordinary people are not truly the ones responsible for these riots. Yes, they – both Muslims and Hindus – do get provoked. Is it the fault of those who get provoked? No, they are just common people. They get provoked because someone else is provoking them. Who are these people inciting violence? Why do they instigate riots? What vested interests do they have? Politicians never try to analyze these questions because if they attempt to control the instigators, they risk losing the next election. Real root of the problem lies here.

The environment for creation of Pakistan was shaped by the Muslim League[6] and Jinnah[7], and the ordinary Muslims got swayed by it. In reality, ordinary Muslims and Hindus, wherever they lived, did not have many differences between them until a Manthara[8] or a Shakuni Mama[9] arrived. When such figures occupied important political positions, divisions were created. Before the Partition of India, ordinary Hindus and Muslims lived together in villages, cities and slums. They did not just co-habit but actively participated in each other's lives. Muslims joined Hindu festivals, and Hindus helped in Muslim celebrations. Everything was going smoothly.

But if Hindus and Muslims remain united, what would happen to the leaders and their politics? So, people were incited, the atmosphere for Pakistan was created, and eventually, Pakistan was formed. It was in the Sindh[10] Assembly that the first resolution for Pakistan's creation was passed. It was introduced by G.M. Syed[11]. G.M. Syed is still alive today. He is around 88 or 89 years old and lives in a village in Sindh. He had even visited India once. He now says, 'I made a huge mistake by supporting Pakistan. I thank God for giving me a long life so I could realize my mistake.' When Dhaka declared war against Islamabad, he became fully convinced that a nation cannot be built on the basis of religion. Today, even within Pakistan, Baluchistan wants to secede,

Pashtun regions want their own state and Sindh wants independence. While today he admits his mistake and accepts that a nation cannot be formed based on a religion, back then, when Jinnah and the Muslim League created such a propaganda wave, people like him too got carried away and supported Pakistan.

Not just divisions between Hindus and Muslims, conflicts are also stirred up between different caste groups like backward and forward castes. Becoming a prime minister or a chief minister wholly depends today on fueling such divisions. What happens to the country does not matter, as long as the leaders can secure power. Until the time that this mindset dominates our leadership, it is natural for people to forget their shared national identity and continue to quarrel.

The Muslims of India did not come from Arabia. They are not the descendants of Babur. They are from among us; they are of this land. They are also the descendants of Shri Ram. Yet, efforts are made to incite them, to make them forget their roots and identity.

In Indonesia, a country with 95 per cent Muslim population, plays based on the stories of Ramayana and Mahabharata are still narrated and remain popular. There, a student may go to the mosque in the morning for prayers, but before entering the examination hall, bows before Lord Ganesha. Once, at an international conference, the foreign minister of Pakistan asked his Indonesian counterpart, 'How is it that, being a Muslim, you still remember Ram, Krishna, the Ramayana and the Mahabharata?' The Indonesian minister replied, 'Sir, we have changed our religion, but not our forefathers.'

If the foreign minister of Indonesia can say this, then why can't the Muslims of India? They share the same bloodline and ancestry as their Hindu brethren. But the reason is that politicians, driven by greed for power, have deliberately made efforts to erase this identity. History shows that if such bonds are broken, even those of the same lineage and blood can end up fighting each other.

Take the example of Rustam and Sohrab,[12] beautifully recounted in a poem by Matthew Arnold. Rustam was Sohrab's father. When Sohrab's mother was pregnant, she got separated from her husband. Rustam went away to another kingdom while Sohrab grew up under different rulers.

As time passed, Sohrab became a great warrior. When he came of age, a war broke out between the two kingdoms. In those days in Iran, before a large-scale battle, the best warriors from each side would indulge in a solo combat. Rustam was chosen from one side, and Sohrab from the other. Neither knew who the other was, even though they were father and son. Matthew Arnold describes their battle in great detail. But in the end, Rustam struck a powerful blow to Sohrab's head, and Sohrab fell.

Rustam was pleased with his victory. Despite being opponents, true warriors appreciate each other's bravery. Rustam was impressed by Sohrab's bravery and rushed to him as soon as he fell down. He took Sohrab's head into his lap. Blood was flowing from Sohrab's wounds, and he was losing consciousness. As he slowly opened his eyes, he looked up and said, 'If only my father Rustam were here, he would have avenged my death.' Rustam was shocked and asked, 'Who are you?' 'I am Sohrab, son of Rustam,' replied the dying warrior. Rustam was devastated – he had unknowingly killed his own son. But it was too late. Sohrab took his last breath. A father had killed his own son because they did not recognize each other.

This story doesn't just exist in a Persian legend. We see similar instances in our own history. Lav and Kush,[13] the sons of Ram[14], were ready to fight against their own father's army and stop his victorious horse because they did not know he was their father. In the Mahabharata, Karna[15] was actually the eldest of the five Pandavas[16]. But because he did not know his true identity, he fought against them. And when his mother finally revealed the truth, it was too late – he had already crossed the point of no return. He told his mother, 'Now, whatever happens will be decided on the battlefield.'

So, if a father can unknowingly kill his son like Rustam did, if the sons of Ram can fight against their own father, if the eldest Pandava can take up arms against his own brothers, then is it really surprising that Hindus and Muslims sometimes fight against each other? The real solution to this conflict is to restore the sense of identity – to recognize that we are one blood, one family and one nation. Religions may differ, and that is perfectly fine. In our country, it has always been accepted that each person can worship God in his own way. Hinduism itself is not a single, rigid religion. There is no one prophet or one book or one form of worship or one ultimate goal. Some are Shaivites[17], some are Vaishnavites[18], some worship Shakti[19], some are theists and some are atheists – and yet, all are considered Hindus.

This is a confederation, not a religion. And the freedom to worship has existed here since time immemorial. Even those who outrightly criticized the Vedas had the freedom to propagate their beliefs. Brihaspati[20], the guru of the gods, was the first material philosopher in our tradition. His doctrine stated: '*Asato sat ajayata*,' meaning 'Existence emerges from non-existence.' This is the first principle of materialist philosophy, which even Western scholars now acknowledge. Thousands of years before the emergence of Democritus[21] in the West, Brihaspati had already developed a materialist doctrine in India. That tradition continued until Charvaka.

In our civilization, there is complete freedom of thought, freedom of expression and freedom of worship. Moreover, we have always believed that the same ultimate reality is referred to by different names – '*Ekam sat vipra bahudha vadanti.*' You may call it Allah, Father in Heaven, Vishnu, Shiva, or if you are more materialistic, you may call it Matter. But there is one ultimate reality, which is called by different names. This has been the fundamental understanding in our tradition.

The unique feature of Hinduism is that it accepts all paths. Unlike other belief systems, it does not say that you are good only if you follow a particular path and bad if you do not. In English, there are two approaches: 'either–or' and 'as well as'. The 'either–or' mindset states that if you follow our path, you are righteous, but if you follow a different path, you are wrong. This is a non-Hindu perspective. The Hindu approach is 'as well as' – this is valid, and so is that as well.

For example, if someone says that salvation is possible *only* through Prophet Muhammad, that is a non-Hindu perspective. But if someone says that salvation is possible *also* through Prophet Muhammad, that is a Hindu perspective. If someone says that salvation is possible *only* through Christ, that is a non-Hindu view. But if someone says that salvation is possible *also* through Christ, that is a Hindu view.

Our ancestors foresaw the emergence of different beliefs – Allah, Yahweh, Father in Heaven, and even 'Matter' as a deity. Anticipating this, Lord Krishna proclaimed in Bhagavada Gita[22]: *Ye'py anya-devata bhakta yajante shraddhayanvitah/Te'pi mam eva Kaunteya yajanty avidhi-purvakam*' (Even those who worship other deities are ultimately worshipping Me, only their rituals are different).

Hence, there is no need for conflicts over religion. Since we share the same blood and lineage, we are one as a society and a nation. This is our true identity. Political leaders have tried to erase this identity leading to confusion. We must recognize this truth.

If we talk about our true identity, this has always been a *Hindu Rashtra* (Hindu Nation) since ancient times. Some people claim that a Hindu Rashtra is being newly established today, but we say that there is no need to establish what already exists. Hindu Rashtra is an eternal truth; it does not require a new foundation. We may have forgotten about it, but history has always referred to this land as a Hindu Rashtra.

In 1857, when Karl Marx[23] sent dispatches to newspapers in New York, he used the word 'Hindu' in both its meanings – Hindu as a religion and Hindu as a nation. Even Sir Syed Ahmad Khan, who was the first to attempt to awaken the Muslim community during British rule, used the term Hindu Rashtra. Although he later altered his policies, he initially accepted that this land was a Hindu Nation.

Today, efforts are being made to erase this identity, and various terms like communalism, secularism and nationalism are being thrown around. But what do those terms truly mean?

The term 'secularism' has been used in many different senses. Pandit Jawaharlal Nehru[24] used this word while drafting the Constitution in a specific sense. This was Nehruvian thinking. The way Nehru used it is not found anywhere else in the world. Nehru's idea was absolutely right – that state, politics and religious affairs should remain separate. Political power should not be in the hands of religious leaders, nor should religious issues be in the control of political power. This was the sense in which Nehru used the term, and it was absolutely appropriate.

However, there was no need to promote this idea so aggressively in India because the Indian state has always been secular. Except for one period – during the reign of Ashoka – the Indian state has always been secular throughout history. If we exclude Ashoka's time, there has never been a theocratic state in India. Hence the term 'secularism' is not really applicable in Indian situation. But Nehru carried the hangover of Partition, which is why he promoted it so much.

Separation between religious authority and state authority is an entirely Western concept. In the early days of Greek and Roman civilizations in Europe, the same authority controlled both religion and politics. When Christianity emerged, it initially maintained this separation, and early Christianity was also secular in this sense. Later, secularism evolved in a different context. In the Gospel of Saint Mark, it is clearly mentioned that Jesus was asked a question to corner him: 'You speak of God, but do you acknowledge the emperor (Caesar), or do you acknowledge God? To whom will you pay tribute?' Jesus replied, as recorded in the Gospel of Saint Mark, 'Give to God what is God's and to Caesar what is Caesar's.' In other words, there is no conflict between the two. Christianity retained this secular outlook until approximately 346 AD. That is why, in the famous Edict of Milan in 312 AD, it was clearly stated that everyone should be free to follow their religious beliefs without any interference.

It was only in 346 AD that this question arose on a large scale. When Constantine accepted Christianity and declared it as the state religion, persecution began against non-Christians, in the same way as the Roman emperors had persecuted Christians earlier. This gave rise to the question: should political and religious authority be the same? This debate began at that time, and all the discussions that followed led to the introduction of terms like 'secular'. That was in the European context. Their historical background necessitated that debate. But in India, such a conflict never arose.

The direct use of the term 'secular' occurred in 1851. A major thinker of that time was Holyoake[25], and his contemporary was another thinker named Bradlaugh[26]. Holyoake coined the term 'secularism' in the sense that political authority and religion should remain separate. However, there was a difference of opinion between him and Bradlaugh. To clarify his stance, Holyoake used the term 'secularism'. Holyoake believed that religion had its place, and political authority and governance had their own place. They were mutually exclusive but not necessarily hostile. In other words, politics and religion are separate from each other, but it is not necessary that they must be opposed to one another.

His contemporary, Bradlaugh, had a different view. He argued that merely stating that religion and politics are separate is not enough. If one tolerates religion and allows its coexistence, then religious influence will inevitably enter the public sphere, and people will start believing in God. Once God's existence is accepted, God will not remain limited only to religious affairs, but will claim authority over material and political matters as well. God will assert himself as the supreme authority, just as the Pope exercised influence over kings. Therefore, if one truly desires a political system where governance and state authority are free from religious influence, then one must completely deny the existence of God. According to Bradlaugh, atheism and secularism were interconnected.

This concept was widely discussed in Europe in the last century. This was also because scientific advancements and discoveries were dismantling many of the claims made in the Bible. As a result, there was an intense conflict between science and religion, as well as a debate over the existence of God versus materialism. Due to all this, the term 'secularism' acquired enormous significance.

Later, Christianity made peace with science. Today, they even have publications like *Christian Science Monitor*. Eventually, this entire issue faded away, and the conflict between science and religion, as well as between religion and political authority, was resolved. By the early twentieth century, Europe reached a point where the term 'secularism' lost its significance.

However, in India, our political leaders have brought it into circulation incorrectly, either due to a lack of understanding or deliberately ignoring its actual meaning. Given today's circumstances, its necessity should be questioned – do we really need it in India? The term itself is good, and our state has always been secular, but we must examine why these conflicts arise.

I recall an event some seven years ago in Lucknow. There was a hall meeting on minority education institutions, chaired by Justice Murtaza

Hussain[27], with only two speakers – him and me. I delivered my speech first, and then he spoke. Justice Hussain, looking at me, remarked that people often accuse Muslims of spreading communalism. He acknowledged the concern but then asked – who is actually responsible for it? He argued that Muslims were not to blame and emphasized that there was never any fundamental issue between ordinary Hindus and Muslims.

Then, he raised the question as to why communalism still persists. He pointed out that in 1947, when we secured Independence, it was expected that our leaders would work towards strengthening the nation, just as the leaders of Japan and Israel did by awakening a sense of nationalism among their people. However, instead of focusing on national unity, their primary concern became securing political power. They realized that Muslim vote bank was crucial for winning elections. Various political parties began attempting to isolate Muslims from the rest of society. They instilled a sense of fear and division within the community, ensuring that Muslims remained separate. Then, each leader approached them with different promises.

When Hindu political leaders, in their pursuit of becoming prime ministers, came to bargain with the Muslim community, should we expect them to act like monks and reject their offers? If politicians are willing to offer so much, why would Muslims refuse? They are not naïve. Thus, he concluded that the real problem did not lie with ordinary Hindus or Muslims. The real issue lied with power-hungry politicians who desperately sought votes and focused on Muslim vote banks. These Hindu political leaders deliberately keep Muslims separate from Hindus. And when competition arises among them, Muslims naturally try to take advantage of it.

He stated that if this problem is to be fixed, the first step should be to correct Hindu political leaders. The day they change their approach, both Muslims and the rest of society would also change. Root cause of the problem is these political leaders; they are greedy for power and dependent on vote banks. I am paraphrasing his views in my own words, but essentially, he stated that Hindu political leaders are the primary cause of division. If they are corrected, Muslims too will understand the reality.

If you look at history briefly, you will realize that modern Indian history effectively begins from 1857. In the 1857 war of Independence[28], Hindus and Muslims fought unitedly – Nana Saheb Peshwa[29], Tatya Tope[30], Rani Lakshmibai[31] and Bahadur Shah Zafar[32] stood together. No politician went to preach about Hindu–Muslim unity then; it occurred naturally. The sentiment always existed.

But history has been misrepresented to current generations. For example, Babur[33] has been portrayed as the 'saviour of Islam'. It is said that he came to Hindustan to protect Islam. Our politicians have propagated this idea so much that even Muslims today believe that Babur was their protector. And when Hindus speak against him, they feel hurt. But Babur did not come to protect Islam. If Islam had been in danger at that time, that is if the Hindu rulers of Delhi followed an anti-Muslim policy, only then could Babur's arrival be seen as an effort to save Islam. But at that time, Delhi was not under Hindu rule; it was ruled by a Muslim ruler named Ibrahim Lodi.[34] Babur's battle to enter Hindustan was not against any Hindu king but against Ibrahim Lodi. That conflict was not for Islam; it was for territorial aggrandizement – to bring more land under his control and plunder wealth from Hindustan.

That is why Babur fought not only against Ibrahim Lodi but also against Rana Sanga and Sher Shah Suri. It was essentially a conflict between Mughal invaders and Afghan rulers. Islam is not monolithic; it consists of different tribes and nations – Afghans, Turks, Mughals and others had their own rivalries. Hence, calling Babur the 'saviour of Islam' is incorrect.

What was the motivation behind Hindu–Muslim unity during the war of Independence in 1857? It was nationalism. What nation was that? When Bahadur Shah Zafar stood against the British, what kind of national unity was he upholding? Towards the end of the rebellion, when it became clear that the British were winning, one of his companions told him, 'There is no strength left in our weapons; now, seek pardon for your life, for, the sword of Hindustan has lost its edge.' But Bahadur Shah Zafar replied, 'As long as there is faith in our warriors, the sword of Hindustan will strike even in London.'

He did not say Pakistan or any other country – he said Hindustan. Later, the British, like all imperialists, attempted to divide and rule. They also aimed at creating an inferiority complex among the ruled, making them feel weak and divided. Our so-called progressive thinkers fail to understand that this was a part of the imperialist strategy.

To give an example, I once had a discussion with a communist leader about the Ram Janmabhoomi issue. He argued that it was a religious matter. I told him that it was not a religious question but a matter of national symbolism. Ram is a national symbol, not just a religious figure. I told him, 'Even your forefathers are Ramji, not Karl Marx.' The attack by Babur was not to protect Islam but to assert dominance over the local people. That, I told him, was a matter of national humiliation.

I gave him another example from Russia. I asked him if he had been to Russia. He said yes. I asked if he had been to Petrograd (Leningrad), where the Winter Palace of the Tsar still stands. He said yes. When we had visited that place as part of a parliamentary delegation, we had noticed that while the old architecture remained intact, certain old statues were replaced by new ones. We asked about those missing statues, and we were told that they were statues of gods – Jupiter, Venus and other Greek deities. One of our delegation members asked, 'But you are Communists; you don't believe in gods. Why did you restore these statues?'

The Russians replied, 'We do not believe in gods, but that is not the issue. These statues were here since the time of the Tsars. We did not install them, but when Hitler's army invaded Petrograd, they destroyed these statues to humiliate us, to hurt our national pride. Hitler's army knew that these statues would not fight against them, but they still destroyed them as a symbolic act of national insult. That is why, when we won the war in 1945, we decided to restore them – not because of religion, but to reclaim our national honour.'

I said that the same applies to the Ram Janmabhoomi issue. He was a communist, but a gentleman, so he did not argue further.

Until 1920, as long as Tilak's[35] era continued within the Congress, the common Muslim population and their leaders remained nationalist. Even Jinnah was initially a staunch nationalist. He stood shoulder to shoulder with Tilak, Annie Besant[36] and Lala Lajpat Rai[37] in the freedom struggle.

Shaukat Ali[38] and Mohammad Ali[39] were also nationalists. In 1919, when the Congress session was held in Amritsar and they were released from Chhindwara jail, they did not stop anywhere but directly reached the Congress session in Amritsar. They touched Tilak's feet and delivered speeches in support of the Congress resolution.

All these leaders were nationalists initially. However, after 1920, Congress' policies changed. Tilak's approach was that while the government might try to create divisions, when it came to strategic negotiations and discussions, only the nationalist Muslim leaders should be engaged at the negotiation table. It was from this perspective that Tilak recognized Jinnah and others. After 1920, Congress adopted a different stance. It declared that 'every Muslim is a bully, and every Hindu is a coward'. Based on this notion, policies were altered. Those who were aligned with the national movement and part of Congress were taken for granted and ignored. Instead, attention was given to those who opposed the nation, fell for British propaganda and sided with fundamentalists.

This shift became evident when Congress supported the Khilafat movement. Jinnah warned that they were making a mistake by encouraging separatist tendencies. However, Congress ignored nationalist Muslims while surrendering to those who criticized it. This policy led to a situation where even Congress-aligned nationalists began feeling sidelined. They felt that if they opposed Congress and criticized it, they would receive attention, whereas if they remained loyal, they will be taken for granted. As a result, Muslim communalism grew, eventually leading to the creation of Pakistan.

After Partition and attainment of *Swarajya* (self-rule), we should have been cautious. But unfortunately, the policies of Jawaharlal Nehru were different from those of Sardar Patel. He acted like an ostrich burying its head in the sand. We achieved Swarajya on 15 August 1947. At that time, we formed the Constituent Assembly. The Minorities Committee of the Constituent Assembly was chaired by Sardar Patel. A meeting of this committee was held on 27 August, just 12 days after Independence. In that meeting, two Muslim members from the Madras Province proposed a resolution demanding separate electorates for Muslims. In response, Sardar Patel said, 'You asked for Pakistan on the basis of religion, and you got it. It would be wrong to raise the Hindu–Muslim question in what remains of India, because you have already secured a separate nation on this very basis.' He further firmly told them, 'Those who make such demands will have no place here. Go to Pakistan!' This was his speech as the Chairman of the Minorities Committee on 28 August.

Had this firm stance been consistently maintained and had Sardar Patel[40] not passed away so soon, the chaotic situation we see today would not have arisen. Unfortunately, the country lost a realist like Patel, and the leadership fell into the hands of Jawaharlal – an eternal dreamer, and a romantic. He propagated '*Hindi–Chini Bhai Bhai* (Indians and Chinese are brothers)'.[41] believing in India–China brotherhood. But when China attacked India, he was completely paralyzed, unable to act. The fate of the nation was placed in the hands of such a romantic idealist.

The same thing happened with Article 370.[42] When Article 370 was introduced, Dr Babasaheb Ambedkar[43], who drafted the Constitution, opposed it. Sheikh Abdullah[44] was sent to convince him, but Ambedkar refused to budge. Eventually, Jawaharlal Nehru used his personal influence to get it introduced. This shows how romantic and unrealistic his approach had been. Ambedkar had also pointed out another issue early on. When the question arose about the division of river waters, such as the Indus[45] and other rivers, a committee was appointed, and Ambedkar was given the responsibility to study the matter. Ambedkar's greatest strength was his intellectual and practical approach. He explained that the sources of these rivers were not within India's control. If India maintained a strict stance from the beginning, Pakistan would have to come to India for its water supply. But if India showed leniency, Pakistan would not recognize India's authority in the future, which would cause problems for India.

During the meeting, discussions took place and Nehru remained silent, but a decision had to be taken. Ambedkar later revealed something shocking. As soon as the committee meeting ended, officials from Pakistan entered the room. Ambedkar's own words were: 'Pakistani troops in the cabinet room.' He was stunned to realize that while Nehru had himself formed the committee, he kept both the committee and the cabinet in the dark and directly informed Pakistan that an agreement could be reached. Ambedkar was deeply saddened by all this and realized that such flawed policies would ultimately lead to serious consequences. As it is said '*Payah panam bhujanganam kevalam vishavardhanam.*' (If you feed milk to a snake, it will only increase its venom.)

The root cause of growing separatist tendencies lies in the unrealistic policies adopted by Jawaharlal Nehru. Patel had clarity about such issues in his mind. He was not anti-Muslim, as he was portrayed to be. He considered the entire nation as one single unit. Things changed later and we see the consequences in the form of growing communalism and communal riots in various places. Unfortunately, no politician dares to speak up against the mischief-makers who incite violence. Instead, they go to preach the poor and misguided people – both Hindus and Muslims. I want to call them as professional secularists. They turned secularism into a business, and they engage in it only to secure ministerial or prime ministerial positions.

Today, even newspapers do not have the courage to present the real truth because they are no longer a medium to protect the nation. Their only obsession is to increase circulation. That is why it is essential to understand what secularism really meant and educate people appropriately. Patchwork solutions – like constantly repeating 'We are all one, we share the same bloodline, we are one family, we belong to one nation' – will not work.

'Hindu' is a term denoting this nation, not any religion. People of all religions can coexist here. Ordinary Muslims understand this, but politicians won't. 'A sleeping person can be woken up, but a person pretending to sleep cannot be awakened,' goes an old saying. It applies to our politicians perfectly. They are not asleep – they are pretending to be asleep.

Hence, we must reach out to ordinary citizens. Interestingly, even Jawaharlal Nehru had sometimes held sound views. When the Communal Award[46] was introduced and elections were held based on it, the stand that Congress took could not be accepted even by its own members. The Communal Award was an obstacle to national integration and unity, so Congress could not openly support it. However, since the award had granted separate electorates to Muslims, opposing it outright would have angered majority members of that community. Congress decided to take an ambiguous stance: 'We neither accept nor reject the Communal Award.' People began to question this – how can such a position be justified? Either you welcome it, or you oppose it. If a thief enters your house, you cannot just stand there and say, 'I neither welcome the thief nor oppose him.' What does that even mean?

This stance seemed obviously flawed. Even Nehru realized that. He felt that the reason why all this was happening was because Congress was not reaching out to ordinary Muslims. Instead of understanding the sentiments of ordinary Muslims, Congress was engaging in negotiations with those who claimed to be Muslim leaders. The solution was to bypass these so-called leaders and engage directly with the Muslim masses. This led Nehru to introduce the 'Muslim Mass Contact' program in 1937. However, Congress did not implement it properly. Instead of genuinely reaching out to ordinary Muslims, Congress leaders just made some statements in newspapers, as politicians always do.

Today also, the situation is same. In the Bharatiya Mazdoor Sangh, we have many Muslims and Christians. When we sat with them, they asked us, 'Who made Syed Shahabuddin[47] a Muslim leader?' This surprised us. They assured us that Syed Shahabuddin's leadership did not emerge from within the Muslim community. He had no real connection with the Muslim masses. Instead, he gained prominence by making provocative statements. Hindu politicians granted him legitimacy, and newspapers amplified his visibility. Ordinary Muslims, seeing him recognized by the media and politicians, simply assumed that he was their leader. But in reality, his leadership was not a product of Muslim society – it was constructed by Hindu politicians.

The greatest threat to secularism does not come from Muslims, but from Hindu political leaders themselves. If they are held to account, within 24 hours, all Muslims will be at peace.

19

'Throughout Indian History . . . Hindu Governance Has Consistently Been Secular in Nature'

DATTOPANT THENGDI

In this speech, Dattopant Thengdi calls for an indigenous approach to building a bright future for India. He argues against falling prey to the influence of the foreign capital and gives a clarion call for a second independence, which he terms as 'the foremost national duty of every patriot'.

It is crucial to clearly define the boundaries of the subject matter at the outset; otherwise, the title may create the misconception that this discussion outlines the framework of a future society. However, that is not the case. A framework is only needed when its implementation becomes feasible. Therefore, individuals engaged in rebuilding a social structure never blindly rely on theoretical knowledge. If that were the case, Lenin, during the early stages of Soviet nation-building, would never have stated that his communism aimed solely at the Sovietization and electrification of Russia and that a technical expert was worth 20 communists.

As for outlining the various stages of development and finding practical solutions to specific issues, Marx and Engels refrained from such discussions, considering them speculative. Marx asserted that the working class does not have a preconceived ideal state to implement, nor is it bound by any particular ideology. Instead, it seeks to liberate the new society from the very elements that cause the declining bourgeois society to suffer.

Communists are not concerned with designing hypothetical structures for the organization of a future society. Therefore, presenting a detailed framework for it is out of the question. Considering how food distribution and living arrangements will be managed in the future is nothing more than an exercise in speculation. Thus, the people of a future communist society will not be concerned with the matters we assume they should be.

Once, when someone asked Pandit Deendayal Upadhyay to present a blueprint for the future society, he responded with a counter-question: 'Do you want to bind the hands of future generations in advance?' Similarly, M.N. Roy, based on his concept of New Humanism, also refrained from presenting an ideal social framework. He believed that doing so would merely depict a hypothetical system, which his followers might accept as the ultimate truth.

This also implied that once such a hypothetical system was achieved, there would be no further scope for progress and development. In other words, society would become stagnant and motionless. Therefore, demanding a structural blueprint is not a practical approach but rather a matter of pure imagination. Until the situation arises where its implementation becomes necessary, worrying about it is nothing more than an unwise step.

Another misunderstanding could be the belief that institutional structure is solely an internal matter. While there is no doubt that it is indeed an internal affair, it does not mean that external elements do not influence it. Similarly, although we have declared that the goal of our foreign policy is to ensure world peace and human welfare while protecting our vital national interests, international circumstances, our relations with neighbouring countries and defence requirements are serious factors that significantly impact this structure.

This is why ancient scholars have stated: '*Shastrena rakshite rashṭre, shastra-chinta pravartate*,' meaning, only in a nation protected by arms can the pursuit of knowledge and wisdom flourish.

At present, our nation's sovereignty faces a more serious threat from the expanding influence of foreign capital and its allied Indian monopolistic capital than from political or military aggression. Foreign entities, leveraging their wealth and advanced technology, are actively expanding their economic empire and unfortunately, many of our political leaders have succumbed to their influence.

Thus, the foremost challenge before our country today is to resist the invasion of foreign economic dominance. The second struggle for independence – the battle against foreign economic imperialism – has now become the national duty of every patriot. As part of *apad-dharma* (duty in times of crisis), the strategy or war tactics adopted for this struggle must inevitably influence our nation's institutional structure in the near future.

For any serious intellectual discourse, appropriate reference points are essential, a fact universally acknowledged. In the present context, the concept of Dharma must be examined first. The term Dharma requires careful interpretation because it is often mistakenly equated with *panth* (sect) or 'religion' and, consequently, perceived as contradictory to *panth-nirpekshata* (secularism). Due to this misunderstanding, even many rational intellectuals have developed an aversion to the word Dharma.

The debate on secularism (panth-nirpekshata) continues to this day. However, unless terms like 'secular', 'religion' and 'dharma' are analyzed with complete conceptual clarity and intellectual honesty, any contemplation on this subject will ultimately prove futile.

The term 'panth-nirpekshata' has been widely misunderstood in our country. This is why debates over its true meaning have persisted from the Constituent Assembly to P.C. Chatterjee's[1] work *Secular Values for Secular India*. The literal meaning of panth-nirpekshata is to be associated with the material world rather than the spiritual or religious realm. It implies a separation from ecclesiastical matters, focusing instead on civic and worldly affairs. This is why secularism is understood as the separation of religion from the state, ensuring that the two remain independent of each other. In the Indian context, the state has historically remained panth-nirpeksh. Revered Shri Guruji[2] often emphasized that throughout Indian history, the state has always been above sectarian divisions and Hindu governance has consistently been secular in nature. Dr B.R. Ambedkar also clarified this concept, stating: 'A secular state does not mean that religious sentiments will be ignored. The only purpose of a secular state is to ensure that Parliament does not impose any particular religion on the rest of the population. This is the only boundary recognized by the Constitution. Secularism does not mean the abolition of religion or religious practices.'

Throughout his life, Jawaharlal Nehru was a staunch critic of everything related to worship, religion or sects. However, in the later years of his life, he wrote about the word 'religion', stating:

> Some words, despite being widely used, never fully express themselves clearly and take on multiple meanings. Perhaps there is no other word – apart from 'religion' (or its equivalents in other languages) – that people interpret in such vastly different ways. This is why, when two people hear or read this word, they do not necessarily experience the same thoughts and emotions. The truth is that the word 'religion' has long lost any definite meaning it may have once had. The varied interpretations of this word only lead to confusion and unnecessary, prolonged debates. Therefore, the best and most appropriate course of action would be to abandon the use of this word entirely and instead adopt more precise and well-defined terms such as theology, philosophy, morality, ethics, spirituality, metaphysics, duty and ritual studies.

In contrast, Mahatma Gandhi held a different opinion on this matter. He said, 'Some people, intoxicated by their intellectual arrogance and rationalism, proudly declare that they have no connection with religion. But such a statement is as absurd as someone claiming that they breathe but have no nose.' Clarifying further, Gandhi stated that 'It is my deep commitment to truth that led me to the field of politics. With complete humility and without any hesitation, I can say that those who claim that politics has no connection with religion simply do not understand the true essence of religion.'

Perhaps it would have been more appropriate for Gandhi to say that most people who seek to separate politics from religion understand the word differently than he did. Gandhi's interpretation makes it clear that he used the term 'religion' in the sense of morality, which is entirely different from how critics of religion perceive it. As a result, the use of a single word with multiple meanings only increases ambiguity and misunderstanding.

In this situation, we are naturally reminded of the words of Jesus Christ, who said, 'The letter kills, but the spirit gives life.' In this context, the following words of William Kape, quoted by Humayun Kabir, are highly thought-provoking: 'The ability of Hindu culture to reconcile and integrate conflicting doctrines, beliefs, and principles is a testament to its unique vitality and eternal strength, more than any other element of its existence. Its remarkable capability to assimilate diverse elements and establish unity in diversity through their synthesis is perhaps unparalleled in all of human history, and we do not find such an example anywhere else.'

Cape further states, 'In reality, the more standards there are for internal mental tendencies and relational boundaries, the more perspectives there will be on the nature of truth and reality. The Hindu mind's inclination towards tolerance is rooted in the internal disposition of this society, which believes that each mental tendency clarifies a specific aspect of reality before us. In contrast, European philosophy rejects opposing categories of thought and attempts to depict reality in clear, definitional terminology, isolating it from other realities as an absolute or ultimate truth. On the other hand, Hindu epistemology does not reject any form of truth but acknowledges its various aspects and categories.'

Cape does not stop at merely comparing Hindu philosophy and European thought. He further asserts, 'European philosophy has attempted to interpret reality in terms of absolute truth or absolute illusion. This has undoubtedly given it depth and firmness, but it has also made Europe's perspective on truth rigid and narrow-minded. In contrast, Indian philosophy has recognized since ancient times that reality or truth has multiple facets and cannot be confined within mutually exclusive, strictly defined intellectual categories. The scale on which Indian philosophy has analyzed truth may perhaps have no equivalent in European metaphysics.'

Against this backdrop, evaluating Indian life structures, circumstances and philosophical thought through Western standards is always fraught with risk. Setting aside the discussion on the development of philosophical thought, it must also be kept in mind that materialist elements are not likely to repeat themselves in Third World countries in the same manner as in European history.

During the Industrial Revolution, a series of coincidental events significantly benefitted the nations of the Western world. These events included the increased geopolitical importance of sea routes before the advent of the aviation era, the abundance of raw materials and the fact that countries with strong marketing capabilities were focused on developing their internal trade and commerce. Additionally, naval power states found favourable conditions for building vast empires, and the economic exploitation of colonies helped sustain their internal economies.

However, for the countries of the Third World, these circumstances will not return. The factors that contributed to the prosperity and affluence of Western nations are no longer available to non-white nations. Therefore, there is no justification for blindly imitating Western countries or considering them as the ultimate model or standard to follow.

In light of the failure of Western models and the clear differences in historical developments, it has become essential for all nations striving for development and progress to set new goals for themselves. Therefore, we must establish our own model of progress and development, taking into account our national culture, ancient traditions, present needs and future aspirations.

We should thoroughly study and analyze Western models and examples and, if possible, benefit from them. However, we must not make the mistake of considering them as the ideal blueprint for our future growth. Similarly, we should not abandon our tradition of drawing inspiration from religion. It is crucial to recognize that equating religion with sectarianism and portraying it as inherently opposed to secularism is a fundamental error that should never be accepted.

The entire controversy surrounding secularism is a product of the Western world. In this context, Saint Mark, proclaiming the doctrine of Christianity, stated: 'Render unto Caesar the things that are Caesar's, and unto God the things that are God's.' With this statement, Saint Mark attempted to draw a dividing line between worldly and spiritual affairs – an approach that differed from the Greek and Roman city-states, where state power controlled both aspects of human life.

The decree issued by the Italian state of Milan in 312 AD affirmed this very doctrine stated by Saint Mark. However, after embracing Christianity, Emperor Constantine[3] declared it as the official religion of his empire and, by 346 AD, ordered the closure of all non-Christian temples. After this, in Europe, the church and the state continuously attempted to establish dominance over each other.

The philosophical foundation of secularism lies in the utilitarianism of Jeremy Bentham[4] and James Mill,[5] which was influenced by the anti-religious radical ideas of Thomas Paine[6] and Richard Carlile[7]. Utilitarianism provided secularism with a dual theoretical foundation: freedom of belief and the development of human personality, along with the complete exclusion of religion from the process of social construction.

To remove religion entirely from the crucial process of social development, it was even argued that 'All the purposes for which a building's blueprint is created by an architect can be fulfilled even without consulting the architect.' The implication was that worldly life could be made prosperous and fulfilling even without the guiding authority of religion.

From a political perspective, the development of secularism can be traced back to the Reform Act of 1832[8] and the turbulent events that followed. It was also partially influenced by Robert Owen's[9] socialism and the Chartist movement[10].

The term 'secularism' itself emerged as a result of the life and efforts of George Jacob Holyoake,[11] who introduced it in 1851 after meeting Bradlaugh[12] in 1850. At that time, Holyoake emphasized that secularism was not based on opposition to religion but rather on maintaining the distinctiveness and autonomy of both religion and the secular sphere. On the other hand, Bradlaugh believed that secularism required the rejection of the existence of God.

In the United States, religious freedom is considered the foundation of all other freedoms, whereas in Europe, it was attained much later – even after the achievement of political freedom. Due to the deep respect for religion in America, religious freedom is deeply rooted in its society and philosophy. In contrast, in Europe, religious freedom was achieved largely due to indifference and opposition towards religion. The official American perspective on secularism can be seen in the First Amendment to the U.S. Constitution in 1791 and, more than a century later, in the 1940 Supreme Court ruling in the case of *Cantwell v. Connecticut*[13].

Therefore, while shaping the institutional structure of future India, it is essential to keep it free from the influence of sects, religions or faiths. Its development should be based on the universal principles of *Sanatan Dharma*. Keeping this in mind, Dr Ambedkar stated that religion (*mazhab* or *panth*) is entirely a personal matter related to an individual, whereas dharma has a broader social dimension.

The difficulty arises when some intellectuals in our country attempt to artificially align the Indian context with the rigid philosophical ideas of Europe. In doing so, they overlook the crucial reality that the historical development of philosophical thought has not been the same in the East and the West.

20

'Babasaheb Ambedkar Firmly Believed That Ideological Transformation and Social Unity Were Only Possible Through Religion'

DATTOPANT THENGDI

In this speech, delivered in 1990 in remembrance of Dr B.R. Ambedkar, with whom he had personal association, Dattopant Thengdi seeks to present his vision and contribution in a new light offering fresh insights into Babasaheb's thinking, which, according to Thengdi, could pave the path for the regeneration of the Indian nation. Thengdi extensively quotes from Ambedkar's speeches and writings to argue that the latter was essentially a Hindu reformer, and not merely a champion of the interests of the Dalits alone.

Thirty-four years have passed since the mahaparinirvana (great demise) of the revered Babasaheb Ambedkar. Yet the dust stirred by the storm of his personality has not settled, making it difficult to evaluate him in a transparent manner. Moreover, the country does not have the right atmosphere for such an assessment. Politics dominates everywhere, and people seem to have forgotten the process of rebuilding the nation. The life values that Babasaheb cherished are now considered outdated – those who claim this are regarded as 'pragmatic' in today's world.

There are many misconceptions among people regarding the role of politics, political parties and state power in the advancement of a nation. Many believe that everything is possible only through state power, and therefore, engaging in politics to seize control of it is the only important task. However, the revered Babasaheb had a different perspective. He believed that human development, transformation of values and social unity are the true foundations of all kinds of progress. Aristotle once said, 'Political science does not create humans; it has to take them as nature has given them.' Babasaheb also used to say, 'We must now purify our hearts and develop an inclination towards virtues – this is how we should become religious. Character is the primary aspect of religion, and morality, dignity and discipline all stem from religion.' He firmly believed that ideological transformation and social unity were only possible through religion. According to him, politics had a limited role in achieving a greater objective.

That is why, after the passing of his wife, Ramabai, on 27 May 1935, Babasaheb spent some time in solitude and decided to prioritize religious matters over politics for the rest of his life. In line with this, on 23 July 1935, he announced that he was retiring from politics. When journalists asked him, 'You have been a relentless champion of the rights of the Dalits. Don't you think you should continue guiding them?' he replied, 'Yes! I have been a determined advocate for their rights, and I have helped them secure those rights. But I no longer believe that my presence in politics is absolutely necessary.'

He was aware that many people found his decision to deprioritize politics incorrect. Many journalists of that time were sharply critical of his decision. For example, when he resigned from Nehru's cabinet, *The Times of India*, on 23 May 1954, wrote, 'Ambedkar's political career is the tragedy of a man who believes that politics values reason and that an argument is worthy of support simply because it is logical. Being a fundamentally rational person, Ambedkar argues from beginning to end in favour of what is logical. However, the majority of politicians have no concern for reason. They, in fact, argue in the opposite manner – they first arrive at a conclusion and then construct premises that align with it. The painful truth is that a politician obsessed with reason will ultimately meet the fate where, sooner or later, that very reason will turn against him instead of his opponents and destroy him. Politics is not a branch of logic.'

This remark reflects the mindset of those who consider idealistic individuals, who assign limited importance to politics, as impractical fools. However, Babasaheb was not one to be disturbed by such comments. He used to say, 'In the progress of society, social and economic aspects hold more importance than politics. Therefore, activists should focus more on these areas. Those who are consumed by the belief that politics is everything start running for tickets to contest as soon as the election period arrives. If they do not get a ticket, they create divisions in society. If they lose the election, they become exhausted and sink into despair. And if they win, they assume their only duty is to sit silently in the legislature for five years, doing nothing.'

On 6 February 1954, while inaugurating the film *Mahatma Phule* produced by Acharya Atre, Ambedkar said, 'Today, there is no character left in the country. A nation without morality faces a difficult future. Whether the Prime Minister is Jawaharlal Nehru or the Chief Minister is Morarji Desai, your future will remain bleak. Ministers do not uplift the nation; only those who truly understand religion can save it. Mahatma Phule was such a religious reformer. Knowledge, wisdom, compassion, character and friendship – each individual should build their character based on these religious principles. I consider an educated person without compassion to be nothing more than a butcher. In the essence of compassion, one must go beyond mutual love between humans.'

Such words of Babasaheb are not given much importance by today's 'practical' individuals, who regard them as nothing more than Sunday sermons in a church.

Later scholars, even if they are authentic, may make the mistake of assuming that past circumstances, events, parties, individuals and their equations were the same as those of today. This is known as anachronism – a chronological misplacement of events. Leaving aside pure literary figures, in the works of great achievers, some aspects remain eternal truths, while others are of only temporary significance – contextual reactions to specific situations and audiences. For example, Swami Vivekananda's advice to the youth to play football instead of reading the Bhagavada Gita does not fall into the category of eternal truths.

Today, a dangerous trend is emerging in the country. Maharashtra claims ownership over Lokmanya Tilak's legacy, Bengal over Rabindranath Tagore and Gujarat over Mahatma Gandhi. Similarly, Sant Dnyaneshwar[1] is considered the legacy of Brahmins, Tukaram[2] of traders, Namdev[3] of tailors, Sant Gora[4] of potters and Chokhamela[5] of the Mahar community. In this way, revered universal figures – whose legacy should belong to all of humanity – are confined within narrow caste and regional boundaries. As a result, the misconception arises that what these great personalities were meant to offer to the world was instead limited to their own communities.

Regarding this trend, Babasaheb used to say, 'The raging fire of casteism has reduced Gautam Buddha, Vivekananda, Dnyaneshwar, Tukaram, and many others to ashes.' Perhaps Babasaheb was also concerned that after his departure, this narrow-minded society might do the same to him.

This thought troubles me, as well as many others, that both Babasaheb's supporters and opponents portray him as a leader of a specific section of society. Comparing him to figures like E.V. Ramasamy (Periyar)[6], Barrister Jinnah[7], Laldenga[8], or Phizo[9] is a grave injustice to him, stemming from sheer ignorance about his true character. Revered Babasaheb was a true patriot, a humanitarian, deeply spiritual and a noble-minded great personality. There was no place for narrow-mindedness in his vast heart. And whenever circumstances forced him into such roles, he experienced immense sorrow.

On 11 January 1950, during his felicitation in Mumbai, he said, 'Until now, we conducted politics based on hostility. I feel that all leaders of the untouchable community have, to some extent, viewed and acted with a narrow perspective. I, too, had some of this flaw. We used to wonder what would happen to us if power came into the hands of the Hindus. But now, we need to change our thinking. Until now, we were only concerned about the welfare of our specific community. We must continue to do so, but alongside that, we must also be concerned about safeguarding the Independence of our country.

Our nation has gained Independence multiple times, only to fall into subjugation repeatedly. We had to endure the slavery of both the Muslims and the British. The need for independence is as essential for the Dalit community as it is for the upper castes. Therefore, if the country once again loses its freedom, it will be an unfortunate fate for all of us. Everyone must consider the protection of national Independence as their supreme duty.'

> When the British ruled our country, the rights given to different communities depended on the rulers. At that time, we remained distant from other communities. But now the British have left. Therefore, we must maintain a sympathetic harmony with other communities and parties. If we wish to progress legally, we must collaborate with some party or organization. We must forget old hostilities. The isolation we practised before will no longer be effective.

After hearing this speech, some people felt that Babasaheb was changing his ideological stance. But that was not the case. Just as in America's struggle for liberation, there were extremists like Bayard Rustin[10] on one side and inclusive leaders like Martin Luther King Jr[11] on the other, similarly, there were two currents among Dalit thinkers in India. One group of leaders believed that all untouchables should unite and wage a battle against the upper castes, while Babasaheb firmly believed that the question of upliftment of untouchables was a concern for the entire Hindu society and that both the upper castes and untouchables must work shoulder to shoulder for this cause.

With this thought, he established the Bahishkrit Hitkarini Sabha on 20 July 1924. Sir Chimanlal Setalvad was its president, and G.K. Nariman, Dr V.P. Chauhan, Dr Paranjape and B.G. Kher were its vice presidents. Babasaheb himself was the working president of this organization. In his inaugural speech, Babasaheb had said: 'We appeal to the upper classes not to exhaust all their energy solely in politics but also to contribute to the upliftment of the oppressed. The untouchable community constitutes one-sixth of India's total population, and as long as such a large segment remains deprived and paralyzed, the country cannot progress.'

On 14 January 1946, in his speech at Solapur, he made an honourable mention of Dr V.V. Mule, saying, 'With his assistance, I began my public work twenty years ago. During the Mahar Satyagraha, he rejected the demand of the Brahmanetar Dal (Non-Brahmin Party) that if I removed all Brahmins from my movement, they would fully support me.' Babasaheb further stated, 'I have no quarrel with the Brahmin community. My struggle is against their wrongful tendency to consider others inferior. A Brahmin who believes in equality is dearer to me than a non-Brahmin who practises discrimination. I cannot exclude such Brahmins who support my movement.'

Once, a professor from Milind College, Prof. Thakar, asked Babasaheb, 'Why are you against Brahmins?' Babasaheb replied, 'Son! If I were against Brahmins and Hindus, you wouldn't be working here (in this job).' His decision in 1936 to embrace Sikhism was, in fact, due to his deep affinity for Hindu society. Prominent Hindu leaders such as Dr Munje, Barrister Jayakar and Shri Yugal Kishore Birla supported Babasaheb's decision.

With great emotion, Babasaheb had said about this decision, 'Many renowned Hindu leaders, including Shri Shankaracharya, have welcomed the decision of the untouchable community to adopt Sikhism. This suggestion was initially made by Hindu leaders themselves, and I accepted it. While choosing this option, my underlying sentiment was that I, too, bear some responsibility for the future of Hindu society.' (It is a different matter that due to certain reasons, Babasaheb had to abandon this decision.)

Later, when Babasaheb decided to embrace Buddhism, he explained his decision by saying: 'Once, while discussing the issue of untouchability with Gandhiji, I had told him that even though we disagreed on this matter, when the time came, I would choose a path that would cause the least harm to the country. That is why, by adopting Buddhism, I am working for the greatest benefit of the nation. Buddhism is an integral part of Indian culture. I have taken care that neither the culture, traditions, nor history of this country suffer in any way. I do not wish my name to be recorded in history as a destroyer of this nation's culture and traditions.'

On 13 December 1947, while speaking in the Constituent Assembly, he said: 'Today, even though we are divided into different camps politically, socially and economically, I still believe that despite the presence of many castes and sects, we will stand as one nation. A day will surely come when even those Muslim groups that once demanded partition will realize that their true welfare lies in an "Undivided India".'

On 31 May 1952, in his speech in Mumbai, Babasaheb said: 'Although I have a somewhat aggressive nature and frequently clash with those in power, I assure you that during my foreign travels, I will never let India's prestige be tarnished. I have never engaged in treason against the nation – my heart has always been dedicated to the country's welfare. Even during the Round Table Conference, I was 200 miles ahead of Gandhiji when it came to national interests.' During the Round Table Conference, Babasaheb had demanded that the Dalit community be referred to as 'Protestant Hindus' or 'Non-Conformist Hindus.'

On 11 January 1950, at his felicitation ceremony in Mumbai, he stated: 'For the past 20 years, I have been called a British agent and a supporter of Muslims. I have been labelled as an enemy of Hinduism. But I believe that when people see the work I have done in drafting India's Constitution, they will realize how baseless and false these allegations were. One day, Hindu society will acknowledge me as someone who has contributed to its welfare and will express its gratitude.'

After the creation of Pakistan, Babasaheb advised the Dalits there to come to India by whatever means and routes available to them. He also warned that trusting the Muslims of India or the Nizam of Hyderabad would be disastrous for the Dalit community. For those Dalits who had been forcibly converted to Islam in Pakistan, Babasaheb assured that upon coming to India, they would be treated with the same brotherly affection as before their conversion.

He advised the Dalit community not to stain the entire Dalit society's reputation by siding with the enemy of India, the Nizam of Hyderabad. His words were: 'The Muslims and the Muslim League, charged as they are with passion to make the Muslims a governing class as quickly as possible, will never give consideration to the claims of scheduled castes. This I speak from experience.'

On 25 November 1949, responding to the debate in the Constituent Assembly, he said: 'It pains me deeply to acknowledge that India has lost its independence multiple times, and that too due to betrayal and treachery by its own people. Will history repeat itself?' Expressing his concern, he stated: 'Hindu society's caste and sectarian divisions have always been its old enemies. To make matters worse, there is now a rise in politically opposing factions, which adds to my worries.' Therefore, he warned the Indian people: 'If these political parties place their partisan interests above national interest, Indian independence will once again be in jeopardy – so much so that it could be lost forever. Therefore, we must resolve to fight to the last drop of our blood to protect our independence.'

Babasaheb's concept regarding the varna system was similar to that of Hindutva adherents. However, those Hindutva followers who shared Babasaheb's views did not have much influence over the upper-caste society. On the other hand, the contemporary political leaders who held greater sway over the traditional upper-caste society failed to understand Babasaheb's role.

Later, in 1969, during a grand conference of the Vishwa Hindu Parishad in Udupi, Karnataka, it was officially declared that 'untouchability is neither religious nor sanctioned by scriptures.' The resolution also affirmed '*Na Hinduḥ patito bhavet*' (A Hindu cannot be fallen) and '*Hindutvah sodaraḥ sarve*' (All Hindus are brothers). If only the religious leaders had made this declaration before the Mahar Satyagraha in 1927, history might have taken a different turn. Unfortunately, at that time, Indian society was heavily influenced by the Congress, which only led to Babasaheb's disappointment.

From the very beginning, Babasaheb wanted the anti-untouchability movement not to take the form of 'touchables versus untouchables' but rather 'Hindu reformers versus Hindu orthodox conservatives'. However, very few people paid attention to the work he did in collaboration with upper-caste social reformers towards this goal.

On 5 March 1928, at Thakarsi Hall in Mumbai, an inter-caste communal meal was organized by Samaj Samata Sangh. Later, on 22 March 1928, under the leadership of Pandit Paley Shastri, nearly 500 untouchables from the Mahar caste underwent the *yajnopavita sanskar* (sacred thread ceremony). During these events, several leaders from upper-caste communities were present alongside Babasaheb. How many people have actually paid attention to this fact?

For the conference held in Mahad on 25 December 1927, even Lokmanya Tilak's son had sent a message of goodwill. At this conference, Babasaheb issued a 'Declaration of Birth Rights of Hindus'. The conference passed a resolution stating:

1. All Hindus should be considered of a single varna.
2. The use of varna-discriminatory terms such as Brahmin, Kshatriya, etc., should be prohibited.
3. Competitive examinations should be conducted for entry into the Hindu priesthood, and only those who pass should be granted a license to perform priestly duties.

In his presidential address, as reported by *The Indian National Herald*, Babasaheb said: 'If we succeed in uniting all Hindus into a single caste through our movement, we will be rendering the greatest service to the Indian nation and, in particular, to Hindu society.'

However, due to the influence of Gandhi-led Congress on the Hindu public, Babasaheb, despite his strong desire, was unable to fulfil this all-inclusive role.

The only Congress session that Babasaheb attended was in 1918, where, for the first time, a resolution for the eradication of untouchability was introduced. The stance of Congress on this issue was as follows: 'As supporters of democracy, we believe that individuals are free to conduct their private affairs within the four walls of their homes. Therefore, we cannot mandate that people allow untouchables to enter their homes, nor can we require others to visit the homes of untouchables. We will not ask anyone to dine with others, nor will we compel others to invite someone to dine with them, as this is a matter of personal freedom. Everyone holds their own caste and religion dear. We will not advocate for inter-caste marriages either. It is not our intention to interfere in anyone's religious beliefs, customs, or interpersonal interactions. We only seek the eradication of untouchability.'

Babasaheb had differences with Gandhi on almost all issues. He was a strong critic of Gandhi's concept of a caste-based social structure. He referred to himself as a 'Protestant Hindu'. He believed that Gandhi's use of the term 'Harijan' placed untouchables in a dependent position. He used to say: 'It is unfortunate that untouchability has been entrenched in this country for two thousand years. I acknowledge that not only in India but throughout the world, there was a period of slavery and inequality. I also recognize that this long-standing disease will not disappear suddenly – it can only be eradicated gradually through a change in the mindset of society. Until then, I am even willing to wait. However, my sorrow is that the educated social reformers who raise their voices against untouchability are themselves not "genuine." In such a scenario, no matter if we wait for fifty or even hundreds of years, I have no hope that untouchables will receive justice.'

A report was published in Nashik's *Kohinoor* newspaper stating that, due to oppression, 500 untouchables had decided to convert to Islam. Responding to this, Babasaheb urged the people of Nashik district: 'They should remain steadfast . . . Whether my efforts succeed or not depends on how much religious sincerity and social conscience exist among the upper-caste society.'

On 20 September 1951, during his speech in Parliament, Babasaheb said, 'By abandoning Sita, Ram committed an injustice.' Upon this, a member accused him of hurting religious sentiments and remarked, 'We also support progress, but if the Law Minister can present his bill without criticizing Hinduism, we would be pleased.' Babasaheb responded, 'If you had mentioned this earlier, my speech would not have contained any objectionable remarks. My intention was not to hurt anyone's feelings, and if I have, I sincerely apologize.' Later, while speaking to a professor at Milind College, Babasaheb said, 'I am the person who protested to gain the right to enter the Kalaram Temple in Nashik. It is you who have pushed me away from Ram. My aspiration has always been to be a reformer of Hindu society.'

An investigation should be conducted to determine whether the bitterness in Babasaheb's stance and statements during the Gandhi era stemmed from 'opposition to Hindutva' or 'opposition to Congress'. In this regard, the book *What the Congress Has Done to the Untouchables* is worth reading.

Babasaheb's reactions towards Hindutva-oriented leaders and Gandhi were always distinct.

For example, in *The Times of India* on 19 September 1933, Babasaheb wrote: 'I am unable to understand the grounds of Mr Gandhi's opposition to the Communal Award. He claims that this award has separated the Depressed Classes from the Hindu community. On the other hand, Dr Moonje, a much stronger advocate of Hindu interests, holds a completely different view on the matter. Since his return from London, Dr Moonje has been insisting in his speeches that the Communal Award does not create any separation between the Depressed Classes and the Hindus. It is, therefore, surprising that Mr Gandhi, who is considered a nationalist and not a communalist, interprets the Communal Award concerning the Depressed Classes in a manner quite contrary to a so-called communalist like Dr Moonje.'

On one hand, repeatedly criticizing leaders like Dr Moonje, who were actively working for Hindu interests, by labelling them as communal, and on the other hand, consistently glorifying Gandhi – this tendency of Hindu society deeply pained Babasaheb. This frustration is evident in his satirical writings.

The warmth that Hindutva-oriented individuals felt for Babasaheb was expressed whenever appropriate. For example, consider this news from *The Times of India* on 3 February 1937: 'In today's *Kesari*, democratic leader Narasimha Chintaman Kelkar published a two-column article, the essence of which was: "Vote for Dr Ambedkar".'

Babasaheb had an intense sense of national unity. Once, during a Constituent Assembly meeting, when it was suggested that the provision for reserved seats for Dalits should be removed from the Constitution, Babasaheb strongly opposed it. He argued that the development of Dalits might take 25 years, and by then, none of the current leaders might still be alive. It was uncertain whether those in power at that time would have the courage to amend the Constitution. In such a situation, this issue could become a serious obstacle in Indian politics. Therefore, he insisted that the provision for reserved seats should be framed in such a way that a proposal could be brought to continue it, but not to abolish it.

21

'Life for Guruji Was an Act of Devotion'

ATAL BIHARI VAJPAYEE

Atal Bihari Vajpayee joined the RSS and became a pracharak in the 1940s. When Dr Shyama Prasad Mukherjee requested Golwalkar, 'Guruji', to lend some workers to work in his fledgling party, Bharatiya Jana Sangh, Vajpayee was among the young pracharaks deputed to work in the political arena under Dr Mukherjee's guidance. Vajpayee continued his close association with the Sangh and Guruji even after he rose in politics to become one of the important voices of the nationalist forces in the country. In 1977, Sangli Municipality in Maharashtra decided to unveil a portrait of Guruji in its office building. Vajpayee, a minister in the Janata Party government led by prime minister Morarji Desai, was invited for the unveiling of the portrait. Vajpayee spoke passionately about his association with Guruji, and also, in the process, highlighted the vision and mission of the RSS as conceived by Hedgewar, 'Doctorji', and Guruji.

Excerpts from his speech are presented here.

Guruji is no longer among us. We can only see him in a portrait now. Today, we are unveiling his portrait. Before his death, he wrote that no memorial should be commissioned in his name. You have placed his portrait today. Tomorrow, someone might attempt to create a statue of him. The day after, perhaps a temple might be built in his memory. But none of these actions would align with his wishes. He even performed his own *shraaddh* (last rites) and departed. Hence it may seem as though he left nothing for us to do, but saying he left nothing would not be accurate. He left us a great legacy of patriotism, an unfinished task of organizing, disciplining and empowering society and a grand vision to elevate India to the pinnacle of ultimate glory.

Like a *nanda deep* he kept burning, illuminating others while sacrificing himself, constantly fighting against the forces of darkness. In this struggle, he never asked for rest, never sought comfort. On the path of duty, he never paused. *Charaiveti charaiveti*[1] – this mantra from the Upanishads seemed to manifest in his life. Every particle of his body and every moment of his life was dedicated to the nation, day and night. However, his concerns for the nation never led to despair. His worries never induced inactivity.

In society, we often encounter people who express concern for the nation, but in a way that spreads hopelessness. They claim India is destined for ruin and that there is no way to save it. These individuals are so disheartened that anyone who comes in contact with them also feels discouraged.

But Guruji was not like that. He was concerned about the state of the nation, but his concern sparked resolve. If the country's condition is not good today, then we will make it better. If we are weak today, if we are struggling with shortages, if any son or daughter of Mother India is unable to live with dignity and prosperity, that is a challenge for us. We must face this challenge and change India's destiny. From his worries emerged this spirit of determination.

Time and again, the image of his last day flashes before my mind. Perhaps, in this large gathering, I am one of the few who met him that morning. At dawn on that summer day, we reached Hedgewar Bhavan after travelling through the night from Jabalpur, hoping to catch a glimpse of him. He was seated after completing his *sandhya vandana* (evening prayers). The practice of prayers never ceased, and the daily Sangh prayers were never missed. After his evening prayers, he met people.

When we arrived, his face held that same divine, enchanting smile – one that captured hearts, dispelled sorrows and eased exhaustion.

No matter how distressed, tired or worried someone was, being in his presence and catching his gaze would make all their fatigue vanish.

That day, too, his health was frail, although anyone who saw him wouldn't have easily noticed it. Still, he greeted everyone warmly and asked, 'Who has come from Jabalpur? What work did you all come for?' He recalled past meetings with remarkable clarity, asking, 'Oh, we met at your home, didn't we? What was the name of that young swayamsevak? How was the program organized in Jabalpur?' When introduced to a doctor among us, he smiled and inquired with curiosity, 'Which type of doctor are you?'

Before the doctor could answer, he began narrating a comic anecdote. 'I know a doctor who once went to see a patient. The doctor asked the patient, "Tell me, what is troubling you?" The patient got annoyed and said, "If I have to tell you what is troubling me, then what kind of doctor are you?" The doctor replied, "Wait, I will call a doctor who can treat you without you telling him anything." The doctor went out and called a veterinary surgeon, saying, "This doctor can treat you. Their patients don't need to say anything; the doctor understands everything on their own."' Then he again asked the doctor who was with us, 'So, what kind of doctor are you?'

This was a humorous anecdote narrated by him at a time when death was at his door, the body was giving up and worldly ties were breaking one by one. Guruji knew that the final call had arrived. Early that morning, he said that the bells were ringing. But for whom? When swayamsevaks arrived, even death seemed to step aside. Guruji endured the pain and ignored the agony of his body. He laughed, joked, met with swayamsevaks and asked for tea. Even tea, for him, was a way to connect with people.

He even remembered who drank tea and who didn't. I had stopped drinking tea due to stomach issues, but after an operation, I resumed. Yet, he still remembered that I didn't drink tea. He said, 'This one doesn't drink tea, bring milk instead.' I told him I had started drinking tea again, to which he replied, 'Good, that means your trouble has lessened.'

For a moment, it felt like he was lying on a bed of thorns, like Bhishma Pitamah[2]. But in the next moment, the thought came that Bhishma Pitamah stood for justice. However, this ascetic, this devoted individual, always fought for Dharma (righteousness) and justice. He was never on the side of the Kauravas[3].

When allegations were falsely made against the organization, even those who accused us knew the charges were baseless, false and rooted in malice. But the accusations were made, nonetheless. Guruji did not lose his composure or become discouraged. He told the swayamsevaks, 'This is a time of trial; remain patient and work diligently.' The ban was lifted after a few months, and when he was released from prison, lakhs of people came out to welcome him. Such a reception had never been seen in many cities of India.

Yet, even after this grand welcome, what did he say? He bore no ill will towards those who had imprisoned him or banned the organization. He said, '*Vayam panchaadhikam shatam*' (We are not a group of five; we are one hundred and five)[4]. For a moment, I thought of Bhishma Pitamah, who had the boon of choosing the time of his death. But in Guruji, I saw a man who understood that death was near, yet he refused to lie down, even on the bed. He remained steadfast and true to his principles until the very end.

Even for essential needs, he never gave up going to the bathroom on his own. The doctors insisted, 'You can stay seated; we will bring a commode,' but he refused. Sitting there, as if in a yogic posture, he breathed his last. In death, he became even greater. Sometimes, those who live with great dignity their entire lives tremble in the face of death. But that was not the personality of Guruji. For him, death was merely a part of the game.

Life for him was an act of devotion. Society, in his eyes, was a manifestation of the divine. National service was as essential to him as breathing. He often said, 'Can anyone live without breathing? If we do not serve the nation, if we do not organize society, if we do not strengthen it by rising above all divisions, if we do not weave our nation into the fabric of unity, then saying we can live is as absurd as saying we can live without breathing.'

He believed a society without unity is no longer a society. Such was his faith in his work that he often emphasized that the means themselves are the end. Devotion itself is the goal of attaining the divine; the path itself becomes the destination. Devotion takes on the form of God. The effort becomes one with the goal. Such harmony and oneness with his purpose were reflected in Guruji's life.

There are many leaders in the country, and there will be many more in the future. I, too, am counted among the minor leaders, which might be why I have been placed on this stage. But the word '*neta*' (leader) means one who leads or carries others along. It comes from the root '*ni*' meaning 'to lead or carry'.

I remember that once when Guruji was invited to Allahabad University, some friends had decided that they would not allow him to speak. Thousands of young students, with a sense of discipline, stood in a semicircle and Guruji remained calm even as he was denied entry into the hall. At that moment, he said, 'What is progress? Every movement forward is not progress. If someone falls from a mountaintop and says, "See how rapidly I am progressing," they may be moving fast, but they are heading into a pit.'

A leader who takes a nation into a pit is no leader at all. True leadership is about taking the country to the summit. And to reach the summit, there are no shortcuts. One must place each step firmly, work hard, sweat, practise discipline and endure challenges. One must burn like sandalwood – releasing fragrance even while being ground down. Only then can one climb to the summit. Yes, there may be shortcuts to descend from the summit, but ascending it requires effort, patience and perseverance.

It is easy to fall after climbing up, but to rise from below requires effort. Guruji's life was an embodiment of continuous hard work, unparalleled devotion, selfless worship and dedication to society. Inspired by his life, millions of people left their homes and families and came forward to serve society. Sometimes, some of them felt despondent when the work did not go as planned. Guruji used to encourage them by saying that if our work isn't completed in this life, 'we will return to this earth in our next life and complete what remains unfinished.'

In this life or the next, the mission remains. That mission is to change the destiny of India and work towards creating a better future for it, wherein the world looks towards India for guidance. In this mission of taking India to its greatest glory, there should be no disagreements.

Disagreements can arise over political and economic issues, and even on how to reconstruct society. In a democracy, differences of opinion are natural – in fact, not only natural but also essential. When there is a churning of ideas, the essence that emerges strengthens society, making it robust and powerful. In our country, we have never restricted the churning of thoughts. Since ancient times, there has been freedom to express different opinions. Criticism and churning have continued, and debates have taken place. However, one thing that was always clear was that those who were defeated in these debates accepted their defeat. But now, things have changed. Today, people say, 'Okay, we may not have the best argument, but look at the numbers, we have the majority.'

Sometimes, the same happens in Parliament. We may be in the opposition and in a minority, but sometimes, the strength in our argument turns the tide. What if the numbers are still with the other side? Should decisions be made solely on the basis of numbers and not logic? If numbers dictate that only judges who support the government should be appointed to the Supreme Court, does that make it a valid principle? Would it be appropriate? Now, one of our friends says, 'There can't be anyone who is impartial. Anyone who takes a seat on the bench brings their own thoughts and values with them.'

Should this be acceptable? Is this true justice? In ancient times, there was a famous debate between Adi Shankaracharya[5] and Mandan Mishra[6] in Kashi. The question arose: who would be the judge in such a debate? Two great scholars were clashing. Human wisdom expresses itself in many forms, and the debates continue. But who will take the responsibility of delivering justice? There were no scholars available! Yet Shankaracharya didn't say, 'Let so and so person become the judge of the debate, and his judgment will be final.' Nor did he say that a spouse would always support their own side.

How can someone be impartial if they hold personal biases? Is true impartiality even possible? Yes, a person can be unbiased, disinterested and detached. In this country, with a population of 56 crores, when someone becomes a judge, they will not consider which family they belong to or who their close ones are. They will make decisions based on the truth, standing by the principles of justice.

If such a situation does not exist, we should consider that the destiny of India is in darkness. But that is not the case; there is no darkness, and there are such people. Guruji used to say, 'There's a difference. Some people like what they like, and what will make others applaud for them. But there's another category, who are about what is good for the public, what benefits the nation.'

'Go after what's right, not what's popular,' he used to advise. He would give an example of a person who craves for spicy food even though it's harmful to his health. It might taste good, but the doctor would advise him not to eat it. Similarly, the right thing is not always what is liked by people, but what is beneficial for them.

Sometimes, even a mother might give a child something harmful just to stop the child from crying. The child might like it, but the doctor would say it's not good. Similarly, Guruji was a realist who did what was best for society, even if it was unpopular. Some people misunderstood him, but when they came closer, they realized how transparent he was and how his transparency came from his deep love for the society. Guruji used to say that if someone does something wrong in society, they must be punished. But the punishment should be given with the mindset that the person is still one of us. The punishment should be like that of a mother to her child – not to destroy, but to reform.

I remember that when Guruji visited Kashi, the city council decided to honour him. The council head was a Muslim gentleman. He asked Guruji what place would Muslims have. Guruji replied, 'Who am I to decide that? Muslims themselves should chose the place they wish to have.' He went on to add, 'We do not have any disagreement with any method of worship. If someone believes that calling God by the name of Allah can lead to the realization of the ultimate truth, then let them call Him Allah. However, beyond the method of worship, in all other matters, they should align with us.

Islam came to India at times through the means of propagation and others through the power of the sword. Some people accepted Islam because they liked its way of worship, while others accepted it because they had no other choice. If they had not, they would have faced death. They accepted it under compulsion. Just as we freed ourselves from the chains of colonial slavery, if anyone now wants to free themselves from religious slavery, we welcome it.'

Later, when the mayor thanked him, he said, 'We do not disagree with the thoughts expressed by Guruji.'

I know that people used to call Guruji 'anti-India'. Was he really anti-India? Anyone who got closer to Guruji realized that there was no animosity towards any community in his heart. Once, there was a big discussion on national unity, chaired by the prime minister. I was a member, along with Fakhruddin Ali, Vice-Chancellor of Aligarh University. A book on Guruji's thoughts was recently published and widely circulated. A portion of it was extracted and placed in the meeting. The prime minister asked, 'Mr Vajpayee, please explain this part.' I said, 'If you want to understand something truly good and sincere, then invite Guruji here.' He replied, 'That means this is a matter of interpretation, and you disagree with it?' I said, 'No, I have no disagreement. I fully support it. But I cannot explain everything. If there is any shortcoming, it wouldn't be right to leave any misunderstanding. So please call him.' The prime minister said, 'No, it's difficult to call him.'

The prime minister used to praise Guruji, and this may seem strange to many of you. I have had many discussions with him. He said once, 'Guruji is very rigid about his thoughts.' I said, 'That's why you should talk to him. It may have an impact on you too, and any doubts you have will also be cleared.' He replied, 'No, no, the thoughts cannot be changed.' I said, 'If you talk to him, maybe things will change. If there is something that needs changing, then what's the harm in it?' He said, 'No, no, it's not right to call him.' Then he asked, 'Does this mean that there will be a place for Muslims in India? It's written that Muslims should merge with the mainstream national life.' I said, 'It's correctly written.' You will be surprised by the words the prime minister used – 'What is mainstream national life?'

I said, if this is the disagreement, then there is no common ground for reconciliation. This nation, born in 1947, was a unified nation even before Muslims came here. When Christians weren't here, India was still a nation. In the Vedas, when we declared that the earth is our mother and we are her children, we also declared that we are a nation.

And the nation's main life force lies in its unity. Many small rivers merge into river Ganga; Yamuna merges into it at Prayagraj, or the Ghaghara joins it in Patna. Even after Patna, Ganga continues without losing any essence. Similarly, the several streams of our national life come from various sources and join the mainstream. Our culture will accept many influences, but it will adapt them and integrate them as its own.

Some people also say that Guruji wanted to maintain the distinction between the upper castes and the Shudras. But I never saw such a thing. There is no space for discrimination in RSS. We know the names of our swayamsevaks and from which shakha they come from. But we don't know which family or caste they belong to. Even Mahatma Gandhi came to a Sangh *shibir* (camp) and said there is no discrimination there.

However, when discussions about social structure were happening, Guruji said that, in ancient times, we had established a system where there were no distinctions between different sections. There was a division of labour, which was useful, and in times of foreign invasions, it also proved beneficial. But over time, some flaws emerged. He said that the old system no longer existed. He said that there should be no place for untouchability, and it should end. Where, then, is the disagreement in these thoughts? However, Guruji never tried to counter these misrepresentations. 'Rather than wasting energy on refutation, it's better to focus that energy on constructive work,' he used to say. 'Those who seek to oppose will eventually become silent on their own.'

He often spoke about an example Dr Hedgewar used to give of the elephant when discussing about wisdom. The elephant moves along its path, and even if the dogs bark, it doesn't stop. Let the elephant continue its journey. Let the spiritual practice proceed. Let it spread fragrance like sandalwood.

Once, during a discussion, someone asked Guruji, 'You don't eat at night, why?' Guruji said, 'I was born in a country where millions of people do not get food for even one meal. That's why I do not eat twice.' There was no declaration of socialism, no slogan to remove poverty, no campaign for elections but simple life example.

I am discussing these things after his departure. When he was alive, we did not have the courage to discuss. He always considered society to be divine and truly important. He worshipped the poor as forms of God and lived a simple life. His economic ideas were revolutionary. He used to say that foreign ideologies should be avoided. Politics should not be allowed to dominate. The social structure should not rest entirely on the foundation of the state. We never allowed it in the past, and it should not be done in the future. Even if the state changes or collapses, the society should remain immortal. In ancient times too, states changed, many rulers sat on the throne of Delhi, but our values and traditions continued. Our *gurukul*[7] and *tapovan*[8] survived, and that is why we remained alive. Greece has perished, Rome collapsed and Babylon is gone, but India remained alive from the time of the Vedas to today and will continue to remain eternal. Guruji used to say that this was the source of our civilizational life force.

It is essential to understand the importance of the state and to build it. It is also necessary that those who run the state are virtuous. However, the entire essence of life should not be tied to the state. If the state falls, what will remain? That is why culture, values, education, gurukuls, panchayats and a self-reliant society – capable of facing external challenges and resolving the country's internal issues over time – are important.

Guruji is no longer with us, but creating the India of his dreams is still possible. He has left those dreams with us in the form of his legacy. We will walk in his footsteps. The essence of life lies in purity, a sense of divinity in society, a deep devotion to the nation and an unwavering commitment to the welfare of society. These are the virtues that, if brought into our own lives, will allow us to claim the legacy of Guruji in the true sense.

I saw Guruji for the first time 34 years ago. I was a young swayamsevak, and Guruji was travelling to Punjab by the Punjab Mail. We, the young karyakartas, had gathered on the platform. It was crowded, and it was hard to make our way through. The train was to halt for about 10 minutes, and many young swayamsevaks were present. He met everyone, placed his hand on some heads, lovingly patted others and offered words of comfort.

That was my first glimpse, the first spark in the eyes of a child, a vision of divine grace.

Thirty-four years have passed, and I've had several conversations with him, been close to him on several occasions, sought his blessings many times and even been reprimanded on some occasions. Guruji is no longer with us in physical form, but his presence is eternal. His timeless influence, his ability to conquer time, his spiritual practices continue to inspire us. The memory of his life will continue to motivate us, especially when we face darkness or exhaustion.

Whenever there is a feeling of weakness, the example of his unwavering dedication will remove all difficulties and weaknesses. By remembering him, we will gain the courage to walk on the path of duty. His glorious presence is not confined to the body; it has spread across countless hearts. His vision is written in every heart, and in its light, we will find our way and fulfil our purpose.

Dr Lohia[9] once came to a shakha. He met Guruji and said, 'Guruji! What a band of swayamsevaks you have! If I had such swayamsevaks, I would not have to strive so hard for securing India's independence.' Dr Lohia had great respect for Guruji.

I am happy that the portrait of Dr Lohia is in this municipal hall, and now, Guruji's portrait is also being unveiled. This is a moment of joy as well. It is true that what arrives will depart; life is fleeting. However, those whose lives were dedicated to the service of the people, the protection of Dharma, cannot be erased by time. They are immortal and eternal. Guruji belongs to that category.

22

'When It Comes to Social Reform, the Sangh Must Take the Lead'

ATAL BIHARI VAJPAYEE

This is the text of a speech delivered by Atal Bihari Vajpayee at the Tritiya Varsha Sangh Shiksha Varga[1] of the RSS at Nagpur in June 1990. In this lecture, Vajpayee dwells at length about the concept of social harmony.

I completed my Tritiya Varsha in 1944. The country was not free at that time; it was under British rule. One part of the country was under Portuguese occupation, and a small portion was ruled by the French. All three powers had come from Europe. They crossed the seas to trade, not to rule. But they turned the scales of trade into instruments of monarchy. England never officially declared war against India. In fact, the British government did not even send troops to fight the Indian army. The East India Company (EIC), which had come to trade, had recruited a few soldiers to protect its trading establishments. But gradually, it raised its own army. Taking advantage of the internal conflicts among Indian kings of that time, EIC began to seize land.

It led to a situation which can be aptly summed up in a slogan frequently heard in Delhi those days: 'The world belongs to God, the country to the emperor, but the rule is of the Company Bahadur.'

Company Bahadur sounds like it was some brave individual. But how did a company become Bahadur? How did this company begin to rule? That the world belongs to God – *haq khuda ka* – is understandable. But tragically, the Mughal emperor remained an emperor merely in name. A handful of Englishmen, who had come under the name of the company to trade, became the de facto rulers of India.

Everyone should read the detailed history of how the British rule was established in India. That history was written by the British themselves. They did not hide any facts. They clearly admitted that the number of British soldiers in India never exceeded one lakh, or at the most one and a half lakh. How did they manage to capture our vast country with such a small force? And after capturing it, how did they manage to keep such a huge nation under their control?

The British were not exceptionally brave. At the time when they were trying to establish their foothold in India, they were actually fleeing from Europe, troubled by Napoleon. The British soldier was not known for his bravery. But while British influence was growing in Europe, a new power was emerging in India. That power was based on deceit, treachery, cunning and the strategy of making brothers fight each other for their own gain. Someone rightly said that the British did not conquer India – rather, Indians sold their own country with their own hands and handed it over to the British. This is one of the most painful aspects of our history.

In the Battle of Plassey, only half a dozen people were killed, yet the fate of India was sealed. More people stood outside the battlefield watching the outcome than those fighting, waiting merrily to see who would become their new master. This was the reason for our downfall. A country divided into small princely states could not come together in unity to resist the foreign power. Did people truly begin to believe that the ruler may change, but they will remain slaves? Did the thought 'how does it matter who the king is; it makes no difference to us anyway' take root in the minds of the people? Did their feeling of nationalism really dry up? And if so, why was there no attempt to reawaken it?

One after the other, states were defeated and fell, while the remaining ones simply waited their turn to be defeated. People intensely resented

British slavery. Some of them, when forced to meet the slave masters and shake hands out of compulsion, would return home and wash their hands as a purification. While there was such intense emotion against the foreigners among the people, there was no organized effort to resist them at the political level. That is why we were enslaved. Even after India's Independence, Portugal continued to hold on to some of our territories while the French had only recently left Puducherry.

At that time, as swayamsevaks, we had a longing, a dream and a vow – to make India free. Those who have not seen that dark past cannot imagine what it was like. There were clubs with signboards that read, 'Indians and Dogs are not allowed.' It was an extremely humiliating situation. The foreigners ruined our industries, destroyed our trade and wiped out our craftsmanship. Today, we are free, and we should be proud of that. But we must also remain vigilant so that we never become slaves again. Today the nation is thriving. The day we gained Independence was also the day we faced Partition. One eye held the joy of freedom, while the other was filled with the pain of division.

Fortunately, all that past aside, today, from Kashmir to Kanyakumari and up to the Andaman and Nicobar Islands, India is united. Culturally, we were always one – even during Mughal and British rule. But we have also achieved political unity today. We have one Constitution, one president and one national flag. Our nation must always remain a republic and a democracy, and it must remain united.

It is our good fortune that we are living in this era. But we must not be under the illusion that our freedom will never again be in danger, or that the country will never face another partition. It is possible that the form of external subjugation may change. A foreign army may not come to occupy us, but foreign influence and foreign culture may infiltrate and continue to dominate us. And above all, there may be attempts to entangle the country in the trap of economic slavery. Today, the nature of imperialism and colonialism is changing. That is why we talk about economic self-reliance and self-sufficiency.

It is important to remember that the reasons why we were forced into slavery have not been completely eradicated. Even today, there is unrest in the border regions. Some people, instigated by foreign powers, and using weapons and money supplied by them, want to secede from India. These are false ambitions and will never succeed. We shall protect our unity and integrity at all costs. But the real question is – why do such sentiments even arise? Broadly speaking, the reason is the lack of nationalism. If a person living in Punjab starts to think only about Punjab and further narrows it down to only his own community, then difficulties will surely arise. In this country, there will be so many communities, castes and sub-castes. Attachment with a community is one thing, but communalism is an entirely another thing. States have been formed on linguistic lines. I do not wish to get into that debate about whether that decision was right or wrong. People prefer that their government functions in their own language. But our loyalty towards our language, our region, our form of worship or our caste should not become so intense that it starts to negatively impact our loyalty towards the entire nation.

In the past, kings fought for their own selfish interests. Even kings belonging to the same caste fought against each other, just to avenge personal insults. In the process they did not hesitate to lay out a welcome path for foreign invaders. Sadly, the foreigners killed their enemies first and then turned on the friends who had helped them as well. History is full of such examples.

It is also true that through all this, the country continued to fight for Independence. There were always some people who paid the price for freedom with their very lives. They kept the flame of Independence burning steadily. In the penultimate years, the Indian army rebelled and refused to fight for the British masters. The Indian National Army (INA) was formed, and there was a mutiny in the navy. The British may have won the Second World War, but they no longer had the strength to hold on to their empire. While leaving, they partitioned the country.

Now, it seems that preparations for another partition are underway. We will have to confront it. And to confront it, it is of utmost importance to eliminate the weaknesses, vulnerabilities and flaws that exist within our society. I wouldn't say that we lack the ability to come together during the times of crisis. We do have the capacity to come together – but if we were to stay united all the time, then crises would not even knock at our doors; those doors would never open, and the crises would have to simply turn back. Unfortunately, our unity emerges in the times of trouble, but as soon as the trouble lessens, that unity also starts to disappear. Our internal differences return to dominate us.

As the RSS, we are working for Hindu unity. I once went to Vrindavan to meet revered Devraha Baba[2]. He has always showered us with immense blessings. He has remained unchanged for the past 50 years. I don't know what kind of spiritual practice it is, or what miracle it is.

So, he asked me, 'Brother, how is the organizational work going?' He knows that I am a swayamsevak of the Sangh.

I said, 'The work is going on well, but we are facing some difficulty in connecting with our Harijan[3] brothers. They're not joining in the numbers they should.'

He asked, 'Why don't they join?'

'They tell us that "you have considered us inferior since birth," and that they won't tolerate it anymore,' I replied.

He said, 'Explain to them – we haven't made them inferior.'

He gave the example of the Purusha Sukta[4] from the Rigveda[5] – Brahmins were born from the mouth, Kshatriyas from the arms, Vaishyas from the thighs and Shudras from the feet. Devraha Baba laughed and said, 'Go and tell them that the sacred Ganga[6] emerged from the feet of Lord Vishnu. They are not inferior, they are sons of Ganga, the purifier. So how can they be impure?'

The Purusha Sukta is often interpreted in a way that conveys the feeling that the Shudras, born from the feet, are inferior. But that is a great injustice to the composers of the Rigvedic hymns. If the description is of a cosmic being, it cannot be that the being has a head, arms and thighs, but no feet. Feet give stability; feet enable movement. We don't worship the head – we worship feet. If people start touching the head instead, it will cause great trouble. Feet are worshipped – they are sacred. The Purusha Sukta is in the tenth *mandala*[7] of the Rigveda. In the first nine mandalas, there is no mention of any *varna*[8] system. Even in the Purusha Sukta, the idea was about the parts and the whole – not about superiority and inferiority. If a thorn pricks my foot, I feel the same pain as I would with a headache. This is just a way of expressing our mutual interdependence. Until the ninth mandala of the Rigveda, there is mention of *jana* (people), but not varnas (castes). There was the mention about five janas, and the *rakshasa*s were also included in that. We think of rakshasas as fearsome beings, but they were also a community – and must have been a part of the society at that time. Back then, there were Brahmins and Kshatriyas, and the rest were called Vish. There was no mention of Shudras.

In the Bhagavada Gita[9], when Lord Krishna says during the Mahabharata period, '*Chaturvarnyam maya srishtam guna karma vibhagashah*' (The four Varnas were created by me, based on the qualities and actions). But it wasn't like that during the Vedic age. During the Mahabharata era, varna was based on qualities and actions, not by birth. There is a mantra in the Vedas in which a *rishi*[10] says, 'My father is a physician, my mother is a grinder, she grinds grain, but I am a poet.' Now, all three have different occupations, yet they belong to the same family. In the Mahabharata, there are examples of people belonging to the same varna doing different kinds of work. There are also examples of people from different varnas living together.

Were the people of Vedic age fair-skinned? Perhaps yes, some may have been light-skinned. But the belief that they were outsiders because of their fair complexion is incorrect. No, they did not come from outside. There's no need to gather too many arguments to prove this. If they had come from elsewhere, they would have brought memories of that land with them. And if they had brought such memories, they would surely have been reflected somewhere in their literature. But we do not find any such reflection. The way the Aryans[11] expressed affection towards the land of the Sapta Sindhu[12] – 'My Ganga, my Yamuna, my Saraswati . . . ' – if they had come from outside, such deep love would not have flowered. They were inhabitants of this very land. People of every skin tone are found here. The varna system cannot be based on skin colour.

Secondly, varna means one who makes a choice (*jo varan karta hai*) – that is, individuals choose their work or profession based on their ability. If someone is born in a family where a certain profession is practised, it is natural that they will be inclined towards that profession. But if a profession can be designated, it also means that it can be changed. In the rigid definition, a Brahmin is supposed to do only worship, perform rituals and *yajna*s – nothing beyond that. But are Brahmins actually doing *only* that? Are Brahmins not taking up jobs? Of course they are. Similarly, Kshatriyas, by definition, are supposed to do nothing but fight. But what should a Kshatriya do if there is no war? If there is no war from outside, should they fight within? Nowadays, when there is war, the so-called 'martial races' alone are not sufficient. The entire nation has to fight. This theory of 'martial race' no longer holds ground.

In some accounts of Alexander's invasion and defeat, it is mentioned that Alexander's army captured some Indian soldiers, and they were Brahmins. How were Brahmins performing the duties of Kshatriyas then? That means a Brahmin could take on a Kshatriya's role, and a Kshatriya could perform some other work too. Sadly, looking at someone as inferior or superior by birth, and treating them accordingly throughout their life has been going on for generations in our country. This is a shameful image of us. What message of equality can we preach to the world?

In Namibia and South Africa, discrimination exists based on the colour of one's skin. There, at least the difference between white and black is clearly distinguishable. However, we have no such distinction here. The colour of our blood is same, and the colour of our skin too is same. Then what is the basis for this discrimination?

They were deprived – they were not allowed to read the Vedas. They were deprived – they could not perform worship in temples. They were deprived – they could not walk on the same streets as others. There would be elevated roads for some, and lower ones for them. And even on the lower road, they were made to wear a pot around their necks – because if they needed to spit, they couldn't spit on the road, as it would be defiled. They had to spit into the pot around their neck and carry their spit along with them. Ah! These things sound like fables, but for so many generations people have had to endure and suffer this system. Its lingering embers still burn deeply in the heart.

I was shocked the other day when, during a Rajya Sabha debate, a very senior leader from the Congress Party said that Chakravarti Rajagopalachari was a Brahmin, but he did not believe in untouchability. However, his elder brother held very rigid views. He wouldn't eat food touched by anyone else. The leader said that once, while they were having lunch, he accidentally entered the room because he needed to collect a piece of paper. Rajaji's elder brother saw him and immediately left his meal. Rajagopalachari said, 'Why did you enter the room? Ah! Now he has to remain hungry.' The man replied, 'But I didn't say anything. I didn't even go near him.' To which Rajagopalachari said, 'My elder brother considers even being seen by someone a defilement – *drishti dosh*.' I don't want to say anything bad about him. But such things cannot continue anymore.

The varna system may have had some utility in the past. Inherited professions may have led to expertise and skill. A son would see the work his father did and learn it from a young age. That could have opened paths to development. But it should not be based on heredity anymore. If someone wants to take a different path, there should be a way for them. Even today, millions of people in this country still carry human waste on their heads. Mechanization has still not been fully achieved. This has been going on for generations. But what hurts them more than the work itself is that they no longer have a bond of affection with us, the kind that once existed. I have seen discrimination and untouchability even in my own village during my younger days. But the man who used to cut our hair, we used to call him '*Nai Chacha*' (Barber Uncle). Today, no one says that anymore.

Even professions were classified separately so that everyone could have a livelihood and people wouldn't interfere in each other's work. We had farmland at home, but we weren't allowed to use the plough. We couldn't bring a spinning wheel into our home or spin yarn with a spindle, because that was someone else's work, and we were not supposed to interfere. But how did that work become inferior?

Forty years have passed since Independence. Many institutions and organizations have tried in their own ways to bring about equality and harmony in our society. The RSS too has played an important role in this. But the pace of this reform must accelerate. The Sangh may not be able to do everything in its official capacity, but we as swayamsevaks of the Sangh can do it. The revered sarsanghchalak has clearly outlined the Sangh's stance in his speech at Pune[13] – we do not believe in untouchability;

we seek to end untouchability in society. There should be no place for untouchability in the conduct of the Sangh. We do not judge anyone as superior or inferior on the basis of birth.

Pandit Kamalapati Tripathi is a senior leader of the Congress. A commemorative volume was published when he turned 75. One of the essays in that book supported the caste system based on birth.

I said, 'Pandit ji, what is this?'

He said, 'I believe in the varna system.'

I replied, 'If you believe in it, that's your choice. But what was the need to write about it in your birthday commemorative volume? That wasn't right. And this is a matter of disagreement. Who would want to be born "lower" by birth? Who would want to be a "Harijan"? Why would anyone want that? The responsibilities they're handling today are, in fact, a favour to us – a favour.'

Panditji got upset with me. He said, 'What kind of Brahmin are you?'

I said, 'Maharaj, I'm this kind of Brahmin.'

I didn't tell him that I go to the RSS. My elder brother and I – descendants of a high Brahmin lineage from Gwalior – went to a Sangh camp once along with a few others. At home, we used to remove our clothes and eat on a separate platform, strictly following untouchability rules. Even in the cold, we would shiver but still remove our clothes before eating. In the camp who would remove their clothes? How would it look if we alone undressed while everyone else ate fully clothed? If religion was at stake, so be it – we wouldn't remove our clothes. Anyway, it was too cold. But my elder brother was with me there. And another person by name Manikchandra Vajpayee too. Manikji was quite orthodox. He said, 'I have come to the camp, but I won't eat with everyone else.'

Our camp-in-charge said, 'Fine, eat separately. But who will cook?'

He said, 'I'll eat food cooked by my own hands.'

'Then go ahead and cook.'

He was given lentils, rice, vegetables, firewood, etc. Once, he managed to light the stove, make some roti and even removed his clothes and ate. But when evening came, we said, 'Now, Mamaji, that's enough. You've defended personal religion in the morning, now defend public dharma.' He didn't cook separately the second time.

But this work must now move faster. There's a conspiracy underway to distance those who call themselves Dalits from the Hindu religion. A calculated effort is being made. Slogans like *'Harijan-Muslim bhai-bhai, Hindu kaun, kahan se aaye!'* (Harijans and Muslims are brothers, who are these Hindus and where have they come from) were being raised. A political party has emerged to put these slogans into action. Although it hasn't gained many votes, it is spreading poison in the society. They are exploiting existing inequalities and trying to deepen them.

There should be equality in food and prayer – at the very least, these two things should have no discrimination. Marriage is a separate issue, but equality in food and devotion is essential. This is followed at RSS gatherings, but what is the situation outside? Even today, there are temples where not all Hindus are allowed entry. Even today, there are wells from which not everyone is allowed to draw water.

Recently, a riot broke out merely because a Harijan groom rode a horse through the village. Why shouldn't he? A groom is a groom, no matter what caste he belongs to. If he rode through the village on a horse, what's wrong with that? Harijan (Dalit) women are not allowed to wear jewellery – such reports have also come in. Although such incidents are decreasing, they are also exaggerated in the media many times. Caution must be exercised about that too. RSS swayamsevaks should be present in such situations and respond appropriately.

A society remains alive only when it continues to work actively and has the ability to change with time. Greece perished, Rome fell, no one even remembers ancient Egypt, Islam took over Iran and ancient Iran vanished and Iraq's former glory turned to dust. But if there is any civilization whose cultural tradition has continued uninterrupted and intact for thousands of years, it is our Hindu civilization and the honour of Hindu identity.

But this does not mean we have not changed – we have changed, just gradually. Dr Hedgewar was a proponent of social reform. His view was simple: the Sangh must always stay one step ahead of society. Keep this in mind: the founder of the Sangh, who once contemplated revolutionary methods for freedom, was also a pioneer of ideological transformation. He never said that we should lag behind in matters of social reform. The Sangh created a system in which caste differences are minimized, equality increases and harmony is nurtured. He clearly stated that when it comes to social reform, the Sangh must take the lead – it should not fall behind. It must lead, and from that position of leadership, observe whether the rest of society is also progressing.

Today, we need to take a big step. Lord Vamana[14] measured the earth, the netherworld and the heavens in just three steps. If the RSS truly wishes, it can cover this entire nation in just one step when it comes to social reform. But our role – as individuals – must also be more impactful. It should be the role of every swayamsevak. Look within yourselves, think deeply. Observe the situation in your own village. Analyze how much damage this social division is causing us. You'll then arrive at the conclusion that this rupture in society must be healed.

Industrialization is happening. Urbanization is happening. Employment opportunities are being ensured for every individual. The gap between 'big' and 'small' should naturally reduce. Yet, some things are deeply ingrained in our blood – they cause great pain. These can only be removed through a transformation of values and mindset.

I remember, back in 1980, we were contesting elections. The Janata Party had broken apart. One faction had separated, and Shri Jagjivan Ram had been made the leader. Under his leadership, we were fighting the elections as the Bharatiya Jana Sangh, and we were hopeful of good results. Once, I was giving a speech in Sitapur. After I finished and stepped down, someone handed me a small slip. I read it after getting into the car. The note said: 'Don't keep mentioning Jagjivan Ram's name repeatedly. People are against it. They say he belongs at their feet, and now you want to place him on your head?' It was a small note – but it hit me hard. I told some of my friends in the Janata Dal that we won't win this election. The public mindset is not yet ready to accept Jagjivan Ram as prime minister. And yes, there were other reasons for the defeat too.

But if this was one of them, then it's deeply concerning. If a Muslim can become this country's president and home minister, then why can't one of the Hindus? I mentioned this in several speeches. Jagjivan Ram called me and said, 'I read your speech. Please don't say such things. It will divide society. Please don't say these things.' He was a true Hindu.

Selfish interests are growing stronger today. Many forces are working to divide society. We know that political unity depends on social unity, and we must take the mantra of unity into the entire society – not just in words, but in action.

I once said in Parliament: 'I do not believe in untouchability. And even if God Himself comes and tells me to believe in untouchability, I will still refuse to believe in it.' And I added: 'My God can never say such a thing. He is the one who sanctifies the fallen; He can never promote such a belief.'

We have taken upon our shoulders a great responsibility – the work of the Sangh. And to fulfil that responsibility, may the Almighty give us strength – this is my humble prayer.

23

'Dharma Is the Nectar-Filled Vessel for the Welfare of All Beings, the Wish-Fulfilling Tree of Global Well-Being'

RANGA HARI

Ranga Hari was a senior pracharak from Kerala who held a number of important positions in the RSS at the provincial level in Kerala as well as at the national level. He served as the Akhil Bharatiya Bouddhik Pramukh for several years. Later, owing to health issues, he restricted himself to the Bharatiya Vichar Kendram in Thiruvananthapuram, Kerala, yet continued his intellectual pursuits like authoring books and delivering occasional addresses.

Here is a speech he delivered at the Tritiya Varsha (Vishesh) Sangh Shiksha Varg[1] at Nagpur in 2011 on 'The Concept of Dharma'. Many misconceptions exist in our society regarding the concept and meaning of Dharma. Through his deep study, serious contemplation and personal experience, Ranga Hari presents the essence of Dharma with clarity and insight.

The desire to understand Dharma is evident everywhere today. Generally, the word 'dharma' is often used by religious leaders. However, nowadays, even political leaders, who crave power, also emphatically talk about the idea of 'coalition Dharma'. Social leaders, who are leading movements against corruption and misgovernance, also speak in terms of Dharma and *adharma*. Those who are fighting for social justice through public interest litigations also claim to be working to restore Dharma in the society. In other words, in today's public life – whether political or economic or social or religious – the 'Dharma' has become common parlance. It has even found its place in the dictionaries of Western languages.

What is this much-talked-about Dharma? What does it really mean? What is its relation to justice and ethics? Finally, is Dharma just a religious term like *punya* (virtue) and *paap* (sin)? What is its relevance in everyday life and in today's democratic international world? Is it a term opposed to the concept of secularism? Such questions arise in the minds of sincere and thoughtful persons.

One commonly heard quotation from the followers of most religions in India – whether learned or illiterate, philosophers or demagogues, priests or scholars, writers or producers: '*Dharma eva hato hanti, d Dharma eva hato hanti, Dharmo rakshati rakshitah harmo rakshati rakshitah*,' which means 'Dharma, when protected, protects; Dharma, when destroyed, destroys.' Many of those who repeat this phrase may not fully understand its meaning, yet they continue to repeat it.

Similarly, there is another verse: '*Yato dharmastato jayah*,' which means, 'Where there is Dharma, there is victory.' This maxim is inscribed in Devanagari script behind the seat of the Chief Justice in the Supreme Court of India. It is the guiding motto of that highest institution. Likewise, many institutions and newspapers in India have also adopted this very motto. This short eight-syllable line has become a widely known saying across the country, irrespective of linguistic differences. This is a statement from the epic Mahabharata. In that priceless text, this line appears 12–15 times, much like a recurring refrain of a devotional song.

For example, in the Udyoga Parva[2], Karna[3] says it to Shri Krishna, and Dronacharya[4] to Duryodhana[5]; while in the Bhishma Parva[6], Rishi Vyasa[7] to Yudhishthira[8]; and in the Anushasana Parva[9], Bhishma[10] to Shri Krishna. Each of them, after analyzing and evaluating the circumstances, arrive at the conclusion, 'Where there is Dharma, there is victory.'

In the same way, there is another well-known phrase: '*Satyam vada, dharmam chara*,' meaning, 'Speak the truth and follow Dharma always.'

Its source may be unknown, but everyone knows it. It is the most valuable instruction that a guru gives to the graduating student who is returning home from the *gurukul*[11] after completing his education. There are hundreds of such examples. The point is simply this: in India, the importance of Dharma is accepted by one and all.

To present the importance of Dharma not just on a theoretical level but also as the foundation of life, our great ancestors set before us the examples of many revered figures as the personification of Dharma. For example, while answering Sage Valmiki's[12] question, Sage Narada[13] clearly states that Dasharatha's[14] son, Rama, is the follower, protector and guardian of his own and his family's Dharma. An ideal human being is expected to be someone who is knowledgeable about Dharma and a protector of it in both personal and public life.

The root of the word Dharma is '*dhru*', which means 'to hold', 'to sustain', 'to grasp', 'to establish' and 'to manage'. The Shabda Kalpadruma[15] dictionary defines Dharma as '*dhaarati lokaan*', meaning, that which holds or sustains all the worlds is Dharma. Similarly, the dictionary by Vaman Shivram Apte[16] repeats this in different words, defining Dharma as '*dhriyate loko'nena, dhaarati lokam va.*'

Here, we must understand the meaning of the root 'dhru' – to hold – correctly. The meaning of this root in relation to Dharma is not merely limited to worldly or physical actions but encompasses a much broader meaning. I will clarify this with an example. There are two words: Muralidhar[17] and Gangadhar. Muralidhar is the one who holds the flute. If seen from this perspective, a person who carries a basket of flutes on his head and goes door-to-door selling them would have to be called Muralidhar. But we do not call him Muralidhar. Why? We know that he only carries the flute for his livelihood.

Beyond the livelihood, there is no connection between him and the flute. Now, let us turn to the real Muralidhar. For him, the flute is an intentional and self-acknowledged effort to make his sweet voice even sweeter, as if the flute is an additional instrument for him. The flute serves the purpose of successfully performing his task. He must keep the herd of cows under control without ropes, lead all the assistant cowherds in harmony and provide charming notifications before the arrival and departure of the teachers of Vrindavan[18]. The means adopted by Kanha[19], the flute he holds, are integrated into his personality and that is how he became Muralidhar. Many people may carry flutes, but the true Muralidhar is only one. This is the deeper meaning of the word '*dhru-dhaarati*'.

Gangadhar is the one who holds the Ganga. If seen from this perspective, especially during the month of Shravan[20], millions of people carrying water pots filled with Ganga water across villages would be called Gangadhar. However, in our minds, there is only one Gangadhar, Lord Shiva, who holds the Ganga in his matted hair. In that holding, there is a goal, a penance. The immense force of the celestial Ganga waterfall required an extraordinarily strong foundation on earth, which Lord Shiva provided with his matted locks. From there, the life purpose of the Ganga – to cleanse sins and provide merit – began. It is for this reason that Lord Shiva became Gangadhar.

The explanation of the word 'dhaarati lokaan' or 'dhaarati lokam vaa' in the etymology of Dharma refers to this type of holding. It is not merely a physical grasp by the hand. It represents the sustenance of the world after its creation. It involves the stability, goodness, protection and nurturing of creation. Hence, it is said, '*dhaaranaat dharmah.*'

In the Vedic scriptures, the word 'dharma' is less frequent than '*rtam*'; in the Rigveda[21], it appears 56 times. In the later periods, starting from the historical and Puraanic[22] era, the 'dharma' gained prominence and abundance, while 'rtam' remained confined to the hymns of the Shruti[23] mantras. However, an important truth to note is that this did not lead to any loss of meaning or significance; rather, 'dharma' and 'rtam' came to be regarded as synonymous. Both were connected to the absolute truth.

Why is dhaaraṇa – sustaining – necessary? It is said, 'dhaaranaat dharmah', or that which sustains is Dharma. But why was this need for sustaining felt? To find the answer, we must look towards the process of creation itself. Imagine, there is a man, and he is alone. He can go anywhere for work, stay anywhere and change his residence whenever he wants. He is his own master, and there is no need or necessity to hold anything or anyone. However, as time passes and the cycle of life progresses, he eventually becomes a successful householder. He becomes the father of 7–8 children, and his family now consists of 10–12 people, including his wife. All the members of the family lead their lives according to their own interests or preferences. Now, if the head of the family ignores everyone and leaves them free, there could be internal conflicts. But coordination is also possible. Ideally, coordination is what is desired, as it will lead to the family's development and everyone's happiness. For this, the head of the family must weave all the members together in the thread of unity, handling them together without conflict or jealousy. Such a necessity did not exist when he was alone. It only became essential to hold and guide many once he manifested as many.

Let us examine the process of creation. It is said that before the expression of creation, there existed only the singular, unique primal energy. Within it, the impulse of desire arose: 'I must become many.' '*Vats* (Oh Child)! In the beginning, there was only *sat*, without the second. It desired, "Let me become many, let me generate,"' says Chandogya Upanishad[24]. That was when the undifferentiated, multi-dimensional expression of *sat* came into being. However, in the many arising from the one, there was an inherent consciousness of fundamental unity, much like how even when a magnet is broken into pieces, each piece retains magnetism.

For the development of that many, without destruction, there arose a need to keep them in harmony and unity. As mentioned in the etymology of 'dharma', it was necessary to uphold and manage the entire creation. In other words, as the primal energy expressed itself in multiplicity, Dharma was also created to uphold and sustain it. Dharma is the eternal force that stabilizes the creation while maintaining its diversity and multiplicity. Therefore, the Brihadaranyaka Upanishad[25] states: 'It created the form of Dharma in the shape of welfare. Therefore, nothing is superior to Dharma. That which is Dharma is undoubtedly truth itself.'

Let us take the example of the solar system. The Earth revolves around the Sun, and the Moon revolves around the Earth. Similarly, other planets also revolve around the Sun. Each of these has a fixed timeline – Saturn completes one revolution in 30 years, and Jupiter in 12 years.

Alongside this, these planets exert mutual gravitational pull on each other. Meanwhile, planets like Earth also rotate on their own axis.

From the beginning of creation till today, this entire solar system operates in perfect rhythm and harmony, with precision and order. The eternal force behind this cosmic coordination is called *Prakriti Dharma* (Nature's Dharma). Without Dharma, this would not be possible. In our own smaller worldly realm, even a small lapse in the observance of Dharma can lead to disasters. Imagine if even a tiny slip occurred at the level of Nature – then an unimaginable catastrophe would become inevitable. This reveals the immense significance of Dharma.

From this, it becomes clear that Dharma is not merely a concept relevant only to humankind; rather, the entire web of creation is bound by Dharma. All forms of existence – living or non-living, conscious or unconscious – depend on Dharma for their very being. It is in Dharma that they find their essence.

This is why it is said: water has its own Dharma, fire has its own Dharma, air has its own Dharma. Without this, their existence would collapse, and their identity in the world would cease. For instance, the Dharma of fire is heat. If something appears to be fire but lacks heat and only emits light, we don't call it fire. The Dharma of wind is motion. If air remains completely still without any movement, who would still call it wind? The Dharma of Earth is to provide support to all. Hence it is also called Dhara, Dharitri, Dharani and Vasundhara. If it ceases to uphold this Dharma, all these names would lose their meaning.

In this vast universe, every tiny element has its own inherent Dharma. Its existence, nature and identity depend on it.

In the same way, living beings too have their own specific Dharma. That is how we recognize them. There's a well-known children's story: A jackal's cub, from early childhood, is raised among lion cubs. One day, a herd of 10 or 12 elephants approach. The lion cubs, overcome with excitement, roar enthusiastically and prepare to attack. But the jackal cub trembles from head to toe. Until then, he had always thought himself to be a part of the lion pack – but now, why was he reacting differently?

Observing the whole scene from outside the cave, the lioness mother smiled and said, 'Son, you are brave, trained, and worthy of being admired

– but you were born in a clan where elephants are not hunted.' What the lioness meant was that the Dharma of a lion cannot be that of a jackal.

The Dharma related to non-human creation is also called *Prakriti* (Nature). This is because, unlike humans, non-human beings do not possess faculties like intellect, mind and discernment. For them, Dharma itself is their nature. Still, every inert object and every living being can be identified only through their innate natural Dharma.

Dharma is the very foundation of both non-human and human existence. Without Dharma, creation cannot sustain itself – it will weaken and dissolve. Therefore, our ancestors and seers have said, 'Dharma is the foundation of all existence in the universe; everything is established in Dharma, and hence Dharma is regarded as supreme.'

Let us now consider the place of Dharma in the human domain. Here, one fundamental truth must be remembered. According to the Indian philosophy, human beings are an integral part of the entire creation. They have no existence separate from it. Nor was the universe created solely for their enjoyment. Although the Creator has endowed humans with the inner capacity to realize *Sat–Chit–Ananda* (existence-consciousness-bliss), his right to live on Earth is equal only to that of a tiny ant.

Therefore, Dharma exists for the stability and sustenance of all. Within its scope, both humans and non-humans are equally included.

That is why Bhishma Pitamah, while instructing Yudhishthira, says:

'Dharma is what binds and sustains all together in a single thread. It is through Dharma that all beings are connected as one. That which unites all is Dharma.'

Humans, owing to their internal faculties like mind, intellect and consciousness, are more evolved than other beings. This enables them to go beyond the mere realm of nature. Depending on their inner qualities, humans can either evolve or regress. The qualities that lead to evolution are called *sadguna*s – virtues, while those that cause degeneration are called *durguna*s – vices. In a positive direction, man can go beyond nature and progress towards culture – *sanskriti*. In a negative direction, he can slip into distortion – *vikriti*. Both tendencies exist within him.

Lord Krishna classified these qualities into two types: *daivi* (divine) and *asuri* (demonic) qualities. The daivi qualities are those which make human society healthy, happy, secure, orderly, organized and harmonious. Hence, they are considered religious or aligned with Dharma. On the contrary, those qualities that lead to illness, disorder, disintegration, tension and conflict are termed adharmic – unrighteous.

Thus, the qualities that nurture and strengthen Dharma later came to be known as 'Dharma' itself. Across the country, ordinary people commonly understand Dharma to mean duty, compassion, charity, non-violence, good conduct, honesty, empathy, cooperation and helpfulness. These qualities are not Dharma itself, but rather emotional virtues that express and uphold Dharma. These virtues enable Dharma to function and succeed. Hence, they came to be recognized as indicators of Dharma and began to be known as Dharma itself.

A human being, unlike an animal, does not think only about themself. They are also a component of society. Therefore, they are called a social being. A society is different from a herd. A herd is driven merely by an instinctive urge for survival and lacks individual personality. But society is that collective where each person, while preserving their distinct identity and selfhood, willingly sets aside personal inconvenience for fulfilling collective needs and joins hands with others for the common good.

Here, the Sanskrit language helps us. In Sanskrit, the word for a herd is '*samaj*'. It is a birth-oriented word. Just as '*jalaj*' means 'born of water', similarly, samaj means born of sameness – where all are identical in impulse and action. Hence the definition: '*Pashunam samuhah samajah*', or, group of animals is called samaj. However, Sanskrit also gives us the word '*samaaj*'. This is an action-oriented term. It means a group of people moving in the same direction towards a common goal. This is possible only for human beings. Therefore, a comparative definition later emerged: *Pashusamananam murkhanam samuhah samajah, pashubhinananam sabhasadanam samuhah samajah*. Or, the group of animal-like ignorant beings is samaj, but the group of wise individuals distinct from animals is samaaj. Thus, samaj is a group of ignorant beings like animals, while samaaj is a group of wise and thoughtful beings.

When contemplating about Dharma, we must keep this distinction in mind. As long as the sense of individuality and collectivity remain interwoven like warp and weft, humans live with mutuality. If this mutuality disappears, they will move towards conflict and 'might is right' becomes the rule. That will be like falling even lower than animals.

The conclusion is that human life can advance only through collectivity. This is clearly guided by the mantra of *sangacchadhvam samvadadhvam* – a call for shared speech, shared thought and shared action. It is a direction to move together towards one goal. For this, support must be taken from Dharma, because Dharma is born for the very purpose of *dhaarati lokaan* – that which upholds the worlds.

Affirming this through past experiences, Bhishma Pitamaha told Yudhishthira: 'It is through Dharma alone that the entire samaaj (society) has continued to live by mutually protecting one another – even without a formal state system, without a king, without punishment and without external compulsion.'

Relying on evolved individuals and shifting from the ego-centred '*aham* (I)' to the collective '*vayam* (we)', human society has advanced – not through external force, but through inner inspiration, both at the personal and the collective level.

When we say that Dharma exists to connect individuals and keep them harmoniously organized, it implies that more than one person is needed for its application. In essence, Dharma is not individual-centric but community-oriented.

Let us analyze this. Words like *maatrdharma* (mother's Dharma), *pitrdharma* (father's Dharma), *patidharma* (husband's Dharma), *gurudharma* (teacher's Dharma) and *shishyadharma* (disciple's Dharma) refer to individuals but are meaningful only in relational contexts. Take pitrdharma as an example – it refers to a father's duty towards his son or daughter. This means that to carry out pitrdharma, at least one child is necessary. More children would only deepen its application. But for someone who is childless, what pitrdharma can there be? Similarly, patidharma requires a wife, gurudharma a disciple and shishyadharma the presence of a teacher. A Sanyaasi (renunciate) has no *patnidharma* (duty as a husband), and a barren woman has no maatrdharma (duty as a mother).

Thus, it becomes evident that for the cycle of Dharma to be complete, more than one embodied being is required. In other words, Dharma is related not to one, but to many. If a lone human being lives in a vast, desolate forest, what kind of Dharma could apply to him? Only that which applies to human existence in general. But forests are inhabited by wild animals, not human society – hence, he will remain untouched by *maanavdharma* (human social duties).

Another unique feature of Dharma is that it is self-regulating. It does not require external compulsion. Through an awakened heart and an enlightened mind, Dharma becomes self-operating. The joy that arises from this itself becomes its driving energy. Law, on the other hand, behaves differently. Law does not possess self-regulating capacity. It originates from an external centre of authority, and without that, it has no real force. Those who follow the law are not necessarily broad-hearted or enlightened. It is mostly the fear of punishment that drives compliance. For example, at a traffic junction, if there is no police presence, no crowd and no signal, a scooter rider inspired by Dharma will still stop, respecting traffic rules. In contrast, a person forced by law may think, 'There is no police – what is there to fear?' and proceed by breaking the rules, possibly ending up in an accident.

A person compelled by law thinks only about himself, while one inspired by Dharma considers others as well. Law is individual-centred; Dharma is community-centred. Dharma is also context sensitive.

Dharma prevents wrong actions, while law punishes after the wrong has been done. Dharma is the green light that leads you on the right path, and law is the red light that prevents you from taking the wrong path. Law is a complement to Dharma, not a substitute. It does not have the same independent, self-sustaining existence as Dharma. Even in the absence of a government, Dharma will survive. But if there is no government, law will cease to exist.

Dharma is not a visible or tangible object. It is a fundamental principle and like all such principles, it is formless. It can only be manifested through a living, conscious human being. The qualities that make Dharma successful and effective reside in humans. The responsibility of cultivating these qualities in individuals primarily lies with the family, educational institutions and sects or creeds (*panth-sampradaay*). It also involves literature, art, history and administration.

From children to the elderly, everyone is drawn to stories. Literature and tales influence young, tender minds with virtuous qualities early on. For example, texts like the Panchatantra[26] and Hitopadesha[27] use small, everyday creatures as characters to plant the seeds of virtues like trustworthiness, friendship, unity, harmony, cooperation and mutual living in the fertile soil of childhood minds. Hence, ethics came to be regarded as synonymous with Dharma.

To curb crimes like theft, smuggling and cheating, the administration created suitable laws. As a result, rule or law (*niyam* or *vidhi*) became another meaning of Dharma. Likewise, when beggars came to doorsteps saying, '*Dharm do, maiya*' (give alms, mother), and the mothers offer them a handful of grains, children perceive Dharma to mean charity.

Thus, due to its various dimensions, Dharma came to mean ethics, charity, duty, law, compassion, service and more. As a result, Dharma became a treasure chest of collective, noble virtues beneficial to society as a whole.

The greatest contribution in shaping Dharma in this way has come from various pantha-sampradaaya. Two key concepts within any sampradaaya are puṇya (merit) and paap (sin). All devout believers across the world, regardless of sect, agree on this idea: *Paropakaarah puṇyaaya, paapaaya parapidanam* (Helping others is merit, hurting others is sin). All the qualities that enable the turning of the *dharmachakrapravartanaaya* (wheel of Dharma) are universally regarded as merit-giving, and their opposites are considered to generate sin.

Puṇya leads to eternal happiness, while paap brings perpetual suffering. This shared and unwavering idea across all sects leads to the inspiration to accumulate merit and gain eternal happiness, and the desire to avoid sinful acts and escape eternal sorrow. In other words, moving forward in a positive, Dharmic direction and turning away from negative, adharmic paths becomes possible due to the strong influence of pantha-sampradaaya. Thus, sects or creeds serve as an enduring source of inspiration for living a Dharma-abiding life.

As a result, pantha-sampradaaya has also acquired the designation of Dharma, just like qualities such as morality, charity and duty. There are many examples where the means, in complete harmony with the ends, assume the name of the ends itself. For example, through an idol (*murti*), the devotee experiences the presence of the formless divine and ultimately begins to perceive the idol itself as God. Dharma holds a similar position.

At this point, a clarification is necessary. It is often said that referring to sects and creeds as Dharma is a distortion introduced by the British. However, upon reflection, one feels convinced that we ourselves are responsible for this error. It was quite likely that our own people had made such mistranslations.

In our spiritual literature, Adi Shankaracharya[28] is referred to as 'Shanmatacharya'[29], not as 'Shadharmcharya'[30]. Great sages like Swami Vidyaranya[31], who were knowledgeable in philosophy, referred to Shankaramat but not Shankardharma (in Sanskrit). This is not an ancient or old concept but something from the fifteenth–sixteenth century. Even today, in the four languages of the South, terms like Hindu *matam*, Christu matam, Muslim matam, Jain matam, Buddh matam, Shaiva matam, Vaishnava matam, etc., are in vogue. The sects and creeds that are mistakenly called religions today are actually *mat* (faith or doctrine). The doctrine of Jesus Christ is 'Christu matam', the doctrine of Muhammad is 'Muhammadiya matam', the doctrine of Buddha is 'Buddh matam', the doctrine of Jain Tirthankaras is 'Jain matam' and the worshippers of Vishnu, based on idol worship, follow the doctrine of 'Vaishnava matam'. At the root of each matam is always a human being. Therefore, matam is human in nature, while Dharma is non-human.

In reality, Dharma is broader than matam; it is the foundation. Dharma is inclusive. It accommodates both theistic and atheistic people, as both are committed and responsible for the well-being of human society. Non-violence, truth, honesty, etc., are rooted in humanity, not theism or atheism. If examined closely, all ten characteristics of Dharma, as defined by Manu[32] in Manu Smriti[33], are related to humanity. These characteristics are – determination (*dhriti*), forgiveness, self-control (*dama*), honesty, cleanliness, control of senses, wisdom (*dhi*), knowledge (*vidya*), truth and non-anger. Careful reflection will reveal that none of these are linked to any particular form of worship. Whether one is a theist or an atheist, these virtues are expected in all righteous men and women.

There are countless references like this in our religious literature. Bhishma Pitamah says to Yudhishthira, 'He who is the friend of all beings and is one with all beings is called Dharmayukta.' This is a characteristic of the global human, the qualities of a global citizen, regardless of being theistic or atheistic. When King Rantidev[34] said, 'I do not want the divine supreme abode, nor do I want the eight divine *siddhis*[35], nor the divine power that takes me beyond the cycle of rebirth. What I want is the ability to share in the sufferings of those who are suffering and help alleviate their pain,' he attained the religious level of the universal human.

Sects and creeds are exclusive. In the worship practices of Vaishnavas, Shaivas are not included; and in the worship practices of Shaivas, Vaishnavas are not included. Their rituals are different. Similarly, in Islamic rituals, Christian rituals are not included; and in Christian rituals, Islamic ones are excluded. Sects are separate, and religion is integrative. Sects are analytical, while religion is holistic. The circle of religion is all-embracing, while the circle of matam is self-chosen.

It is not mandatory that a theistic person is always righteous, and an atheistic person is unrighteous. This is because a devout and faithful person, like Ravana[36], can also be unrighteous. It is essential to understand that Dharma is based on values, not on whether a person is theistic or atheistic. The concept of Dharma is uniquely Indian, and hence, its worldview naturally aligns with Indian philosophy. This is fundamentally different from Western and Semitic philosophies, which hold that the duration of life is only until death. After death, the soul has to wait in the grave until the day of final judgment. However, in Indian philosophy, the journey of life is infinite. Death is not the end of life; it is merely a pause before the next birth. Life is a chain made up of the links of this world and the afterlife. The journey continues until liberation (*Moksha*) is attained through one's actions. This is the Dharma-centric worldview of life. Therefore, Dharma does not only consider the material world but also the afterlife. This is what spirituality refers to. Hence, naturally, spirituality is part of the domain of Dharma.

In his commentary on the Bhagavada Gita, Adi Shankaracharya says that Dharma is the cause of the world's existence ('*Jagatah sthitikaranam*'), and at the same time, it is the cause of the progress and ultimate well-being of all beings ('*Praninam abhyudayanishreyasehetu*'). *Abhyudaya* means progress in this material world, and *Nishreyasa* means Moksha, the ultimate spiritual goal. Thus, Dharma is the means of progress in both this world and the afterlife. To attain that state, an individual can follow any path of worship based on their feelings and emotions. Dharma does not interfere with this. However, it does firmly state that 'the ultimate goal of a human is Moksha, and its foundation is Dharma.'

According to Indian philosophy, human life is like a river, and its water and flow represent the pursuits of *Artha* (wealth) and *Kama* (desire). This river has two banks: Dharma and Moksha. In order to be beneficial, the river of life must flow between these two banks, without crossing or ignoring them. The relationship between Dharma and spirituality is clearly illustrated by this example.

Dharma is directly related to practical life, and a human being, constrained by his circumstances, creates smaller and larger circles around himself, due to which his Dharma too takes on smaller or larger dimensions. First and foremost, being an individual, a person has individual Dharma (*vyaktidharma*). As he evolves into a family, he gains a family Dharma or household Dharma (*kutumbdharma*). Similarly, around him grow the circles of caste, village, province, country, nation, world, etc., and as a result, he becomes associated with various kinds of Dharma. To fulfil these, in addition to vyaktidharma, there is also caste Dharma, village Dharma, national Dharma, global Dharma and professional Dharma such as business Dharma, legal Dharma, medical Dharma, teacher's Dharma and so on.

No level of Dharma is separate or different from the other, as all have the same goal – 'dhaarati lokaan' (to uphold the world in an orderly manner). However, sometimes a conflict arises between two Dharmas, and the person caught in between becomes restless or confused about what to do. This is called a moral dilemma – *dharmasankat*.

A dharmasankat is different from indecisiveness – *duvidha*. Duvidha is the inability to make a decision: whether to go to the cinema or not, whether to eat dinner at night or not, whether to wear a khadi kurta or a silk one for the wedding. This is not a conflict, but a matter of mental uncertainty.

But a dharmasankat arises when both actions are right and necessary. However, doing one goes against the other. Both are Dharma; neither is adharma. In other words, this is not a conflict between Dharma and adharma but between two equally valid Dharmas. Because both are Dharma, a person finds himself in a crisis. This is what is called dharmasankat.

There is an old story. Sage Matanga[37] was meditating under a tree. A distressed traveller, with a bag of money in his hand, came running and said, 'Maharaj! Please save me! A robber is chasing me.' At once, Matanga told him to hide inside the hollow of the tree. After a while, the robber came and asked the sage, 'Have you seen someone running this way?' Now the sage was in a dharmasankat. His life's vow was truth and non-violence. What should he say now? If he told the truth, it would lead to violence, and he would be complicit, thus becoming a sinner. If he told a lie, he would become a sinner for speaking untruth. He immediately reflected and concluded that protection of life is the highest Dharma, and he lied to the robber. The story tells us that no sin was attributed to Sage Matanga.

There is a similar story in the Karna Parva[38] of the Mahabharata, with a slight difference in narrative. There was a truth-speaking Brahmin named Kaushika[39]. He was meditating near a confluence outside the village. One day, some travellers, fleeing from robbers, took shelter in his hermitage. A little later, the robbers came asking. The ascetic Kaushika told them the truth. As a result, all the travellers were caught and killed. Though he had spoken the truth, the Brahmin became a participant in the sin of violence, and he fell from grace.

There is another well-known story of the devotee Prahlada[40]. His father was Hiranyakashyapa[41]. The father asked, 'Didn't your teacher tell you not to disobey your father's command?'

Prahlada replied, 'Yes.'

'Then why do you keep spreading the name of Narayan[42] against my wishes?'

Prahlada answered, 'Father, sometimes there is a conflict between a greater Dharma and a lesser one. In such situations, one must abandon the lesser and uphold the greater. Otherwise, the crisis will escalate and lead to total destruction.' This statement from Prahlada is invaluable for public life.

The same principle is expressed by Indra[43], in the form of a dove, to King Shibi[44]: 'O King, one must decide between Dharma and adharma by assessing what is significant and what is secondary. One must recognize the appropriate importance of things and make a Dharma-based decision.'

This is the same principle adopted by Sage Matanga. When a conflict arose between the two Dharmas – protection of life and truthfulness – he considered protection of life as the higher Dharma and chose it, letting go of the lesser one. In contrast, Kaushika clung to the lesser and abandoned the greater, thus becoming a participant in sin. Especially today, in a democratic environment where there is uproar over issues such as human rights, freedom of thought, caste rights, linguistic pride, regionalism, nationalism and global humanity, such a discourse on Dharma becomes immensely valuable.

Among the means that reinforce Dharma, the most significant are the religious paths and sects. The great saints who promoted these paths have, through simple allegorical tales and engaging anecdotes, revealed to us the importance of Dharma. By giving the formless Dharma a tangible form and presenting it through characters in stories, they introduced it to society.

When the noble daughter-in-law Draupadi[45] was being disrobed, Lord Krishna, moved by her heart-wrenching plea, took on the invisible form of Dharma and protected her modesty. In an extremely perilous situation, Dharma assumed the form of a Yaksha[46] and asked Yudhishthira, 'What are the gateways to Dharma?' The answers he received were – *ahimsa* (non-violence), *samata* (equanimity), *shanti* (peace), *daya* (compassion) and *amatsara* (absence of envy). Upon receiving this response, the Yaksha revealed his true form and granted the boon, 'You will remain safe from the Kauravas during your exile.'

Similarly, Dharma, in the form of a dog, came to test Yudhishthira during his final journey to the Himalayas. Deeply satisfied by the unwavering adherence of Yudhishthira to Dharma, he said: 'O best of the Bharatas! You have attained supreme greatness.'

In the Bhagavada Purana[47], an allegorical tale concerning Dharma appears, which is highly enlightening. The names of the characters in the story themselves signify the importance of Dharma. These are all names that denote qualities. The events in the story are also symbolic. With a little reflection, the deeper meaning becomes easily comprehensible.

Dharma is the son of the Creator, Brahma[48]. He was born from the right breast of the life-giver. The Prajapati[49] gave his 13 daughters in marriage to Dharma. They all became his *sahadharmacharini*s (righteous consorts). Their names are – Shraddha (faith), Maitri (friendship), Daya (compassion), Shanti (peace), Tushti (contentment), Pushti (nourishment), Kriya (action), Unnati (progress), Buddhi (intellect), Medha (wisdom), Titiksha (forbearance), Hri (modesty) and Murti (form). The last daughter, Murti, had two children; the others had one each. Thus, there were a total of fourteen children.

From Dharma and Shraddha was born Shubha (auspiciousness), from Dharma and Maitri came Prasada (grace), from Dharma and Daya was born Abhaya (fearlessness), from Dharma and Shanti came Sukha (happiness), from Dharma and Tushti was born Muda (joy), from Dharma and Pushti came Smaya (pride), from Dharma and Kriya was born Yoga, from Dharma and Unnati came Darpa (arrogance), from Dharma and Buddhi came Artha (wealth), from Dharma and Medha was born Smriti (memory), from Dharma and Titiksha came Kshema (welfare) and from Dharma and Hri (modesty) was born Prashraya (humility and grace). From the union of Dharma and Murti, the twins Nara and Narayana were born.

In truth, this tale is a narrative interpretation of the line quoted at the beginning of this essay from the Brihadaranyaka Upanishad. In the tale, the primordial energy takes the form of the Creator, Brahma; and through him, Dharma is born as his son. The subsequent storyline is self-explanatory.

There is also an allegorical tale related to adharma (unrighteousness), which is equally beneficial to understand, as it clarifies our conception of Dharma even further. According to the Bhagavada and Padma Purana[50],

Adharma is an anti-Dharmic being born from the back of Brahma. That is, while Dharma emerged from Brahma's right breast, Adharma came out from the back. His wife was Mrisha, meaning falsehood. The offspring of Adharma and Mrisha were Dambha (hypocrisy) and Maya (illusion). These two became a couple, and from them were born Lobha (greed) and Vikrita (deceitful duplicity). Later in that lineage were born Krodha (anger), Hinsa (violence), Bhaya (fear) and Yatana (torture).

What is the message of these two allegorical tales? Both Dharma and Adharma were born from the same body – Dharma from the nourishing breast that provides the elixir of life, and Adharma from the back, which expels waste. The virtues born from Dharma and his consorts are beneficial for humanity, elevating humans from nature towards culture. On the other hand, the traits born from the union of Adharma and Mrisha – such as hypocrisy, greed and anger – are harmful to humanity, leading it from nature towards distortion. In essence, Dharma is the righteous path (*sanmargi*), while Adharma leads one astray (*kumargi*).

Dharma is eternal and unchanging because it is meant to keep the entire cosmos firmly and properly organized. However, due to differences in time and place, it must offer guidance in practical life in a way that is suited to each era and location. Therefore, from a philosophical point of view, Dharma is stable, but from a practical point of view, it is dynamic. This is what is meant by *sanatan* (eternal). The way it is understood today – as orthodox, harsh or regressive – is not the correct interpretation. The word 'sanatan' is formed from two roots: '*san*', which means ancient, and '*tan*', which means current. So, sanatan means that which, although ancient, is ever new. Wise people often give the example of sunrise. It is the oldest phenomenon, yet always new – therefore, it is sanatan.

In the Brahmavaivarta Purana[51], the nature of Shri Shakti[52] as *sanatani* is described. Translating those Sanskrit words into refined Hindi, it states: 'That which exists in all times is called *sana*, that which is present is called *tani*, and that which is present at all times and in all places is sanatani.' This clarifies the meaning of the word sanatan. Dharma is undoubtedly sanatan – ancient yet current, stable yet dynamic, immortal yet everlasting.

Dharma is the foundation of all creation. The human society composed of diverse men and women of various forms and temperaments can only be sustained on that very foundation. Dharma is not individualistic, it is reciprocal. It is not divisive but inclusive, embracing all. The sphere of Dharma may vary in size according to different units of society, but it always strives to expand towards the greater good. Dharma is self-motivated and leads towards culture. It is not harsh, it is *sanatan*. Dharma is India's unique and invaluable gift to the world.

According to the saintly scholar Bharat Ratna Dr Bhagwan Das[53]:

> Dharma is that which upholds a thing, preserves its essence, prevents the weakening of its natural qualities and actions, and primarily maintains its very existence. Dharma is the natural law that binds various parts of the universe through cause-and-effect relationships – it is the organizing principle of the cosmos. It is the set of rules and principles that, emerging from the distinct emotions and feelings of individuals, weave together their actions, rights, and duties to sustain society. Dharma is the way of life that, based on the Vedas, guides human society towards both material prosperity (abhyudaya) and spiritual liberation (nishreyasa). In short, from a scientific viewpoint, Dharma is the inherent nature of a thing; from a moral and legal viewpoint, it is duty; from a spiritual and psychological viewpoint, it is a path or tradition; generally, it is righteous conduct and order; and above all, it is the highest obligation.

From this, it becomes evident that Dharma is as deep as it is lofty, as individual-centred as it is universally encompassing, as ancient as it is modern, as eternal as it is dynamic, as multidimensional as it is focused. It is the nectar-filled vessel for the welfare of all beings, the wish-fulfilling tree of global well-being.

Thus, even while lying on a bed of arrows, the venerable Dharma-knower Bhishma Pitamah begins his profound and infallible discourse on Dharma with this auspicious invocation: '*Namo dharmaya mahate namah krishnaya vedhase.*' In other words, 'Salutations to the great Dharma. Salutations to Krishna, the Creator.' What a meaningful and weighty invocation to the one who upholds Dharma!

24

'*Sarvangina Unnati* Means Holistic Progress in All Facets of Life'

DATTATREYA HOSABALE

Dattatreya Hosabale is a senior pracharak, currently serving as the sarkaryavah[1] of the RSS. After his education, Hosabale spent many years in the Akhil Bharatiya Vidyarthi Parishad (ABVP), prominent student organization in the country, rising to serve as its national organizing secretary, before being co-opted into the national team of the RSS in 2003. Since then, he has held several positions in the organization and was elected as its sarkaryavah in 2021. Besides occupying himself with the onerous activities of the topmost executive responsibility of the world's largest voluntary organization, Hosabale continues to pursue his passion of engaging with the intellectual world, and guides and mentors many individuals and organizations in that field.

He delivered a lecture on Hindutva at an RSS event in Bhopal, seeking to provide a contemporary interpretation of it.

This subject is not new to any of us, but its interpretation keeps evolving. In our prayer, we seek '*param vaibhav*', which is the highest level of magnificence or prosperity; and in our pledge, we speak of '*sarvangina unnati*', or what is balanced, integrated development. Both of these are expressions of the concept of development in Hindutva.

Everyone understands '*vaibhav*' to mean prosperity or material progress. However, 'param vaibhav' refers to progress that is attained not just materially, but also with altruism and spirituality. It is a higher kind of advancement. 'Sarvangina unnati' means holistic progress – progress in all facets of life, which includes both the animate and inanimate.

The word '*vikas*' (development) is widely used nowadays. Development and good governance are now widely discussed as primary objectives of state power everywhere.

At the core of modern development lies economic progress, often regarded as its backbone. It is measured by the increase in the production and consumption of goods and services, which is known as gross domestic product (GDP). We all know that considering economic progress alone as development has led to numerous crises for individuals and nations alike. It is important to understand the nature of those crises.

1. *Destruction of Natural Resources:* This is one of the gravest challenges in the world today. This issue is widely discussed from school textbooks to international conferences.
2. *Distortion of Food Grains and Agriculture:* The food we consume has become toxic, giving rise to many diseases. Similarly, agricultural land is also turning poisonous. This has impacted not just farming, but also the life, culture and community that depend on it.
3. *Adverse Impact on Society:* Growing economic disparity has led to disorder and fragmentation in the social order.
4. *Impact on Cultural and Biological Diversity:* Due to the so-called globalization, many local drinks across the world have disappeared and brands like Pepsi and Coca-Cola have become symbols of 'progress' for our youth. The same applies to entertainment and sports as well. Thanks to our association with the Sangh, we have had the opportunity to engage in a wide variety of games. However, when we look at the broader society, this diversity in sports seems to have disappeared. Games promoted by the media and the West have now become dominant. Sports have become a major business. This business, backed by big money, has destroyed local games.

Various surveys and studies, conducted globally, have assessed the grim world situation. A glimpse of it is as follows:

Environmental disasters

- Excess fossil fuel consumption leading to scarcity by 2050.
- Natural gas and coal to be scarce commodities by 2080 and 2100, respectively.
- As much as 25 per cent increase in pandemics, epidemics and other communicable diseases in 10 years.
- Sea-level rise due to polar ice melt could submerge hundreds of islands globally by 2050, creating over 3.5 million refugees in India and Bangladesh alone.
- By 2050, Ganga glacier melt would affect more than 4 million people in the Gangetic delta. Even if they are not rendered homeless, their lives will certainly be impacted.
- As high as 38 per cent of earth's surface area is used for agriculture. Rise in sea levels is expected to reduce a minimum of 5 per cent of it by 2050.
- Every year, 13 million hectares of forests are lost globally, contributing to climate change and global warming – this will only continue to rise. These are the harmful outcomes of the path of technological and economic progress we have chosen. Even experts have now begun to acknowledge this.
- Nearly 17,000 species of biodiversity are under threat, and more than 1.5 billion people are directly dependent on this biodiversity for their livelihood – this data paints a frightening picture.

Impact on Society

- Around 9 million children under the age of 5 die due to lack of access to healthcare, and 100 million children globally are homeless and sleep on the streets. There is no food – and if there is, it is not nutritious. Future of these children is steeped in darkness.
- Globally, 2.6 billion people lack access to sanitation.

- Across the world, 75 million children (55 per cent of whom are girls) have never been to school. In addition, 776 million adults – 16 per cent of the adult population – lack basic literacy skills, and two-thirds of them are women.
- In Bharat, the number of divorces has doubled in the past 10 years, and there has been a 3.6 per cent increase in the crime rate. We can clearly understand the impact this is having on Bharat's cultural and family life. Similarly, crimes against women have risen by 17 per cent, and crimes against children (child abuse) have increased by 10.2 per cent.
- There has been increased urbanization. By 2050, more than half the world's population will live in cities. Today, 33 per cent of the urban population lives in slums. The new government is talking about developing 100 smart cities. But due to urbanization, villages have emptied out, and slums in cities have expanded – worsening living conditions for many.
- Not only in Bharat, but also in Europe and America, we all saw what happened in the name of economic progress. In Bharat, the average household has 5.5 members, which requires one house per family. In contrast, America's average is 2.35 – which means that for Bharat to reach the American average, we would need double the number of homes, proportionate to population. Due to the trend towards smaller families, the number of houses required in Bharat is around 45 crores. Earlier, two or three generations lived together under one roof, but now even parents are not living in the same household. This puts pressure on government expenditure for social security. In America, the government has to spend as much as 60–65 per cent annually on social security. If the same trend takes hold in Bharat, how can the governments cope? From natural, cultural, social and economic perspectives, its harmful consequences are already visible.
- For instance, people from Kerala initially migrated to neighbouring states. Later they started going abroad. This led to cultural fragmentation and a rise in stress levels. A similar situation was seen in Bihar. Although the situation in Bihar improved slightly due to better law and order, migration from Odisha is still continuing.

People want to stay connected to their roots, but due to unfavourable environment, they are forced to move.

- People used to migrate for work for 8–10 days, or even for a month in the past too. Yet, they remained connected to their social and cultural moorings. But now, migration has acquired a more permanent form, resulting in social and cultural fragmentation.
- In Bharat, cyber fraud has increased by 44.9 per cent over the past decade, with 61.2 per cent of the offenses committed by people in the age group of 18–30.
- More than 350 million people belonging to indigenous (*swadeshotpanna*) communities, which constitute 6 per cent of the global population spread across 72 countries, are facing the threat of extinction.
- Out of around 8,000 languages spoken globally, more than 11.5 per cent (900 languages) have fewer than 150 speakers, and 95.2 per cent of the languages are listed as threatened worldwide. This is the result of the last 100 years. Even in our own country, the new generation is unable to speak in their mother tongues or native dialects. This is the outcome of linguistic homogenization.
- Due to the dominance of English as the sole communication language, the multilingual system and identity are under threat, and by 2050, it will become the only global lingua franca.
- Culture industry (even if it's not an industry in the traditional sense, it is treated as one) accounts for 3.4 per cent of global GDP – this is the economic promotion of culture. It includes cinema, theatre, orchestra and so on.
- With the breakdown of the social fabric and the rise in violence, 20 million people are displaced every year.
- Three billion people rely on fast-disappearing traditional medicine as their primary form of health care.
- There has been a homogenization of food consumption. In the past two decades, there has been a 94.5 per cent shift towards rice and wheat, leading to a sharp reduction in crop and food diversity.

Impact on Food Grains and Agriculture

- Even in food, local items are vanishing. Pizza, burger, chips – these are what the new generation and people in corporate lifestyle prefer. Slowly, the practice of cooking at home is also declining. This has harmful consequences from all perspectives.
- Globally, one billion people are undernourished.
- There has been a 40 per cent reduction in global soil productivity; chronic food scarcity is expected by 2050.
- Depletion in genetic diversity is an issue. For instance, in Bharat, before the Green Revolution, 4,200 varieties of rice were cultivated. Today, fewer than 500 varieties remain.
- By 2025, 40 per cent of the earth will face physical scarcity of fresh water.
- In 2007, 70 per cent of fresh water was used for agricultural production. And by 2025, more than 30 per cent decline in freshwater availability is expected.
- Global warming is projected to reduce wheat production by 30 per cent and irrigated rice production by 15 per cent in developing countries by 2050.
- Global grain reserves have been declining sharply since 2000, reaching their lowest point in 2009.
- In Bharat, landless rural livelihoods saw a constant increase, reaching 22 per cent in 2008.

Understanding the impact of development paradigms through new 'development indicators'.

Many countries have explored alternate ways to measure economic development. There are more than 20 alternative indicators in use today. Some of the major ones include:

1. Human Development Index (HDI)
2. Ecological Footprint
3. Happy Planet Index
4. Gross National Happiness

All these indicators have some limitations. None are complete in themselves. So far, GDP remains the primary metric of progress in Bharat. However, due to its limitations and inconsistencies, GDP has faced criticism. To understand this, consider an example. A woman working in a household is paid wages, which are added to GDP. But if she becomes the wife of the householder and performs the same or even more dedicated work without payment, it no longer counts towards GDP. This reveals the inconsistencies of the metric. Many such contradictions exist.

In Bharat, previous Five-Year Plans have primarily considered GDP as the main indicator. It is a measure of progress and economic growth. It represents the total value of goods and services produced in a year, and can be considered as national income, national product and average demand. GDP per capita, on the other hand, is the total GDP divided by the population. It is only an aggregate monetary measure – its aggregated nature prevents it from reflecting actual realities.

A large set of services are not accounted for; many genuinely useful societal services are not included. For example, small village storytellers provide valuable service to society. They teach lessons, entertain and are well-respected. People even contribute financially for their livelihood. Yet, such services are not included in the GDP framework. Such examples abound.

There are several other limitations of GDP. It cannot measure welfare objectives, nor can it account for natural resources and environmental structures. It offers no space to include culture and values (*sanskar*s).

Gross National Happiness (GNH)

Gross National Happiness (GNH) was conceptualized by the King of Bhutan, his daughter (a Harvard graduate) and a few Buddhist monks. The focus was to measure the quality of life in a holistic manner. This indicator tries to explain life quality more integrally and psychologically than GNP (Gross National Product).

GNH has been implemented in Bhutan since 2004 and is based on a Buddhist worldview. It believes that material and spiritual development together constitutes true development; it considers both *samutkarsha* (material upliftment) and *niḥshreyasa* (spiritual wellbeing). Being rooted in Buddhist thought, it is close to Hindu philosophy and reflects glimpses of *Ekatma Manav Darshan* (Integral Humanism). It is increasingly gaining attention across the world.

The four pillars of GNH are as follows:
1. Promotion of equitable and sustainable socio-economic development.
2. Preservation and enhancement of cultural values.
3. Conservation and nurturing of the natural environment and ecology.
4. Establishment of good governance.

GNH has nine domains:
1. Psychological well-being
2. Health
3. Time-use: are we just constantly running all day, or is there pause? Pause is essential for culture and civilization. It also strengthens the feeling of family.
4. Education
5. Cultural diversity and resilience
6. Good governance
7. Community vitality and virility
8. Ecological diversity
9. Living standard.

Sankat Ka Mool – Drishti Dosh (Faulty vision is the root of the problem).

The prevailing development thinking is solely tied to economic progress. Economic progress generally overlooks social, cultural and environmental issues. Some ingrained concepts arising from the so-called 'modern' Western worldview are:
1. *Humanity:* This is the belief that humans are superior to all creation and that only humans should survive, while the rest can live or perish. Everything is for human happiness and is subservient to it. This is the biblical view.
2. *Nature:* Resources are seen as an unlimited storehouse, while nature indeed has its limits.

3. *Materialism and consumerism as paths to happiness:* This is a false notion because consumption leads to increasing desire.
4. *Individual-centred perspective*: In America, the individual exists along with the government, while family, lineage and community have been destroyed. In India, this system is still intact.
5. Treating family, community and local environments as non-essential and attempting to universalize them.

A patchwork approach will not solve the crisis; the solution lies in a holistic approach. The prevailing concept and vision of development must be totally abandoned. Mere repair will not suffice. We must think about life in a different way, even if people say that we are 200 years behind. Adapting it to the modern age depends on our capacity. A comprehensive change in perspective is necessary.

Beyond economic progress, something else can exist. Happiness can come even beyond economics. This idea exists in the Indian worldview. Environmental welfare, social well-being, culture and society should also occupy central roles in the development plan. Therefore, they must also be included within the economic framework of development.

Up until the year 1700, India was at the forefront of economic affairs in the world. Back then, we balanced economic progress with nature and life. We did not destroy them. Life was joyful and fulfilling. Thus, Indian thought or worldview could serve as an essential foundation for development. Pandit Deendayalji[2] also mentioned this in his Integral Humanism philosophy. That concept is even more relevant today.

Indian (Hindu) Worldview:

- The entire universe (cosmos) is an expression of the same universal consciousness at various levels.
- Chiti (universal soul) exists from the individual to the universal, and we experience this at different levels. This is the concept of interdependence, interconnectedness and complementary unity of the whole.

- *Purushartha chatushtaya*: Dharma (righteousness), *Artha* (wealth), *Kama* (desire) and *Moksha* (liberation), these will guide the establishment of a duty-based, moral, social, economic system.
- Uncontrolled consumption of Artha and Kama has led to a crisis in our culture and community. This is a point we need to reflect upon.
- Earning with a sense of duty, without accumulation and detachment – this leads to an increase in wealth. This is clearly stated in Gandhiji's concept of trusteeship, and in Jain and Buddhist thoughts as well.
- Dharma: Freedom, truth, non-violence, altruism, charity, renunciation, etc.
- *Dritih kshamaa damo'steyam shaucham indriya-nigrahah. Dhir vidyaa satyam akrodho dashakam dharma-lakshanam.* (Manusmriti) This verse means that patience, forgiveness, self-control, non-stealing, purity, control of the senses, wisdom, knowledge, truthfulness and absence of anger – these 10 characteristics are essential in all aspects of individual, family, societal and national life. Only through these can eternal happiness be attained. This is the foundation of life. It should also be integrated into economic progress.
- *Ishavasyamidam sarvam.* (Ishavasyopanishad – 1) Or, all wealth belongs to God. Therefore, no one has the right to monopolize it.
- *Sabai bhumi Gopal ki.* In other words, since all land belongs to God, it should be utilized with us as its trustees.
- Restraining consumption: Emphasizing on savings, not just for oneself but for society and future generations. By reducing consumption, we can save water, forests and the environment. This saving is necessary from an individual, family and social perspective.

Protection of our Environment and Surroundings:

- Individual, family, community (society), nation, world, and ultimately, the entire creation are all interconnected (*akhand mandalakar*). In this interconnectedness, individual's happiness is ensured, and there is no conflict or struggle. Today, the modern Western model has made the individual the basis for conflict with all others.
- All components (units) are independent, autonomous, complementary, unified, self-motivated, self-regulated and are not merely the parts of

a large machine but rather biological organs. This prevents any desire to eliminate one another in conflict. All should work to support and strengthen each other.

- Protection of the individual within the family: Society must protect and nourish the children, the elderly, the disabled, the unemployed, the sick, the weak, the fallen and the abandoned. It is the responsibility of the society, and not some specialized institutions, to protect them. From a humane perspective, just because they do not earn, are they a burden? The Hindu perspective does not view them as a burden; instead, society has the responsibility to nourish and protect them.
- This unique thinking is not just for the benefit of India but for the entire human race. Chanakya had said the same – 'The science of economics has been created keeping in mind the welfare of the entire world (*Prithivyah labhapalanopayashastram arthashastram iti*).' This is India's vision.

Inspired by this worldview, India became a powerful economic force with remarkable material development. Economic historian Paul Bairoch found this fact while reviewing the General Agreement on Tariffs and Trade (GATT). He reviewed the global economic output between the years 1700 to 1980. In the period from 1700 to 1800, India's share of global output was 24.5 per cent, while that of Europe was 23.2 per cent.

Economic historian Angus Maddison conducted an Organization for Economic Co-operation and Development (OECD) survey. He studied global GDP and population from 1 AD to 2000 AD. From 1 AD to 1700 AD, India was always a highly successful and influential economic power. For a thousand years, India contributed more than one-third of the world's total production.

In the Hindu worldview, there has been a system of four varnas, four ashrams and the four purusharthas, along with a life built on Dharma and decentralization. This system led to the development of 64 arts. The architecture of thousands of temples, the water and agricultural systems, the textile industry, which had exports to over 50 countries, and the educational system where thousands of foreign students studied in Indian universities – all of this existed in our country. The invention of electricity happened only 150 years ago, but the development of civilization dates back by many millennia. In the US, the Amish community, who are European and white, still do not use electricity or motor cars, yet their life is joyful. They remain disconnected from the American glitz and glamour but are still content and peaceful. They allow children over 18 to live independently, yet most of the community stays together.

Direction for Humanity

- *Arthik manav nahi, ekatma manav* not an economic man, but an integral man.
- Focus on social, cultural and human (so-called non-economic) aspects in the development process.
- Distributive justice: The basic needs of everyone must be met along with social justice. There should not be extremes where some have unlimited wealth while others have none. Wealth must be distributed equitably.
- Environment-friendly, human-faced technology.
- Contextual technological reforms, suited to the age. Imports should be domestically suitable – adapt foreign technology to local needs. This was the vision of Pandit Deendayalji.
- Sustainable development demands sustainable consumption. We must control consumption to ensure long-term sustainability.
- New Economic System:
  a. Self-reliant, decentralized, people centric
  b. More production, less consumption
  c. Agriculture-based (agricultural industry)
  d. The creation of village clusters: Small villages are not effective in development individually, so they should unite into groups to facilitate economic progress.
  e. Emphasis on village industries and cottage industries
  f. Family as a socio-economic unit based on values, such as weavers, fishermen, potters, etc. In Japan, family-based corporate structures exist.
  g. Economy driven by people, not governments or markets

h. At all levels, coordinated efforts from farmers, small industrialists, scientists, technologists, administrators and social workers (teachers, trainers, motivators) are required to build an integrated structure, methodology and tradition.

Pandit Deendayalji expressed all of this in his concept of Integral Humanism, which is based on the following foundational concepts.

a. Integral human: The balanced, holistic development of body, mind, intellect and soul
b. Yajna chakra: Mutual coordination of the individual, society, creation and the Creator
c. Purusharth chaturthya: The four fundamental objectives of human life – Dharma, Artha, Kama, Moksha
d. *Sadhan chaturthya*: Education (not only governmental but also society-based), freedom (by authority), peace and courage (from society), from which higher achievements can be attained

For the overall development of the nation, the following is necessary:

1. The self-confidence and determination of the society: The activities of the Sangh are intended to cultivate this.
2. Ethical leadership: Leaders in politics and across all sectors of society must be committed to the welfare of the nation

Good governance should fulfil the basic needs of individuals. Such a system is known as *dharmarajya*, otherwise, it will be called *adharmarajya*.

In the epic *Raghuvansha*[3], while describing King Dilip[4], Kalidasa[5] said, 'By ensuring the sustenance, protection, promotion and education of his people, he became their true father. Other fathers were merely those who gave birth.'

When we talk about supreme glory in prayers, its prerequisite is the protection of Dharma. But how to protect Dharma? For this, we can rely on the organized strength of people, which can lead to prosperity and welfare. Sometimes people say that the idea is good, but where is the blueprint? Pandit Deendayalji said, 'We don't need a blueprint, we can provide the vision. We don't want to bind the hands of the next generation'

When Savarkar[6] met Lenin[7] in India House[8] and enagaged in conversation for several days, Savarkar asked him, 'I don't believe in your communism, but once you take power, what kind of governance will you establish? What will Russia look like?'

Lenin replied, 'We will think about it once we have power! Right now, we have a vision, but no means. Once we have the means, we will tell you'

Shri Guruji[9] said, 'Considering the current circumstances, Hindus have every right to create the societal structure they deem necessary. However, it is crucial that any such structure necessarily aligns with the eternal principles of *sanatan* values.'

We cannot provide a complete blueprint. However, if there is vision, a firm foundation, awareness of our heritage, determination to act, spiritual insight, ethical leadership and self-confidence, then people with talent and hard work will emerge on their own to develop the model of development. In the end, it is talent, hard work, vision and determination that will enable us to present ourselves as a worthy example to the world.

25

'The Curriculum and Syllabus Be Redesigned to Reflect India's Contributions, India's Philosophies and Indian Thought'

SURESH SONI

Suresh Soni is a senior RSS pracharak who as of 2025 is a member of the national committee of the organization. He has earlier held several key positions, including that of Sahsarkaryavah.[1] Widely regarded in the organization as a thinker and ideologue, Soni has guided many of Sangh's allied organizations engaged in educational and intellectual work.

In this essay, he reflects on the impact of the British education system – often called as the Macaulay system – on India's rich traditional education and learning systems, and argues for a return to those indigenous methods and practices.

Today, it is universally accepted that if a nation – and indeed the entire world – wants to progress, the only way forward is to educate every individual in society. As a result, there has been a significant growth in educational systems across the globe.

If we consider India specifically, we observe that at the time of Independence, there were only 17 universities. By 2009, that number had grown to 410. Alongside this, there are around 21,000 different types of institutes and colleges, along with approximately 1,500 research institutions, including IITs, IIMs and various others. Thus, we can say that education has indeed expanded. And when such growth is visible in India, it is only natural to assume that similar developments are taking place in other countries as well.

However, while education is expanding on the one hand, some serious problems are also emerging on the other. In the United States, for example, as the importance of education has grown within colleges and schools, so has the prevalence of gun culture. Likewise, the number of teenage pregnancies has increased, and boys as young as 15 or 16 are testing positive for HIV. These trends are on the rise.

This creates a paradox: why are such negative trends increasing alongside the expansion of education? You might have recently read about a university student who shot and killed 35–36 people on campus. Thousands of such incidents occur within a year.

In India too, we observe that although education has expanded, the systems being built by educated individuals – whether in politics or administration – are failing to bring happiness and well-being to society. Despite being educated, these systems are plagued with corruption, causing distress throughout the country. Education is increasing, but so is corruption.

In cities like Delhi, incidents of rape are occurring in broad daylight even within medical and engineering colleges. This raises a serious question: if education is expanding, why are such incidents happening?

This is not a problem unique to India; it is a global issue. The cause, description and consequences of the current tragedy have been analyzed by Theodore Roszak in his book *Where the Wasteland Ends*. Roszak says that today's education aims to create individuals who are multi-headed engineers – someone who is a techno-political-econo-socio expert.

The tools used for this are the internet, closed-circuit TV and laboratories. When modern mechanical devices replace the warm and personal relationship between teacher and student, when technology takes the place of a teacher's thoughtful guidance, then a spiritual and psychological emptiness begins to grow within the younger generation.

Instead of inspiring transformation in a student's life through personal example, society now puts into the teacher's hands electronic, individualized, computerized, audio-visual multi-instructional consoles. This attempt to replace a living, breathing human being with a mechanical process is precisely what leads to the imbalance and tragedy described above.

In such times, the question arises: what is the path forward, and why has this kind of education emerged? UNESCO gave this issue considerable thought, and after deep reflection, stated in its report that the root cause of all these problems is a distorted vision of man and the universe.

One of the key features of this distorted vision is considering the foundation of the universe to be purely material – when the world is seen through a material lens, thought becomes fragmented. This fragmented thinking gives rise to a broken or partial worldview, and the ultimate motivation behind such a view becomes *Artha* (material wealth) and *Kama* (sensual pleasure). So, we see three main issues: first, a materialistic foundation; second, fragmented thinking; and third, motivation driven by wealth and pleasure. All problems stem from these.

Until now, in the context of education, UNESCO promoted the slogan 'learning to do'. But later, it recognized the need for change and introduced a new slogan: 'learning to be'. But what does it mean 'to be'? What kind of person should one become?

This naturally raises the question among thinkers: in this situation, what is the way forward? And in the search for that path, their attention inevitably turns towards India.

When we reflect on Indian educational thought, the first question that arises is: what is education? The essence of our traditional thinking was beautifully expressed in modern terms by Swami Vivekananda. He said, 'Education is the manifestation of perfection already in man.' So, what should be the ultimate aim of any form of education? It is to bring forth the perfection that already exists within a human being. True education is that which allows a person to grow, expand and ultimately manifest this inner perfection.

How is this perfection to be attained? Indian sages and thinkers addressed this, and Swami Vivekananda summarized their insights by saying, 'Every soul is potentially divine, and the goal of life is to realize this divinity.' How can this divinity be realized? He answered, 'By controlling nature – both external and internal.' Through the regulation of both the inner self and the outer world, this divinity can be attained.

How should this be done? He said, follow any path, be it *Karma Yoga* (path of action), *Bhakti Yoga* (path of devotion), *Jnana Yoga* (path of knowledge) or even through mental discipline. One may choose a single path, multiple paths, or all paths, but the ultimate aim must be the realization of this inner divinity. Everything else – doctrines, dogmas, rituals, books, temples, forms – are secondary.

It is with this understanding that our systems and institutions were developed, and from them, our culture evolved. This cultural heritage must be passed down from generation to generation, and it is education that plays the crucial role in carrying it forward.

Thus, an educationist once rightly said, 'Education is the principal instrument in the hands of social groups,' – and by social groups, we include the family, the traditional *gurukul* system and so on – 'by means of which people inherit, modify and transmit culture to the next generation.'

Education is the means through which the entirety of our cultural heritage is transmitted to the next generation. From this perspective, education is the system that enables the manifestation of the inner perfection within a human being, the paths that guide one towards that perfection and the culture that emerges from it – not just for an individual, but for the entire human society.

Another distinctive feature of our tradition was that education was independent. This was one of its greatest strengths. In Indian educational thought, the teacher or guru held the highest place in society. Naturally, the systems that existed at the time were supported economically by the wealthy members of society and the kings, who would bear the full cost. However, decisions about the curriculum and the content of education were ultimately made by the teacher alone. This was a significant and unique characteristic, and because of it, society produced self-respecting, independent thinkers engaged in various domains of life.

A further important concept is: what kind of system was designed to support this? After all, a human being is not a unit that can be educated within a fixed age limit. From the moment of birth – even before knowing how to speak – a child begins observing the world around them. Using all five senses, the child attempts to understand their surroundings. Therefore, education does not begin only when a child enters school. Our ancestors believed that education should not be thought of in fragments.

Accordingly, our traditional system was built on three foundational pillars:

1. The family: Within the family, the child received their initial and most vital development. The attitudes, behaviour and values instilled by parents played an essential educational role.
2. The gurukul: What we now call schools and colleges. These were formal spaces of learning under the guidance of a teacher.
3. The yajna institution: In ancient times, this was a spiritual and social space, often associated with temples today, where sages and saints would visit and enlighten the general public.

Thus, from childhood to the end of life, there existed a three-pillared system that supported continuous development in a well-defined direction.

What should be the foundation of education? According to UNESCO, today's problems have emerged from a distorted vision of man and the universe. This distorted vision is rooted in three aspects: a materialistic foundation, fragmented thinking and motivations driven by artha and kama. In contrast to this model, our ancestors emphasized that for the holistic development of an individual and society, the foundation must be spiritual.

Spirituality teaches that the entire universe is pervaded by one single essence. When there is one essence at the core of all existence, the perspective through which we view the world remains unified, not fragmented. This very inspiration is what we call Dharma.

In the Indian life tradition, it is believed that a life based on Dharma is rooted in spiritual experience and the realization of unity. Hence, Dharma holds an unparalleled significance in our culture. Some time ago, there was a legal dispute about whether religious education should be imparted or not, and this matter even reached the Supreme Court. In its verdict, the Supreme Court upheld that the teaching of religion is essential, because Dharma is the element that elevates a human being from animalistic tendencies towards divinity.

Thus, in our tradition, Dharma is not merely a ritualistic practice or method of worship – it permeates all aspects of life. For example, Charaka authored the *Charaka Samhita*, a foundational text of Ayurveda, and when asked about its purpose, he responded: '*Dharma prapti* (the attainment of Dharma).' Chanakya wrote the *Arthashastra*, an authoritative text on economics and politics, yet he clearly stated that its analysis was done in the service of Dharma. Rishi Kanada composed the *Vaisheshika Darshan*, a treatise on atomic science, and its very first aphorism is: '*Yatobhyudaya nihshreyasa siddhih sa dharmah*' (That which leads to worldly prosperity and ultimate liberation, that is Dharma). Similarly, Maharshi Jaimini's *Mimamsa Darshan*, a work on the philosophy of karma (action), begins with the aphorism: '*Athato dharma jijnasa*' (Now, therefore, the inquiry into Dharma).

This is the mindset embedded in our culture. Even when someone buys a new computer, they apply a *tilak* (sacred mark); when starting a new vehicle or machine, they offer a *namaskar* (salutation). These actions stem from deep-rooted *sanskar*s (cultural impressions). Why is this so? Because in our tradition, Dharma is seen as the force that uplifts a human being above animalistic tendencies.

Pujya Guruji was once invited by a branch of the International Lions Club. Before Guruji began his speech, the club president addressed the gathering and said, 'I request our esteemed guest to kindly avoid speaking on two topics – dharma and politics.'

Guruji stood up and said, 'Your president has asked me to speak, excluding two topics. I have no particular interest in politics, especially not in today's politics, so I won't speak on that. But he also asked me not to speak on dharma. Now I am faced with a dilemma. He says don't speak on dharma, while our ancestors have said: "*Ahara, nidra, bhaya, maithunani, samanyam etat pashubhir naranam* (Eating food, sleeping when tired, feeling fear in danger and procreation; these four acts are common to both animals and humans). *Dharma hi tesham adhiko visheshah* (It is only Dharma that distinguishes humans from animals)." If we remove Dharma, then: "*Dharmena hinah pashubhih samanah* (Without Dharma, humans are no different from animals)." And since the president has said I must not speak in Dharma, I feel the name of your club – Lions Club – is truly apt.'

This incident illustrates just how important Dharma is considered in our tradition. It is regarded as the very foundation.

A third point that sometimes comes up in discussions is that education in our tradition was solely focused on renunciation – on religion, philosophy and detachment. But that was not the case. Both *nivritti* (renunciation) and *pravritti* (engagement) were included in our education system.

In the Chandogya Upanishad, there is an account where the celestial sage Narada[2] approaches Sanat Kumara and says, 'I am deeply troubled. Please impart to me the knowledge of the Self.'

Sanat Kumara replies, 'First tell me what you have studied.'

Then, Narada begins to list his studies: 'I have studied the Rigveda, the Yajurveda, the Samaveda. I have studied the Itihasa and the Purana, which are regarded as the fifth Veda. I have learned astronomy, mathematics, rituals of ancestral offerings, *bhuta vidya* (the science of spirits), military science, astrology, logic, ethics, divine sciences, dance, sculpture, music . . .' – and the list goes on.

In the same way, you may have heard of the 10 disciplines (*dashashastra*), the 32 arts (*vidyas*), and the 64 skills (*kalas*). These 64 skills included everything from sports and child-rearing to the governance of a state, city planning, architecture, shipbuilding, mineral science and even aeronautics.

All these subjects were taught and studied. This fact clearly shows that our education was not only about renunciation. Rather, both material and spiritual knowledge were part of the curriculum.

A key feature of the Indian education system was its emphasis on holistic thinking. Even when considering the human being, it approached the subject from a comprehensive perspective. According to Indian philosophy, a human being is made up of five layers (*pancha kosha*), and true development must encompass all five.

These five layers were analyzed systematically. The first is the *annamaya kosha* – the physical body – which is visible and is sustained by food. Behind it lies a subtler element called *prana*, or life-force energy. This is the *pranamaya kosha*. Today we see how fluctuations in this life-force affect health. The popularity of figures like Baba Ramdev[3] is largely due to their focus on developing and balancing this vital energy through breath and yoga. Development must happen with an understanding of this pranic dimension. Then comes the *manomaya kosha* – the mind. It is the mind that causes inner imbalance in people. Hence, mental development and education are essential. The *vijnanamaya kosha* follows – this is the intellect. Education must also foster the development of wisdom. And beyond that lies the *anandamaya kosha*, the sheath of bliss, which relates to the soul (*jivatma*).

Beyond all these layers lies the Supreme Consciousness (*Paramatma*).

These five layers correspond to the body (annamaya and pranamaya), mind (manomaya), intellect (vijnanamaya), soul (anandamaya) and the Divine (beyond the five). Thus, if we aim for a complete or holistic development, it must be pancha kosha–based development. Education must strive to achieve this.

So then, what is the purpose of development?

The answer is given in our tradition:

'*Sa vidya ya vimuktaye*' (True education is that which liberates). It should free the human being from all forms of bondage and lead them towards unity and wholeness.

What kind of liberation is required? Our organs of action (*karmendriyas*) must be freed from laziness and lethargy. Education should not make one indolent. It must promote the right habits and food, and a lifestyle that counters sluggishness. Our organs of perception (*jnanendriyas*) must be freed from insensitivity. We see things, but our mind is unaffected; we hear things, but they don't move us – if society becomes like this, genuine empathy and connection will vanish. Hence, education must awaken sensitivity. Our mind must be freed from desire and craving. Our intellect must be freed from ignorance and lack of discernment. Our soul must be liberated from its identification with body, mind and intellect.

To achieve all this, a well-thought-out system was developed. Through such a system, a person's relationship with self, family, village, society and the nation was shaped holistically. The ultimate aim of our education system, then, is to build a society that lives by the highest ideals of life.

A question often arises: 'Were we like frogs in a well, refusing to accept ideas from the outside world?' The answer is, absolutely not. Our ancestors clearly stated: '*Ano bhadrah kratavo yantu vishvatah*' (Let noble thoughts come to us from all directions of the world). This means our windows must remain open to ideas from across the globe. What we choose to accept or reject is ours to decide. But the flow of thoughts from all sides must continue.

To bring all these values into actual life, a remarkable system was developed – the system of sixteen *sanskar* (sacraments or cultural rites). These sanskars were designed to integrate these values into the life of the individual, the family and society at large. This system was incredibly scientific. In this context, Dr Snehalata Deshmukh, former vice-chancellor of the University of Mumbai, conducted an experiment. She referred to the Mahabharata, where it is mentioned that Abhimanyu[4] learned the technique of breaking into the Chakravyuha[5] (a military formation) while in the womb. She wondered – is it really possible for a child to grasp thoughts and emotions in the womb?

She studied the *Vagbhata Samhita*, an ancient Ayurvedic text, where it is stated that a foetus, in its fifth month, begins to absorb thoughts and emotions. Inspired by this, she and a team of doctors launched a project in a nursing home, focusing on the effect of external stimuli on unborn children.

They used two musical ragas – Kedar and Yaman – that are known for their soothing, joyful nature and absence of sorrowful tones. They recorded the *bansuri* (flute) tunes of Pandit Shivkumar Sharma[6] and requested pregnant women to listen to the music with deep attention.

To observe the impact of the music on the foetus, they used 4D sonography machines. The results were extraordinary. When the music played and the computer button was pressed, a six-month-old foetus appeared on the screen. As the tune played, the child became visibly happy – lips smiling, eyes blinking, facial expressions glowing with joy. After the child was born, the mother shared: whenever the child cried, playing that same tune would immediately calm him.

Another foetus, also six months old, showed a different response. The face remained neutral, but the hands started moving. That child is now four years old and is an excellent tabla[7] player. A third foetus, again six months old, had a still face, unmoving hands, but its fingers were gently moving. That child is now six years old and plays the veena[8] beautifully. Dr Deshmukh concluded, 'This Hindu system of sanskars – this is the most scientific system.' This shows that the transformation in human life is deeply influenced by the power of the sanskar system.

In the same way, for these sanskars to be meaningfully expressed in everyday life, the tradition of *panch yajnas* (five sacred duties) was established in the life of a householder.

1. *Brahma yajna*: the duty of continuous learning and study
2. *Deva yajna*: the practice of worship, rituals and spiritual discipline
3. *Pitri yajna*: performing rites for ancestors such as *shraddha*
4. *Bhuta yajna*: care and compassion for all living beings including animals and birds. That is why we see practices such as keeping water pots outside the house the house for birds, building small ponds or troughs outside, offering a piece of roti (bread) to cows or feeding flour balls to fish. These daily actions are expressions of bhuta yajna.
5. *Nara yajna*: ensuring no human being remains hungry or unhappy. This inspired the tradition of hospitality and charity.

All of these practices ensured that life remained free of distortion and aligned with the greater good of society. Based on the moral compass of Dharma, a system of do's and don'ts (*vidhi–nishedh*) was developed.

Therefore, when a student completed their education in the gurukul and was ready to step into worldly life, the teacher would give a final sermon: Speak the truth (*satyam vada*), walk the path of dharma (*Dharmam chara*), do not neglect self-study (*swadhyayan ma pramadah*), revere your mother as divine (*matru devo bhava*), revere your father as divine (*pitru devo bhava*), revere your teacher as divine (*acharya devo bhava*), revere your guest as divine (*atithi devo bhava*).

They were also advised to care not just for themselves but for all of humanity and the entire creation. Thus, the structure of life was built in such a way that it created a holistically developed individual, a holistically developed family, a holistically developed society and ultimately a welfare-oriented worldview for the entire universe. This is the essence of Indian educational philosophy.

So far, we have reflected on the completeness of Indian education. The current educational framework we follow today is based on a Western model, and we are living within its structure. However, India once had its own ancient educational system, which was still functioning even when the British arrived. Those who are interested can refer to the book *The Beautiful Tree* written by Dharampal[9]. During the Second Round Table Conference in 1931, Mahatma Gandhi had referred to the Indian education system as a 'beautiful tree'.

The British set up four commissions to study the Indian education system: The Munro Commission Report, Adam's Report, Litner Report and a report from the Bombay Presidency. These four reports collectively revealed that India had around 500,000 schools at that time, and teachers from all castes were involved in education. These reports help dismantle the common misconception that education in India was limited to upper castes. In fact, records compiled by the British themselves stated that teachers belonged to all communities – including potters (Kumhar), oilpressers (Teli), cobblers (Mochi), washermen (Dhobi) and barbers (Nai). The percentage of students from what are today categorized as OBC, SC and ST communities was as high as 70–78 per cent, while students from what are now termed upper castes made up only 16–22 per cent.

All these details are mentioned in Dharampal's book mentioned earlier. But These weren't just claimed by him, in 1853, John Bright[10], a member of the British House of Commons, stated in a speech that in every Indian village, teachers could be found as easily as one would find a village headman or *patel*. Unfortunately, this beautiful educational system was completely destroyed, and no alternative system was put in place. As a result, the entire Indian population began to suffer from poverty and deprivation. John Bright even criticized the British in their Parliament by saying: 'We collect £29 million from India and return only £6.6 million.' Such was the injustice inflicted, and the beautiful structure that once existed was entirely dismantled.

The education system we follow today, where did it actually come from? In May 1792, Charles Grant[11] wrote a report called *Observations*, in which he discussed how to gain complete control over India. Building upon that report, in 1835, Macaulay[12] presented a plan. Without going into too many details, one important line from his proposal stands out. He said that the kind of person this new education would produce would be 'Indian in blood and colour, but English in taste, in opinions, in morals, and in intellect.' This meant that the person might look Indian on the outside, but in his thinking and values, he would be completely British.

Today, we can see the impact of that idea. If two highly educated individuals greet each other with '*Ram Ram*,' it feels outdated or village-like, as if someone from the sixth century has shown up. But if someone says 'Hello' or 'Hi', it is immediately seen as modern and progressive. Macaulay had said that the tastes of Indians would change – and that has clearly happened.

Looking at morals and values, earlier even wealthy individuals wore simple clothes. That didn't mean they lacked money; it meant they chose to spend it on noble causes – on donations, religious activities, community service and charity. Macaulay had stated that these values would gradually fade. When Lord Bentinck[13] received information that, as a result of the new education system, the rich in India were giving up their so-called 'bad habits' like donating to the poor, building dharamshalas and running community kitchens – and instead were spending their money on comfort, luxury, and entertaining Europeans – he saw it as a sign of progress.

This model of change had a deep and lasting impact. As Max Müller[14] once said, 'India has been conquered once, but India must be conquered again – and that second conquest should be a conquest by education.' That educational conquest, in many ways, is still shaping the mindset of modern India.

And then, an economy-centric framework was created – completely disconnected from Indian values and way of life. On this very foundation, curriculums were developed that lacked any sense of Indianness. There was neither Indian thought nor acknowledgment of Indian contributions. As a result, over the course of the past seven to eight generations, the people who have emerged from this system now find it extremely difficult even to engage with questions like Indian educational philosophy or the Indianization of education.

In such a complex situation, how can the Indianization of education take place? We cannot simply bring back the old system, and from this perspective, there are certain key points around which a public awareness needs to be built. The first and foremost of these is that education must be made independent. One of the most significant things the British did was to take education in India – which was originally autonomous and self-sustaining – and turn it into a government department. Just as there are departments for agriculture and irrigation that deal with inanimate things, they made education – a field that deals with conscious human beings – just another department. That was their first move.

The result of this was that the acharya of a gurukul was pushed to a secondary position, while the education secretary – a government officer – became the primary authority. This is why, even though we call universities 'autonomous' and 'independent', today anyone who wants to become a vice chancellor has to run after the education secretary and the minister. Can such a person instil a sense of self-respect in students?

Another thing they did was introduce the system of registered societies. Earlier, gurukuls did not require any royal order to function. But now, if you want to run an educational institution, you must form a registered body, and that body becomes the owner. The management of the institution gained control, and the guru was reduced to just a 'teacher'. This was the second major issue.

The third problem came with the introduction of the 'grant-in-aid' system. The government would provide funds, but only if institutions agreed to its terms and conditions. As a result, education – meant to be independent – became bound and restricted. This is one of the biggest challenges we face today. On the other hand, under the banner of globalization, all kinds of invasions are taking place. Education is increasingly being stripped of its humanity, reduced instead to a purely technical, economic and management-driven structure focused solely on maximizing profit. In this entire context, there is an urgent need to liberate education.

Some have suggested that just as the Election Commission, despite many flaws in the current system, is a constitutionally independent body and not controlled by the government – thus able to assert some influence and authority during elections – the same should be done for education. An independent Education Commission should be established with a proper budget, and it should be led not by bureaucrats, but by educationists.

An argument often made is that the government does not have enough money. But even compared to earlier times, the current spending on education by the government has reduced. In such a situation, corporate houses, charitable trusts and society at large must understand their responsibility. Alongside the government, different societal groups and organizations must step in to ensure that quality higher education reaches the masses. Creating an environment that supports such a social role could be one effective effort in this direction.

Another major need is to reconnect education with Indian soil, Indian traditions and Indian thought. Currently, our education system is completely disconnected from these elements, and it must be reconnected. For that, the entire syllabus needs to be transformed. Every subject in the curriculum should reflect India's contributions. In history, we must highlight our past. In science and various disciplines, we should acknowledge what our ancestors contributed. The entire heritage passed down by our forefathers should become a part of the curriculum across different subjects.

Moreover, while we are currently teaching modern content in our courses, every subject has some gaps or issues. In such a situation, we must ask: what alternatives can be introduced? What kind of structure and policies can be built based on Indian thought? These questions and their possible answers should also become a part of the syllabus. To find a model or a path forward, it is essential that the thinking class of the country becomes actively involved with the education system. This is the need of the hour.

The third and most important point is that in India, education was never dry or mechanical – it was always value-based. A scholar without values held no importance in Indian society. Was Ravana[15] not a great scholar? In his time, there was likely no one who could match his intellect. Yet, despite being a towering scholar, he was rejected by society. Why? Because he lacked values. That is why, in our tradition, values were considered supreme. Education and values were never treated as separate. Hence, the concept of Dharma was central, because Dharma is the source of values. Today, there is an urgent need to reconnect education with values. The current lack of this connection is the root cause of all problems – corruption, violence, crime and inhuman behaviour.

Nowadays, there's a lot of talk about literacy. Everyone is saying, 'Increase literacy.' But in our tradition, it was clearly understood that if a man becomes literate but has no sense of values, what good is that? The answer lies in an old saying: *'Saakshara vipareetaashcha eva raakshasa bhavati'* (If you reverse the word *saakshara* [literate] you get *rakshasa* [demon]). The entire system today has removed value education, and this is what has led to the present crisis.

An example can help understand the consequences well. Some college students once visited a village for a survey. There, they observed a traditional water-lifting system: a bullock was tied to a device, and as it moved in circles, water was drawn from a well. A bell was tied to the bull's neck, and as it moved, the bell rang, letting the farmer know the bull was working. The farmer, meanwhile, was engaged in another task. A student asked him, 'You left the bull alone – how do you know if it's working or just standing still?' The farmer replied, 'I've tied a bell around its neck. When it moves, the bell rings – I know it's working.' The student then asked, 'But what if the bull just stands and moves its neck to ring the bell?' The farmer smiled and replied, 'My bull would never do that – because it hasn't studied in a college.'

This is the crisis we face today – education that is devoid of values. Justice Rama Jois[16] once made a poignant observation. He said, 'The country is unnecessarily worried. Corruption is increasing, crimes are rising and everyone says things are going wrong – but what's really wrong?' Our ancestors told us to walk the path of dharma; all education used to teach us that. But our political leaders say, 'Be secular.' So society follows what its leaders say – how can we say it is in the wrong?

He gave another example. Our ancestors said, 'Speak the truth. That is Dharma.' Today's leaders say, 'Be secular,' which in practice means lie, cheat and be dishonest. So, people are doing just that. Our forefathers taught us to treat another's wealth as if it were dust. There's an old story of a couple, where the husband sees some gold that belongs to someone else and, fearing his wife might be tempted, he covers it with mud. When she asks what he's doing, he replies honestly, 'It's someone else's gold. I didn't want you to be tempted, so I'm covering it with mud.' The wife replies, 'You fool! You're just putting mud on mud.' That was our life philosophy – to see others' wealth as worthless.

But today, people say, 'Be secular,' which now seems to mean: 'my money is mine, and so is yours.' And how is that money acquired? Through corruption, kidnapping, robbery even murder. It's all being normalized. Our ancestors taught us to regard every woman as a mother. But now, in the name of secularism, harassment is brushed aside and society looks the other way. And we still ask – what's wrong with that?

The erosion of value-based education has led us here. That's why it is essential that education reconnects us not just with Indian identity but also with these eternal values – our *sanatan* values.

Along with everything else, there's another important point. The current examination system does not encourage in-depth study of any subject; instead, it creates a kind of mental stress. The question is not how knowledgeable a person has become in a subject, but rather how many marks they can score. The entire effort is directed towards marks. 'Learn for marks,' and once the exams are done, everything is forgotten. In essence, it's time to reflect on how this system aligns with the broader journey of life.

P. L. Deshpande, a renowned humorist and satirist from Maharashtra, once shared an incident. He said, 'I went to a college and gave a speech on the "Dnyaneshwari" After the speech, I was sitting in the principal's office when a student came to the door and asked, "May I come in, sir?" I said, "Come in." The student recited a verse (*ovi*) from the Dnyaneshwari and asked me to explain its meaning. I was overjoyed – imagine, a college student in this modern era showing interest in the Dnyaneshwari! I asked, "Have you read the Dnyaneshwari?" He replied, "No." Then I asked, "So why are you asking about it?" He said, "Sir, because this verse is definitely going to come in the exam." I asked him, "How many marks is the question for?" And he replied, "Sir, at least two and a half marks."'

While narrating this story, Deshpande concluded by saying, 'If the value of Dnyaneshwari in today's system is 2.5 marks, then what would be my value?' This is the kind of examination system that needs to be reconsidered.

In our traditional system, the focus was not merely on marks. There were two main types of examinations. One was the *shalaka* system. Suppose someone claimed, 'I am a scholar of this philosophy,' for example, the philosophy of *nyaya darshan*. How would they be tested? The examinee would bring the book, and the teacher would also have a copy. Shalaka refers to a pointer, similar to what we might call a fountain pen today. The teacher would randomly insert the pointer anywhere in the book, open it and read the first line.

From that point, the examinee had to recite the rest of the text word for word, exactly as it appeared, until the teacher asked them to stop. That was the first part of the exam. In the second part, the teacher would again point randomly, open the book and the student would have to explain the passage and also describe how different scholars have interpreted it. In the third round, the pointer would be placed once more, and the student had to express a viewpoint different from all the interpretations that existed so far. Only after completing this level of study would one be recognized as truly knowledgeable.

The second examination system was the *ghatika* system, where ghaṭika meant a pot. In this system, a pot contained slips of paper with various questions related to the subject. The student would pick one and continue answering until the examiner was satisfied. This method encouraged deep and thorough study of the subject. As a result, society developed a sense of trust in such scholars. We need to reflect on these traditional methods and what we can learn from them.

Along with everything else, there is another important issue – education has become disconnected from its surrounding. Vinoba Bhave[17] once said that when the British came, they instituted mandatory holidays on Sundays so that Christians could attend church. But is this necessary today?

Secondly, since they came from a cold country and couldn't bear the heat, they introduced the concept of 'summer vacation'. The British have long left, but the summer vacation system still continues. As a result, students from villages who go to study in cities have holidays during the summer – the very time when there is no work in the village. But during the monsoon, when there is work in the fields, they are away in cities for studies. That means they get completely disconnected from village life, from farming, from their roots. Overall, education has become separated from its natural environment. Rethinking this disconnect is what true Indianization of education means.

In today's times, there's a widespread misconception that only someone with a formal degree is knowledgeable. As a result, many naturally gifted individuals who never went to school are undervalued in society. But who awarded Newton[18] a degree? What degree did Edison[19] have? The numerous inventions made by such individuals were not done by degree holders. Therefore, even today, there are many such talented individuals. There's a need to create systems that include and recognize them as well.

Alongside all other issues, the issue of language is a complex one. However, the it is universally accepted that a human being is a living entity, and during the early stages of life, our senses can grasp things more easily in a natural environment and a familiar language. Therefore, placing an additional linguistic burden on a child during the primary phase, can hinder their overall development.

All psychological studies affirm that primary education should be imparted in one's mother tongue. At times, there are conflicts on this issue, but in life, there are certain matters on which we must take a firm stand.

When the British established Hislop College in Nagpur, students from upper castes joined in large numbers. A year later, a student from a Scheduled Caste was admitted, and all the upper-caste students became furious. Out of nearly a hundred students, all demanded that the management remove that one student. The management refused, saying, 'We will not expel him.' The parents responded, 'Then we will withdraw our children.' The management stood its ground: 'Do as you wish.' All the upper-caste students withdrew from the college. The entire institution ran with just that one student for a whole year – such was their commitment.

Similarly, in Meghalaya, when English-medium schools were first introduced, Bengali was the dominant medium of instruction, and for several years, no students enrolled in the English-medium schools. But the schools persisted. As a result, over time, the entire education system transitioned to English medium.

Today, even though struggles and complexities remain, it is essential to build a larger consensus and cultural atmosphere around this issue.

Ask the greatest scientists of this country – from Dr A.P.J. Abdul Kalam[20] to Dr R.A. Mashelkar[21] – what language their early education was in. Each one of them has said that their primary education, up to the tenth grade, was in their mother tongue. This is also a subject that deserves serious thought.

While contemplating the Indianization of education, it is important that the entire system be independent, and the curriculum and syllabus be redesigned to reflect India's contributions, philosophies and thought. Textbooks should be developed with this in mind, and education should be rooted in value-based understanding. Education systems should aim to make individuals true scholars of their subjects. Learning must be aligned with the local environment and made socially relevant.

Gandhiji had said that education should be a combination of learning and productivity. After gaining a certain amount of knowledge, a person should develop the capability to earn a livelihood. It is from this perspective that we must reflect on this issue today.

In all the ups and downs of the world, we see that whether the world desires it or not, the hardships and experiences of life push humanity towards improvement. Today's circumstances are leading not only the people of India but also people around the world towards Indian thought. Therefore, the idea of holistic Indian thinking must be expressed through education. We must examine how this can be done in today's context and develop a noble vision of education in our minds.

Kaka Kalelkar[22] gave a beautiful description of education that encompasses all these ideas. He envisioned education as a goddess, who says:

I am not a servant of power.
I am not a slave of the law.
I am not a doorkeeper of art.
I am not a companion of science.
I am not a maid of economics.
I am the return of Dharma.
I am the sovereign of human intellect, heart and all the senses.
Psychology and sociology are my feet.
Art and craftsmanship are my hands.
Science is my head.
Dharma is my heart.
Logic and observation are my eyes.
History is my ears.

Freedom is my breath.
Enthusiasm and enterprise are my lungs.
Patience is my vow.
Faith is my consciousness.
In this way, I am Jagadamba, the universal mother, the nurturer of the world.
My devotee shall never be dependent on anyone.
By my grace, all their desires shall be fulfilled.

This is the divine form of Indian educational thought. May it inspire us to build a new India in every sphere of life in the times to come. Let us create such an atmosphere, engage in such reflection and strive in this direction.

26

'As You Call Yourself *Rashtriya* Swayamsevak Sangh and Not Hindu Swayamsevak Sangh . . . It Is My Desire That You Should Be Instrumental in Bringing About a Revolution in India'

JAYAPRAKASH NARAYAN

Jayaprakash Narayan, popularly known as J.P., was a renowned freedom fighter and a close aide of Mahatma Gandhi. During the Congress' movement for Independence, he was also influenced by socialist ideals, and continued to uphold them after Independence. He was a critic of the Rashtriya Swayamsevak Sangh for many decades. However, in the 1970s, when popular resentment against corruption and authoritarianism in the Congress Party under the leadership of Indira Gandhi – first in Gujarat and later in Bihar – took the form of a people's resistance movement called the Lok Sangharsh Samiti, Jayaprakash emerged as the guide and philosopher for that student- and youth-led movement.

That movement for restoration of probity and democracy had major participation of students and youth associated with the RSS and its affiliates like the Akhil Bharatiya Vidyarthi Parishad (ABVP). Jaya Prakash came into direct contact with senior RSS and Bharatiya Jana Sangh (BJS) leaders during that movement and subsequently during the Emergency imposed by Indira Gandhi. That engagement brought about a total transformation in him – from a bitter critic of the organization to an ardent admirer.

Here is his address to RSS swayamsevaks in Patna on 3 November 1977, in which he called the RSS a 'revolutionary organization' that has taken up the 'challenge of creating a new India', and insisted that he had 'great expectations' from it.

I am very grateful to you for inviting me here and for honouring me in this way. Perhaps this is the time to clarify what I have already said, because some of my statements have led to certain misunderstandings. I have said it before, and I say it again today that it appears to me that there is a need for a fundamental change in the role of the Sangh and maybe there is even a need for a modification of its aims and objectives. Though it is not actually so, people still identify it with Hindu communal and caste interests. But I know that a lot of discussion is going on between your organizer and the cadres about associating the followers of other religions – especially of those religions which were not born in India, such as Islam and Christianity – who are as Indian as we Hindus are. Their forefathers were also Hindus, and through conversion their numbers increased, as did a feeling of separatism, which was exploited by British imperialism.

The imperialists were successful in dividing India into two parts. Later on, with the creation of Bangladesh of its own accord, they became three. But I believe that including Bangladesh and Pakistan, we are one nation. Our states can be separate, but our nation has always been the same – *Bharatiya*. Iqbal himself, a great poet of Urdu and Persian, has said: '*Kuchh baat hai ki hasti mit-ti nahin hamari*' (There is something perennial about us that has not allowed our existence to be wiped out).

So, friends, there is something special about us, and we have to hold on to it as something invaluable. In spite of being divided into three states today, the biggest of these parts, Bharat, has to conduct itself in such a way, and has to have such a vision, that we should be able to win the hearts of the two parts separated from us in the east and west. These states may remain separate – as has been the case in the past, when Bharat was divided into many states – but even then, our *Bharatiyata*, or Indianness, should be retained. People in the other two parts should consider Bharat their own, just as we Hindus do. We have to work towards that end.

Apart from this, we Hindus have to acknowledge and address to the rank injustice and weaknesses in Hindu society that divide us, create feelings of high and low and uphold untouchability, thereby presenting Hindu Dharma in a perverted form. Instead, we should foster a feeling of oneness among Harijans, Brahmins and others. The feeling that 'we are Hindus, as well as Bharatiya,' must also be cultivated among those whom we have long treated as separate and inferior. Muslims and Christians are also Bharatiya. Thus, there is a definite task before the RSS – to consolidate the nation, so that a spirit of national unity is infused in all of us, and the nation gains the strength to accommodate all the differences and diversities within itself.

We Hindus have no holy centre like Mecca, Medina or Rome outside India. For us India is everything, and all our devotion is centred here. But our brethren who embraced other religions – and thus were separated from us as co-religionists – are Bharatiya still. There were cases of forcible conversion too, where some even embraced death to avoid such conversions. Those who converted to other religions have places of worship outside India, and maybe some have even found inspiration outside. For our Muslim brethren, there is Arabia and cities like Mecca and Medina; for Christians, Rome is a holy city – Constantinople is another. For religious inspiration they may look outside, but their national inspiration is Bharat.

The Germans, French, British, Italians and Spanish are separate nations, although their religion – Christianity – is the same. Some follow the Pope, while others, such as the Protestants, have different religious centres. Yet, in spite of religious differences, they have the feeling of being one nation. They consider it their good fortune to get a chance to sacrifice their everything for the nation.

The days of religious crusades are over. So many battles have been fought in the name of Islam and Christianity and other religions in India and elsewhere. But now the sentiment of nationalism dominates all over the world. There are so many different nations in the world today. Nowadays there is a move to bring them together even while retaining their diversity. For some reason, man's intellect tends towards unity. God is one, and all human beings are His creatures. All philosophies point to unity in diversity. Each seeks to identify some binding link among the various nations of the world. President Wilson of the US initiated the League of Nations, and today we have the United Nations – a forum to bring together all the nations of the world onto a common platform. While we cannot say that One World Government is in the offing, but there is no doubt that the ultimate aim is the idea of one world, despite religious, racial, linguistic and geographical differences.

But that is a far-off goal. In spite of the many diversities among the people of India and the existence of so many states in the past, the unity of India has been maintained. During the times of the Mauryas and the Guptas, these very cities of Pataliputra and Kusumpur served as the capitals of the whole of India under Emperors Ashoka and Chandragupta. Thus, empires have existed in this country. These empires eventually disintegrated, for it appears we have historically been weak in statecraft. But with due deference to those among you who profess different religions, I may say perhaps no other religion can match the catholicity, the nobility, the loftiness and the depth of Hinduism as found in its scriptures and philosophical texts.

In other religions there is often one book or holy word, by repeating which you would be initiated into the particular religion and become its devotees. But among us, those who put faith in the Vedas and even those who decry them are Hindus. In fact, the word Hindu is not an ancient one and is not found in any of the ancient books. It was others – who pronounced 's' as 'h' and 'Sind' as 'Hind' – who called us Hindu. In fact, it had nothing to do with any religion and had only a geographical connotation.

So, friends, there are many tasks before the RSS, and some of them are very difficult. Take the caste system, for example. I cannot say what the Sangh is trying to do to break this system. I can understand someone being called high or low according to their action, but we in actual practice have made such a society in which we have dubbed someone as 'untouchable' and someone else as 'Brahmin', fit to be worshipped as a god. The 'Brahmin devta' may be a '*chandaal*' by action, still he remains a Brahmin. In the villages, we see people greeting a Brahmin by expressing the desire to touch his feet. 'Panditji, *paye lagi.*' 'Oh scholar! We touch your feet,' they say. But such an honour is never given to an untouchable, however noble he may be.

Thus, I have great expectations from this revolutionary organization which has taken up the challenge of creating a new India. I have welcomed your venture wholeheartedly, sometimes I have offered you my advice and have even criticised you, but it was as a friend. This is because I understand my strength and your potential. There is no other organization in the country which can match you.

The task of building up the character of the youth is a very urgent task in the country today. We had a big youth movement recently, and I had the good fortune of accepting their leadership at their insistence. I agreed with great reluctance, as I told them that I was ill and that they should be satisfied with seeking my advice whenever necessary. But when they insisted that I would have to take up their leadership, I agreed. They have achieved something. But now the movement has slackened. Its revolutionary content has been dissipated. It does not have the capacity anymore to change the society – though there remains the need for change in society in every sphere, be it economic, social or political. I have an unshakable, faith that we can be one nation even while fulfilling the demands of our different religions and communities. Even while carrying out the necessary rituals, we can be united in our hearts to form one nation.

As you call yourself *Rashtriya* Swayamsevak Sangh and not *Hindu* Swayamsevak Sangh, and this name has been decided upon with due deliberation, therefore it is my desire that you should be instrumental in bringing about a revolution in India. The revolution ushered in by you will command greater respect because people of your standing in the higher rungs of the caste hierarchy, like the Brahmin and Kshatriya classes, will enjoy wider acceptability. Such acceptance will not be easily extended to organizations such as the Chhatra Sangharsh Samiti and Lok Sangharsh Samiti, at least not within the Hindu Society.

On this occasion, I want to point out that we are passing through revolutionary times today. The traditions handed down to us by our ancestors are great. We should go ahead with the task of changing ourselves first, discarding all that is wrong, evil or outdated, while retaining that which is noble in our heritage. Those who do not change themselves and their life, have no right and no power to change others. Those who cannot transform their own lives have no right to ask others to do so. You are committed and devoted people – disciplined and imbued with many qualities. It is my expectation of you and, as an elder, it is my prayer, that God may bless you with enough strength to give a new shape to India – to create a new India where human beings treat one another as brothers, and where there is no distinction between high and low, rich and poor. This is possible, and this should be done!

Even though I know that it is difficult to wipe out poverty – and in any case it is not something that can be achieved in a few days – it is a task worth accomplishing. There are so many households today in which children do not get their fill; they go to sleep crying with hunger. Whatever little food grains they get are of the lowest quality. It is such a painful situation. How shall we change it? The Rashtriya Swayamsevak Sangh should think over this: how to bring about economic transformation? How to transform the village? All our leaders, including Mahatma Gandhi, have worked for it.

You have included Mahatma Gandhi in your morning prayers, and he is indeed worthy of being remembered every morning. This is a very good step you have taken. If he had lived a little longer, he would have guided us a little more to remove untouchability and other evils from the Hindu society. But the way is clear now, and I beleive that you are more capable than I am of undertaking this mission. You are better equipped, because you think and deliberate upon the various aspects of our traditions, our culture and Dharma constantly.

Therefore, I appeal to you to consider every moment valuable for the purpose. We want to see our country in such a condition where Brahmins and Harijans treat each other as brothers and embrace each other without hesitation; where the distinction between rich and poor is wiped out; and where people have direct control over the administration. This is not an idle dream; it is truly possible. It may not be possible in other countries, but it is possible in this ancient land where the institution of Gram Panchayats has functioned for thousands of years and where they are still playing a role in some form or the other. Their condition may not be excellent today, but they are a standing reminder of what they once were.

So, this society, its glorious history, the heritage of our forefathers, the sacrifices of the builders of this country, their achievements and the freedom that we have won – you are the inheritors of it all, and it is for you to make the best use of it. I say this not to flatter you but to bring home the reality of the situation. Your word has a far-reaching effect. There is the force of spiritualism behind us. You are also in the forefront of the transformation that is taking place before our very eyes. The results of this change are also at your disposal.

Friends, I am overwhelmed when I think of the matters concerning the country. I know that I don't have long to live. I am living on borrowed time and am at the brink of death. Even then I am determined to serve my country, my society, my people and the poor and the suffering of this land until the last ounce of my energy and the last breath in my body. I commend to you the ideals of service, renunciation and sacrifice. I have no doubt that you are already imbued with these ideals and are of self-sacrificing nature and noble conduct. A vast country lies before you – here is your arena. You can accomplish much. May God give you strength and may you live up to such expectations.

Part 3

Sangh in Conversation

27

M.S. Golwalkar's Conversation with Saifuddin Jilani

M.S. Golwalkar, 'Guruji', met an Iranian scholar Saifuddin Jilani in 1972. Those were the times when the Rashtriya Swayamsevak Sangh was accused of anti-minority attitude. The Indianization call given by a leader of the Bharatiya Jana Sangh too created an uproar in the country with several leaders attributing it to RSS' design to de-Islamize Muslims. It was in this context that Golwalkar explained the position of RSS on all these questions in this very important interview. This conversation took place less than a year before the demise of Golwalkar, thus forming part of the organization's views on all such questions for the future.

Complete text of this interview is reproduced here.[1]

Dr Jilani: **Don't you think that a solution to the Hindu–Muslim problem must be found, especially at this critical moment when the country is faced with dangers from all sides?**

Guruji: As far as the work for the country is concerned, I do not distinguish between Hindus and Muslims. But how do people look at this problem? Probably these days everyone thinks that he would be able to push forward claims or privileges for his own community by exploiting political situations. If this could be remedied and the people became patriotic – hold only a patriotic-point of view – then all troubles will end in no time.

***Dr Jilani:* Has this problem anything to do with the Muslim grievance that they are not getting their due share in the country's affairs?**

Guruji: I can understand that the Muslims should be given their due share, as everyone else. But this does not mean demanding various rights and privileges. I have heard about the demand for a Pakistan in every state. The president of a Muslim organization was reported to have said that he planned to see his flag fluttering over the Red Fort. He never contradicted the report. Such are the things which irritate those who think in terms of the country as a whole.

Look at their stance on Urdu. Fifty years ago, Muslims in various states spoke and studied the local languages. They never thought that they had a different 'religious language' of their own. Urdu is not a 'religious language' of the Muslims. Urdu is a hybrid product that evolved during the Mughal rule. It has nothing to do with Islam. It was in Arabia that Islam was born. The Holy Koran is in Arabic. If at all there is a 'religious language' for the Muslims, it is Arabic. So, why this emphasis on Urdu? It is because, on the strength of one common language Muslims are sought to be united into a political force. That is all. Such a political force is bound to run counter to the interests of the country.

Some Muslims say that Rustom is their national hero. But Rustom was a Persian hero. He has nothing to do with Indian Muslims. He was born long before Islam. If he could be considered a hero by the Muslims, why not Shri Rama? I say, why don't you accept this history?

Pakistan celebrated the 5000th birth anniversary of Panini who was born in that part which is now in what is called Pakistan. If Pakistanis can claim Panini as one of their great forefathers, why should not our local Hindu Muslim – I call them 'Hindu Muslims' – say that Panini, Vyasa, Valmiki, Rama, Krishna are all their great ancestors? There are many people in the Hindu Dharma who do not believe in the divine incarnation of Rama and Krishna. But they believe that they are great personalities, worthy of emulation. So, how does it matter if Muslims do not believe that God incarnated Himself? Why should they not consider such personalities as their national heroes?

According to our ways of religious belief and philosophy, a Muslim is as good as a Hindu. It is not claimed that the Hindu alone will reach the ultimate Godhood. Everyone has the right to follow his path according to his own persuasion. Let me give you the instance of the previous Shankaracharya of the Shringeri Math,[2] His Holiness Shri Chandrasekhara Bharati Swamiji. An American approached him to be converted to Hinduism. Swamiji asked him the reason. The American replied that he was not satisfied with Christianity, that it left his spiritual longing unquenched. Acharya asked him: 'Have you honestly practised Christianity? Try it first. If it does not satisfy you, then come to me.'

That is our attitude. Ours is a non-proselytizing Dharma. In almost all cases, proselytization is motivated by political or some such gain. We reject it. We say: 'Here is the truth. If you believe it is right, then accept it. Otherwise just leave it.'

While I was travelling in the South, some people came to see me in Madurai. They discussed the Muslim problem and wanted to know my opinion on this issue. I said to them, 'I am happy meeting you. We all must remember that all of us have common ancestors. We are their descendants. You all should follow your respective religion diligently. But we all must be on the same page on issues related to our nation. We should stop demanding such rights and concessions which are detrimental to the interests of our nation. Since we are Hindu, we never ask for special rights and concessions. In such a situation if some people demand that "We want to separate, we want a separate state," then we are not going to tolerate this.'

This so-called 'minority' problem is not one of Muslims only. It is also within Hindus themselves. For example, we have the Jains; we have what is known as the Scheduled Caste people some of whom followed Dr Ambedkar and became Buddhists and are trying to claim that they are separate. In our country, each minority is given certain political privileges. Therefore, many groups are claiming to be a 'minority' and demanding certain privileges on this ground. This will divide our country into so many pieces. It will be a disaster. We are heading in the same direction. When some people look at things from the point of view of political aggrandizement, dangerous problems crop up. But once this aggrandizement is given up, our country will get united and then we can meet the challenge of the whole world.

Dr Jilani: **Materialism in general and communism in particular threaten to engulf our country. Don't you think that Hindus and Muslims, as believers in God, should act as a united bulwark against these dangers?**

Guruji: A similar question was put to me some time ago by a gentleman from Kashmir. I think his name is Nazir Ali. I met him at Aligarh at the residence of my advocate friend Shri Mishri Lal. He said to me that this threat of atheism and communism are trying to attack us. Therefore, all of us who believe in God should join hands to meet this danger.

I said to him, 'I agree with you. But the difficulty is that we all have broken the image of God into so many pieces and each one of us is holding his own piece. You think of God in one particular way. The Christians think in another. The Buddhist says there is no God; there is only nirvana. The Jain will say that everything is like a *shoonya*. Then so many of us will say that we worship God in the form of Rama, Krishna, Shiva, etc. So, how do we ask all these people to believe in one common God? Do you have any recipe for this?' He was a Sufi gentleman, and I believed that the Sufis have faith in God and are thinking persons. You will be surprised to know his answer. He said, 'Then why don't all of you embrace Islam?'

I replied, 'Then some of them will say why don't you convert to Christianity.' I – as devoted as I am to my Dharma – may also say, why not all become Hindus? It comes to the same thing, and the problem will never end.'

He then asked me what my suggestion was. I said, 'Follow your own religion. But there is one substantial philosophy that does not belong exclusively to the Hindu or to the Muslim. Call it whatever you like. It says that there is one Single Power, one Single Existence which is Truth, which is Bliss. It is the Creator, Sustainer and Destroyer. All our conceptions of God are only our own limited conceptions of that Ultimate Reality. This basic truth does not belong exclusively to any one religion, but is universal. So that bedrock of ultimate reality can join us all together. This concept of God can unite us all. In reality, all religions take us towards God. So, why don't you realize that the God of Muslims, Christians and Hindus is the same and we all are His disciples? As a Sufi you should accept this.

Dr Jilani: **Both Hindus and Muslims have a vast amount of goodwill for each other. In spite of this, occasional clashes of varying magnitudes do occur. What steps, in your opinion, should be taken to minimize or altogether stop these fights?**

Guruji: In your writings, you mention that one of the causes of these frictions is the cow. Unfortunately, our people and our political leader don't think about this reason. As a result, it generates a feeling of hurt among the majority community of our country. I do not know why the Muslims should go on harping upon their so-called right to slaughter the cow. They need not. As a matter of fact, Islam does not issue any injunction for cow slaughter. That was only a way of humiliating the Hindus in the old days. Why should it continue now?

There are many other similarly petty issues too. Can't we share each other's festivals? Our most popular festival which brings various strata of society together is Holi. Suppose in this Holi festival, a Muslim is sprinkled with a little colour, do you think any injunctions of the Koran are violated? Why not regard this as a social affair? The Hindus have been taking part in various Muslim festivals like the Moharram. They even participate in a big way in the Urs[3] in Ajmer. But suppose we ask Muslims to come and take part in Satyanarayana Puja,[4] what will happen? Once, the DMK party[5] leaders took a Muslim minister to Rameshwaram. He was accorded all the conceivable honours by the temple authorities. But when the *prasadam*[6] was offered to him, he threw it away! Why should he do so? Suppose he had taken it, would it have violated his religion? There are many small issues like this. We have to learn to adopt an attitude of respect for one another.

What we practise is not just tolerance. Tolerating what others practise is one thing; but holding respect for what others have faith in and what they practise is far greater than tolerance. Holding respect for others' faith is good for the entire humanity. Our faith is not '*sahishnutavaad*' (tolerance-ism), but '*sammanvaad*' (respect-ism). If you learn how to respect others' faith, then tolerance will automatically come in.

Dr Jilani: **Who do you think is best equipped to pioneer this effort of bringing about harmony between Hindus and Muslims – the politicians, the educationists or the religious leaders?**
Guruji: The politician appears to be the last man in this sequence! The same could be said of the religious leaders as well. At present, in our country, there are religious leaders in both communities who are extremely narrow-minded. We need a third type, individuals who will be religious in spirit, who are interested in political leadership, but carry an integrated national concept in their minds. Religious faith is surely important. Take the example of Ramakrishna Mission. This organization promotes a wider and holistic religious attitude. Today we need to adopt a similar attitude and practice so that instead of hurting or destroying different religious faith traditions, we respect them and help in preserving and promoting them.

Politicians are playing their own game by dividing the people more and more. It is they who emphasize caste and accentuate tensions related to languages and religion like 'Hindu–Muslim tension'. In matters related to castes, the real villain of the piece is the politician. Unfortunately, the politician has become the leader of the masses, whereas persons of great merit, character and devotion to God should have been the real leaders of the people. But such people don't have any space in this matter. Those who occupy the place of leadership have been reduced to political animals. Therefore, we need to awaken the people. Two days ago, I said in Prayag that people should not follow politicians. Rather, they should follow those good people who are dedicated to God, who have character and whose vision is large.

Dr Jilani: **Don't you think that the Hindus, as the majority community, have a special and greater responsibility to create an atmosphere of inter-communal harmony?**
Guruji: Yes, certainly. But consider the difficulties. Our leaders are prone to put all the blame upon the Hindus and absolve the Muslims. This

encourages the minority community, that is, the Muslims, to commit communal violence. This is why I say that both communities must share the responsibility.

***Dr Jilani:* What immediate steps do you suggest on the part of both the communities to bring about harmony?**

Guruji: It is difficult to immediately suggest something specific. But it must be given a serious thought. Real religious education on a wider scale can be one such step. Not the Dharma-less education that is being imparted nowadays by our politicians. But true, good, religious education that lets people understand the true wisdom of Islam and Hindu Dharma. People should be taught that every religion guides an individual to be true, pure and welfare-oriented.

Then, the second step is to teach history as it was. Today, we are taught a distorted version of history. If there was aggression from the Muslim invaders in the past, say so, and also clarify that the aggressors were foreigners and that they belong to the past. Muslims today should be told that they belong to this country, and that this aggression is not their heritage. Instead of being taught what is true, the Muslims are today taught a distorted and false version. But truth cannot be hidden for long. However long you hide it, it ultimately comes out and creates far worse feelings only. Therefore, I say that history should be taught truthfully. If Afzal Khan was killed by Shivaji, say that a foreign aggressor was killed by a national hero because of their tense relations. We should tell them that we all belong to this nation, and hence Afzal Khan was not our heritage. But no one has the courage to say so. I have already condemned this mutilation of history many times, and I condemn it again today.

***Dr Jilani:* Much has been said about 'Indianization' and a lot of confusion has arisen over it. Could you please tell me how to remove the confusion?**

Guruji: 'Indianization' was of course the slogan given by Jana Sangh. Why should there be confusion? 'Indianization' does not mean converting all people to Hinduism. Let us all realize that we are all children of this soil, and we must have our allegiance to this land. We belong to the same society, and that our ancestors are common. That our aspirations are also common. Understanding this is Indianization in the real sense.

Indianization does not mean that one should be asked to quit his religion. We neither said this, nor we are going to say so. Rather we believe that a single religious system for the entire human society is not suitable.

***Dr Jilani:* You said it right. It's 100 per cent right. Therefore, I am thankful to you for this clarification.**
Guruji: Still I doubt if I've really been able to clarify all points or not.

***Dr Jilani:* It doesn't matter. You have clarified it from your side quite well. Any thinking person and gentleman would not disagree with you. Don't you think it is high time that a meeting took place between you and such Muslim Indian leaders who would cooperate with you in finding ways and means to remove this communal discord once and for all? Would you like to meet such leaders?**
Guruji: I would not only like it, but I also welcome it.

28

Golwalkar on Governance and Constitution

Through his 33-year leadership of the Rashtriya Swayamsevak Sangh, Golwalkar gave a number of interviews and answered questions on various topics. Compiled here are some of his responses to questions relating to politics, the Constitution and intercommunal relations.

Interview with Pressmen in Calcutta, October 1949

***Q*: How do you view our leaders proclaiming our state as secular?**
A: Emphasizing a state as secular, from the point of view of a Hindu, is superfluous. For centuries, we have been able to maintain religious harmony in the country. The state was only keeping a close watch to see that the people did not fall out, thus rendering the state weak. Otherwise, all had their freedom of worship, etc. That was the concept followed by Hindu ideology.

But it was only in the interim period of the Buddhist era that the state was non-secular, that is, theocratic. During that period, the resources of the state were being used for propagation of a particular persuasion, while dissuading others from practising their own. All these unfortunate things were done by the state in the name of Lord Buddha, that is, out of a misunderstanding of what he has said. This was only an exception in the great current of our national life. Therefore, the qualifying word 'secular' is superfluous and unwanted from our point of view.

Interview with Pressmen in October–November 1949 on the Constitution

***Q*: Why are you critical of the Constitution-making process which is under progress and modelled on several Constitutions in the world?**
A: Because, if we go on always receiving from the world, what shall we give them? In fact, the Constitution should evolve naturally in tune with the traditions of our cultural heritage. It should never be imposed from above. Right from 1909 onwards, constitutions based on foreign models have been imposed upon us. Now, where is the need to follow the same process of imposing the Constitution? Let us take from the foreign countries only that which is essential and proper.

***Q*: If we have to wait for the natural evolution of the Constitution, there will be a period when there will be no constitutional arrangement at all for the country.**
A: Till then, some common principles and articles can be decided upon as a working arrangement.

***Q*: According to you, how long will it take for such a natural evolvement?**
A: As a matter of fact, the evolvement will never come to a halt. But with consistent efforts, four to five years should suffice.

***Q*: Are you opposed to the federal set-up?**
A: Yes. Especially during the transition period, distribution of central power among the states will be positively harmful.

***Q:* So, you are for saddling the centre with increasing powers?**
A: No. I desire more powers for the Panchayats.

Conversation with Friends in 1949

***Q:* Where is the harm in fashioning our newly won *Swarajya* on a foreign model?**
A: How can we call it *swatantrata* (freedom) when it has no *swa* – or,

our genius in it? Then it is only *paratantrata* – dependence on others. If Lenin is kept as the ideal, it becomes 'Lenin-tantra' and not swatantrata! In fact, the protection and propagation of our national life-values, that is, our dharma and *sanskriti*, has always been held in our historical tradition as the raison d'être of swatantrata.

Interview with Pressmen in 1955

Q: **Don't you consider the various amendments to our Constitution as necessary?**
A: My only regret is that the government is setting bad precedents in the formative years of free Bharat. The articles of people's faith and objects of their reverence are being weakened one by one. The Constitution could have been made into a unifying and strengthening factor. They began wrongly by framing an elaborate Constitution, too cumbersome for reverence. Even so, it could have been developed into an object of respect if the government itself had any regard for it. But nothing of the sort exists. There is an amendment every year. People get the impression that you can play with the Constitution as you like. Its sanctity has been violated.

I wish they had given an honest trial to the Constitution for at least 10–15 years. Then we would have known how it worked as it was, and where to amend it for improvement. The government has been hammering away at it without any second thoughts. That is why I said that the government is setting bad precedents.

Q: **Sikhs are demanding a separate state because they have some grievances. What is wrong in granting their demand?**
A: Who does not have grievances? But are we to give a separate state every time someone has grievances? If you yield in one place, you have to yield all round. Will the government meet the 'grievances' of Dravida Kazhagam[1] as well, by yielding to its demand for secession? We must put our foot down against all fissiparous tendencies, whenever or wherever they may crop up. There is no other way to a strong, united and happy Bharat.

***Q:* You have suggested that the Hyderabad State should be divided and distributed among the three neighbouring states on linguistic basis. Previously, you had advocated for a unitary state. What has brought about this change in your attitude?**
A: There is no question of a change. I still hold that there should be one state for the whole country. But in the meanwhile, if there is to be a federal structure, and if the government and the people want a particular basis for the reorganization of states, then logic demands that the same principle be applied to all parts of the country.

Interview with the Editor of *Organiser Weekly* in June 1968 on Communal Riots and the Debate on Secularism

***Q:* The government proposes to have special intelligence men, special investigators and special courts for riot cases. Is it necessary?**
A: That amounts to the government's lack of confidence in its normal administrative apparatus! It will be ruinous for its morale.

***Q:* Why do you think the government withdraws all riot cases after some time?**
A: Obviously because they have no evidence against the Hindus, and they do not want to proceed against the Muslims.

***Q:* Why do you think the government suppressed the Jabalpur riot inquiry report?**
A: Evidently, because it went against the Muslims. An analysis of all the riots will show that the first overt act came from the Muslim side. They are always the first to attack. In Nagpur, they started collecting arms and evacuating their families two days before the violence started. They had planned it that way. The police know all this. But they cannot act for fear of the displeasure of their political bosses.

A few years back I said that Muslims were collecting arms in mosques. This ruffled some gentlemen, and they said that I should be prosecuted under Section 153A of the Indian Penal Code. An officer of the central

CID came to me and asked why I did not report the offending mosques to the government. I told him that if I did so, the offending Muslims would be informed of it even before the police went to search the mosques. I named a mosque some 40 miles from Nagpur. The officer rushed to the place immediately and found truckloads of arms. They never talked of using Section 153A again!

Interview with Pressmen in Bangalore, February 1973, on the Reorganization of States

***Q:* What is your reaction to the present Andhra turmoil for the separation of Andhra and Telangana?**
A: About 20 years back, it was thought that language was a great cementing force, but now that theory has imploded. People with the same language want to separate. That trend has been there among the Marathi-speaking people already. The present upsurge in Andhra is also of the same nature. The belief that a linguistic entity would be homogeneous has now been belied.

***Q:* What do you suggest as the way out?**
A: Declare a unitary type of government by suitably amending the Constitution. The country may be arranged into various zones from the point of view of administrative convenience. The zones may be a few or many, that does not matter.

***Q:* But as things stand, the unitary type appears to be a far cry. What is the next best?**
A: If the present federal structure is to continue, then it is essential that a definite policy based on well-defined principles be initiated and adhered to. If there are smaller units, with language as only one of the basic factors and not the sole deciding criterion, then that should be welcomed. States with more than one language, or multiple states sharing the same language, may be formed, keeping in view the overall national interests. Smaller units need not always be harmful.

***Q:* Is your suggestion for the division of Andhra into two or three states not a contradiction of your earlier remark that there should be a unitary government for the whole country?**
A: I have given the precondition that if you insist upon having a federal structure, then only smaller states are preferable.

***Q:* But will there not be more expenditure because of more legislatures, more governors and so on?**
A: Some expenditure is bound to increase. If we opt for a federal structure, we have to submit to that particular difficulty. Otherwise, as I have said, if they have sufficient courage, let them amend the Constitution and say that this federal system goes lock, stock and barrel, leaving a single unitary government for the whole country.

***Q:* When you say India should be one unitary state, can you think of any situation in the past when India had been ruled by one government? Will such a thing happen?**
A: Well, that which has not happened in the past should not be ruled out as unlikely to happen in the future.

29

Prof Rajendra Singh in Conversation with Tavleen Singh

Prof Rajendra Singh, fondly remembered as Rajju Bhaiyya, was the fourth sarsanghachalak of the RSS. He taught nuclear physics at Allahabad University before deciding to dedicate his full life to RSS work in the 1950s. He served in various capacities within the organization and rose to succeed Balasaheb Deoras as the chief of the organization in 1994, a post he held until 2000.

In this rare interview given to journalist Tavleen Singh in 1996[1], Rajju Bhaiyya candidly answered questions on contemporary issues with ease and elegance.

Tavleen Singh (TS): (Intro) The Bharatiya Janata Party (BJP) is often accused of communalism, and a key reason cited is its association with the Rashtriya Swayamsevak Sangh – the RSS. Political parties that define themselves as secular often argue that the BJP is just a front, and the real force behind it is the RSS. And if it is so, today, we are unveiling this face to you. Presenting to you, sarsanghachalak of RSS, Prof. Rajendra Singh, also known as Rajju Bhaiyya.

(To Rajju Bhaiyya) What was it that drew you to the RSS?
Rajju Bhaiya (RB): There are four things that drew me in. First, the kind of character I found in people – strong moral character. They were ready

to endure all kinds of hardship. They were learned, intelligent and well-read. Unlike what I had seen in other organizations, the swayamsevaks I met were genuinely capable.

Second, there was a vision – one rooted in India. While others looked to America or England, or were influenced by communism, here was a vision for Bharat, for how to shape India.

***TS:* And how do you see India in that vision?**

RB: In that vision, India becomes the greatest nation in the world – not necessarily the richest, but the most noble, character-driven and prosperous in a holistic way. A country strong enough not to need to beg before anyone and capable of offering a message of peace and fraternity to the conflicted world.

***TS:* While many consider the RSS fascist and communal, you believe that this image was cultivated by Congress propaganda – propaganda that started even before Gandhi's assassination. If it is merely propaganda, why are so many Indian Muslims afraid of the RSS?**

RB: Because we don't indulge in flattery. We tell them, 'You too are citizens of this country. If everyone is suffering, you must endure it as well.' Why should we expect a special place?

***TS:* A special space was given for those who are backward. The Muslims who were not backward left for Pakistan.**

RB: A friend of ours in Lucknow studied the curriculum of the madrasas. In five years, they teach a hundred biographies, and only four are Indian: Maulana Azad, Zakir Hussain, Mahatma Gandhi and Nehru. The rest are Harun al-Rashid, Suleiman, Omar, Hazrat Ali – all from outside India. They don't even know about Swami Vivekananda, Ramakrishna or Bankim Chandra. Their educational institutions don't spend on changing this; they take foreign funds and spend them on mosque renovations.

***TS:* But even your schools – like the Shishu Mandirs – aren't secular. They teach Hindu dharma.**

RB: Because Hindu dharma, in truth, is universal and expansive. It's not sectarian. It teaches humanity. We teach Ramayana, Mahabharata

... Even during British rule we had institutions that taught Indian traditions.

***TS:* But what about the morning prayers? Those are Hindu traditions.**
RB: Only Saraswati Puja is done, because Saraswati is considered the goddess of education. Look at Pilani, Roorkee – Saraswati is considered the goddess of education there. Even Indonesia considers her the deity of learning.

***TS:* As we returned early morning from the shakha, you pointed to the portraits of great personalities. I noticed none of them were Muslim. Why are there no Muslims in your pantheon of great personalities?**
RB: You probably missed them. We count four: Kabir[2], Rahim[3], Raskhan[4] and Jayasi[5]. They are part of our studies too. But that spirit was interrupted by the politics of the British and the Congress. Had that unity continued and Congress did not behave how they behaved, things may have been different. Many would have drawn inspiration from Ashfaqulla Khan – the one who said, '*Kuch arzu nahin hai, hai arzu to ye hai. Rakh de koi zara si khaak-e-watan kafan mein* (I have no desires. But if I have one, let someone place a little dust of the motherland in my shroud).'

***TS:* Many believe that Hinduism is embedded in RSS's nationalism. For Muslims, this fear may seem natural. But you feel that Muslims must earn the goodwill of Hindus, and that can only happen if they return three disputed religious sites.**
RB: In Hyderabad, I addressed a big gathering. Many Muslims came thinking, 'This is a dangerous man.' But after listening to me, they found my arguments reasonable. I said, 'Look, millions of Hindus visit three places. They mean little to you in religious terms, but everything to us. If you give them back and we build temples there, it will reduce suspicion and tension. It will foster goodwill.'

That evening, a few Muslims visited me. They said, 'We are genuinely afraid.' I said, 'What can be done to remove this fear. Look, there are 7 lakh villages, 25,000 police stations in this country – no one can protect everyone. Goodwill of Hindus is your best shield.' And how can this goodwill be achieved? Simply by giving back these three religious places. Just this one gesture will change the perception of millions of Hindus, and they will think that Muslims in our country respect and listen to our sentiments. We want to give such a message to the masses – mutual understanding and respect towards each other, no one should have any sort of fear. But this fear is nurtured and propagated by political parties as per their will, so that they support them. So, it has become a political game.

***TS:* The first ban on the RSS was imposed after the assassination of Mahatma Gandhi. After Gandhi's assassination, RSS was banned. Congress said Nathuram Godse was a swayamsevak. But you say that if we call Godse a member of the RSS, then we can also say that he was a member of the Congress, because even before joining RSS, he was a member of the Congress.**

RB: It is a very interesting thing. Earlier, he was a part of the RSS. But he had been in Congress before joining the RSS, and he left the RSS in a year or two – in around 1937 – to join the Hindu Mahasabha. He was associated with the Hindu Mahasabha for some time, but later on criticised that the process was very slow, and he left that as well. He later criticized the RSS in his own publication. So how can someone who insults the RSS be called its member? This would be the same as saying Jinnah is a part of Congress because he once belonged to the party.

***TS:* Why did such details about him being part of Congress never come to light?**

RB: Ah! It has come up at times. We are not publicists or propagandists. But we've always said that Gandhi ji visited our camps. And all the things Gandhi ji stood for – cow protection, swadeshi, local languages, village upliftment – we are the ones carrying forward that work. Even Sardar Patel wrote in his biography that, within 26 days, he declared that no organization played any role in Gandhi's assassination. But the propaganda overshadowed it all.

***TS:* Such is the negative perception of the RSS that even when Congress president Sitaram Kesri recently claimed that the RSS tried to kill L.K. Advani in Coimbatore, many secularists believed it. You see this as an attempt to appease Muslims.**

RB: Imagine if we said that Indira or Rajiv Gandhi were killed for Congress to win elections – how would they feel? Just to appease Muslims, if they say that the RSS did it, then it is only going to increase animosity.

Let's agree on some basics – we won't lie or act unjustly. Babri Masjid – what was it really? For 50 years, no one offered namaz there. It wasn't a functional mosque – it was a structure. And yet they argue about it just to gain power.

***TS:* The RSS is also criticized for its regressive ideology. The country suffers gravely from the problems of poverty, sanitation and education, but the RSS seems more focused on issues such as the cow-slaughter ban, rebuilding temples, etc.**

RB: When does a person actually do something? The first step is to increase self-esteem amongst people. Of course, pride awakens the spirit. Without self-respect, we become beggars with a bowl, waiting for foreign aid. Instead, inspire people. A proud nation can do anything. Our belief is that the spirit of action and self-respect in this country must be awakened. Once that happens, everything else becomes possible.

***TS:* How will issues like cow-slaughter ban and abrogation of Article 370 instil that confidence?**

RB: Foreigners destroyed our sacred places, killed cows – symbols of our faith. And today, even in independent India, we have no rights to prevent cow slaughter. What kind of freedom is this?

***TS:* But roads, electricity – these need massive funding. National pride alone can't build infrastructure. Though India needs crores of rupees for development, Indian businessmen do not have that sort of capital as of now. Yet, you believe the RSS's ideology of *swadeshi* and character-building can play a major role. You also believe that we need not export so much.**

RB: We don't need massive exports. Our people can consume most of what we produce. What remains should be truly exceptional goods – those made with labour and care. Even today, foreign countries import hand-crafted Indian goods.

***TS:* But before anything, we need infrastructure – roads, power, water. Without this infrastructure, our country cannot progress. And for this infrastructure, we need a lot of investment.**

RB: We need the money for infrastructure, but along with it, we need integrity. Corruption eats up the money. Roads are built too narrow. Self-respect must accompany funding.

***TS:* And cow protection – how does that link to self-respect?**

RB: The first thing is to study the cow. It is central to India's economy, for organic fertilizer, milk and, even today, for transportation – 40 per cent of rural transport still uses bullock carts.

***TS:* But we shouldn't be proud of it, in fact, it's a matter of shame.**

RB: No. We should be proud, because for petroleum, you are dependent on Western or Gulf countries. So, the day they stop the supply, the industry will freeze. Today, you will be surprised to know that European countries like Germany are importing vegetables grown with organic manure. Mad cow disease has shown the West the perils of their ways. In Hong Kong, we see chicken disease. Similarly, some are suffering from pig disease. Our country had vegetarianism and was never required to kill animals.

***TS:* While the RSS's economic ideas haven't shaped BJP's policies significantly, its cultural and social vision certainly has. That's why accusations of communalism persist. Does the BJP take directions from the RSS? Is it just your political wing?**

RB: No. We don't 'control' them nor are they our 'wing'.

***TS:* What do you mean by Sangh Parivar?**

RB: It is a family of 'shared values'. We share values, a common vision for India – one that honours our ancient culture. That's what *parivar* (family) means: people with shared ideals, striving together.

***TS:* Among all political parties, is the BJP the one most closely aligned with the RSS's ideology?**
RB: Yes.

***TS:* There's no doubt that Indian Muslims have long viewed the RSS with fear. But is that fear now becoming baseless? Is the RSS, too, seeking to transform itself the way the BJP has over the past five years? Your words seem to suggest something along those lines.**
RB: Hindus have never been driven by communalism.

***TS:* But one could be, some are in fact communal.**
RB: There might have been a few exceptions, but a Hindu state has never been governed on the basis of religion. It has always treated everyone equally. In contrast, Christian and Muslim states have historically been communal. Hindus today form around 80 per cent of the population – there seems to be a deliberate attempt to fracture Hindu unity. To break the 80 per cent Hindus, a narrative is being pushed, one that tries to pit Muslims and a section of Hindus known as Dalits against the Sangh, portraying it as anti-Dalit and anti-Muslim.

But take the example of the recent Charkhi Dadri[6] plane crash – it was Sangh swayamsevaks who rushed to help. There isn't a single place where the Sangh hasn't stepped forward to help, nor is there any instance of discrimination.

***TS:* You aren't just about patriotism and religion – you've got a few hobbies too?**
RB: Yes, I enjoy watching sports, like cricket, and I used to play as well. I read books on the history of our country or Dharma, as you can see, there are dozens of books on the shelf. I also read *Reader's Digest* and listen to old classical music or film songs that inspire service to the nation, such as 'Desh Ki Naiya Tumko Sambhalna'. Even this morning, you saw how music and poetry hold an important place in Sangh's daily practice.

30

K.S. Sudarshan in Conversation with Karan Thapar

K.S. Sudarshan was the fifth sarsanghachalak of the RSS, holding that position from 2000 to 2009. Having joined the organization as a pracharak after graduating in engineering, Sudarshan made valuable contributions to its growth in difficult and far-flung regions such as the Northeast, before rising to occupy an important position in the national leadership. An avid reader and a profound intellectual, he was forthright and fearless in expressing his views, but always in a rational and logical manner.

This is an interview given to journalist Karan Thapar, in which Sudarshan spoke about topics ranging from Hindu Rashtra and the RSS to secularism and the Constitution.

Karan Thapar (KT): **Mr Sudarshan, your critics say that the RSS is a Hindu militant fascist organization with an orientation that is anti-Muslim, anti-Christian. How do you describe the RSS yourself?**
K.S. Sudarshan (KSS): First of all, it is not militant. Just having a certain drill does not make you a militant organization. Secondly, it can never be fascist, because for fascism, power is a must. Ours is a voluntary organization. How can a voluntary organization be fascist? Thirdly, we are not anti-anybody, neither anti-Muslim nor anti-Christian.

***KT:* The RSS prayer commits its members to the fulfilment of a Hindu Rashtra. What is a Hindu Rashtra, and how central is it to your ideology?**
KSS: First and foremost, 'Rashtra' is not a political entity. It's a geo-cultural entity. It evolved that way over a long period.

***KT:* So you see India as a culturally Hindu entity? Is that central to your belief?**
KSS: Yes, it is central to our belief. We say that it is a Hindu nation, and it's not a new nation. It is the most ancient nation in the world.

***KT:* You have said of India, and I'll quote, 'Till such time that there is even one Hindu left, it will remain a Hindu Rashtra.' Are you saying that, in fact, in your eyes, India by definition is Hindu?**
KSS: India by definition is Hindu. The culture of this country is Hindu. Because Hindus form the backbone of this nation.

***KT:* So then, where in this concept of a Hindu Rashtra do Indian Christians and Indian Muslims fit in? They are also part and parcel of this national line.**
KSS: They are not from outside.

***KT:* But they are not Hindus.**
KSS: Maybe, because, Hindu, does not mean a particular religion. Hindu means a particular culture.

***KT:* You define Hindu not by religion, but by culture.**
KSS: Yes, we do. And that culture is based on the concept of unity in diversity.

***KT:* Are you also saying that all Indian Christians and Muslims, at some point in time before they converted, were in fact Hindus, and therefore the core identity of this entire country's population is Hindu?**
KSS: Yes, that is true. Their forefathers were Hindu. And so is the blood flowing in their veins; and the blood of their forefathers was Hindu,

because they have only changed the mode of worship. That does not alienate them from their cultural bonding.

***KT:* Genetically, they are Hindu. That's what you are saying.**
KSS: They are Hindu, definitely. Moreover, even the Muslims in this country, when they go outside, are termed as Hindus. Those who go to Saudi Arabia, they are all called Hindus. They are Hindus.

***KT:* And therefore, you are saying that is proof that their core identity is Hindu.**
KSS: Core identity is Hindu, and it is the national identity of the people, irrespective of whichever religion they may subscribe to.

***KT:* One of your predecessors, Mr Golwalkar, in his book *We Are Nation Defined,* said that Indian Christians and Indian Muslims cannot but be foreigners until they discard their religion and culture. Do you subscribe to those views today?**
KSS: No. First and foremost, they do not have a separate culture. First and foremost, the culture is always of the majority. And the people following different religions, they also should subscribe to the same culture. Because that is what democracy means.

***KT:* So, there is no such thing as a Muslim or a Christian culture. Indian Christians and Indian Muslims are Hindu in cultural terms.**
KSS: Yes. Only thing is that they should accept that. I give the example of Pandit Jawaharlal Nehru. Jawaharlal Nehru delivered a convocation address in Aligarh University in 1948. In that he said, 'I am a Hindu. You are a Muslim. We may belong to different religions. And we may have no religion also. But do you feel the same thrill about our cultural inheritance, which I feel belongs to me as much as it belongs to you?'

***KT:* But there is a difference, Mr Sudarshan. He talked about that as the Indian culture. You are calling it a Hindu culture. You are actually associating the culture with the Hindu religion.**
KSS: Hindu is not a religion at all. When you say it is a religion, it is a relationship with God. There are so many religions in Hindu society.

***KT:* Isn't that what a religion is? A relationship between the individual and God, whether it is a Christian religion or a Muslim religion. That is religion by definition. So, Hinduism is as much of a religion as Islam or Christianity.**

KSS: It's not. Because amongst Hindus, there are people who subscribe to God. But there are agnostics and atheists too, who are also called Hindus.

***KT:* Forgive me for interrupting. There is a catch to what you are saying. You are saying that Indian Christians and Indian Muslims remain in a sense peripheral to your concept of a Hindu Rashtra unless they are prepared to accept your central tenet, which is that their core identity, regardless of their religion, remains Hindu. If they make that acceptance, they become part of a Hindu Rashtra. If they don't make that acceptance, they are peripheral to it.**

KSS: What I mean to say is that ultimately, they will accept it. What is happening right now is that, because of the competitive politics among different parties, they are more concerned about their vote banks.

***KT:* You wish to persuade them rather than coerce them. Okay, let me put it like this. If you define India as a Hindu Rashtra, then how does the RSS relate to the present Indian Constitution, and in particular, how do you relate to its political philosophy of secularism and special minority rights for Christians and Muslims?**

KSS: The Hindu concept of state has always been secular. And therefore, the state is different from what we call Rashtra. I do not equate it with nation.

***KT:* Do you accept the Constitution as it is?**

KSS: No. This Constitution does not reflect the basic ethos of this nation.

***KT:* Precisely. M.S. Golwalkar, your predecessor, in his book *A Bunch of Thoughts*, says there is nothing in the Constitution which we call our own.**

KSS: This whole Constitution is based on the Government of India Act of 1935. Some of the things from other constitutions have been added to it. It is not an evolved one. Are you saying it is alien to India's character and thinking? True so. It does not reflect it.

***KT:* Is this what you meant when just after you became sarsanghachalak, you were widely quoted in the press as saying we should scrap the Constitution?**
KSS: I did not say, 'Scrap the Constitution.' When the question was asked, it was in the context of the Constitution being reviewed – 'What is your opinion?' I told them that they say that the basic structure of the Constitution should not be touched. But they have not defined the basic structure. If the basic structure is democracy, then there is a wide range to discuss. Because there are so many forms of democracy.

***KT:* If the basic structure is special rights for minorities to give them a sense of security . . .**
KSS: We do not accept the concept of minority at all. They are not minorities.

***KT:* Hence there is no need for special rights either in your eyes?**
KSS: True. There should not be.

***KT:* Would you also go further? Would you say that, in fact, secularism therefore is irrelevant because Hinduism is secularism, as you said a moment ago?**
KSS: True so. Throughout our history, our state has never differentiated anybody on the basis of their religion.

KT: So, you are saying that there is no need for the Constitution to be actually secular? Hinduism guarantees that?
KSS: A political state will always be secular because it deals with secular matters. So, therefore, you need not specially call it 'secular'. And there was no such word in the original Constitution. It was inserted into it during the Emergency. This country is secular only because the Hindus are a majority. And this thing was repeated by Sonia Gandhi also.

***KT:* You think the Constitution should therefore be amended to reflect this?**

KSS: Yes. We should evolve our own Constitution. The Constitution cannot be imposed on us. Since 1909, the whole Constitution has been imposed on us. We have not evolved it. It must evolve.

***KT:* So, you want a thorough review of the Constitution to reflect India's actual Hindu character?**

KSS: Not only me – even Dr Ambedkar said the same thing in his concluding speech on the Constitution. He said, 'Each generation is a nation in itself. It can bind itself, by the will of the majority, to a particular legal system. But it cannot bind the coming generation.'

***KT:* You are not feeling bound today by a Constitution that was created 50 years ago.**

KSS: What I mean to say is that it needs a proper review. It must be reviewed completely to understand if whatever we started with is fulfilled or not.

***KT:* That's the first question. And the second question with which this review must happen is to reflect what you call the essential, unchangeable Hindu character of the people. That's your second reason. You are in fact saying that you would like a Hindu review of the Constitution, to put it like that.**

KSS: When you say Hindu review, again you are misinterpreting Hindu for a particular religion.

***KT:* No, I'm saying Hindu in the terms in which you mean it now. A review of the Constitution to reflect the Hindu cultural character of the people.**

KSS: Our constitution should reflect our national ethos.

***KT:* And at the moment you're saying it doesn't?**

KSS: Definitely.

***KT:* And so, when Indian Christians and Indian Muslims and other minorities turn around and say, don't touch the Constitution, we are very happy with it, what do you say to them?**
KSS: Those people who are being averse to this review of this Constitution have themselves tampered with the Constitution for the last 15 years. Several political parties, including even the Communist Party, have passed resolutions calling to scrap this Constitution. Today they are defending it.

***KT:* So, you're saying, they have no right to object.**
KSS: Definitely, they have no right to object.

***KT:* At the very core of the ideology of the RSS is the belief that Indians are Hindu and India is a Hindu Rashtra. That is the unshakable central core of your belief.**
KSS: That is our article of faith.

***KT:* In 1925, when the RSS was founded by Dr Hedgewar, it was a single organization. Today you have a full *parivar* consisting of a lot of others. Let me put this to you. What is the relationship between the RSS and the Bharatiya Janata Party (BJP)?**
KSS: Our relationship is only with the swayamsevaks. Because the Bharatiya Janata Party and the RSS are autonomous organizations, they have got different constitutions and different objectives.

***KT:* But it is part of the same parivar.**
KSS: You can say it is part of an ideological construct.

***KT:* Of which the RSS is the centre, the mother?**
KSS: True. Because many of the leaders who formed the Jana Sangh first, which was converted into the BJP afterwards, came from the RSS stock.

***KT:* Quite right. And would I therefore be right in saying that the Bharatiya Janata Party was formed to realize further and create a political opportunity for the RSS ideology to be fulfilled?**

KSS: What we say is that the Hindu ethos should reflect in every walk of social life. Of which one is the political field as well. So, our members have gone into each and every field of social life with this objective.

***KT:* So as you said, the BJP exists to reflect the Hindu ethos in the political field.**
KSS: Yes.

***KT:* Okay, so then, when in 1998 and again in 1999, the BJP put its political ideology on the back burner to come to power, in your eyes, was that clever politics or was it a mistake?**
KSS: When you are in politics, many times you have to make compromises. And you must allow them to do this. And they are doing that.

***KT:* So, compromise is essential to come to power, is that what you are saying?**
KSS: Not that. But whenever there are certain political situations like that, where you have to make compromises, you must give that much space to them to do it.

***KT:* But, nonetheless, as we said, the RSS is the core of the ideological circle within which the BJP lives. That being the case, was the BJP right to give up its commitment to the abrogation of Article 370, to the creation of a Uniform Civil Code, to the building of a Ram Temple and in giving it up, has it strengthened itself or has it weakened its identity?**
KSS: I don't believe that the BJP has left all those things. It is only the NDA government . . .

***KT:* The BJP has officially said it has put it on the back burner.**
KSS: What we feel is that BJP is a political party. And as a political party, it must educate the public about its different programmes, which gave it a special niche in the hearts of the people. And therefore, it should not tie itself solely to the NDA agenda. In the NDA government, there are other political parties that have not left their programmes – but the BJP has set aside its own.

So, the BJP has put its agenda on the back burner as far as the government is concerned. Otherwise, the BJP should be free to educate the public or expand its organization according to its own agenda.

***KT:* But is it doing that?**
KSS: We feel they should do that. If they don't do it, because at the moment they are unable to, it is up to them to decide.

***KT:* Tell me something. When compromises are made, they are judged at the end of the day by whether they paid off or not. As you see it, will this compromise deliver results, or do you think the BJP could be the net loser?**
KSS: That we'll have to see when they complete the five-year term. Are the BJP supporters, well-wishers disillusioned with the party? We will have to wait and see. When they go to the hustings, then it will be decided whether people are disillusioned or not.

***KT:* You are suggesting, Mr Sudarshan, that in fact people, when they go to the hustings, won't vote for the BJP the same way again.**
KSS: They may or may not vote. Ultimately, it is the public who have to decide whether they are disillusioned or not. And they will also ultimately know it from the decision of the public only.

***KT:* The tone and tenor of everything you're saying suggests that you yourself are disillusioned. You keep saying the BJP has to decide what it does, but you don't sound as if you're convinced by what it has done.**
KSS: What I mean to say is, we understand their compulsions. That in the present set of circumstances, they have no other choice. They have to act under certain constraints. And particularly, there are three constraints under which they have to work.

***KT:* Quite right. The constraints are, of course, well known. Forgive me for interrupting. But what I'm trying to understand from you is, do you think those compromises were worth making, or has the BJP lost**

something that made it different? Has it ceased to be the party with the difference?

KSS: As things stands today, we do not feel that it is acting as a party with a difference. And therefore, it is for the BJP to decide and assess the pulse of the people. If they fail to do so, they may lose touch with public sentiment – and that responsibility lies with the party, not the government. Ultimately, it is the party that must go to the people and understand what they think of it. It is for them to decide.

***KT:* You are also suggesting that the party has lost its ability to feel the pulse of the people.**

KSS: Now, unless and until they lay more stress on their organization, and try to educate the people, and try to know from them what ultimately the people are thinking, they will be cut away from the public.

***KT:* Mr Sudarshan, you are saying that, by coming to power in the circumstances in which they did, the BJP organization and the BJP's ability to reflect the mood of the people are both suffering.**

KSS: At the present moment, it appears like that.

***KT:* You are actually sending out an important message of correction if they listen to you, aren't you?**

KSS: It is for them to ultimately decide whether they will listen to us or not.

***KT:* Sometimes they don't listen to you?**

KSS: We cannot force anybody to listen to us. They are an autonomous organization, they have to decide for themselves. We can only suggest. They may accept our suggestion, or they may not. We cannot force anybody to do what we say, and we do not claim that whatever we say must be accepted by them.

***KT:* You give me the feeling that there are many occasions when you try to make suggestions, and they haven't listened to you. Is that the case?**

KSS: Maybe, because ultimately, we make our suggestions according to the feedback that we get, and according to the perception that we have. They may have a different perception, and they may have a different feedback also. So, they may decide differently.

***KT:* And you are also saying that the longer they don't listen to you, the greater the danger that, when the next election comes, they will lose seats.**

KSS: No, I cannot say that.

***KT:* But it's a danger.**

KSS: I just suggest that we will have to look into these things, and to listen to their cadre and the general public also, know the pulse of the public and then decide what they have to do. The only thing is, even in the present constraints, if they can provide at least a good measure of a good government, only then can people say, 'Well, till now we did not get a good government.'

***KT:* Let me put that to you. Are they giving good government? Are they giving corruption-free government?**

KSS: As far as the central government is concerned, we cannot say anything.

***KT:* Why?**

KSS: Because they are working under constraints. But in Gujarat, they have done some very good experiments.

***KT:* Let me come back and continue with the central government. The RSS believes that Article 370 should be abrogated. Far from abrogating it, this government is today talking to Hizbul Mujahideen without constitutional preconditions. Do you approve of that?**

KSS: When the people are coming to the talking table, this should be welcomed.

***KT:* But without preconditions?**
KSS: Maybe. But ultimately, whether what they propose is accepted or not – it is for the government to decide. But what is the harm? Let them put forward their views.

***KT:* In between, you were questioning the BJP and their decision, but now you are supporting thc way they are handling the Kashmir talks. Is that correct?**
KSS: Because ultimately it is for them to solve the problem, and the best way to solve the problem is to have a dialogue. Then they themselves are coming forward to have a dialogue. Let them have a dialogue.

***KT:* What about the prime minister's statement, as he put it, that we can have a dialogue in the name of humanity? Do you think that is a welcome remark, or is that a dangerous precedent?**
KSS: Let us see that . . . The path of humanity is all right. But ultimately, it all depends on what comes out of the talks. That is important. Ultimately what comes out from the talks is important. Unless and until you talk to them, unless you try to know what their problem is, you will not be able to understand how to solve it. And even today in Kashmir, only one-sixth of the valley holds a different opinion. The rest – Jammu and Ladakh – want full integration of the state. And there are movements going on in that area for the trifurcation of the state.

***KT:* On Kashmir, your central belief is that the government is wise to talk without preconditions. But would you say that the outcome has to be within the parameters of the Indian Constitution? And so, is there not a danger that if the talks are without preconditions, the government could find itself pushed against its will?**
KSS: Not necessarily. There is no danger. It ultimately depends on the sagacity of the government to steer clear of the pitfalls that may arise there in such talks.

***KT:* Are you confident that this government has that sagacity?**
KSS: Yes, we are confident.

KT: **Because a moment ago, very clearly you were saying that this government has disillusioned its cadres and its supporters. It runs the risk of losing votes at the next election. It runs the risk of having made compromises without delivering results. And now when we move to Kashmir, your entire attitude has become supportive and understanding. You believe that, in fact, there is no danger in holding talks without preconditions. There is almost a 180-degree U-turn here.**
KSS: As a matter of fact, you cannot always deride all the policies of the government. Some of the policies that the government has put in place are good. And whatever policies are beneficial to the nation, you must support them.

KT: **A new voice of the RSS is speaking up. The dragon, if I may use that phrase, is deliberately presenting itself in a better, kinder, gentler light. Is this deliberate? Or is it simply that up till now we have misunderstood it?**
KSS: I think it is because of misunderstanding. Because the problems in this country have to be talked out and solved. Without talking and solving, you will not come to any understanding at all. Let them talk. You do not constrain, restrict them when they talk to the people. Let all these things come forward. Then we shall decide what happens.

KT: **A moment ago, you said that on many things where you advise the government, they don't listen. Is this an area where you think they will listen to you on Kashmir?**
KSS: We never expect the government to listen to us. What we say is that we, in our perception, suggest certain things. Perhaps, they have broader feedback and may be thinking in another direction. It is for them to decide. Ultimately, whatever the government does, it is according to its own decisions. For us, as a volunteer organization, as a nationalist organization with the interest of the nation at heart, the touchstone is whether any decision of the government is in the interest of the nation or not. So ultimately, whatever comes out of the talks will have to be judged on the basis: is it in national interest or not? Let them talk. Let them come out.

Notes

Introduction

1. TNN. 2018. "'Nehru Invited RSS To '63 R-Day Parade, Indira Attended 1977 Event'." The Times of India. The Times Of India. May 29, 2018. https://timesofindia.indiatimes.com/india/nehru-invited-rss-to-63-r-day-parade-indira-attended-1977-event/articleshow/64376602.cms.
2. Mirror Now Digital. 2018. "When Lal Bahadur Shastri Invited RSS' Shri Guru Ji to All-Party Meet during 1965 Indo-Pak War." @TIMESNOW. Times Now. June 7, 2018. https://www.timesnownews.com/mirror-now/in-focus/article/lal-bahadur-shastri-rss-shri-guru-ji-all-party-meet-1965-indo-pak-war/236863.
3. Mehta, Nalin. 2017. "'Indira Gandhi Put RSS's Guru Golwalkar on Cow Slaughter Committee … Wound up after 12 Years without a R." Times of India Voices. Times of India. June 15, 2017. https://timesofindia.indiatimes.com/blogs/academic-interest/indira-gandhi-put-rsss-guru-golwalkar-on-cow-slaughter-committee-wound-up-after-12-years-without-a-report/.

2. 'Doctorji: A Steady Lamp in the Cause of the Motherland'

1. A shakha is a daily gathering of swayamsevaks from different age groups at a designated ground or meeting place, lasting for one hour. The routine activities include physical exercises, patriotic songs, group discussions on a wide range of subjects, and a prayer for the motherland.
2. All-India executive committee of the RSS.
3. General secretary; the executive head of the organization who conducts the affairs of the Sangh. Currently, Ma. Dattatreya Hosabale is the general secretary of RSS.
4. Literally means 'one who serves voluntarily'.
5. Ekadashi is considered to be an auspicious day; it takes place on the eleventh day of the two lunar cycles of the month.
6. Shivaratri is a festival commemorating Lord Shiva's marriage to Goddess Parvati; the word literally translates to the 'Night of Shiva'.
7. Dr Balakrishna Shivram Moonje.
8. This is a metaphorical reference to the Mahabharata. Yudhishthira, the eldest of the Pandavas, known for his truthfulness, was so morally upright that even Drona – or Dronacharya, his teacher and commander on the opposing side – trusted his word about his son, Ashwathama's demise. Yudhishthira called Duryodhana, the chief antagonist of the epic, by the respectful name Suyodhana, reflecting his own nobility.
9. Literally, one without enemies; another name for Yudhishthira.
10. Derived from the root 'tap', which means to heat, to burn or to shine; *tapasya* is the inner fire generated through self-discipline, penance and focused practice.

11. Shibi, a legendary king from Indian epics, is celebrated for offering his own flesh to save a dove – a symbol of ultimate self-sacrifice. Dadhichi, a sage in Hindu mythology, willingly gave up his life so that his bones could be used to create a weapon to defeat the demon Vritasura. These metaphors underscore Doctorji's ideal of total self-offering for society's well-being.
12. Shyama Prasad Mukherjee (1901–53) was an Indian political leader, academic and activist, best known for his role in the foundation of the Bharatiya Jana Sangh, the precursor to the Bharatiya Janata Party (BJP), and is often remembered for his advocacy of integrating Jammu and Kashmir fully into India.
13. In Hindu tradition, Sri Krishna is revered as the eighth incarnation of Vishnu and is a central figure in the Bhagavata Purana and Mahabharata. Gokula is the pastoral village where Krishna spent his early childhood among cowherds. Yashoda is Krishna's foster-mother, known for her deep affection and for raising him as her own child, unaware of his divine origin.

3. 'What We Lacked Was the Consciousness of Fundamental Hindu Unity'

1. RSS training camps.
2. Purushottama, also known as Porus, was an ancient Indian king who fought against the army of Alexander and defeated him.
3 Seleucus Nicator was a Greek general and officer under Alexander the Great. He was defeated by Chandragupta Maurya in the northwestern region of India.
4. Chandragupta Maurya was the founder of the Maurya Empire. Coming from a humble background, and guided by his advisor, Chanakya, he rose to overthrow the Nanda dynasty. He is known for unifying much of the Indian subcontinent and establishing one of the most powerful empires in ancient Indian history.
5. He was a twelfth-century Rajput king of the Chauhan dynasty, known for his victory in the First Battle of Tarain (1191) against Muhammad Ghori. In the Second Battle of Tarain, he was defeated and captured. It was an important moment in Indian history marking the establishment of Muslim rule in northern India.
6. Coming from the Ghurid dynasty in present-day Afghanistan, Muhammed Ghori was a twelfth-century Muslim ruler who defeated Prithviraj Chauhan in the Second Battle of Tarain. Following this, Qutb al-Din Aibak, established the Delhi Sultanate.
7. East India Company (EIC) was a British trading company established in 1600.
8. A thirteenth-century Turkic military general under the Delhi Sultanate, Khilji is known for destroying the ancient university of Nalanda.

4. 'Cow Slaughter Is an Anti-India Act'

1. Gopashtami is a Hindu festival celebrating Lord Krishna's transition from a cowherd of calves to a caretaker of cows, symbolizing love and reverence for the cow.
2. Pandit Jawaharlal Nehru (14 November 1889 – 27 May 1964) was India's first Prime Minister.
3. Vijayadashami, also known as Dussehra, is a Hindu festival symbolizing the victory of good over evil, commemorating Lord Rama's triumph over Ravana and Goddess Durga's victory over Mahishasura.

4. Lord Ram is a diety in Hinduism, known as the seventh incarnation of Vishnu, embodying virtue, courage, dharma and is celebrated as the hero of the epic Ramayana.
5. Acharya Vinoba Bhave (11 September 1895 – 15 November 1982) was a spiritual leader, social reformer and Gandhian who initiated the Bhoodan movement.
6. Maharshi Dayananda Saraswati (12 February 1824 – 30 October 1883) was a Hindu reformer and founder of the Arya Samaj.
7. Lokmanya Bal Gangadhar Tilak (1856–1920) was an Indian nationalist leader and freedom fighter.
8. Renowned scholar and spiritual leader.
9. Spiritual head of one of the four cardinal mathas (monastic centers) established by Adi Shankaracharya in the 8th century to preserve and propagate Advaita Vedanta.
10. 10-15 million.
11. A town in Uttar Pradesh, India where Lord Krishna was raised by Yashoda and Nanda.
12. Shri Mahadev Haribhai Desai (1 January 1892 – 15 August 1942) was the devoted personal secretary, confidant and chronicler of Mahatma Gandhi for 25 years.
13. Chhatrapati Shivaji Maharaj was a legendary Indian warrior king and founder of the Maratha Empire, known for his military tactics, progressive governance and the establishment of a strong, independent kingdom in western India, which challenged the dominance of the Mughal Empire.
14. Prabhudatt Brahmachari (1885–1990) was a nationalist monk, Sanskrit scholar, and Gauraksha activist who participated in the freedom struggle, opposed the Hindu Code Bill, and contested the 1951 election against Nehru to defend traditional Hindu values.

5. 'The Objective of the Sangh Is to Organize Hindu Society and Make It Powerful'

1. Marshal Philippe Pétain (1856–1951) was a French general and political leader.
2. Admiral François Darlan (1881–1942) was a senior French naval officer and political figure. (Marshal Pétain, once a WWI hero, led the collabourationist Vichy regime during WWII, while Admiral Darlan, initially loyal to Vichy, abruptly switched allegiance to the Allies in 1942 before being assassinated – both becoming controversial figures in France's wartime history.)
3. Winston Churchill (1874–1965) was the prime minister of the United Kingdom (UK) during WWII.
4. Clement Attlee (1883–1967) was the prime minister of the UK from 1945 to 1951.
5. Chhatrapati Shivaji Maharaj was a legendary Indian warrior king and founder of the Maratha Empire, known for his military tactics, progressive governance and the establishment of a strong, independent kingdom in western India, which challenged the dominance of the Mughal Empire.
6. Sambhaji Maharaj was the eldest son of Chhatrapati Shivaji Maharaj and the second ruler of the Maratha Empire, known for his bravery, scholarship and fierce resistance against Mughal emperor Aurangzeb.
7. Rajaram Maharaj was the younger son of Chhatrapati Shivaji Maharaj and the third ruler of the Maratha Empire, who kept the Maratha resistance alive against the Mughal invasion after the death of his brother Sambhaji by relocating to Jinji and leading a guerrilla struggle.

8. Aurangzeb was a Mughal emperor (1658–1707). He is known for expanding the empire to its greatest extent and enforcing Islamic policies.
9. Santaji Ghorpade was a legendary Maratha general known for his daring guerrilla warfare tactics against the Mughals during the late seventeenth century, playing a crucial role in keeping the Maratha resistance alive after Chhatrapati Sambhaji's death.
10. Dhanaji Jadhav was a prominent Maratha general and close associate of Santaji Ghorpade.
11. Robert Clive was a British officer who laid the foundation of British rule in India by winning the Battle of Plassey in 1757.
12. Napoleon Bonaparte was a brilliant French military leader who rose to become the Emperor of France.
13. The Battle of Waterloo, fought on 18 June 1815, was a decisive battle in which Napoleon Bonaparte was defeated by the Duke of Wellington (British-led forces) and Prussian troops, marking the end of the Napoleonic Wars and Napoleon's final downfall.
14. Shankaracharya is the title given to the heads of the four cardinal monastic institutions (mathas) established by Adi Shankaracharya, the 8th-century philosopher and reformer.
15. The Ku Klux Klan (KKK) is a white supremacist hate group founded in 1865, notorious for its violence and terror against African Americans and other minorities, particularly during the Reconstruction and Civil Rights eras.
16. Vinayak Damodar Savarkar (28 May 1883 – 26 February 1966), popularly known as Veer Savarkar, was a revolutionary freedom fighter, nationalist thinker and a key ideologue of Hindutva.
17. An individual who is inspired by the mission and objective of the Sangh and dedicates his full time to carry forward this mission.

6. 'May All of Us Sincerely Feel That the Hindus Must Unite and the Basis for That Unity Can Only Be Social Equality'

1. Dr. B. R. Ambedkar (14 April 1891 – 6 December 1956) was a jurist, economist, social reformer and chief architect of the Indian Constitution.
2. Panchāyatan is a traditional form of Hindu worship and temple architecture in which five deities are worshipped together.
3. Hindu festival dedicated to Lord Shiva.
4. Rahu is one of the nine celestial bodies (navagrahas) in Vedic astrology, representing the north lunar node.
5. Ketu is one of the nine celestial bodies (navagrahas) in Vedic astrology, representing the south lunar node.
6. Rishyashringa, Vishwamitra and Agastya are three ancient Hindu sages.
7. Aitareya Brahmana is a prose text that explains the rituals, ceremonies and meanings of the Rigveda hymns, forming part of the Aitareya corpus associated with the Rigveda and composed by the Aitareya family of sages.
8. Dwija means 'twice-born' and refers to members of the three higher Hindu varnas – Brahmins, Kshatriyas and Vaishyas – who undergo the sacred Upanayana ceremony, symbolizing their spiritual rebirth and eligibility to study the Vedas.
9. Jabala is an ancient sage mentioned in Hindu scriptures, best known for the Jabala Upanishad, which discusses the nature of renunciation (*sannyasa*) and spiritual liberation.

10. Upanayana is a sacred Hindu rite of passage (also called the "sacred thread ceremony") marking a boy's formal initiation into spiritual education and his entry into the study of the Vedas.
11. Shri Guruji, also known as M. S. Golwalkar (Madhav Sadashivrao Golwalkar) (19 February 1906 – 5 June 1973), was the second Sarsanghchalak.
12. A historically oppressed caste.
13. Pandit Bachhraj Vyas (1916 – March 1972) was an Indian politician and stalwart of the Bharatiya Jana Sangh.
14. General Secretary.
15. Prant Pracharak is a regional head responsible for overseeing the organization's activities within a specific geographic area, known as a 'Prant'.
16. Bharatiya Jana Sangh (BJS) was a political party founded in 1951.

7. 'We Aspire to Build an India That Is Self-Respecting, Self-Reliant and a Beacon of Wisdom for the World'

1. Hindu saint, poet and philosopher best known for composing the Ramcharitmanas.
2. Ajamila is a figure in Hindu mythology, found in the Bhagavata Purana, who, after living a life of sin, was redeemed at the time of his death simply by chanting the name of Lord Narayana (Vishnu).
3. Narayan is another name for Lord Vishnu, one of the principal deities in Hinduism, known as the preserver and protector of the universe.
4. Valmiki is a prominent Indian sage and the author of the Ramayana.

8. 'We Have Forgotten Ourselves, and Those Who Forget Themselves Are Vulnerable to Any Attack'

1. Caliph Umar ibn al-Khattab was the second caliph of the Rashidun Caliphate, ruling from 634 to 644 AD after the death of Abu Bakr, the first Caliph.
2. Muhammad bin Qasim was an Umayyad general who led the first successful Muslim conquest of India in 712 AD. He invaded the Sindh and Multan regions (in present-day Pakistan) under the orders of the Umayyad Caliphate, then ruled by Caliph Al-Walid I.
3. A series of religious and military campaigns launched between eleventh and thirteenth centuries by European Christians aimed at reclaiming the Holy Land (Jerusalem) from Muslim control.
4. A prominent Indian historian specializing in medieval history.
5. Nineteenth-century Indian philosopher and monk, he played a key role in introducing the Indian philosophies of Vedanta and Yoga to western audience. He is best known for his inspiring speech at the 1893 Parliament of the World's Religions in Chicago.
6. Nineteenth-century Indian philosopher.
7. Thirteenth-century Marathi saint, poet and philosopher from Maharashtra, India, he is known for his Dnyaneshwari, a Marathi commentary on the Bhagavada Gita.
8. Indian politician, writer.
9. 'Prithvi Sukta' is a hymn from the ancient Indian scripture dedicated to Prithvi, the Earth goddess.

10. The Atharvaveda is one of the four main Vedas in ancient Indian scripture, alongside the Rigveda, Yajurved and Samaveda.
11. A famous Hindu pilgrimage to the Sabrimala temple in Kerala, India, dedicated to Lord Ayyappa.
12. Pandharpur is a famous pilgrimage town in Maharashtra, India, known primarily for the Vithoba (Vitthal) temple, dedicated to Lord Vithoba, a form of Lord Krishna or Vishnu.
13. The month of Shravan is a holy month in the Hindu calendar, usually falling in July or August.
14. Devotees who take part in the annual pilgrimage to collect holy water from the Ganges River during the month of Shravan. They carry this water in special pots called kanwars on their shoulders and travel long distances.
15. The Amarnath Yatra is an annual Hindu pilgrimage to the Amarnath Cave.
16. A pilgrimage site located on Trikuta Mountain in the state of Jammu and Kashmir, believed to be the abode of the goddess Vaishno Devi, a manifestation of *Shakti*.

9. 'We Must Perceive, Understand and Manifest [Mahatma Gandhi's] Idealism in Our Lives'

1. Albert Einstein (1879–1955) was a theoretical physicist.

12. 'True Swarajya Is Emotional and Spirited'

1. Bharatbhumi (भारत भूमि) literally means "the land of Bharat", referring to the Indian subcontinent as a sacred, cultural and spiritual geography. The term is deeply rooted in civilizational, philosophical and dharmic traditions.
2. Mirabai (c. 1498 – c. 1547) was a 16th-century Hindu mystic poet and one of the most prominent female saints of the Bhakti movement in India.
3. Purushartha concept in Hindu philosophy that outlines the four goals or aims of human life.

14. 'The Program of Our Sangh Is to Revive the Healthy Flow of National Life'

1. An ancient sage and lawgiver, traditionally regarded as the author of the *Manusmriti.*
2. Albert Einstein (1879–1955) was a theoretical physicist.
3. Pandavas are the five heroic brothers in the Hindu epic Mahabharata –Yudhishthira, Bhima, Arjuna, Nakula and Sahadeva – known for their righteousness, bravery and central role in the Kurukshetra war.

15. 'Akhand Bharat . . . Is the Foundation of Our Entire Philosophy'

1. In present-day Pakistan (Punjab province); historically, the northwestern frontier of India.
2. City in Odisha, eastern India.
3. Region in Gujarat, western India.
4. Ancient kingdom/region in Assam, northeastern India.

5. Northern-most region of India.
6. Southern tip of mainland India (Tamil Nadu).
7. Puranas and Upanishads are ancient philosophical texts.

16. 'In Our Tradition, the Nature of the State Has Always Been Envisioned as a Dharma Rajya – A Righteous State'

1. Extracted from Rashtra Chintan by Deendayal Ji.
2. In hinduism, these are the four goals of human life – duty, wealth, desire and liberation.
3. Galileo Galilei (1564–1642) was an Italian astronomer, physicist and mathematician.
4. Caliphate is an Islamic political and religious state led by a Caliph.
5. The Papacy is the office and authority of the Pope, the spiritual leader of the Roman Catholic Church.

17. The Answer to World's Problems Is Not Socialism, but Hindutva'

1. Extracted from Rashtra Chintan by Deendayal Ji.
2. 1955 annual session of the Indian National Congress, held in Avadi, Tamil Nadu.
3. Hindu Mahasabha is a right-wing political organization founded in 1915 that advocates for Hindu nationalism.
4. Jayaprakash Narayan (1902–1979) was an Indian freedom fighter, socialist thinker and political leader.
5. M. N. Roy (1887–1954) was an Indian political thinker, and the founder of Indian communism.
6. Karl Marx (1818–1883) was a German philosopher, economist and best known for developing the theory of Marxism.
7. Prince Peter Kropotkin (1842–1921) was a Russian aristocrat-turned-revolutionary.
8. René Fülöp-Miller (1891–1963) was an Austrian cultural historian, journalist and writer known for his critical studies of Russian culture, mysticism and totalitarianism.

18. 'Some People Claim That a Hindu Nation Is Being Established Today, but We Say That There Is No Need to Establish What Already Exists'

1. An individual who is inspired by the mission and objective of the Sangh and dedicates their full time to carry forward this mission.
2. Vishwa Hindu Parishad (VHP) literally means World Hindu Council. Founded in 1964, the VHP is a Hindu organization that aims to promote and protect Hindu dharma (religion and way of life) across the world.
3. Ram Janmabhoomi means the birthplace of Lord Ram, and refers to the site in Ayodhya, Uttar Pradesh, where Lord Ram was born.
4. E.M.S. Namboodiripad was a prominent Indian communist leader and the first chief minister of Kerala.
5. It means United Front and refers to a political coalition of multiple parties that come together – usually with leftist, regional or anti-Congress/anti-BJP leanings.
6. The All-India Muslim League was a political party founded in 1906 in British India to represent the interests of the Muslim population. It played a central role in the Pakistan Movement, advocating for the creation of a separate Muslim state, which eventually led

to the partition of India and the formation of Pakistan in 1947.

7. Muhammad Ali Jinnah (1876–1948) was a lawyer, politician and the founder of Pakistan.
8. Manthara is a character in the Hindu epic Ramayana, known for manipulating Queen Kaikeyi into demanding the exile of Prince Rama and the coronation of her own son, Bharata.
9. Shakuni Mama was the uncle of the Kauravas in the Mahabharata, known for manipulating the game of dice that led to the downfall of the Pandavas.
10. Sindh is a region located in present-day southern Pakistan. Earlier it was a part of undivided India.
11. Ghulam Murtaza Syed, popularly known as G.M. Syed, was a prominent Sindhi nationalist, politician and intellectual, born in Sann, Sindh (now in Pakistan).
12. The story of Rustam and Sohrab is a tragic tale from the Persian epic *Shahnameh* by Ferdowsi.
13. Lava and Kush were the twin sons of Lord Rama and Sita in the Hindu epic Ramayana.
14. Rama is considered the seventh avatar of the god Vishnu, known for his virtues of righteousness, courage and compassion.
15. Karna is a key character in the epic of Mahabharata. He was born to Kunti before her marriage (making him elder to the Pandavas).
16. The Pandavas are five brothers – Yudhishthira, Bhima, Arjuna, Nakula and Sahadeva – central to the epic of Mahabharata. They are known for their courage and sense of dharma. They fought the Kurukshetra war against their cousins, the Kauravas, with guidance from Lord Krishna.
17. Shaivites are devotees of Lord Shiva.
18. Vaishnavites are followers of Lord Vishnu and his avatars, especially Rama and Krishna.
19. Such devotees worship various forms of the goddess, such as Durga, Kali, Lakshmi and Parvati, etc.
20. Brihaspati is the Hindu god of wisdom and is regarded as the guru (teacher) of the gods (Devas). He is also associated with the planet Jupiter in Hindu astrology.
21. Democritus was an ancient Greek philosopher (460–370 BC), best known for developing the concept of the atom as the smallest, indivisible component of matter.
22. The Bhagavada Gita is a Hindu scripture in which Lord Krishna guides Arjuna on duty, righteousness and the path to self-realization during the Kurukshetra war.
23. Karl Marx was a nineteenth-century German philosopher, political theorist and economist.
24. First prime minister of India.
25. George Jacob Holyoake (1817–1906) was a British thinker, writer who coined the term 'secularism'.
26. Charles Bradlaugh (1833–91) was a British political activist, atheist and member of parliament.
27. Justice Murtaza Husain (1920–2012) was an Indian jurist who served as a judge of the Allahabad High Court and later as the Lokayukta (anti-corruption ombudsman) of Uttar Pradesh.
28. The 1857 War of Independence, also known as the Indian Rebellion of 1857, was a massive and widespread uprising against the British East India Company that marked a turning point in Indian's colonial history.

29. Nana Sahib Peshwa was a prominent leader in the Indian Rebellion of 1857, which is often regarded as India's first War of Independence.
30. Tatya Tope, a close associate of Nana Sahib Peshwa, was one of the most prominent generals of the Indian Rebellion of 1857.
31. Rani Lakshmibai (1828–1858), also known as the Queen of Jhansi, was one of the warriors of the Indian Rebellion of 1857.
32. Bahadur Shah Zafar (1775–1862) was the last Mughal emperor and a symbolic figurehead of the Indian Rebellion of 1857.
33. Founder of the Mughal Empire in India and its first emperor.
34. Ibrahim Lodi (reigned 1517–26) was the last Sultan of the Lodi dynasty and the last ruler of the Delhi Sultanate before the establishment of the Mughal Empire in India.
35. Bal Gangadhar Tilak (1856–1920) was an Indian nationalist, freedom fighter, scholar and social reformer, often called 'Lokmanya Tilak'.
36. Annie Besant (1847–1933) was a British-born social reformer, theosophist, educationist and a prominent freedom fighter in India.
37. Lala Lajpat Rai (1865–1928), also known as the 'Punjab Kesari (Lion of Punjab)', was a prominent freedom fighter, social reformer and leader of the Indian Nationalist Movement.
38. Shaukat Ali (1873–1938) was a prominent Indian Muslim leader, known for his role in the Khilafat Movement alongside his brother Mohammad Ali Jauhar.
39. Mohammad Ali Jauhar (1878–1931) was a key leader of the Khilafat Movement in British India.
40. Sardar Vallabhbhai Patel (1875–1950), known as the 'Iron Man of India', was a key leader in India's struggle for Independence and the country's first deputy prime minister and home minister after Independence.
41. Coined in the 1950s during the early years of friendly relations between India and China.
42. Article 370 was a provision in the Indian Constitution that granted special autonomous status to the region of Jammu and Kashmir.
43. Dr Bhimrao Ramji Ambedkar (1891–1956), also known as Babasaheb Ambedkar, was an Indian jurist, economist, social reformer and politician. He is considered as the architect of the Indian Constitution.
44. Sheikh Abdullah (1905–82) was a political leader and founder of the National Conference, a political party in Jammu and Kashmir.
45. A river flowing through Tibet, India and Pakistan.
46. The Communal Award was a British government decision announced in 1932 by the then Viceroy Lord Ramsay MacDonald. It aimed to provide separate electorates and political representation to various minority communities in British India, including Muslims, Sikhs, Christians, Anglo-Indians, Dalits (then called 'Depressed Classes') and others.
47. Syed Shahabuddin (1935–2017) was an Indian politician and diplomat.

19. 'Throughout Indian History . . . Hindu Governance Has Consistently Been Secular in Nature'

1. P.C. Chatterjee (Phanindranath Chatterjee) was a notable Indian scholar and legal historian.

2. Madhav Sadashiv Golwalkar, known as 'Guruji', was the 2nd Sarsanghchalak of RSS (1940–1973).
3. Constantine the Great (c. 272–337 AD) was the first Roman emperor to convert to Christianity and played a crucial role in making it a dominant religion in the Roman Empire.
4. Jeremy Bentham (1748–1832) was an English philosopher, jurist and social reformer.
5. James Mill (1773–1836) was a Scottish historian, philosopher and economist.
6. Thomas Paine (1737–1809) was an English-American political thinker, revolutionary and writer.
7. Richard Carlile (1790–1843) was a radical English writer, publisher and free speech activist who championed freedom of the press, secularism and political reform.
8. A landmark British law that expanded the electoral franchise, reformed parliamentary representation and reduced corruption in the electoral system.
9. Robert Owen (1771–1858) was a Welsh social reformer and industrialist.
10. Demanded political reforms to make the parliamentary system more democratic and representative of the working class.
11. George Jacob Holyoake (1817–1906) was an English social reformer, writer and co-creator of the term "secularism".
12. Charles Bradlaugh (1833–1891) was a British political activist, atheist and reformer who championed secularism, free speech.
13. Cantwell v. Connecticut (1940) was a landmark U.S. Supreme Court case that incorporated the First Amendment's protection of religious freedom to apply to state governments through the Fourteenth Amendment.

20. 'Babasaheb Ambedkar Firmly Believed That Ideological Transformation and Social Unity Were Only Possible Through Religion'

1. Sant Dnyaneshwar (1275–1296) was a Marathi saint, poet and philosopher known for composing the Dnyaneshwari.
2. Sant Tukaram (1608–1650) was a Marathi saint and poet of the Bhakti movement.
3. Sant Namdev (c. 1270–1350) was a Marathi and Punjabi saint-poet of the Bhakti movement.
4. Sant Gora Kumbhar (also spelled Gora, lived circa 1267–c. 1312) was a Marathi saint and poet of the Bhakti movement.
5. Sant Chokhamela (c. 14th century) was one of the earliest Dalit saints and poets of the Marathi Bhakti movement.
6. E.V. Ramasamy (1879–1973), popularly known as Periyar was a social reformer and activist from Tamil Nadu who led the Self-Respect Movement.
7. Muhammad Ali Jinnah (1876–1948), known as Barrister Jinnah, was a lawyer, politician and the founding father of Pakistan.
8. Laldenga (1927–1990) was a Mizo political leader and founder of the Mizo National Front (MNF).
9. Angami Zapu Phizo (1913–1990) was a Naga nationalist leader and the key figure behind the Naga independence movement.
10. Bayard Rustin (1912–1987) was an African American civil rights activist known for masterminding the 1963 March on Washington.

11. Martin Luther King Jr. (1929–1968) was an American civil rights leader.

21. 'Life for Guruji Was an Act of Devotion'

1. 'Charaiveti' is a Sanskrit term meaning 'keep moving' or 'go on'.
2. Bhishma Pitamah, born as Devavrata, was the grandsire of the Kauravas and Pandavas in the Mahabharata, known for his vow of celibacy and commitment to dharma. Gifted with the boon of *ichha mrityu* (death at will), he chose to die on a bed of arrows after imparting deep wisdom to Yudhishthira on statecraft and righteousness.
3. The Kauravas were the 100 sons of King Dhritarashtra and Queen Gandhari, with Duryodhana as the eldest. They were the main antagonists in the Mahabharata, who opposed their cousins, the Pandavas, in the epic Kurukshetra war.
4. The phrase appears in the context of the Mahabharata, specifically during a moment when the Kauravas and Pandavas were together before the tensions that would eventually lead to the Kurukshetra war. The phrase symbolically refers to the 100 Kaurava brothers (sons of Dhritarashtra and Gandhari) and the 5 Pandava brothers (sons of Pandu and Kunti), together making a total of 105 princes.
5. Adi Shankaracharya was an Indian philosopher and theologian, known for consolidating the doctrine of Advaita Vedanta, which emphasizes non-dualism – the belief that the individual soul (*Atman*) and the supreme reality (Brahman) are one and the same.
6. Mandan Mishra was a Mimansa scholar and Vedic philosopher who lived during the time of Adi Shankaracharya. He is best known for his legendary philosophical debate with Shankaracharya on the nature of reality, ritualism and liberation.
7. A gurukul was the traditional Indian system of education in which students (*shishya*) lived with their teacher (*guru*) in an ashram-like setting, often located in forests or villages.
8. Tapovan (from *tapas* = penance and *vana* = forest) were sacred forests in ancient India where sages and seekers performed intense spiritual practices, such as meditation, to attain higher consciousness or liberation.
9. Dr Ram Manohar Lohia (1910–67) was a prominent Indian freedom fighter, socialist thinker and political leader.

22. 'When It Comes to Social Reform, the Sangh Must Take the Lead'

1. Third-year training camp or batch organized by the RSS.
2. Devraha Baba (circa 1900s–1990) was a revered Indian yogi and saint known for his long life, spiritual wisdom and influence over political leaders and common people alike.
3. Harijan is a term popularized by Mahatma Gandhi to refer to the Dalits or 'untouchables'.
4. The Purusha Sukta is a hymn from the Rigveda.
5. The Rigveda is the oldest of the four Vedas, composed in Sanskrit
6. A holy River in India.
7. A mandala (मण्डल) refers to a book or division. The Rigveda is divided into ten mandalas, each comprising a number of hymns (suktas).
8. The varna system is a social classification described in ancient Indian texts, especially the Purusha Sukta of the Rigveda. It divides society into four broad categories based on qualities and functions, not birth.

9. The *Bhagavad Gita*, a 700-verse Sanskrit scripture within the *Mahabharata* (Book 6), is a philosophical dialogue between Prince Arjuna and his charioteer Krishna, an incarnation of Vishnu.
10. A rishi is an ancient Indian sage.
11. Aryans were an ancient Indo-European people who migrated into the Indian subcontinent around 1500 BCE.
12. Sapta Sindhu refers to the ancient region described in the Rigveda, meaning 'and of seven rivers'.
13. A city in the state of Maharashtra, India.
14. He is the 5th avatar of Lord Vishnu.

23. 'Dharma Is the Nectar-Filled Vessel for the Welfare of All Beings, the Wish-Fulfilling Tree of Global Well-Being'

1. Third Year (special) Officers Training Programme.
2. *Udyoga Parva* is the fifth book of the Mahabharata, detailing the preparations for the Kurukshetra war.
3. Karna is a key character in the epic Mahabharata. He was born to Kunti before her marriage, making him the eldest Pandava.
4. Royal guru (teacher) and Master of Advanced Military Arts in the Mahabharata.
5. Eldest son of the Kauravas. An antagonist, who opposed the Pandavas' rightful claim to the throne.
6. *Bhishma Parva* is the sixth book of the Mahabharata and primarily describes the beginning of the Kurukshetra war. It also includes the famous Bhagavada Gita conversation between Lord Krishna and Arjuna.
7. Rishi Vyasa, also known as Vedavyasa, is the legendary sage credited with composing and compiling the Mahabharata.
8. He is the eldest of the five Pandava brothers in the Mahabharata.
9. *Anushasana Parva* is the thirteenth book of the Mahabharata, primarily focused on moral instructions, duties and codes of conduct given by Bhishma to the Pandavas during his final days on the battlefield on a bed of arrows.
10. A warrior in Mahabharata. Known for his vow of celibacy and a unique power of '*iccha mrityu*' – the ability to choose the time of his own death.
11. A traditional ancient Indian residential school system where students (shishyas) lived with their teacher (guru).
12. A sage, poet and author of Ramayana.
13. A sage, messenger. Known for travelling across the worlds with news and wisdom.
14. Dasharath was the king of Ayodhya in the ancient Indian epic Ramayana, best known as the father of Lord Rama.
15. Shabda Kalpadruma is a Sanskrit dictionary and lexicon compiled by the scholar Sir M. Rajaram Shastri in the twentieth century. It is widely regarded as one of the most authoritative works in Sanskrit lexicography.
16. An Indian lexicographer and professor of Sanskrit at Fergusson College, Pune, he is known for compiling Sanskrit–English and Sanskrit–Hindi dictionaries.
17. Another name for Lord Krishna. *Murali* means flute, therefore, Muralidhar literally means 'the one who carries and plays the flute'.

18. A sacred place in Uttar Pradesh, India, where Lord Krishna spent his childhood
19. Another name for Lord Krishna.
20. The month of Shravan is a holy month in the Hindu calendar, usually falling in July or August.
21. Rigveda, the oldest of the sacred books of Hinduism, was composed in an ancient form of Sanskrit around 1500 BC and contains over 1,000 hymns.
22. Puraanic relates to the Puranas, a genre of ancient Indian texts that contain mythological stories, legends.
23. Shruti mantras refer to the mantras and verses found in the four Vedas.
24. The Chandogya Upanishad is one of the oldest and most important Upanishads. It is part of the Sama Veda.
25. The Brihadaranyaka Upanishad is one of the oldest and largest Upanishads, forming a key philosophical text in Hinduism that explores the nature of reality, the Self (*Atman*) and ultimate knowledge (*Brahman*).
26. An ancient Indian collection of interrelated animal fables and stories designed to teach moral lessons and practical wisdom through simple, engaging tales.
27. A classical Sanskrit text composed of fables and stories similar to the Panchatantra, aimed at teaching practical wisdom, moral values and political strategy through simple narratives.
28. An eighth-century Indian philosopher, theologian and spiritual teacher who consolidated the doctrine of Advaita Vedanta – the philosophy of non-dualism – and revitalized Hinduism by establishing monasteries (*matha*s) and promoting the study of the Vedas and Upanishadas.
29. Teacher or acharya of the six philosophies (shanmata) – Nyaya, Vaisheshika, Sankhya, Yoga, Mimamsa and Vedanta.
30. A Shadharmacharya is someone who teaches or upholds the six fundamental duties or virtues prescribed in Hindu dharma – Satya (truthfulness), Ahimsa (non-violence), Asteya (non-stealing), Brahmacharya (self-control), Shaucha (purity) and Daya (compassion).
31. A fourteenth-century Hindu philosopher, saint and scholar who played a key role in the revival of the Vijayanagara Empire.
32. Manu is the mythic first human and lawgiver, believed to have established the principles of dharma and social order for humanity.
33. The Manu Smriti, also called the Laws of Manu, is an ancient Hindu legal and ethical text that outlines the social laws, duties and moral codes governing individuals and society.
34. King Rantideva was a noble ruler famed for his boundless charity and compassion.
35. Siddhis are supernatural powers or spiritual abilities.
36. Ravana was the ten-headed king of Lanka, a learned and mighty ruler, and the main antagonist in the Hindu epic Ramayana, known for his immense strength, intelligence and devotion to Lord Shiva, but also for his arrogance and the abduction of Sita, which led to his eventual defeat by Lord Rama.
37. A Vedic sage.
38. Karna Parva, one of the books (parvas) of the Mahabharata, details the battles fought by Karna during the Kurukshetra war and also narrates his death.
39. A sage.

40. A great devotee of Lord Vishnu and the son of demon king Hiranyakashyapa.
41. A demon king known for his hatred towards Lord Vishnu and for being the father of the great devotee Prahlada.
42. Narayana is a form of Lord Vishnu.
43. Indra is the king of gods.
44. King Shibi was a righteous and compassionate his death known for sacrificing his own flesh to protect a dove.
45. Draupadi is a central character in the Mahabharata, born from fire, married to the five Pandavas and a key force behind the Kurukshetra war. The *vastraharan* of Draupadi was a disgraceful incident in the Mahabharata in which she was dragged into the Kaurava assembly and an attempt was made to disrobe her, but Lord Krishna protected her by endlessly extending her garment.
46. Yakshas are nature-spirits or supernatuural beings in Indian mythology, often depicted as guardians.
47. The Bhagavada Purana is a sacred Hindu scripture that discusses devotion (bhakti) to Lord Vishnu – especially through the life and teachings of Krishna – while narrating stories of creation, cosmology, saints and divine incarnations.
48. Brahma is the Hindu god of creation, part of the Trimurti alongside Vishnu (the preserver) and Shiva (the destroyer).
49. The Prajapati is the Lord of creatures.
50. The Padma Purana is one of the major eighteen Mahapuranas in Hinduism, composed in Sanskrit. It primarily highlights Lord Vishnu and his avatars, especially Lord Krishna, and contains extensive stories on cosmology, mythology, pilgrimage sites (*tirtha*s), rituals and ethics. The text also includes sections devoted to Shiva and Shakti, reflecting its syncretic nature.
51. The Brahmavaivarta Purana is composed in Sanskrit and focuses primarily on Krishna, Radha and the divine feminine. It is known for its Vaishnava and Shakta synthesis, presenting Radha as the supreme goddess and Krishna as the supreme god.
52. Divine feminine energy.
53. Dr Bhagwan Das (1869–1958) was an Indian philosopher, educationist and freedom fighter, best known for co-founding the Kashi Vidyapith and being awarded the Bharat Ratna in 1955 for his contributions to philosophy and literature.

24. 'Sarvangina Unnati Means Holistic Progress in All Facets of Life'

1. General secretary.
2. Pandit Deendayal Upadhyay (1916–1968) was an Indian philosopher, economist, political thinker and one of the key leaders of the Bharatiya Jana Sangh (the forerunner of the BJP).
3. *Raghuvansha* (Lineage of Raghu), is a celebrated Sanskrit epic poem composed by the great poet Kalidasa.
4. King from the Ikshvaku dynasty in ancient Indian tradition, best known as the ancestor of Lord Rama and the father of King Raghu.
5. A classical Sanskrit poet and dramatist.
6. Vinayak Damodar Savarkar (1883–1966), popularly known as Veer Savarkar, was an Indian freedom fighter, nationalist thinker, historian and social reformer.

7. Vladimir Lenin (1870–1924) was a Russian revolutionary, political theorist and the founding leader of the Soviet Union.
8. India House was a residence and political hub in London that served as the centre of Indian revolutionary activity in the early twentieth century. Founded in 1905 by Shyamji Krishna Varma, it provided shelter and support to Indian students and acted as a base for anti-colonial thought and activism.
9. M.S. Golwalkar, the second sarsanghchalak (chief) of the Rashtriya Swayamsevak Sangh.

25. 'The Curriculum and Syllabus Be Redesigned to Reflect India's Contributions, India's Philosophies, and Indian Thought'

1. Joint General Secretary.
2. Narada is a sage (Devarishi) in Hindu mythology, known as a cosmic messenger, musician and devotee of Lord Vishnu.
3. Indian yoga guru and entrepreneur.
4. Abhimanyu is a warrior in the epic of *Mahabharata.*
5. Chakravyuha is a complex, circular military formation described in the *Mahabharata*, designed to trap and confuse enemies, famously associated with the warrior Abhimanyu.
6. Pandit Shivkumar Sharma (1938–2022) was an Indian classical musician renowned for popularizing the santoor.
7. Tabla is a pair of small hand drums used in Indian classical music.
8. Veena is a traditional Indian stringed musical instrument.
9. Dharampal (1922–2006) was an Indian scholar and social reformer known for his research on indigenous Indian education and critiques of colonial education policies.
10. John Bright (1811–1889) was a British politician and orator known for his advocacy of free trade, parliamentary reform and opposition to the British Corn Laws.
11. Charles Grant (1746–1823) was a British East India Company official and reformer who advocated for the spread of Christianity and Western education in India.
12. Thomas Babington Macaulay (1800–1859) was a British historian and politician who played a key role in introducing English education in India.
13. Lord William Bentinck (1774–1839) was a British Governor-General of India known for his social reforms, including the abolition of sati and efforts to modernize Indian administration.
14. Max Müller (1823–1900) was a German-born philologist and Orientalist.
15. Ravana is the legendary demon king of Lanka in the Hindu epic *Ramayana.*
16. Justice Rama Jois (1932–2021) was an eminent Indian jurist, former Chief Justice of the Punjab and Haryana High Court.
17. Vinoba Bhave (1895–1982) was an Indian advocate of nonviolence and human rights, best known for initiating the Bhoodan Movement.
18. Sir Isaac Newton (1643–1727) was an English physicist and mathematician who formulated the laws of motion and universal gravitation, founding classical mechanics.
19. Thomas Edison (1847–1931) was an American inventor and businessman.
20. Dr A.P.J. Abdul Kalam (1931–2015) was an Indian scientist and the 11th President of India, renowned as the "Missile Man of India" for his work in aerospace and defense.
21. Raghunath Anant Mashelkar is a renowned Indian chemical engineer.

22. Kaka Kalelkar (1885–1981) was an Indian independence activist, social reformer and writer.

27. M.S. Golwalkar's Conversation with Saifuddin Jilani

1. Narendra Thakur and Vijay Kranti, *About RSS (Rashtriya Swayamsevak Sangh)*, Vimarsh Prakashan, 2023, pp. 31–40. https://www.archivesofrss.org/books/About per cent20RSS-1.pdf
2. Shringeri Math is one of the four original monasteries established by Adi Shankaracharya in the 8th century to preserve and propagate Advaita Vedanta philosophy.
3. Urs is the annual death anniversary celebration of a Sufi saint.
4. Satyanarayana Puja is a Hindu ritual dedicated to Lord Satyanarayana (a form of Vishnu), performed to seek blessings for prosperity, peace and fulfillment of wishes.
5. Dravida Munnetra Kazhagam (DMK) is a major political party in Tamil Nadu, founded in 1949 by C.N. Annadura.
6. Prasadam is food that is first offered to a deity.

28. Golwalkar on Governance and Constitution

1. Dravida Kazhagam (DK) is a social reform and political movement founded by Periyar E.V. Ramasamy in 1944 in Tamil Nadu.

29. Prof. Rajendra Singh in Conversation with Tavleen Singh

1. Friends of RSS, 'Rajju Bhaiya's Exclusive Interview with Tavleen Singh,' YouTube, 24 October 2018, https://www.youtube.com/watch?v=ix8YYYbFkeM. Accessed on 26 June 2025.
2. A 15th-century poet and saint whose dohas emphasized devotion, morality and a synthesis of Hindu and Islamic thought.
3. Abdur Rahim Khan-i-Khana, a Mughal courtier, poet and scholar known for his Hindi couplets.
4. A Muslim devotee of Krishna and poet who composed bhakti poetry in Braj language.
5. Malik Muhammad Jayasi, a 16th-century Sufi poet best known for his epic Hindi poem Padmavat.
6. The Charkhi Dadri(Haryana, India) mid-air collision occurred on 12 November 1996 between a Saudi Boeing 747 and a Kazakh Il-76, killed 349 people.

Index